CORSICA:
Portrait of
a Granite Island

CORSICA

CORSICA:
Portrait of
a Granite Island

by Dorothy Carrington

THE JOHN DAY COMPANY

An Intext Publisher

NEW YORK

For Jean Cesari,
catalyst, guide and friend

FIRST AMERICAN EDITION 1974
COPYRIGHT © 1971 *by Dorothy Carrington*

Library of Congress Cataloging in Publication Data
Carrington, Dorothy.
  Granite island.

  Reprint of the ed. published by Longman, London.
  Bibliography: p.
  1. Corsica. I. Title.
DC611.C81C27   1974   914.4'945'0483   73-17015
ISBN 0-381-98260-2

CONTENTS

LIST OF ILLUSTRATIONS

AUTHOR'S NOTE

CORSICA has changed while I have been writing this book. During the last decade twentieth-century civilisation has been unleashed onto the island, backed by massive capital investment and the resources of modern technology. The result is exactly what one would expect in a beautiful, underpopulated, hitherto under-developed and – at last – easily accessible area of the Mediterranean: hotels, shops, filling-stations, bungalow villages, bungalows, all designed to accommodate an inrush of summer visitors that gathers volume year by year. At the same time the French government has fulfilled an old promise to promote Corsican agriculture, and in so doing has transformed some neglected districts almost out of recognition.

The obvious gain, for the Corsicans, is in prosperity: almost everyone is better fed, dressed, housed. The villages, released from their immemorial isolation, have become less preoccupied with past feuds and dramas, less introverted; and there are none, today, so necessitous as those where on my first journey to the south I came to know the essential virtue in hospitality.

Travellers can now enjoy the island in comfort, sometimes in luxury. But there is less to be enjoyed. Hasty building has deformed the ancient towns and dese-crated strips of the coastline (though some remains mercifully unimpaired). On the other hand certain mountain regions, abandoned by their inhabitants, are now even more serenely desolate than when I first saw them. If the new *Parc Naturel Régional* does its work these at least will be preserved.

Yet there is probably not a single person, however secluded, nor a locality, however remote, still unaffected by recent change. Not long ago I visited, with Jean Cesari, a part of the south, of no interest to tourists or farmers, that seemed wholly immune to the contemporary world. We were talking with some elderly people about their prophetic dreams and visions. I noticed that nothing they des-cribed seemed to have taken place within the last few years. When I asked them the reason they fell silent, and looked grieved. 'We don't see or dream any longer,' one of them eventually explained, 'it's because of the modernism.'

'The modernism' has done more than improve conditions and degrade appear-ances, more, too, than alienate the Corsicans from certain realms of experience: it has brought down a traditional way of life with an integrated pattern of values, customs, attitudes and loyalties, in fact what amounted to an insular culture. That culture is my subject; not because it was Utopian but because it has existed and been ignored. It had its roots in the Neolithic era, came to maturity in the mid-eighteenth century and then decayed slowly until it received its death-blow in the 1960s. Yet its essential values – a cult of egality and justice, a belief in the human potential – are more than ever relevant today. To lament its collapse would however be futile; most Corsicans do not. For them the ending of the old order means escape from various kinds of drudgery and from a social code that had become outdated and cramping.

This book is based on the observations of my first journey, before the moderni-sation of the island had got under way, interwoven with later experiences, re-searches and studies. Conversations were noted in day-to-day diaries.

ACKNOWLEDGEMENTS

I T is impossible for me to thank individually all the people who have been of help in the writing of this book; since its subject is Corsica, almost every Corsican I have met has in some degree affected its contents. Nor can I mention all the many people who went out of their way to show me local curiosities and antiquities, accompanied me on long walks across country, gave me lifts in their cars and sheltered and fed me in their homes. Some I never knew by name; others prefer to remain anonymous. I think especially of the priests who welcomed me to their parishes and showed me the forgotten treasures of their churches, and the shepherds whose spontaneous hospitality made every mountain excursion memorable.

I have to thank the Préfecture de la Corse and the different administrative services of the *département* for information on various subjects courteously supplied; I am particularly indebted to the Direction Départementale des Services Agricoles. To M. Pierre Lamotte, Directeur des Services d'Archives de la Corse, my gratitude is unbounded. His precise erudition, generously dispensed through the years, has been beyond price. I wish also to thank the members of his staff.

My very sincere thanks are due to M. Jean Leblanc, Conservateur des Musées d'Ajaccio and Conservateur du Musée de Morosaglia, and to Madame Leblanc, Conservateur du Musée d'Histoire Corse, at Corte; to M. Etienne de Leca, Conservateur de la Bibliothèque d'Ajaccio and to Madame de Leca; to Madame Serafini-Costoli, Conservateur du Musée d'Ethnographie Corse, in Bastia, who have freely given me their time and expert advice. I also offer my thanks to the personnel of SOMIVAC.

In preparing the archaeological sections of this work I have been greatly indebted to the specialists who have generously communicated to me the results of their researches and allowed me the exhilarating experience of seeing their work in progress: M. Roger Grosjean, Directeur du Centre de Préhistoire Corse; M. François de Lanfranchi, Correspondant de la Direction des Antiquités; Professeur Jean Jehasse, Directeur des fouilles d'Aléria, and Madame Laurence Jehasse, Conservateur du Musée Jérôme Carcopino, Aléria; Madame Geneviève Moracchini-Mazel, Conservateur des antiquités et objets d'art en Corse and Directrice des fouilles de Mariana.

I acknowledge my gratitude to M. le Sénateur François Giacobbi, Président du Conseil Général de la Corse, and to those people in Corsica and elsewhere who have kindly given me information on matters in their special fields of knowledge: Dr Marcelle Bouteiller, authority on witchcraft; the botanist Mme Marcelle Conrad; Professor John Grenville, University of Birmingham; Professor Leonard W. Labaree, Yale University; the anthropologist Dr John Layard; the archaeologist Commandant Octobon, Nice; Sir Francis Rose, who accompanied me on several Corsican journeys and gave me his valued opinion on various works of art; Signor

Salinas, Soprintendenza ai Monumenti e Gallerie della Sardegna; the musical scholars M. Jean-Claude Sillamy and M. Felix Quilici.

It is with pleasure that I recall my excursions in Corsica with Mlle Janine Renucci, of the University of Lyons, who most generously communicated to me her findings for her thesis on Corsican economy, to appear shortly.

I offer my warm thanks to the following people who have assisted me by their intimate knowledge of particular subjects and places, lent me rare books and in other ways facilitated my researches. In Ajaccio: M. le Chanoine Giudicelli, Vicaire Général du diocèse d'Ajaccio; M. Martin Baretti, Président d'Honneur de la Fédération Départementale des Syndicats d'Initiative; M. Victor Franceschini, director of A Sirinata Ajaccina; Maître Georges Morelli; my guides and companions in the high mountains, M. Jean Bianchetti and M. Jean Angelini; M. Pierre Poggi; Mme Barbara Benedetti, *voceratrice* of Ota; Dr Luciani, of Moca-Croce, Conseiller-Général; in Sartène, M. Joseph de Rocca-Serra; Mme Valère de Susini Musso; M. Caius de Peretti of Levie; M. Rossi of Bonifacio, Directeur d'Ecole; at Chera the bard Jean-André Culioli and M. Charles-André Culioli. At Aléria, M. Jean Luisi, Président of Les Amis d'Aléria; in Bastia, M. Louis de Casabianca, architect; the writer and journalist Francis Maure; M. François Pietri, architect; M. Dominique Vecchini, formerly Conservateur de la Bibliothèque de Bastia. In the Castagniccia, M. Dominique Mosca, Sécretaire administratif de la Fédération des Oeuvres Laïques en Corse; M. Jean-Joseph Pinelli, of Cervione, Conseiller-Général; Mme Pietri, Maire de Giocatojo; Mlle Charlotte Rocchi and members of her family. At Corbara, M. Tito Franceschini Pietri; Comte Savelli de Guido. M. Julien Allegrini of Sant'Antonino; M. Charles Colonna d'Anfriani, of Monte Maggiore, formerly deputy for Marseilles. At Calvi, M. Etienne Millie, Président du Syndicat d'Initiative de Calvi; M. Augustin Canava; M. Etienne Marini. In the Niolo, M. Peppu Flori, poet, of Lozzi; Maître Padovani, notary of Casamaccioli. At Corte, M. le Chanoine Casanova, now Archiprêtre de Bastia; at Venaco. M. André Moreau, who kindly allowed me the use of his splendid library.

My great debt to Jean Cesari, Charles-Antoine Cesari and members of their family will be apparent in the pages of this book.

This work has been a long time in preparation, and it is my grief that so many who helped and encouraged me in its early stages are no longer here. I think particularly of the late Duc Joseph Pozzo di Borgo, of Comte Peraldi, Président du Syndicat d'Initiative Régional d'Ajaccio et de la Corse, of the historian Pierre Rocca, the erudite M. Jean Alessandri and M. Francois Levie, of M. Attilius Marcangeli, Chef du Bureau Communal des Archives d'Ajaccio, the photographer M. Toussaint Tomasi, Maître Musso of Bonifacio and M. François Franzini of Pietralba, Conseiller-Général.

During my years in Corsica I have owed very much to Valerie Duchesse Pozzo di Borgo and members of her family.

I have to thank Mr Tom Van Dycke for his generous encouragement during this long task.

I am much indebted to the Musée des Arts et Traditions Populaires, Paris, the National Portrait Gallery, London, and to the London Library which has given me constant and invaluable assistance.

Finally, I wish to mention my gratitude to Miss Diana Buist, of Calvi, who has read my text with unusual perceptiveness and offered many helpful suggestions, and to Miss Violet Thayre, who typed and retyped it in a spirit of loyal cooperation.

1 THE IMPERIAL CITY

In sight of Corsica – Ajaccio – Victorian visitors – Genoese
nucleus – the Corsican past – the Bonaparte

CORSICA came into view with the dawn. Almost colourless, its outlines uncertain, it swam in the early morning mist, a creation half-materialised, an
ectoplasm of the sea in trance. I hurried out of my stifling cabin to find the
couple I had been talking to the previous night already at the rail. There we
stood in silence, watching the island taking substance between sea and sky.
They had spent many years in Madagascar, and at dinner, sailing out of Marseilles, they had been eager to tell me about their colonial experiences; but
now all that was forgotten: they were coming home at last.

This first sight of Corsica allowed me to imagine the sensations of Captain
Cook discovering some marvellous, improbable South Pacific island. The
mountains surged into the sky, behind, beyond, above one another, ending in
rows of cones and spikes and square-topped knobs like gigantic teeth. Their
lower slopes, smothered in vegetation, looked uninhabited and impenetrable.

What would I find there, besides rock and forest? I knew little of Corsica,
then, except what I had gleaned from conversations with Jean Cesari, a
Corsican I had met by chance in London. In the evenings of that bitter,
gritty spring he had spoken to me of his home. Of his uncle, a shepherd, and
his aunt, a brilliant raconteur in the Corsican dialect; of their ten children and
the little house they had built for themselves by the sea. He had told me of the
chestnut gathering, in the mountains, in the snow, and of hunting wild boar;
of old men and women who had prophetic visions, dreamed the future, could
foretell deaths. And he had described some huge stone statues of great age,
lying forgotten under the olive trees. These statues were what stood out most
vividly in the curious mixture of homely and magical themes that made up his
talk, what stirred my curiosity most. Did they exist, or did they belong to the
realm of dreams and visions? Was it really likely that huge stone statues were
lying about, ignored, in a province of France, a country that gives so much
expert attention to its antiquities?

'Come and see for yourself,' Jean had said to me, 'I'll show them to you
when I go to Corsica next summer. You and your husband could stay with my
uncle and aunt. The statues are quite near where they live, on the property of
my cousin, Charles-Antoine.'

I

And so it happened that we found ourselves in early summer on a ship bound for Ajaccio, the Corsican capital. In the meantime I had read such books on Corsica as I could lay hands on: Mérimée's *Colomba*, a dramatic tale of blood vengeance; Boswell's exhilarating account of his visit to Pasquale Paoli, the Corsican leader who had freed his country from Genoese rule and given it a liberal constitution much in advance of his time. I had also read lives of Napoleon that mentioned his obscure, frustrated youth in Ajaccio, and some travellers' reminiscences of rough journeys, fine landscapes, a proud, fierce hospitable people and bandits who were looked upon as heroes. We had arranged to meet Jean at the home of his uncle and aunt and see the statues and stay there awhile, after which my husband and Jean would return to England while I toured the rest of the island.

Details came into focus as we drew towards land: ridges, crests, chasms, promontories, the shadows of the mountains on the water; but few works of man, few houses or fields or roads. Only a lighthouse and an ancient watch-tower appeared on the Iles Sanguinaires, a chain of barren pyramidical islands flung out from the bay of Ajaccio like a bastion. It was then that we caught the scent of the maquis, borne out on a warm land breeze. This is the scent of all Corsica; bitter-sweet, akin to incense, heady, almost, as an anaesthetic after rain. The maquis is a dense jungle of aromatic evergreen plants and shrubs: arbutus, myrtle, cistus and lentisk, rosemary and lavender and thyme. It covers the land except where fields are cultivated and forests grow, and at present the forests are dwindling and the cultivated fields are few so that the maquis spreads over more than half the land. It may be useless except as a hideout for guerrillas and bandits, but it is a perpetual and potent enchantment; one sleeps and wakes with its fragrance which is like no other. Napoleon recalled it with nostalgia in St Helena when, humbled at last, he became like any Corsican ending his life in exile, his memories not of his palaces and triumphs but of the maquis-scent of childhood.

Ajaccio, set deep in a curling bay enclosed by high mountains, came as a surprise, a neat white classical-looking little town quite out of keeping with its wild setting. It suggested nothing so much as an eighteenth-century engraving, cut out and pasted on a photograph of this tremendous landscape to make a surrealist collage. Later, as we steamed into the harbour, the severe houses fronting the still water recalled, for a moment, Canaletto's views of the Grand Canal. But at close quarters I saw that Ajaccio was neither so neat nor so elegant as it had appeared from a distance: stucco had fallen from the tall façades, exposing black and red patches of rotting brick and masonry; washing was swinging and sagging between drainpipes and balcony privies; ferns and shrubs sprouted from decaying fortifications, ramshackle sheds straggled about the quay.

The docks were packed; hundreds of people had gathered to see the ship come in. I stepped off the gang-plank into a crowd of dark eager faces; sturdy old peasant women in black boots and kerchiefs embraced homecoming sons in new town suits and dashing ties. The sunlight had a ripe golden quality;

the air was rich with mingled scents – of maquis, wood-smoke, sea-salt – so that I felt I was breathing some powerful narcotic into my lungs.

A taxi took me through a square, shaded by palms and plane trees, along an avenue, bordered by cafés and palms; we skirted another square, enormous, flooded with the radiance of sun and sea. Then came more palms and plane trees and yet more cafés; the town seemed to consist almost entirely of cafés; I had reached that deep zone of the Mediterranean where people sit about drinking all day long. We passed a rambling leafy garden screening the gaunt walls of the old Grand Hotel; but I was bent for another, further up the avenue, where the town runs into the maquis. Here the bushy mountainside rose so steeply behind the building that one felt it might at any moment topple its load of vegetation onto one's head. The hotel garden was sweet with freshly watered flowers, morning glory, magnolia, orange blossom, hibiscus, datura; immediately below, white houses framed three bands of blue of differing tones: the sea, the mountains far off across the bay, the un-clouded sky.

A starched maid took my luggage; I was shown to a room with a polished brass bedstead, served coffee in a dark-pannelled bar smelling of beeswax; the illusion of Victorian England was poignant. As I later learned, until the Second World War the hotel catered for a predominantly British clientele. Ajaccio was one of those southern resorts where retired army men and faintly eccentric single ladies congregated to spend comfortable annuities. They changed for dinner, they played bridge and hunted wild boar, they were entertained by bandits; one of the ladies painted the charming watercolours of rock and forest that still decorate the hotel's walls.

The immediate surroundings of the hotel, too, bear the stamp of the old-fashioned British expatriate, remind one of corners of Mentone, as I discovered as I wandered through streets where trees made shadow-pictures on wide pavements and wistaria nodded over the railings of villa gardens. And there I came upon the Anglican church of the vanished British community, one of those to be found dotted about the Mediterranean, stranded amid palm trees and oleander and murmuring imperturbably of yew trees and harvest festivals and apple-faced children's choirs.

A Miss Thomasina Campbell was responsible for building it, a fearless Scottish spinster who discovered Corsica back in the 1860s and also built herself the largest of the neighbouring villas, one with high gables and a summer-house aping a Gothic tower. Undismayed by the savage aspect of Corsica, by reports of bandits and bad inns and malaria, she journeyed all over the island in hired carriage and stage-coach and wrote a book about her experiences called *Southward Ho!* It is an informative, sensible book which sails smoothly along on the breeze of her wholesome temperament; but for the magic and mystery of Corsica one must look elsewhere. No hint of this disturbed her as she identified wild flowers, assessed the value of wood, citrus fruit and coral exports, enjoyed local hospitality and revelled in seven-course meals. But she did befriend a traveller more sensitive than herself: Edward Lear of the *Non-*

3

sense Rhymes, and his *Journal of a Landscape Painter in Corsica* does convey the grave hard splendour of the island, untainted, then, by foreigners' ways; a place of vast untenanted wooded landscapes and brooding heights of rock and snow such as he evokes in his superbly romantic engravings.

Between them, Miss Campbell and Lear made Corsica fashionable, and the British soon began to settle there. They built themselves villas near Miss Campbell's which they referred to, modestly, as cottages. In fact they seem to have lived in style. The Corsicans remember them mainly as a people who wore top-hats, which had never been seen in the island before.

Mindful of their health, these Victorian expatriates chose the coolest and cleanest part of the town. As I followed the avenue down towards the harbour the air became heavier, enclosed between high, dilapidated buildings. Yet I could understand why the British had felt at home in Ajaccio. There is a feeling of artificially created privilege about the place, reminiscent of some of the smaller British outposts, such as Aden, or Gibraltar. Ajaccio was an inconsiderable town, a minor Genoese fortress until Napoleon, in 1811, made it the administrative capital. After which the French enlarged it, laid out squares and avenues, built a Préfecture in the classical style set back behind iron railings and ornamental trees that recalls many a Government House. Yet Ajaccio remained a very small oasis of civilisation: a century ago the population numbered hardly more than eleven thousand, and it is still below fifty thousand today. Avenues lead to nowhere: to the maquis, to the sea; either one finds oneself looking out across the bay at the blue ranges receding into undefined blue distances, or back at the wooded mountains that seem to shoulder their way into the end of every street.

The inhabitants, I thought, were engaged in a conspiracy of keeping up appearances. The cafés, now, were full of solemn-faced men in dark suits; Corsicans, presumably, for no holidaymaker could possibly endure such stuffy clothes. Grouped round the little tables, they were conversing with extreme seriousness. What subject, I wondered, could possibly assume so weighty an importance on a golden summer's morning in this quietly crumbling town? Local politics, I was later to learn. The Corsicans' passion for *la politique* is innate, rooted in a tradition of local democratic government that goes back to the Middle Ages, inherited from centuries of political tension and insecurity, stimulated by a taste for intrigue, and a craving for authority on however small a scale. So the men of Ajaccio (as in the other towns and even the villages) go day after day to a café to plan and manœuvre public affairs. The consequences sometimes strike beyond the limits of island life. It was in a café of Ajaccio, in May 1958, that some sixty citizens, siding with the insurgents of Algiers, plotted the bloodless revolt which overthrew the legal government of the island and supported de Gaulle's return to power.

Meanwhile the women of Ajaccio, that summer morning, were sauntering under the trees. Respectable women having not yet won the liberty to go to the cafés (a victory of very recent years), they were then obliged to look for much of their social pleasure walking about the streets. There was nothing

4

in the least peasantish about those I saw. Like the men they wore very formal clothes, the current Paris fashions interpreted in a hard sleek style of their own. No concessions had been made to the shabby décor – the fallen plaster, the pot-holed pavements – their pride was in ignoring the shortcomings of their town. Tropical birds of bright plumage, they picked their way unconcernedly over the rubble and rubbish. Most were very small women, fine-boned as orientals, and they had added five or six inches to their height with spike-heeled pumps in delicate colours, like flowers on their feet.

My walk had brought me back to the main square, oversized, theatrical, where Napoleon in bronze, on horseback, got up as a Roman, is surrounded by his four brothers, in togas, standing at the four corners of the ponderous monument. A line of decaying houses, six and seven storeys high, looking like battered stage scenery, complete the solemn dignity of the scene. They mark the boundary of a tiny ancient city, the Genoese nucleus of Ajaccio.[1] I entered it, that blazing summer morning, with the sensation of stepping into a grotto, for the tall buildings cover the narrow streets in a nearly perpetual shade. Balancing on paving-stones rounded by the passage of feet through many centuries, I slithered through dusky alleys, curiously silent in spite of the multitudes stacked in the great tenements, flaunting their laundry on poles, like banners, from windows high above. These, evidently, had once been aristocratic homes; several bore marble escutcheons over Renaissance doorways. Now the ground-floor rooms with fine rib-vaulted ceilings had become carpenters' workshops and cafés. Workmen were pottering about in blues, and a few women in cotton wrappers; these people were dressed haphazardly without seeming really poor. But then one seldom sees real poverty in Corsica; never the conscience-burning destitution of Sicily, no signs of hunger or desperate need. If there is a certain lack of ready money everyone eats sufficiently; the enormous blessing of a country with a population too small for its size.

A glow of sunshine at the end of a canyon street led me to the fishing port, brilliant as a stained-glass window. The sea, almost purple, lay beneath a sky tinted china blue; among the fishing boats moored along the jetty was a little pleasure yacht with a dazzling lilac sail. The view across the sea, seen from a new angle, was magnificent. Here the bay appeared as a vast lake, ringed by mountains rolling back into the *terra incognita* of the hinterland. They rose in tumbled ranges, tier above tier; one could hardly tell how many, for their middle slopes were barred with a blue incandescent mist so that only the foot-hills were distinct, and the topmost peaks touching the small, tufted, clouds.

Seen against this noble background the people on the quay were miniature figures, like those in Guardi's waterscapes. Under a plane tree, just below the ruined fortifications, fishermen were boiling pine bark in a cauldron for dyeing their nets; others were sitting on the ground repairing nets, each length to be mended stretched between hand and big toe. Boats were cutting in across the harbour, returning with their catch; fishermen were carrying fish to the market in baskets cushioned on thickly curling hair, stepping barefoot over the paving-stones with a disdainful tread. Others crowded the little bars,

5

calling for coffee and eau-de-vie. They were less stereotyped than the dressed-up café-sitting gentlemen. The sea life, which had sharpened their features, giving to each face an exaggerated individuality, seemed to have operated in the same way on the totality of their physique: here were men lean and laconic, tubby and jovial, thick-shouldered bruisers, boys handsome as film-stars, old men who incarnated the very essence of decrepitude.

Later, when I came to know these people, I grew familiar with the recurrent topics of their conversation. Except at election times, politics are excluded; the fishermen, who form a caste apart, are uninterested in the details of public affairs. Their talk, like that of Jean Cesari, is an unexpected mixture of the homely and the fabulous. The cost of nets, the price of fish, where to put down the nets at sea (the areas that give the best results are known as 'meadows of the fish'); such everyday subjects are passionately discussed for hours and hours. But so are less common matters: a waterspout, for instance. The fishermen I was dining with one night – on a desert beach, under a crescent moon, squatting round a camp fire where our *bouillabaisse* was cooking – were eager to describe that hair-raising phenomenon: how the cloud came down, how the water went up, how it whirled round and round all the way from sea to sky. Words were inadequate to express its horror; hands and arms twisted in frantic imitation; a boy, his eyes stretched in terror as they must have been at the time of the experience, sprang to his feet and began spinning round the flames like a dervish, or, as he intended, like the waterspout; one after another his companions rivalled him until an old old man tottered into action, whirling clumsily, frenziedly, like a damned soul until he fell on his back in the maquis amid taunts and laughter.

Or they will discuss the habits of fish. Their natural history belongs to the same category as that of Lyly's *Euphues* or the mediaeval bestiaries. The *murène*, that sinister mottled sea-serpent with a bite that can be dangerous, exists, so they maintain, only in the female sex; the female *murène* slides ashore to couple with grass snakes; nearly all the fishermen I know claim to have seen this unholy love-making.

Late at night, those almost sleepless nights when one lies in the boats on baroque couches of ragged oriental carpets and sacking, waiting to pull in the nets at dawn, minds may wander to larger subjects: death, for instance; Corsican conversation is always likely to come round to our universal ending. If the fishermen's natural history is mediaeval, so is their faith. 'What, you are afraid of dying?' a young, high-spirited fisherman once said to me when we were speaking of shipwrecks. 'You, who write, and even for the newspapers?' Many of the fishermen are illiterate, having skipped school to go to sea in their fathers' boats as boys. 'But did no one ever tell you?' he continued, pityingly. 'When the body falls down the spirit flies away. So you see, there's nothing at all to be afraid of.'

That fisherman meant exactly what he said. Later he was in fact lost in a storm at sea. A week he was missing, with his boat and crew. For once there was no oratory in the quayside cafés. Day after day, while the waves smashed

6

over the jetty, the fishermen sat huddled at their drinks in silence, united in a solidarity that goes beyond friendship or sympathy: what happens to one can happen to all. In fact I heard only a single comment on the situation. The words had the ring of Elizabethan tragedy: 'His wife came down to ask for news. You should have seen that woman! Her face was black; she has drunk of the blood of his heart.' Blessed are the illiterate, who can spontaneously express themselves in such apt and opulent imagery! More than once in Corsica I was to marvel at the command of words by those who can neither read nor write them. But perhaps this was general in the days before universal education began mass-producing minds. I have often wondered how far the Elizabethan writers were indebted to the virile, vivid speech of an illiterate majority.

On the seventh day the fisherman came back, with his crew, 'No, I didn't suffer,' he told me. 'I said to myself: if the boat capsizes I have my revolver, see?' He gleefully displayed a very old, very large pistol, pressing it to his forehead in the manner of one performing a parlour trick. That fisherman had never learned to swim.

The day was advancing rapidly while I dawdled on the port; it was time to call on Comte Peraldi, President of the Syndicat d'Initiative, an organisation that deals with visitors. Although he had never heard of my existence he greeted me as though he had been impatiently awaiting my arrival for years. 'Excellent! Excellent!' he cried, 'I'm so very delighted to see you! The English have always favoured us. You once even ruled us for a year or two, but you found us too expensive. I'm joking, you know. We had many English visitors here before the war, but now, since the bandits have disappeared, we are less attractive to you. The English are very romantic. There was a Mrs Nelson – yes, her name was truly British – she fell in love with the bandit Spada and had honeymoon with him in the maquis and paid a lawyer to defend him when he was on trial for half a dozen murders, but they guillotined him just the same. But I'm joking again. Now tell me, where are you planning to go?'

I told him I had arranged to go to the south of the island, with my husband, to stay with Jean Cesari's family. 'Admirable! Admirable!' he replied. 'It's wonderful to be the guest of our peasants! Precisely because they're not peasants. They are great seigneurs and accomplished hosts; they are poets and musicians and sportsmen and sometimes bandits, but never peasants; they never bore one talking about their crops. In truth they have practically no crops; only just what's needed to supply the family table.'

I tried to explain that according to Jean's report the Cesari were a very industrious family; but Count Peraldi was swept along by his theme. 'They're not interested. No. All they want is to go to the Continent or abroad and become postmen and customs' officials, if not gangsters. And then when they retire to their villages they're too tired to do anything more. But it's not altogether our fault!' he exclaimed. 'The French government has given us so very little! The roads, the schools, and both are in a lamentable state of repair, but no dams or irrigation systems, nothing to help the peasants improve their land. The situation can be called dramatic. Soon everyone will have gone abroad and the island will become an uninhabited pile of rocks in the sea!'

All over Corsica I was to hear the same complaints; the French government had neglected the island and now it was dying from lack of capital investment. And this, when I first went there, was certainly true; it is only within the last few years that Corsica has begun to receive anything like a fair share of public money. As the Corsicans often bitterly contend, the island could have become prosperous long ago if the French had sunk into it a fraction of what they squandered on their ungrateful colonies. But until very recently the French never admitted the urgency of doing so. A peculiar insensitivity to Corsican affairs made them unable to appreciate that Corsican backwardness is not an immutable natural condition, correlative with the soil, the climate or a racial character, but the logical outcome of the island's history.

Yet reading this history with an unbiased mind one can hardly fail to realise how far material progress was paralysed by centuries of war and misrule. When the French conquered Corsica just two hundred years ago the capital wealth represented by generations of toil in more peaceful countries simply did not exist. The people who under Pasquale Paoli had operated the most advanced representative government of their time had not succeeded in building a single carriage road. Conditions, of course, have improved since then; but the scars of fifteen hundred years of political disturbances are still apparent. Every ruined house in the marshy bed of a derelict valley is linked to a chain of cause and effect reaching back to the fall of Rome.

Corsica has paid the penalty of being too much coveted. A dozen seafaring states at different times laid claim to the island, which provided safe harbours, unlimited timber for shipbuilding, and gave its possessors a controlling strategic base in the western Mediterranean. Rival powers raided it and invaded it, colonised and exploited it, bought and sold it, fought over it against the inhabitants and each other until they nearly destroyed the prize, so that Corsica became a depopulated island almost without trade, industry or agriculture, where the harbours sheltered only a few fishermen and pirates and the inhabitants had come to believe that their inescapable destiny was privation and war.

Greeks from Asia Minor, Carthaginians and possibly Etruscans had already made colonies on the coasts before the Romans conquered the island after fighting local resistance for the best part of a century. They gave the pre-civilised pastoral Corsicans the olive tree, the vine, new cereal crops, irrigation, a law, the Latin language and, eventually, Christianity; they built a chain of ports round the coasts and a scattering of inland towns. The seven centuries of their domination provided a span of peace and prosperity the Corsicans have never known since. Subsequent invasions – of Vandals, Ostrogoths, Lombards – destroyed the civilised way of life they had implanted, which an interval of extortionate Byzantine rule did nothing to restore;

8

Saracens from Spain and North Africa invaded the island from the eighth century and kept it in a state of alarm and anarchy, practically cut off from the European mainland, for some three hundred years. By then the Roman ports, repeatedly battered, ransacked and burned, had been abandoned; the inhabitants had moved inland and reverted to their ancestral pastoral economy; the fertile coastal plains had become waterlogged and malarial, as they remained until the Second World War.

The Corsican dark ages ended in 1076 when the Pope, titular sovereign of the island since the time of Charlemagne, assigned its defence to the Bishop (succeeded by the Archbishops) of Pisa. The Pisans revived Christianity in a campaign that has left its mark all over the island in hundreds of severely handsome churches. But the Genoese, who had collaborated with Pisa in the expulsion of the Saracens, contested the arrangement; conflict between the rival trading republics was constant until the destruction of the Pisan fleet in 1284. To replace the Pisan overlordship, the Pope gave Corsica, along with Sardinia, to the kings of Aragon, and thereby inaugurated another long period of war, with the Corsican nobles supporting, on the whole Aragon, the people republican Genoa. Again Genoa emerged victorious; but the Corsican nobles were not subjugated till the early sixteenth century after a sequence of reckless revolts in which they virtually fought themselves to extinction.

It was one thing to wrest the island from foreign competitors and local warlords and quite another to govern it. The Genoese, relentlessly mercantile, the so-called Aberdonians of Italy, were in fact singularly unfitted to handle the Corsicans or win their respect. Equally stubborn and arrogant, but attached to different values, the two people were fatally predisposed to misunderstand and despise each other. When Henri II of France, in the course of his struggle against the Emperor Charles V, invaded the island in connivance with a celebrated Corsican mercenary, Sampiero Corso, he rapidly conquered it with the collaboration of most of the population. But the advantages of a French administration were barely felt before Corsica was returned to Genoa, having been bartered against Calais to the enemy allies by the Treaty of Cateau-Cambrésis.

For the next hundred and sixty years, including all the seventeenth century, the Genoese ruled Corsica unchallenged. They may not have been guilty of the inhuman tyranny described in some Corsican history books; but their system was certainly despotic and their officials, mostly black sheep in their own country, exceeded the contemporary norms of corruption. While magistrates sold themselves to the highest bidders, the vendetta – parallel, primitive form of justice – increased appallingly; the peasants were crushed by taxation, the population declined. Not that the regime was wholly negative. The rural Corsicans were left free to run their own affairs; the Genoese never swarmed over the interior; they remained in their six fortified towns on the coasts: Bonifacio, Calvi, Bastia, Saint-Florent, Ajaccio, Algajola (built in that order). When they interfered with rural life it was to encourage agriculture, and this campaign was sufficiently successful to create a new class of well-off, well-educated rural notables. These were however the very people who most resented Genoese colonial trade monopolies and became the most dangerous enemies of the Republic.

National rebellion broke out, spontaneously, in 1729; the Genoese were soon confined to the coastal towns, where they remained. Sporadic fighting none the less dragged on during the next forty years in accordance with the now familiar pattern of colonial wars. Both sides were aided, at different times, by foreign powers; at intervals settlements were proposed and rejected; meanwhile Corsican leaders came forward, national constitutions were adopted and the Corsican nation took shape by a process of trial and error. A fanciful episode was the eight months' reign of Theodor von Neuhof, a beguiling international crook who induced the rebels to crown him king. But in Pasquale Paoli the Corsicans found a leader to match their aspirations; elected head of state in 1755 he gave the country a constitution in keeping with the most enlightened ideas of the age. But this courageous experiment came to nothing: Genoa sold her sovereignty over Corsica to France; French troops poured into the island; in 1769 the patriots were defeated and Paoli fled to England.

Corsica had become a province of France. But there was no integration of the two peoples before the time of Napoleon. The French Revolution brought about the last political disaffection. Paoli, returned from exile, fell foul of the French revolutionary government, declared Corsica once again independent and appealed for protection to Britain. The British went further than he had bargained for: an Anglo-Corsican kingdom was proclaimed by George III with Sir Gilbert Elliot, not Paoli, as Viceroy. This bungling treatment of the 'father of the nation' was a cause of understandable discontent; Paoli had to be re-exiled, and when the war in the Mediterranean turned against the British they promptly evacuated Corsica while Napoleon sent in troops, unopposed.

Since then the Corsicans have been loyal and conspicuous citizens of France, energetically participating in her politics, pioneering in her colonies, fighting in her wars. While the French have done little, till now, to improve Corsica, they have welcomed Corsican manpower, in the civil service, above all in the armed forces. Some twenty thousand Corsicans, it is said, died in the First World War; in the second they organised a redoubtable resistance which helped to free the island from enemy occupation as early as September 1943.

Corsican history, tale of recurrent discords and disappointments, explains much about Corsica. It accounts for the empty coasts where ruined watch-towers and citadels are still the only noteworthy buildings for miles on end; the forbidding villages on mountain peaks and crests where nearly every house looks like a fortress; the untilled valleys and the acres and acres of uninhabited maquis. Yet its effects were not wholly disastrous. The Corsicans drew pride and strength from their struggles; they learnt to fight for what they valued. In Napoleon's words, they knew that 'death is one of the states of the soul', but that slavery is the soul's 'abasement'.[2]

Against overwhelming odds they defended their fundamental liberties.

Justice was vindicated by the brutal code of the vendetta; thousands were unjustly killed but the principle of justice was upheld. Inefficient and oppressive governments stimulated bold innovations in political organisation; the eighteenth-century constitutions (Paoli's, and several rudimentary ones preceding it), with their *avant-garde* features, were among the consequences of Genoese misrule. The Genoese had indeed actually encouraged liberal institutions by crushing the insular nobility and so facilitating a democratic, collective system in the villages that served as a basis for the eighteenth-century constitutional experiments. The prevailingly egalitarian character of Corsican society ensured that there was no landless proletariat, no hard-and-fast class structure, and in spite of a general low standard of living, no destitution. Alone among the peoples of Europe the Corsicans avoided feudal and capitalist oppression.

Poverty, equality and frustration made up the Corsican birthright; some accepted it with dogged stoicism, others reacted dynamically. The Corsicans have always oscillated between fatalism and a burning will to self-assertion. Resistance to foreign domination encouraged cunning, and Machiavellian methods that often defeated their own ends; but it also fostered bold designs. Ambition has in fact been the undoing of nearly all the outstanding Corsicans: they attempted too much; but they achieved great things before they failed. Those who tried to realise their aims at home usually ran into disaster early, for they were hampered by too many leading actors on too small a stage. Corsica is richer in human material than in any other commodity. But those who made their careers abroad, trained in the hard school of Corsican guile and courage, were often brilliantly successful.

In the old town of Ajaccio, just behind the fishermen's cafés, is the house where the most successful of them all was born. The *Casa Bonaparte* is a large, plain, seventeenth-century building giving on to a narrow alley. The family apparently occupied only the first floor. When I visited it, the day of my arrival in Ajaccio, I was a little depressed by its chilly, genteel air. The rooms, darkish in spite of their high windows, are stiffly furnished with French eighteenth-century furniture, not of the best quality; large bleak mirrors in varnished wood frames hang on walls covered in dull brocade. The only object acquired as a work of art is a marquetry model of the Nativity with ivory figures which Napoleon is supposed to have sent to his mother in the early years of his career; the gift, I felt, of a parvenu son to a bigoted provincial woman, both of them lacking in taste.

But later, when I had grown more familiar with Napoleon's early life, I came to feel a very poignant quality in this stuffy family home with its rather pathetic pretensions, where an impecunious couple struggled to lead a polite life in a rough country and give their eight children a privileged start in the world. Napoleon's parents come alive in this stilted setting: Carlo Bonaparte, a handsome, restless, thriftless lawyer, a shrewd, gambling politician, and his handsome wife Letizia, a dauntless, disenchanted Corsican woman, possessed of all the hard, rather narrow determination of her kind.

Together they weathered the recurrent political crises and with Corsican astuteness contrived to use them for their advancement. Their eldest son, Joseph, was born at Corte, the independent upland capital where Carlo Bonaparte was acting as secretary to Paoli. Letizia was already six months' pregnant with Napoleon when the Corsican patriots were defeated by the French. Retreating from the advancing army, Carlo and Letizia had to ride their mules over the savage heights of the central mountains to reach Ajaccio. If prenatal influences count for anything, this odyssey would seem to explain much in Napoleon's character.

Carlo Bonaparte however sensibly accommodated himself to the new regime and lost no time in securing recognition of his noble origins; ironically enough he was descended from a Genoese soldier with patrician Florentine ancestors who had settled in Ajaccio in the late fifteenth century, with the foundation of the town. Noble status opened the way to the favour of Comte de Marbeuf, the French military governor, to a visit to the court of France as delegate of the nobility of the Corsican Estates, to a scholarship for Napoleon in the French military academy at Brienne and the *Ecole Militaire* in Paris. Carlo Bonaparte even obtained from Marbeuf promises of protection for Joseph, and another scholarship for his daughter, Elisa, at St Cyr, then a school for young ladies; a very privileged upbringing at this period when Corsican girls were rarely taught even to write or read.

This, then, was the background of Napoleon's childhood: grand protectors, keeping up appearances, insecurity, debts; the necessity to succeed. As in many Corsican families success was regarded as a duty of children to parents, and to the group as a whole. But little could they imagine, Carlo and Letizia, as they pushed and wangled and schemed, that those children who gathered round the circular dining-table for the simple country meals – of kid, lamb, goat's cheese, cherries from the family orchard[3] – were destined to be kings and queens, or that the son who brawled in the neighbouring streets (Ribulione – the troublemaker – was his nickname) would become emperor of the French and one of the most formidable soldiers the world has known.

The interior of the Bonaparte house has changed considerably since Napoleon lived there as a child. When Pasquale Paoli, returning from his first exile in England, broke with the French revolutionary government and declared Corsica independent for the second time, the Bonapartes found themselves on the losing side. Menaced by Paoli's partisans, Letizia – then a widow – escaped by night into the maquis with her younger children, while the Paolists looted their home. The family, rescued by Napoleon, fled to Toulon, apparently ruined. Four years later, Paoli and the British having left Corsica, Letizia and Joseph were back in Ajaccio redecorating the house to suit the improved status of the family now that Napoleon had victoriously concluded the Italian campaign. But Napoleon spent only a week in this new décor, banqueting with old partisans and retainers, when he visited Ajaccio, for the last time, on his way back to France from Egypt in 1799. By then Letizia had already moved to Paris and no Bonaparte was ever again to inhabit the family home.

Napoleon's mortifying experiences, when he was hounded out of the island with his family, marked him for life. In his youth he had been an ardent Corsican patriot, as his writings of the period abundantly show. To be forced to fly for his life and his family's, his home ransacked, his reputation blackened, his position ruined and his future jeopardised, was a humiliation of an intolerable kind. It accounts, I think, for what can hardly fail to astonish any visitor to Corsica: his neglect of his homeland. It is true that he reduced taxation;[4] but one would expect to find some visual evidence of his favour. Having made Ajaccio the capital he might, after all, have redesigned it with pleasure gardens and fountains and triumphal arches, or at least embellished it with some of the loot of Italy, and so given it an appearance more in keeping with the name it later received from the Corsicans: 'The Imperial City'. But the improvements carried out to his orders were strictly utilitarian: a new water supply, the planning of new streets; these are works more suited to a conscientious mayor than to the Emperor of the French. Only a very bitter memory of his early experiences can explain such indifference. It was very late, too late for Corsica and himself, before this grudge was dissolved in deeper humiliations; in the days of his exile at St Helena when he remembered the scent of the maquis, and expressed the wish that if burial in Paris were refused him he should lie beside his ancestors in the cathedral of Ajaccio, as is inscribed on a plaque close to the font where he was baptised.

Later, a bronze cast of his death-mask was given to the town. The face is nobler and thinner than it appears in his later portraits. One can see it, now, in the *Musée Napoléonien*, an upper room of the Town Hall that looks less like a museum than an old-fashioned drawing-room, full of busts and portraits of generations of Bonaparte, from Napoleon's parents to the ill-starred son of Napoleon III, killed in the Zulu war. The least convincing is Gérard's lugubrious, oversized painting of Napoleon in his coronation robes.

If there are souvenirs, in Ajaccio, that evoke with an acute intimacy Napoleon's first and last days, there is little enough to recall his image in the prime of life. The Roman emperor on horseback in the main square, the First Consul outside the Town Hall, wearing a toga, crowned with a laurel wreath and surrounded by fubsy-faced lions: these pompous pseudo-antique figures bear no relation to the man who wooed Josephine in passionate letters from the Italian battlefields and returned from Elba to rally a war-weary population to his desperate cause.

Only the most recent monument to him, above the town, up beyond the Anglican church and the British cottages, gives any idea of the man. The statue is a replica of the bronze figure that once stood on the column of the Place Vendôme, with cocked hat and hand stuffed in waistcoat; but it is the setting that touches the imagination. Napoleon stands on a high granite ramp against a background of olive trees and maquis-covered hills. Planted on his native rock, he stares sombrely out to sea, symbol of that determination of the Corsicans, illustrated all through their history, to overcome obscurity and isolation, to impose themselves on circumstances, men, the world.

2 THE FIRST HEROES

Capital cities – Fesch, a great collector – quest for antiquities –
travelling south – peasant families – Filitosa, images of heroes

WE lingered several days in Ajaccio, bathing, sight-seeing, relaxing in the
corrupting subtropical climate. I was planning the route I would follow after I
left the Cesari and my husband returned to England. With Comte Peraldi's
help I worked out an itinerary: southwards from the Cesari's home to Sartène,
the head town of that area (known as the Sartenais); northwards along the
east coast past Aléria, site of the abandoned Roman capital, to Bastia,
capital during the Genoese ascendancy; then over to the west coast for a spell
in the tourist resorts, Ile-Rousse and Calvi, before making my way to the remote pastoral Niolo and back to Ajaccio through Corte, Paoli's capital in the
highlands. My journey round this island 114 miles long by 52 wide, where the
population was said not to exceed twenty per square kilometre, took me from
capital city to capital city. Each of the foreign powers that tried to rule it
created a new one, on the seaboard, as near as possible to its homeland; the
independent capital, like Ankara, was placed high in the native interior.

Comte Peraldi recommended hotels and gave me letters of introduction to
friends in places where hotels were lacking. Martin Baretti, proprietor of the
one we were staying in, gave me a pot of anti-mosquito paste for the east coast
while at the same time assuring me that the dreaded anopheles had been eliminated by DDT since the Second World War. Travelling in Corsica, I realised,
was still regarded as something of an adventure. I determined to make a detour in the south to see Carbini, a village said to have been occupied in the
Middle Ages by a group of heretics who held all their possessions, including
women and children, in common, and celebrated strange orgies in a Pisan
church of unusual architectural distinction. Count Peraldi was discouraging;
I should find nowhere to stay, he told me. My husband spotted an advertisement for a hotel at Carbini with bathrooms to every room; a luxury rare in
Corsica at that time and unheard of in the villages. 'It must be a practical
joke,' Count Peraldi said, 'but you'd better give it a try.'

On his advice we visited the Fesch museum. This gloomy pile in a dilapidated street near the port houses, surprisingly, a collection of Italian paintings classed as the finest in France outside the Louvre. Paintings were the
ruling passion of Joseph Fesch, Napoleon's step-uncle, son of a late second

14

marriage of his maternal grandmother to a Swiss officer in Genoese pay. And Fesch, who began life as an obscure ecclesiastic in Ajaccio, was in a marvellous position to satisfy his tastes after Napoleon had appointed him Archbishop of Lyons, Cardinal, and Minister-Plenipotentiary to the Holy See. Never was there a period, moreover, so favourable to an art collector. Churches, monasteries and chateaux had been rifled during the French Revolution, the possessions of the émigrés confiscated and sold; the legendary cities of Italy and the Low Countries had been looted in the wars: French, Dutch, Flemish and Italian masterpieces, concealed for generations, flooded the market.

A collection that would illustrate the entire history of European art: this, no less, was Fesch's aim. By the end of his life he had almost achieved it; to judge by contemporary records he had acquired examples of almost every outstanding European painter. How many pictures he owned no one knew, not even himself; he thought he might have thirty thousand.[1]

What would happen to them when he died? Fesch, never lacking in political acumen, let it be known that he would bequeath the entire collection to the town of Lyons provided he were reinstated as archbishop, a title he had in fact never resigned. Louis-Philippe was however not prepared to have Napoleon's uncle at the head of the Catholic Church in France. When this became apparent Fesch devised another, more genuinely philanthropic scheme. He would found an academy of learning in Ajaccio and leave a thousand of his paintings, representing the different schools, to be exhibited there for the instruction of the pupils. The academy was duly built, but was not yet in use when he died. Whereupon Joseph Bonaparte, his residuary legatee, greedy for a lion's share of the masterpieces, seized this pretext to oppose the will. An agreement was eventually reached; but it was his choice of pictures, not that envisaged by Fesch, that was finally sent to the town.

Time, however, has given the citizens of Ajaccio a revenge. When Fesch died, in 1839, the sixteenth- and seventeenth-century masters stood highest in public esteem. These, naturally, were the works withheld by Joseph Bonaparte. But Fesch, with an *avant-garde* taste that bewildered his contemporaries, had particularly valued the then-neglected Italian primitives. Works of Daddi, Bellini, Andrea da Firenze, Botticelli, Bocatti, Cosima Tura, and some magical panels of the school of Rimini were included in the cargo shipped to Ajaccio, where they now hang, resplendent, in the little-known museum.

We found the conservator, Jean Leblanc, with his wife, working on card indexes in a back room in a minute space left between stacked canvases and piles of Roman amphorae. 'We've only room to hang a couple of hundred paintings at most,' he complained, 'the rest of the building's used as a school.' 'Corsica's like that,' said his wife, 'full of treasures nobody sees or knows.' I mentioned the statues described by Jean Cesari. 'I should certainly take a look,' she said, 'there must be any amount of antiquities hidden in the maquis: prehistoric, Graeco-Roman, mediaeval, all kinds. Nobody's gone to work here systematically since Prosper Mérimée. You knew that of course? *Colomba* was only a byproduct of his journey; he came as Inspector of Historic Monuments. But as he went round the island in about seven weeks at the pace a horse can go one can imagine he missed a good deal. Come to think of it, he saw a primitive kind of statue; but to the north of Ajaccio, not where you're going.[2] But it could be something similar. There's an engraving of it in his report; let's take a look.'

The engraving was of a large block of stone carved to suggest rather than represent the human form. A pointed face, eyes and nose and mouth were roughly delineated; shoulders, a protruding ear, were cut from the block; but the rest of the body was merely hinted at, without arms or legs, by the tapering shaft of stone. It seemed a weird, barbaric and rather frightening image.

'Mérimée classed it as Roman or Phoenician,' Jean Leblanc commented, 'but there's no doubt it's much older. Odd he didn't associate it with the menhirs he saw down in the south; that's surely the period it belongs to.' There were many menhirs, he told me, in the deserted south-western Sartenais, and some dolmens. 'One doesn't really know how many; archaeologists never stay here long enough. And then the problems of research in a country like this! The maquis covers everything. There's a lot more to be found, of that I'm certain. Perhaps you're on your way to making an archaeological discovery; one never knows.'

I walked out into the drowsy sunlight exhilarated but dazed. The books I had read on Corsica had said little or nothing about antiquities, leaving me with the impression that the arts had never flourished in this island of nearly perpetual war. I had assumed, too, that such antiquities as there were had long ago been located, studied and classified as in other parts of France; I had envisaged only the slenderest chance that Jean's statues – if they really existed – had escaped attention. And now I was told I might discover almost anything.

Yet I was far from measuring the negligence and indifference that had blinded the public to the variety and quality of Corsican antiquities. Prehistoric archaeologists had in fact given attention to the island since Mérimée, but their researches were fragmentary. Subsequent Inspectors of Historic Monuments made harassed, unrevealing tours: six or seven travel hours a day, bandits, malaria, paralysing heat in summer, snow in winter, bad inns or none; it was hardly surprising if they missed some of the best monuments, many of them miles off the roads. Fashions in taste were almost as great a handicap as the awkwardness of travel. The nineteenth-century eye, which dictated a happy elimination of paintings from the Fesch bequest, looked coldly on what is most distinguished in Corsican art and architecture. Not that this is often the work of Corsicans: a sequence of invasions since prehistoric times reduced local talent either to flat imitation or a popular idiom. Yet Corsica has impressed a particular stamp on the styles introduced by its foreign overlords: that of a rigorous austerity. Whereas Sicily – another much-conquered Mediterranean island – stimulated a flamboyant luxuriance in the

16

art of its invaders, the influence of Corsica was just the contrary: to reduce every style to its barest expression. The harshness of the environment, the hardness of the granite that was often the only available building stone, poverty and war: these and other factors, fused with the underlying temper of the people, led to a shedding of ornament, a concentration on basic form that was uncongenial, even offensive to nineteenth-century taste.

It was not until well after my first visit to Corsica that the contemporary sensitivity to functional design, elimination and abstraction, began to set a value on the Corsican artistic climate. A time, for me, of mounting excitement. I had freed myself from obligations in England; I was discovering Corsica village by village, mile by mile. There were expeditions with Jean Leblanc and his wife, when equipped with cameras, masons' measures, undersea swimming apparatus and a sound recorder, we noted, recorded, collected whatever came our way. The booty of each outing was heterogeneous and unpredictable: a photograph of an unlisted Pisan church on a disused mule track; a note on a fifteenth-century altarpiece badly in need of restoration; a haunting air chanted by a bearded patriarch, an amphora drawn from the sea bed.

Later I took to travelling weeks on end alone, reporting results to Jean Leblanc, and to Pierre Lamotte, the archivist, who became my adviser and friend. These expeditions were all memorable, for their byproducts no less than for what I found (byproducts such as gave Mérimée the matter of a masterpiece). There were the long, long bus journeys through bewilderingly noble scenery; the arrivals in isolated villages; visits to the priests and monks whom I came to know as lonely, pioneering men, without exception irreproachably poor. My nights were usually spent in the homes of widows, deprived but respected members of their communities who eke out minimal incomes renting rooms; and there I was initiated into the warmth and the anguish, the dense emotional content of Corsican domestic life.

Days went by exploring dust-smothered churches, and their sacristies, which often proved to be veritable storehouses of religious art; others were spent walking through country so desolate that the sound of a voice drifting across a valley assumed the momentousness of the pealing of a bell. The finds came after many hours alone with the rocks and maquis: dolmens and menhirs, and other perplexing works of prehistoric man, Pisan churches, Roman pottery and tiles that marked lost towns on abandoned shores, where I bathed in blessed cool water, lay stretched on beaches, my body dissolving, so I felt, into the rock and sand.

At a time when this prospecting work seemed most overwhelming specialists took it in hand. Looking for a book, one day, in the Bastia library I ran into Geneviève Moracchini, now the author of an important thesis, who was then methodically walking over the island listing and studying the Pisan churches. We were to visit very many together, some of them in spots so forlorn that one could hardly imagine that a congregation large enough to fill them had ever existed there. Later the prehistorian Roger Grosjean arrived to begin a long-term programme of research. Finally a pair of classical archaeo-logists, Jean and Laurence Jehasse, obtained funds for excavating Aléria, the Roman capital.

The results went beyond anyone's expectations. Genevieve Moracchini, starting from a list of the dozen Pisan churches so far recognised, ended by finding over three hundred. Excavations at Aléria have already shown the unsuspected splendour of the Greek settlement, and that the Roman city was much more than the bleak colonial outpost imagined by some pessimistic local antiquarians (Boswell, echoing his hosts, referred to its inhabitants as 'the dregs of the Romans'). But the most startling discoveries belong to pre-history. Roger Grosjean was able to tell an astonished public that pre-Graeco-Roman Corsica, far from being sunk in abysmal barbarism, had produced two vigorous and wholly original cultures, one the work of a race of master-builders, the other of a metaphysical, visionary people, whose sculp-tors, about a millennium before Praxiteles, groped their way, unaided, towards the classical Greek ideal. Corsica's prophetic role in the genesis of European civilisation, hitherto totally unsuspected, began to be revealed; but this story must be told separately. It began with my first visit to Jean Cesari's family. Yet when I took the bus to the south, that shining summer's morning, nothing suggested that the journey was to have such weighty con-sequences; nothing, that is, except faint, unformulated hopes that now and then brushed the rind of my consciousness, like the wings of swifts in flight.

The bus carried mail and freight all over the south of the island, and it took a long time loading; post bags and crates of beer, an old domed trunk and a roll of wire, a bunch of fishing rods and a perambulator and a couple of bi-cycles had to be thrown, heaved, shoved, hauled on to the roof and roped down in uneasy juxtaposition. We rumbled out of town, at last, into a stream of incoming traffic: donkey carts piled high with brushwood for the bakeries; fast-trotting gigs driven by dark-skinned, black-hatted countrymen; ancient tinny cars and trucks recklessly hooting in mid-road. All these people were on their way to the Ajaccio market: peasants from neighbouring valleys with eggs and vegetables for sale; shepherds from further afield who produce only cheeses, coming up to town to sell them and buy provisions. For though the country to the south is fertile enough, very little of it is cultivated. A mile or so from Ajaccio there was nothing to show for the possibilities of the soil except the extreme density of the natural vegetation. The mountains, heaving into the sky on every side, were covered with evergreen oak right up to their rocky summits. The sun's rays, striking the tree tops, turned them silver, the glossy leaves reflecting the light like metal. But these trees, domeshaped as the trees a child will draw, were widely spaced between undergrowth, and this undergrowth, with their lower branches, was in deep shadow, so that every slope appeared hatched with perpendicular bars of darkness. Such black, secretive forests, I thought, were the preserves once attributed to the prim-eval gods.

The landscape unfolded in vistas of mountains, detached formations, ragged pyramids and cones springing haphazardly from different levels. Naked rock walls crowned them, like the bastions of gigantic castles, gleaming pink in the early sun. As we swung upwards and inland the peaks first seen descended to eye level, their prodigious granite outcrops becoming accessible and unintimidating, while massifs hitherto invisible, still bearing snow, floated up like smoke from the expanding horizon. The holm oak and maquis thinned as we rose. Chestnuts, growing from turf, stood scattered near the first pass, where an old, solitary inn by a wind-bent pine recalled a whole category of romantic paintings and travellers' tales. Beyond, we looked into a vast bowl, walled, to the south, by an impossibly high range, vaporous as mosquito netting in the heat haze.

Down in the circular valley the maquis disappeared. The landscape, here, was dream-like and opulent, reminded me of Sidney's *Arcadia*. In fact the much-quoted opening description gives an almost exact picture of it: hills 'which garnished their proud heights with stately trees', valleys 'whose base estate seemed comforted with refreshing of silver rivers', meadows enamelled with flowers and 'each pasture stored with sheep feeding with sober security'. There were even houses 'all scattered, no two being one by th' other'; 'a show, as it were, of accompanible solitariness, and of a civil wildness'. Nothing was lacking except the shepherd boy piping as though he should never grow old, and the young shepherdess knitting; for no one seemed to be tending the long-legged sheep, either all white or all black, that grazed in the rolling pastures dotted with clumps of holm oak. The houses, too, looked empty; square, stone-built, earth coloured, set apart on grassy knolls and surrounded by shade-spreading trees. Human life has ebbed from this idyllic upland valley no less than from the harsher areas of the Corsican interior. Few people appeared on the road: a boy driving a mule laden with planks; a couple of men with a dog reclining in the wayside grass in poses borrowed from Graeco-Roman sculpture and who indeed looked so like statues that one was surprised to see them wave as one went by.

The feeling of being a tourist progressively slipped away as I penetrated ever deeper into the silent, enveloping countryside. At every village we stopped to exchange passengers and mail bags, to take on freight. Tall houses, built of roughly hewn granite blocks, gave straight on to the streets, without gardens. There was nothing cosy or cottagey about these Corsican homes, patrician, if not elegant, uncompromisingly severe. They were hard to date: seventeenth century, eighteenth, early nineteenth? The villages had an overall appearance of indefinable age. Of the pre-industrial era, anyhow; only the telegraph wires that had accompanied us, like a convoy, all the way from Ajaccio, reminded one of the contemporary world. Few shop windows were to be seen, and not a single advertisement.

The inhabitants – not numerous – were either elderly or young: old men in dark, red-sashed corduroys, old women – the First World War widows? – wearing long skirts, gathered at the back, usually black, with black kerchiefs, elaborately folded, framing beaky features. Young girls were large-eyed and slender; boys had long refined faces and incongruous mops of lusty dark hair. Aloof, composed, old and young sauntered about the streets or crowded to the bus stops to meet returning relatives and friends. There was the kiss on either cheek, the sharing out of parcels and luggage, but no exclamations or discussions: they kissed, shouldered burdens, and made off with a firm, purposeful tread. This was a people self-contained, self-assured; not rich, not poor; absorbed in a life alien to all I knew.

The stops were long; there was always time to go to a café. We filed into dark cool rooms, usually windowless, where the wood of the bar counters was polished chestnut brown by use and age. Sausages and hams hung from the beams; fireplaces were heaped with wood-ash; guns were slung on the walls; one breathed a rich odour – peculiar to Corsican country homes – composed of stale wood smoke and smoked sausages and hams. The proprietors were courteous, but unservile, uninterested, so it seemed, until they refilled one's glass, unasked: 'This one on the house, for the road. Until next time!' Such is the undemonstrative friendship of the Corsican country people, reassuring to those who wake at 3 a.m., alone in the universe, rejected and despised.

At Olmeto, a large, particularly ancient-looking village clinging to a hillside amid olive groves, the driver warned us that the next stop would be ours (he had agreed to drop us at the Cesari's house which stands out in the country between villages). A change of direction brought a view of the sea, invisible since leaving Ajaccio; one of the breathtaking, unanticipated Corsican views. Immediately below, the long low waving coastline of the Golfe de Valinco enclosed a band of water of an incredible dense, chalky blue. Propriano, the port, was a blaze of whiteness far up its further shore. But here, at the square head of the gulf, where the sand was piled like a snowdrift, only two buildings were to be seen: a wooden shed on the beach, and on the roadside a neat stone red-roofed doll's house. Spruce, ingenuous, and ideally placed just above the sea, could this be the Cesari's home? It was.

The driver drew up at the door; the Cesari were greeting us, reaching for our luggage with strong brown peasants' hands. And there was Jean, very pale by comparison, and urban-looking in his slick new English clothes. 'I was almost tired of waiting for you,' he said. 'I was afraid you'd changed your minds.'

We entered a small room, spotless, sparely furnished with a circular dining-table and kitchen chairs. A cooking pot on an open fire emitted appetising odours. Family photographs hung on the pale blue walls, and a framed *'Médaille de la Famille Française'* awarded to Madame Cesari because she is the mother of ten children.

Only three of them had so far left home: a son and a daughter, who had married, and another son who was learning tailoring in Marseilles. The others were all sitting round the table, pressing us to eat dry sweet cakes flavoured with aniseed, known as *canistrelli*, filling tiny glasses with a homemade liqueur in which whole grapes floated. There was Antoine and François and Jean-Baptiste, lean, swarthy young men with soft singsong voices contradicted by

20

their darkly glittering eyes; Marie, the eldest daughter, still handsome in a tousled, gypsy style; Antoinette, black-haired and vivacious; Blanche, pale and withdrawn; Pierrette, the youngest, still at school, a lovely dusky-skinned blonde. She was planning a career in one of the government services, so she told me in her particularly pretty, precise French, choosing and pronouncing each word with fastidious relish; she was studying very hard for her coming exams. Meanwhile Madame Cesari, in a long-skirted dress, her hair piled on top of her head in an apple-sized bun, presided over the table, throwing out occasional phrases in Corsican dialect with a conviction so incisive, an intimation of humour so engaging that I could only regret understanding so little of what she said (she spoke no French).

Had we made a good journey? Did we find seats on the bus? Had we been comfortable in Ajaccio, and in good health? When the exchange of civilities was over Jean took us out to bathe. We slithered down a sandy cliff; five goats sleeping in the shade of a rock started up at our passage to peer at us with bright black gold-rimmed eyes. The sea, lake-calm, was a benediction; the beach, where driftwood logs made polished ivory backrests, was potently scented by one of the most inconspicuous of the maquis plants, the grey-leaved golden-everlasting that grew all over the sand.

Jean had not failed us (no Cesari has ever failed me, they are people of their word). 'Tomorrow we shall go to see the statues,' he said. 'It's all arranged. My aunt is lending us the donkey cart; we must leave at dawn.' To my surprise he spoke of Madame Cesari, not her husband, as the head of the family. The husband, who appeared for the midday meal, was a gentle old man with a long white prophet's beard. His voice was soft and his movements curiously graceful in spite of his heavy boots and bulky corduroys. His personality was that of a superior diplomat or minor sage. Madame Cesari, on the other hand, had the grand histrionic manner of an actress of the old school. No one could more visibly belie the foreigners' theory that Corsican peasant women are crushed, oppressed, broken creatures. Whatever contest of wills had ever taken place between them must long ago have been settled to the satisfaction of them both. They rarely spoke to each other, so I noticed; sitting side by side at the circular table surrounded by their chattering children and guests, they seemed linked in a telepathetic union.

The simmering pot was taken off the fire; it contained a mutton stew, thick with vegetables. But first we had plates of smoked ham and several varieties of smoked sausage, and tomatoes and raw onions swimming in the local unrefined olive oil which gave to all this food a provocative musty flavour; and afterwards came a homemade cheese of ewes' milk, oddly tasting of nuts, and finally small, very sweet melons. Corsican peasant food, if rather repetitive, can be delicious; but the marvel of it is in the quality of the products, all freshly taken from the land and yielding, often, subtle, unexpected flavours in which aroma can hardly be distinguished from taste. At the Cesari's table I felt I was enjoying meat and fruit and cheese for the first time.

The meal led to a siesta, the siesta to another bathe, with the sun westering towards the open sea, transforming the gulf into one of Turner's gilded mythical estuaries. We went to bed early in preparation for the next day's start at dawn, after plates of a nearly solid soup of dried broad beans and cabbage spiced with ham, standby of peasant homes. But that night I could hardly sleep in my little iron bed for excitement. For hours I lay looking through my window opening on to the mountainside, watching the lights of Olmeto disappearing one by one. Jean had promised to knock on our door well before sunrise; but several times I woke of my own accord, thrust up into consciousness by the nightmare panic fear that the others had gone, leaving me behind, to find only the huge black shape of the mountain against the star-lit sky, and the night dead silent save for the croaking of frogs.

The last time I woke light had already come. Had Jean, perhaps, changed his mind? My husband and I threw on our clothes and rushed downstairs. Madame Cesari's shrewd kindly smile reassured me. 'The donkey strayed in the night,' Marie explained, as she lifted the enamel coffee-pot from the iron tripod in the fireplace. 'He was ill-mannered, he went off to sulk in the maquis.' Marie has a naturally quaint, vivid turn of phrase. 'But the men have caught him now,' she told us. 'Take your breakfast with light hearts.' All the same I was not really lighthearted until I actually found myself in the donkey-cart with my husband and Jean and Antoine, rattling towards Olmeto in the first rays of the sun.

The beams were still level with the pearl-coloured sea as we rounded the head of the gulf and branched down a sandy track running along its further shore. The landscape was empty and desolate, with ancient olives, large as English oaks, rising above the maquis. Long ago, Jean told me, the town of Valinco had stood on this coast; but it had been completely destroyed by the Saracens who put the inhabitants in barrels studded with nails pointing inwards and rolled them into the sea. The Sartenais, more than any other part of the island, is haunted by such tales, which suggest – in the absence of documents – that it was here that the Saracens established themselves most firmly and stayed longest. One can seldom tell, however, whether these dreadful memories refer to the Saracen invasions of the early Middle Ages or to the later raids of North African pirates, known locally as the Turks, the 'Barbaresques' or the Moors. The two series of disasters are confused in the popular mind; and understandably, for it seems that the first Saracen invaders occupied parts of the coast as late as the twelfth century and that the North African Moors began their incursions as early as the fifteenth. These continued until about four generations ago; in fact the Sartenais has been victimised by the Muslims through most of its post-Roman history.

The consequences are still apparent; not only in what the invaders destroyed but in what they implanted: a sly kind of violence, born of dark brooding; fatalism, contempt for women. They contributed nothing in the way of learning, art or technical skills. The Saracens, like the later Moorish pirates, must have come as plundering adventurers: in Corsica – as in Crete – not a single trace of a Saracen mosque has been found.[3] Yet the Arab imprint

22

jumps to the eye; a cast of features, most common in the Sartenais, leaves little doubt that the invaders settled in the country and intermarried with its inhabitants. In fact a Genoese official of the eighteenth century reported that the people of the south greatly resembled the Moors in their dress and their 'way of wearing a turban';[4] and still today one sees many long brown melancholy desert faces for which turbans would be appropriate.

The sun was up and shining dazzlingly when we crossed a spur of the coast guarded by a Genoese watchtower and veered into the wide valley of the river Taravo. On the far side of its estuary a cluster of houses could be seen: the tiny fishing port of Porto Pollo, shining white and delectable. But now, turning our backs on the sea, we were creeping inland up a track parallel with the river that sprawled through the valley between overhanging poplars and shoals of sand. Rich, fertile land lay around us: fields of green maize; cornfields already reaped by hand with the stubble standing knee-high; pastures dotted with coneshaped haycocks, the hay twisted round a central pole, looking like the sort of sweets children suck at fairs. Wild fig trees, deeply scented, shaded our passage. At a fountain feeding water into a stone trough we stopped to rest, washed in its water, and ate the bread and sausage Madame Cesari had stowed in the cart with a bottle of wine. A very tall golden-skinned young man appeared from nowhere like an errant Greek god and helped us finish the bottle.

The track, twisting gently uphill, was bringing us back to the more familiar landscape of rocks and maquis. Scattered houses stood on the slopes with old men and women sitting on logs and stones outside. They remained motionless as we passed, as though they had been sitting there always.

The houses were stark rectangular stone boxes, disproportionately high. Windows and doors were placed with a wilful contempt for symmetry; in one house high and narrow as a tower the door and two windows were set one above the other at the extreme edge of the façade, leaving the rest of its surface unbroken. Several had exterior stone stairways slashing the walls obliquely, leading to doors on upper floors. Corsican rural houses conform to an immemorial tradition of building in stone. Their lack of any features that the Victorians would have thought picturesque has blinded most visitors to their bleak, bold type of beauty. The more elaborate are designed with complex arrangements of interconnecting outer staircases, loggias and arcades that make dramatic patterns of light and shadow; but this highly original local architecture has had to wait for the generation of Picasso and Le Corbusier for its mere existence to be recognised.

The hamlet known as Filitosa consisted of half a dozen such houses clustered near the dust-road. Jean brought the donkey to a halt under a tree. A dark thin young woman came running to greet us through the chickens, Françoise, a daughter of the Cesari's who, in accordance with deep-rooted Corsican custom, had married a cousin, Charles-Antoine. Greeting us warmly, she led us into a house where we found her husband, with his father and sister, and his four little children playing, barefoot, on the beaten earth floor.

Charles-Antoine was the first Corsican I had seen with a really fine physique. Tall, husky and fair-haired, he belongs to a type characteristic of the mountains, from which the Cesari originally came. With his light, piercing eyes and wide smile he gave an impression of splendid primitive panache in his tight white jersey and brown corduroys gathered into a thick leather belt in which was stuck a revolver and a long-bladed knife. His father was a formidable old man with eagle nose, flowing white beard and flashing blue eyes. The unmarried sister, fair, middle-aged, speaking no French, arranged some straw-seated chairs in a circle, and we all sat down, ceremoniously, to drink coffee and exchange news.

We were in the main room, which filled all the ground floor, with an enormous fireplace at either end. There was a large iron bed, a large circular dining-table, a dresser, a wooden chest (used for kneading and storing bread), the straw-seated chairs, and that was about all. Wooden casks for water stood under a rudimentary sink beside a basket full of onions and tomatoes, a sack of salt, and one or two cooking pots. No ornaments were to be seen, and no personal possessions whatsoever except guns and cartridge belts hanging on an unpainted wall.

When we had talked about the weather and the health of the different members of the family Jean told Charles-Antoine that we wanted to see the statues. 'But of course! We'll go immediately!' cried Charles-Antoine, laughing, as though humouring some hilarious foreigners' caprice. And he pulled on a wide-brimmed black felt hat, strapped a cartridge belt to his waist and took a gun from the wall. The father, too, seized a gun; in out-of-the-way parts of Corsica it was still considered unwise to leave home unarmed. And no doubt with good reason. This particular district, at any rate, has been a trouble centre: a man was found mysteriously murdered at Filitosa well after my first visit.

We walked out into the hot sun, down a footpath into a valley, Charles-Antoine striding beside us, the father skipping ahead, his gun held ready as though spoiling for something to shoot. The landscape was spellbinding by its air of deep antiquity. Oversized olives grew out of rank grass all over the slopes and hollows, their trunks twisted and knotted by age, their branches covering the ground with a continuous fluttering lacelike shade. Huge boulders, fantastically shaped, rose between them, in which the action of the weather had scooped many shelters and shallow caves. One could imagine them to be the homes of those who inhabited these hills; and once, perhaps, they were.

'What a marvellous thing, an olive tree!' exclaimed Charles-Antoine, picking up a little shrivelled black olive from the ground. 'See! One has nothing to do to make it make money. The olives fall of their own accord and then one gathers them and carries them to the nearest press and then one sells their oil. And it's good, my oil; you'll taste it.'

'That's true,' Jean said. 'Charles-Antoine's oil is very good and he has a great many trees. He's a very rich man, you know.'

24

This, by local standards, was true. All the same the methods described by Charles-Antoine, which were then followed all over Corsica, are not really the best for making olive trees earn money. The olives lie on the ground until enough have fallen to be worth gathering – this intermittent harvesting continues on and off from November till April – with the result that many of the olives are overripe by the time they go to the press and the oil has a peculiar musty, fruity flavour which townspeople dislike. Moreover, many of the presses are the old, beautiful, inexpert machines of wood and stone, worked by hand or by mule, which by modern standards do not sufficiently filter the oil. In consequence there is no regular market for Corsican olive oil; it is disposed of according to the immemorial practices of subsistence farming: a man who produces mainly oil sells it to one who produces mainly cheese, or wine. Many, in fact, do not bother to gather their olives at all, for the cost of labour hardly allows for a profit. So all over Corsica one comes upon neglected groves of centennial trees with their produce rotting at their roots.

We crossed a little stream, full of watercress and wild flowers. The hills enclosed us; like waves, so it seemed, for the silvery foliage of the olives gave an unbroken rippling surface, as of water, to every slope.

Jean was pushing ahead, up a grassy bank, towards a granite outcrop covered with maquis vegetation. 'It's here!' he called.

I had been prepared for disappointment, right up to the instant when I reached the spot where he stood. But the block of granite lying before us on the ground, six feet long or more, was without doubt carved by the human hand in the human form. And certainly it had some resemblance to the statue found by Mérimée. The head was clearly shaped: a large round head with protruding ears, sinister close-set eyes and a faint indication of mouth and nose. Neck and shoulders were carved from the block; but the body was simply a flattened shaft of stone, with a ridge, just discernible, crossing it diagonally: not an arm, it seemed, but a sword. It was still monstrously impressive, this hero-image lying on its back in the maquis, worn by uncounted centuries of wind and rain. The head recalled nothing I had seen so much as one of Picasso's more brutal drawings.

'You see!' Jean gasped, and sat down; he had lost the habit of uphill midday walks in the maquis. 'And there are several others somewhere around here,' Charles-Antoine told us.

We found them. One, lying close by in a thicket, was more crudely carved, but the facial features were unmistakable. The other two were embedded, like steps, in the slope falling towards the stream. One had deeply hollowed eyes and a nose in faint relief; the other, exceptionally long, appeared to be featureless.

And so the object of much speculation, of hoping against hope, had easily, almost automatically, fallen into my hands. The statues which in London had seemed almost as insubstantial as the prophetic visions Jean had described with equal conviction, really existed: four of them, lying close together on Charles-Antoine's land. 'We call them the "paladini",' he said to me. Paladins: knights of Charlemagne; and warriors they certainly did seem to represent, but of a more remote antiquity.

Few works of art have ever made so strong an impression on me as these enigmatic, rudimentary human figures. They were uncouth, they were barbaric; yet their impact was sharpened by what I recognised as familiar in their strangeness. For they were not alien and unintelligible, like the stelae of the Mayas. The clumsy but vigorous effort to carve the human body in its true proportions, to portray man in his physical strength and dignity, foreshadowed, crudely but unambiguously, the high victories of Grecian sculpture. They moved me in the acute and disturbing way of things long lost and suddenly rediscovered, which is more poignant, far, than the shock of what is altogether unknown.

Like witnesses of a mortal accident we stood gathered round the huge stone bodies; my husband and I, Charles-Antoine and his father, Antoine and Jean. 'Are they very old?' Charles-Antoine asked me. 'Extremely,' my husband answered, 'several thousand years.' 'And whom do they represent?' he enquired. 'Warriors, heroes,' I hazarded, 'the chieftains of those times.' 'Ah!' cried Charles-Antoine, suddenly vehement, 'and no doubt they were like the chiefs we have had in Corsica since then. They were foreigners, those so-called noblemen, and they came over from Italy to drive out the Saracens. But we all fought the Saracens, so they couldn't pretend to any special glory for that. And then they set themselves up as lords and built themselves castles and became great landowners. You'd like to know how? I'll tell you. They stole the land from the shepherds, the land that had always been free for all of us for grazing our flocks. They took all the land within sight of their castles and then they collected taxes and called themselves counts. That's how our chiefs behaved, and no doubt those paladini were just as bad.'

'Very probably,' I answered. I was unwilling, at that moment, to be drawn into a discussion of Charles-Antoine's shrewd, untaught and probably accurate account of the formation of the Corsican seigneurial domains. Conversation with a Corsican is always likely to be sidetracked into politics; and politics, even early mediaeval politics, were far from my mind as I stared at those figures of the Corsican heroes; heroes before the coming of the Romans, or the Greeks.

3 BIRTH OF A MYTH

In search of statue-menhirs – the lost sanctuary of Filitosa –
the megalithic faith – Mother Goddess and hero – megalithic
tradition

I HAD a premonition, at Filitosa, that I had stumbled on a find of great significance. Yet for a long time those statues – or rather statue-menhirs – were a
source of acute personal frustration. I reported them to the Leblancs and
Comte Peraldi on my return to Ajaccio; Comte Peraldi mentioned them to
some Corsican antiquarians; the antiquarians were interested, but there were
no qualified archaeologists in Corsica at that time. I returned to England; my
work led me into other paths; when I eventually went back to Corsica nothing
more was known about the statue-menhirs than before.

In the interval I had however by good fortune met a specialist on statue-
menhirs, Commandant Octobon, a distinguished archaeologist living in Nice.
In his magnificently illustrated work[1] I discovered the number and variety of
those weird anthropomorphic images that appeared in western Europe from
the end of the Neolithic Age till the coming of Etruscan and Graeco-Roman
civilisation. I learnt that they are dispersed over a vast area that includes the
Channel Islands, Portugal and northern Italy, with some fifty in mainland
France, the latter enigmatic, barely representational figures very different
from those I had seen at Filitosa. I learnt too, that other statue-menhirs had
been located in Corsica since Mérimée's journey, noted by visiting archaeologists; half a dozen in all.[2] I walked in search of them on my return to the
island, and found several (those that had escaped being broken up for building
stone): a featureless stele laid horizontally in a boundary wall on the despair-
ingly desolate plateau of Capo-di-Luogo, in the deep Sartenais;[3] a mysterious
totem-like figure,[4] still standing upright, close to a Pisan church at Cambia
in the central north, with a wide open mouth: laughing? Prophesying? I
found my way to the statue-menhir reported by Mérimée.[5] Meanwhile another,
much over life-size, was discovered in the maquis-waste to the south of Calvi,
with a crudely carved face and a formation of the back of the head that seems
intended as phallic.[6]

At this period of roaming the island in search of antiquities the occasional
meetings with those stone figures were always exhilarating. The Italianate
churches, altarpieces and saints' statues I saw in the villages invariably
impressed me with their foreignness; I could never forget that they were

subdued versions of prototypes created by and for much wealthier, urban societies. Only the statue-menhirs, rude, vigorous and archaic, spoke the authentic insular language. But their message was unintelligible, the culture they had sprung from tantalisingly obscure.

Organised prehistoric research in Corsica had to wait for several years, until the arrival of Roger Grosjean. Together we went to Filitosa. We saw the statues Jean Cesari had shown me; we rolled over the long, apparently featureless stele lying under the olives. Hardly impaired, a face that had lain pressed into the ground, perhaps for millennia, stared up at us in the hard sunlight with earth-filled, deep-socketed eyes. A dagger appeared carved in sharp relief on the upper part of the body.[7]

Then began a time of almost daily discoveries: of dolmens and menhirs and statue-menhirs, found and since forgotten in the lower valley of the Taravo, or unnoticed or unrecognised.[8] The country that at first had seemed so alien to me gradually became as familiar as the ground-floor room in Charles-Antoine's house where I now slept on a camp bed, to be woken every morning before dawn when Françoise, coming down from the upper room, lit the oil lamp and made coffee for the family. By that queer contraction of the landscape that comes by living continually out of doors the surrounding ranges seemed as homely as those walls, and I sometimes had the fancy, as darkness fell, that I had only to reach out my hands to draw them round me like a blanket.

Meanwhile our expectations rose. Each find seemed to presage a more important discovery. Little by little we grew convinced that a key to the enigmatic data we were collecting lay somewhere concealed in the acres of dense, shimmering maquis. Daily we were hoping that a turn in one of the footpaths twisting through the cistus and prickly pears, a rent in the vegetation, would lead us to the creative centre of this local culture, some settlement or sanctuary. The hoped-for discovery came; but not before I had left Filitosa and Roger Grosjean was preparing to go. The centre we were looking for was found precisely where our searches had begun, at Filitosa itself, on Charles-Antoine Cesari's property.

On the evening of his intended departure Roger Grosjean's curiosity was excited by the look of a flat stone he was sitting on with Charles-Antoine, close to the house, under a tree. 'That's nothing,' Charles-Antoine told him, 'I've been sitting on this stone for twenty years.' But the familiar seat turned out to be a very large statue-menhir lying face downwards. The face is delineated in the very most economical manner possible by two superimposed Vs carved in relief (a shorthand symbol which Picasso, plunging to the roots of western European tradition, has revived); on the body a long, vertical sword, and a dagger in its sheath, are carved with painstaking realism. The back of the statue shows engraved lines apparently representing shoulder-blades and spine.[9] These anatomical details appear on several of the Filitosan statue-menhirs, distant prefigurations, perhaps, of the Greek vision of the male body naked and unadorned.

28

Statue-menhir at Filitosa with dagger. (*Jean Bailet*)

Statue-menhir at Filitosa with dagger. (*Jean Bailet*)

Statue-menhir at Filitosa with sword; the first seen by the author. (*Jean Bailet*)

Bust of a statue-menhir at Filitosa standing on Toreen monument in which it was found. (*Jean Bailet*)

Roger Grosjean was preparing to leave Filitosa for a second time when Charles-Antoine casually remarked that there was an old monastery on his property, hidden in the maquis. He took his guest to a densely wooded spur overlooking the stream, within sight of the four statue-menhirs I had seen on my first visit. Grosjean at once realised that the wall which could be glimpsed through the tangled vegetation was not the work of any mediaeval craftsman: it was composed of the colossal blocks of stone used by prehistoric men in the technique of building known as 'cyclopean'. Here, Roger Grosjean judged (and correctly), was the cultural nucleus he had been searching for. Clearing and excavations began there the following summer.

Private affairs took me away from Corsica while the work was in progress. By this unlucky accident I missed the incomparable excitement of seeing the lost sanctuary of the Taravo emerge from the rocks and maquis. But I had my compensation. When I returned, in mid-August, the first excavations were completed. But the news that was to send visitors bumping along the dust roads to Filitosa had not yet broken into the press. Roger Grosjean had left; a heat-wave had spread over the island that kept people lying down and indifferent. I reached Filitosa late in the afternoon, hitch-hiking in a van freighted with the first grapes. Charles-Antoine took me to the site in the still scorching sunset hour. We passed a fragment of wall at the neck of the spur, built of giants' stones. The ground had been cleared of all vegetation except the larger olives. Dust hung thick, turning gold, in the motionless air.

Strange beings were crowded under the trees: stone figures starting out of the ground at waist level like ghosts rising from their graves. A stately, aristocratic face confronted me, a face of intimidating authority, with deepset eyes under level brows and a long straight nose.[10] Features, neck and shoulders were carved in bold clean lines with a mastery of symmetry, a true appreciation of the ideal human form. It was as though the concept that struggled for expression in all the primitive statue-menhirs I had seen scattered about the island had here triumphantly forced its way through the granite.

The companion figures were inferior beings, with rudimentary faces, flat-topped heads, eyes close and small, secretive little owl-like creatures each fixing us with an inscrutable gimlet stare. But each had its own individuality. There was no copying of a standard model in the Corsican statue-menhirs; some seventy have now been found in the island, twenty of them at or near Filitosa, and no two are identical.[11]

The statues, or rather busts, had been set upright round a circular stone construction occupying the centre of the spur. All of them were broken at waist level. Stone blocks of various sizes were propped beside them; fragments of unsculptured menhirs or of their own bodies. One statue, broken into three portions, carried a thick sword placed vertically on the body. The head, hardly damaged, was astonishingly, disturbingly realistic: the prominent brow, coarse nose, heavy jaw and small tight mouth made up a physiognomy of brutal power, the likeness, it seemed, of some formidable warrior, some prehistoric Tamberlane.[12] The intention, here, was evidently far removed from that which produced the unpersonalised, semi-abstract statue-menhirs of mainland France; the sculptors of Filitosa, one can hardly doubt, aimed at portraiture.

The spur ended in a rocky escarpment. A curving stone wall appeared built against the cliff; the remains of a conical tower. Looking across the valley we could see the four statues Jean had first shown me, now set upright. Another full-length statue found in the neighbourhood, topped by an oversized, featureless head, had been added to the group.[13] Backed by a clump of gnarled olives they cast long shadows down the slope still gleaming with an unearthly brilliance in the setting sun.

Charles-Antoine and I, of course, could not see the statue-menhirs of Filitosa as they were intended to be seen; we could only guess their significance; never could we recapture the overwhelming impact they must have made on primitive men. But at least we saw them in their own setting, one that had been hardly impinged on by the civilised world. As we sat there, smoking in the hot dusk, we became increasingly conscious of the stone figures surrounding us, staring at us, pressing in on us, the intruders. Charles-Antoine summed up my feelings: 'It's easier,' he said, 'to imagine that those men are still here and alive than that they are all dead.'

Who were they? When had they lived and died? Why had they carved these stone images in their own likeness? Such questions were without answer, then and for a long time to come. Years of archaeological research were needed before any dates or cultural context could be proposed for Filitosa, and mystery still clings to the site, for certain features are still only tentatively explained.

It is now accepted that the statue-menhirs, at Filitosa and elsewhere, are a late manifestation of the megalithic faith in Corsica, the faith associated with the dolmens and menhirs. They represent Corsica's original contribution to the art of the great prehistoric religious movement that can be traced from Palestine to the Orkneys, that scattered Europe with some of the most impressive monuments ever created and left a spiritual heritage powerful enough to linger on, here and there, into modern times.

Few subjects can have given rise to so many romantic, conflicting theories as the megalithic faith. And small wonder. The dolmens, those barbarous card-houses brooding over the heaths and downs of western Europe, the man-dwarfing circles of standing stones, such as Avebury and Stonehenge, the ranks of menhirs advancing miles across country like armies with half their men fallen in the field: these monuments can leave no one quite unmoved. Everything about them is awe-inspiring: their immense antiquity, their extravagant size and massiveness, their relation to barbarous, unexplained rites and ceremonies, their air of belonging to a race of supermen or giants. Imagination may take fire when one learns how many there are in the world, and where: more than fifty thousand in western Europe alone, and uncounted others in North Africa, the Caucasus, Palestine and desert Arabia, and yet further afield in Abyssinia and the Sudan, Persia, Baluchistan, Kashmir, southern India, Borneo, Melanesia, Korea and Japan.[14]

Before archaeology became a science many wild guesses were made as to what master race erected them: ancestors of the adventuring Vikings? Or of the Spaniards, prehistoric conquistadores? The migrating Children of the Sun from Egypt, perhaps? Or, as was for a long time firmly believed in connection with western Europe, the Celts of mystic inclinations? But archaeology has demolished the master race theory. The dolmens, once regarded as sacrificial altars on which Druids slaughtered human victims, are now known to have been collective tombs for members of families or clans, and the human remains found in them have been shown to belong to various races.[15] Moreover, modern techniques have revealed that the megalithic monuments in different areas of the world belong to dates so far apart that they cannot possibly be considered as expressions of a single, integrated culture: in western Europe they date from before 3000 to c.1500 B.C.,[16] in Mysore from 200 B.C. to A.D. 50; in Melanesia megaliths are still being raised today. Megalithic building, that is, the use of large, usually undressed stones, not superimposed in courses but arranged in a card-house type of architecture,[17] is a simple (though far from easy) technique for creating very durable and imposing monuments, and it developed at widely different periods in different parts of the world.[18]

All the same, the European megaliths are thought to be the expression of a single culture, or rather religion: one that prescribed that the dead should be interred collectively and honoured with imperishable stone monuments (both burial and cremation were practised). Archaeologists are now pretty well agreed that the megalithic faith came to western Europe from the East. The movement must have been seaborne; the great megalithic centres are on the coasts, the peninsulas and the islands.[19] From the Aegean area or the Near East, it is supposed, shiploads of adventurers set out to explore, exploit and colonise the barbarous West. They went in search of living-space, trade and, increasingly, metals;[20] and they took with them their religious beliefs, just as Europeans later carried Christianity to the Indies. Professor Gordon Childe contends that the motivation was primarily religious, and speaks of 'megalithic saints', analogous to the Celtic saints of the Middle Ages.[21] Sibylle von Cles-Reden argues, persuasively, that the megalithic faith originated in Palestine, source of world religions, where hundreds of megalithic tombs can be seen, some dated to the fourth millennium B.C., and hosts of menhirs proclaim a belief in supernatural forces dwelling in stone.[22]

At all events the megalithic monuments, all over western Europe, attest similar religious concepts, which were current in the Palestinian area and also in the Aegean: collective burial; a Great Goddess, at once giver and taker of life; the sacred fertilising serpent of the underworld, her symbol and companion; the bull, revered as the incarnation of male procreativity from Mesopotamia to Crete. The goddess, archetypal mother, serene and protective in the Mesopotamian religions, gracefully dithyrambic in Minoan art, underwent a transformation in the more primitive West. Here her chthonic aspect is

31

particularly emphasised, and her image, often demoniacal, may be reduced to a pair of glowering eyes.[23] Perhaps, as Gordon Childe suggests, the spirits of the dead were thought of as potent intercessors with this unmerciful deity, and so the collective tomb became a shrine.[24] But it cannot be doubted that the dead were also revered for themselves, perhaps increasingly, as subservience to the Terrible Mother gradually gave way to a confidence in the human potential. And it is hardly possible to reject Sibylle von Cles-Reden's suggestion that the megalithic faith offered men a new promise of immortality provided their remains were suitably venerated: nothing less, one feels, could have unleashed the tremendous creative impulses of megalithic art or inspired such 'fantastic efforts in the service of the dead'.[25]

At the opposing extremes of Europe, on the shores of the Mediterranean, the Atlantic, the Baltic and the North Sea, generations of men quarried, hacked, shaped, lifted, dragged, rolled and elevated colossal stones: titanic designs for tomb and temple were conceived and executed; Europe's first monumental architecture came into being. Over the long period of the megalithic ascendancy – longer than the duration of Christianity to date – each area evolved its own style of building, its characteristic art and symbols corresponding with particular interpretations of the mysteries of death and life. Native imagination flowered, stimulated by the coming and going of traders, colonists, migrating peoples. Arid little Malta was covered with grandiose temples by a population using only stone implements, and undermined with labyrinthine catacombs; statuettes of a Buddha-like Mother Goddess were created there, whereas the rock-cut burial chambers of Sardinia present bas-reliefs of the horns of the sacred bull. In Brittany, where a thousand and ninety-nine menhirs were erected in processional formation at Carnac, an abstract art was developed with enigmatic motifs suggesting ideograms; Stonehenge became a majestic open-air temple to the sun and moon. Corbel-vaulted tombs akin to the Aegean *tholoi* were built in southern Spain and on Orkney, at the extreme edge of the habitable world.[26]

The bearers of the megalithic faith reached Corsica, according to Roger Grosjean, around 3000 B.C.; where exactly they came from is uncertain. Some of the Mediterranean islands are known to have been colonised later than the mainland areas; they must have become ports of call as a two-way east–west sea traffic developed. The discovery, among the very few objects left to archaeologists in the much-plundered Corsican tombs, of five bell-beakers, point to connections with Spain.[27] At all events the south of Corsica is where their monuments are most numerous, with spectacular groups in the south-western Sartenais.[28]

The missionary-navigators found the island already inhabited, by a Neolithic population that had been there thousands of years. A site recently excavated in the central south by François de Lanfranchi gives the astonishingly early dates, obtained by carbon-14 tests, of 6610 and 5350 B.C. These people made a decorated pottery with impressed designs, and used arrowheads of obsidian, a stone not found in Corsica which they must have procured either from the Aeolian isles or Sardinia. Stone querns show that they knew agriculture; their arrows must have served for hunting.[29] During obscure millennia the Neolithic Corsicans apparently flourished; their sites, not yet precisely dated, have been found scattered about the island from sea level to high mountain plateaux. Perhaps, as Roger Grosjean suggests, they were also pastoralists who drove their livestock up and down the mountain spine according to the seasons, as the Corsican shepherds have continued doing to this day.[30]

Of their religious beliefs nothing is certainly known except that they may have venerated the Mother Goddess in the form of small stone idols of which a few specimens have been found.[31] With the coming of the megalith builders the populations near the coasts, at least, must have been converted to the new faith. The megalithic monuments were erected in valleys and on plateaux only a little distance from the sea; the lines of menhirs, the isolated dolmens, still dominate those deserted landscapes. None is very large: the menhirs seldom rise above thirteen feet, the dolmens average about six feet by eight and six feet high; in Corsica there was no tendency to the gigantism that obsessed so many of the megalithic peoples of western Europe. The Corsican monuments have a much rarer distinction: an exceptionally careful treatment of the stones. The menhirs, and the components of the dolmens, are most often shaped and dressed, and sometimes even polished, and they are designed with an eye to symmetry and proportion. The granite has weathered very little over the millennia, so that many of these monuments appear almost in their primal barbaric elegance. Probably the dolmens were meant to be seen and admired from afar; unlike the majority of European megalithic sepulchres they do not seem ever to have been covered by cairns.[32] Often menhirs were erected in sight of them, as though each commemorated a human being whose remains lay in the neighbouring tomb.

The prevailing north–south direction of the alignments discourages the idea that the menhirs were associated with a sun cult.[33] Menhirs served various purposes in the megalithic world: in Brittany, it seems, they were used to mark out ceremonial avenues, in Britain, certainly, to enclose circular sacred grounds, at Stonehenge, it is assumed, to plot a pattern related to astronomy; but it can hardly be doubted that in some contexts they were intended as symbols of dead people and that in Corsica this was their significance.[34] Many are in fact vaguely human in shape; an obelisk of rectangular section with a slightly rounded summit was the preferred model of the Corsican megalith builders.[35] Though they cannot compete in overwhelmingness with the colossi of Brittany and Britain, they have a peculiarly disturbing presence: in the great alignments of the Sartenais, the scores of standing stones, only a little over man-size, set close together, sometimes nearly touching, evoke the idea of a crowd of ghosts or half-created men.

Occasionally an intelligible, unmistakable human image is achieved. To the south-west of Sartène a finely built chamber tomb, the dolmen of Fontenaccia, stands, almost intact, on a gentle rise. The wide, undulating valley can have changed little since the megalithic seafarers occupied it; rare shepherds' cabins, reached by earth tracks, are dwarfed by piles of boulders; dark groves of holm oak still harbour memories of the earlier inhabitants. In a black little copse dozens of menhirs are assembled near a broken dolmen, upright or crazily tilted or heaped pell mell on the ground. These have been known to archaeologists since the last century; so has an alignment of menhirs in a boundary wall, smothered by maquis.[36] When Roger Grosjean recently cleared the vegetation obscuring this group, he found four anthropomorphic figures in the ranks of the unsculptured menhirs. Two have well-carved, quite realistic faces; swords are shown hanging vertically on their bodies above triangular shapes apparently representing loin-cloths.[37]

Roger Grosjean believes that statue-menhirs began to supersede the menhirs in Corsica towards the middle of the second millennium B.C. A carbon-14 test relative to a site that includes round-topped or 'proto-anthropomorphic' menhirs gives the date 1870 B.C.[38] At Filitosa the new art developed with a particular freedom and audacity.[39] Heads, disengaged from the stone shafts, were sculpted in the round; portraiture came into being. The variety of facial features leaves no reasonable doubt that individuals are represented. At least half carry daggers or swords. The sculptors' intention, here as elsewhere, was evidently to honour and commemorate famous men, outstanding warriors or chieftains.[40]

The transformation of menhir into statue-menhir might seem so natural as to be inevitable. But in fact it took place in only a few areas of megalithic Europe, and nowhere so completely as in Corsica. The statue-menhirs of mainland France, which are mostly dated to the second millennium B.C., are far more archaic, in concept and in execution. Eyes and nose, but not mouth, arms, and sometimes legs and female breasts, are indicated on roughly shaped blocks; though sometimes both sides are carved there is no attempt to reproduce the human contour. The faces, often grotesquely small, appear as though set in a monstrous mound of flesh composing the whole body; arms and legs, carved as flat bands, seem to belong to corpses. The inhuman aspect of these images, which must surely be deliberate, has led to the conclusion that they represent supernatural beings; a divine couple, speechless and inscrutable, the Mother Goddess and her spouse. The god is defined by axe, bow and arrows, or a mysterious ritual object; yet this menacing deity never rivals the gruesome majesty of the goddess. One must look to Mexico, to Polynesia, to find images as terrible as hers. Beak-nosed, the eyes hideously underscored with horizontal tattoos, the gross bodies bedizened with several-stringed necklaces above protuberant breasts, they exude a dense, lethal kind of sensuality recalling tales of elementals, or the worst nightmares. The creator and consumer of life is here invested with her maximum significance as an archetype of the collective unconscious, charged with nameless fears.[41]

The Corsican statue-menhirs proclaim a dramatic breakaway from the ancient servitude to the Universal Mother. All seem to be male. The goddess, venerated by the old Neolithic population, was apparently dethroned by

34

a dynamic development of the megalithic faith. Though memories of her dread dominion may have echoed down the millennia in certain popular attitudes and beliefs, the counter-movement that came into play with the creation of the statue-menhirs affected the whole future of Corsican culture. At that period insular society must have assumed the strongly patriarchal character it maintained into the present age. An ideal of masculine prepotence is conveyed by the uncompromising stone figures, larger than life, displaying their meticulously carved weapons.

They in no way resemble the divine bridegroom, that enigmatic figure who, even less than the goddess, offers any semblance of a human being. The Corsican statue-menhirs are explicitly, triumphantly, human. Though survivals of megalithic symbolism can be detected, the drive towards naturalism is uppermost. The faces, always disproportionately big,[42] betray an intense struggle to recreate the human countenance, the human expression; the figures, even the crudest, respect the human contour. Alone among western Europeans the Corsican megalith builders believed that man was an object worthy of realistic, monumental portraiture. Their imperfect achievement carries the germ of Greek humanistic sculpture and of the aesthetic principles that have inspired European art as a whole.

That Corsica – obscure, peripheral Corsica – should have brought forth the central concept of European art at so early a period is something many people have been hardly willing to believe. Yet this monumental portrayal of the human being would seem a natural enough expression of the megalithic veneration of the dead, practised in an area isolated from other religious influences and there pushed to extremes. The artistic innovation issued from a spiritual development, one that implied the emergence of a new concept of man. That man should seek to glorify and immortalise his kind in art marked an increased recognition of his own value. Confident in his power to stand up to forces seen and unknown, he assumed the vocation of the hero. Death consecrated the hero, perpetuated his virtue; man, in fact, could become god.

The vision was prophetic; it has fascinated Europeans, swayed our culture, notwithstanding Christianity. But it was not diffused from Corsica. Other races, Greek and Roman, Celtic, Teutonic and Scandinavian, rediscovered and propagated the hero myth with a haunting awareness of the hero's limitations that has provided the tragic matter of many European masterpieces. No ancient people, it seems, went so far towards substituting man for god as the megalithic Corsicans. Yet this intrepid upsurge of consciousness, so modern in character, passed unnoticed. The statues of Filitosa were not the heralds of an expanding culture radiating overseas. Like other Corsican achievements (in different periods and different spheres), they remained, in all probability, unknown to the outside world.

What happened to the megalithic people of Corsica? Why did their art have no sequel? Roger Grosjean believes that towards the end of the second millennium B.C. they were defeated in war. Their enemies, he maintains, were a people of another race who reached Corsica from the eastern Mediterranean about 1500 B.C. and first settled near Porto-Vecchio. Roger Grosjean has named them the Torréens, because their characteristic monuments are locally known as *torri*, towers. These are conical structures built in dry-walling, sometimes with stones of cyclopean dimensions; they were roofed with corbel vaults or large stone slabs laid across inclined walls. Most often they consist of a central chamber with side chambers or recesses, sometimes reached by curving corridors. Archaeological evidence suggests that they were used for cremating the dead; one even has a smoke-blackened flue designed to draw the air from the entrance opening across a central hearth. Dozens have been located in southern Corsica during the last years, though none in the northern part of the island. In style and design they are related to a widespread category of Mediterranean protohistoric monuments; particularly they resemble the Sardinian *nuraghi*, fortresses which during the first millennium B.C. attained a real architectural magnificence.

The Torréens were master-builders, but not sculptors; they produced a characteristic type of pottery and brought with them from the eastern Mediterranean objects in bronze, which among the megalithic Corsicans was still rare or unknown.[43] According to Roger Grosjean they introduced bronze weapons: the daggers and swords carved on the statue-menhirs. These weapons have been one of the major puzzles of Corsican archaeology. No specimens of them have been found at Filitosa or other sites associated with statue-menhirs, in fact practically no metal at all.[44] The statue-menhirs seem to have been the work of a technologically backward society.

Typological comparisons have convinced Roger Grosjean that the daggers and swords shown on the statue-menhirs represent bronze weapons manufactured in the Aegean around 1450 B.C.[45] The Torréens, he contends, introduced them to Corsica. The megalithic people could have captured them from the Torréens in time of war, or obtained them by barter in periods of peace. Roger Grosjean however believes that the armed statue-menhirs were portraits of Torréens killed in battle. The idea is derived from Aristotle who relates that the Iberians – by which he could have meant any of the western barbarians – erected obelisks round their tombs representing the enemies they had slain.[46] According to this theory the armed statue-menhirs would have had the value of trophies.

Equipped with these superior weapons the Torréens, so Roger Grosjean believes, moved westwards across Corsica, victoriously building and fighting. At Filitosa a decisive battle took place; the Torréens won. Like conquerors of all periods they thereupon set about annihilating the culture of the conquered race. They occupied the site, fortified it, erected their own cult monuments there and destroyed those of the defeated enemy. The sacred images of the dead were broken up with iconoclastic brutality and incorporated in the base of a *torre* in the centre of the spur. It was there that the truncated figures were discovered, including two masterpieces of Filitosan art. The monument would therefore illustrate the clash between two peoples, two cultures.[47] A more elaborate *torre*, with a complex of subterranean passages and alcoves, was erected on a stone-faced platform on the edge of the escarpment.[48] Stone dwellings were also built; the foundations of their weirdly shaped curved rooms have been recently unearthed, and several clay hearths. Stratigraphical excavations apparently confirm that a Torréen occupation succeeded that of the megalithic people;[49] carbon-14 tests indicate that it lasted until between 1200 and 1000 B.C.[50] After which, according to Roger Grosjean, the Torréens emigrated to Sardinia and built some of the early *nuraghi*.[51]

The vanquished megalithic people, he believes, moved to the north of Corsica, where the Torréens had never penetrated,[52] and there continued to practise their art until the early Iron Age. Twenty statue-menhirs are known in this area; none is armed; the representation of necklaces points to peaceful preoccupations. Some of them certainly appear to belong to this late period. Two, geographically far apart (in the valley of the Gravona and near Saint-Florent), have astonishingly realistic heads; the firmly carved three-dimensional oval faces with level brows and very deep-set eyes are strong, straightforward portraits of a type of Corsican one may see today.[53] A bodiless head found in the north-west on the deserted plateau of Capo Castinco, noble in expression and classical in proportions, is considered by some to reflect Graeco-Roman influences.[54]

Such, in outline, is Roger Grosjean's working hypothesis. It has not been unanimously accepted. Certain archaeologists and others are unconvinced by the evidence for the Torréen-megalithic war, reject the explanation of the armed statue-menhirs derived from Aristotle, and maintain that they are in fact what they seem to be: memorials to the dead warriors and chiefs of the people who created them. The archaeologist François de Lanfranchi, in a thesis shortly to be published,[55] affirms that Torréen sites continued to be occupied after 1000 B.C.; in one he has identified bronze ornaments belonging to the sixth century B.C. of types also found at Graeco-Roman Aléria. Thanks to his researches the relics of the Corsican Iron Age, formerly neglected, are being progressively brought to light. Etruscan influence is detected in certain ornamental objects found in various parts of the island, but there is no sound evidence that the Celts ever reached Corsica.[56]

This divergence of views may lead to a reconsideration of the *torri* and their occupants, but in no way diminishes the significance attributed to the statue-menhirs. Their original connection with megalithic beliefs is not in question. If some should be shown to be later in date than has been supposed, the early examples remain an astonishing manifestation of monumental anthropo-morphic sculpture at a period when the concept was altogether alien to the art of western Europe. That this unique Corsican art should have persisted into the Iron Age merely gives added proof of its vitality, and of the authority of the ideas that inspired it. The Corsican megalithic phenomenon can be seen as a religious movement cutting right across the established stages of cultural evolution. Brought, it seems, to a Neolithic people by foreign navigators who were apparently themselves without metals, it flourished and developed through the Copper and Bronze Ages of Corsica, and was perhaps still creative in the early Iron Age, several centuries after 1000 B.C.

Nor was it destroyed by the impact of civilisation, which first reached Corsica with the Greek colonists of Aléria about 560 B.C. The megalithic monuments, indestructible, remained objects of popular veneration long after they had ceased to be erected, in spite of the Greek colony and the Roman conquest, in spite of invasions, in spite of Christianity. Gregory the Great complained that the Corsicans still worshipped stones;[57] what was true in the sixth century was probably still true in the twelfth: the open-mouthed statue-menhir by the Pisan church at Cambia was Christianised with a cross incised on its body; Geneviève Moracchini-Mazel found two statue-menhirs inserted as cornerstones in the base of the ruined Pisan cathedral of Sagone.[58] They cannot have been used for convenience; the Pisan craftsmen invariably shaped and polished their facing stones; they must have been immured in the Christian edifice to demonstrate the victory of one faith over another.

It is easier to degrade images than beliefs: there is evidence to show that the megalithic faith lived on in the deeper layers of the Corsican psyche, affecting customs, attitudes, values, almost to the present time. Funeral rites from the deep past, with wailing, verse-improvisation and dancing, though frowned on by the Church, were performed until recent years; they enshrined an authentic indigenous art of a hardly bearable intensity. The dead were often collectively buried in the vaults of churches; the rarity of coffins cannot be attributed to excessive poverty but rather to a tradition dating back to megalithic times which decreed that the dead should lie in promiscuity. Fragments of mediaeval Italian pottery found in the vault of a Pisan church in the Nebbio suggest that megalithic ritual was unforgotten;[59] the custom of laying the dead to rest among their possessions may have persisted through the generations. In a few villages the dead were interred together in a building erected for the purpose; these communal sepulchres remained in use until the beginning of the present century.[60] By then elaborately designed family mausoleums, often built on family properties, had generally superseded the unhygienic church vaults; the larger ones contain little altars, so that the tomb is also a kind of shrine.

These burial methods made for a particular cohesion in family or tribe, based on the metaphysical union of all its members, the living and the dead. In the Middle Ages and even later village assemblies and tribunals took place in a spot known as the *arringo*, round a slab of stone – the *petra l'arringo* – laid over a tomb or above a burial ground; the custom, which may derive hardly distorted from megalithic times, must surely include the belief that the spirits of the dead could direct the judgment of the living.[61] The idea that the dead watch over their descendants and influence their lives permeates traditional Corsican thinking. The mild Christian attentions to the dead – the visiting and flowering of tombs – assume a propitiatory significance; unauthorised local rites – including offerings of food and drink – betray the deep fear that mingles with reverence for the departed. In popular belief their spirits punish as often

38

Bust of a statue-menhir; the masterpiece of Filitosa. (*John Donat*)

Alignment of menhirs at Palaggiu. (*Jean Bailet*)

The dolmen of Fontenaccia, at Caouria. (*Jean Bailet*)

as they protect and guide; their apparition forbodes death; the dreams, visions and supernatural manifestations by which the dead communicate their usually baleful messages to the living were within the common experience of rural Corsicans until after the Second World War. Some of these beliefs have surprisingly close parallels in distant areas of megalithic Europe; in Brittany, Scotland and Wales.[62]

The hero-myth, which in the latter phases of the Corsican megalithic faith mitigated the obsessive preoccupation with the future life, became self-generating; the Corsicans never went back on their early realisation of the potential of the individual man. Napoleon is the lineal descendant of the warriors of Filitosa. All through history Corsica has produced heroes and honoured them; their deeds have been celebrated in ballads and chronicles (the cult of the dead gave Corsica many historians), their bronze and stone images dominate the village squares. Many were victims to their vocation; undone by hubris they ended assassinated, in prison or in miserable exile.

These men, of course, were the exceptions; for the average Corsican faith in human value was translated into an unshakeable consciousness of personal worth and dignity, an absolute refusal of contempt, tyranny or exploitation. A respect for justice, noted, with admiration, by Diodorus Siculus,[63] is an aspect of the Corsican estimate of what is due to the human being; so is an acute concern with status and prestige, the cult of heroism reduced to the cult of honour. The contending claims of individuals and families gave rise to rough-and-ready democratic institutions; democracy, in Corsica, does not represent the triumph of one class over another, still less a philanthropic ideal, but rather a truce between men free and equal all aspiring to pre-eminence. The breaking of the truce meant the vendetta, a life for a life, with the dire dead participating: the murdered men cried vengeance from their graves.

Yet democratic cooperation, often backed by the Christian Church, uniquely in Europe held its own and developed: the collective, egalitarian organisation of the rural communes was its early triumph.[64] From these age-old usages issued, in the eighteenth century, a succession of national constitutions; the last, conceived by Paoli (least warlike of Corsican heroes) formulated the central Corsican social creed. 'The General Diet of the people of Corsica ... legitimately master of itself': so runs the opening phrase of that historic document. With this noble declaration the primitive insular faith in man was brought into line with the ideals of modern Europe.[65]

More than three thousand years probably separate these two demonstrations of Corsican values: the statue-menhirs and Paoli's constitution. Both prefigured concepts that determined European civilisation, and both were rudimentary: Paoli's constitution, too, was imperfect. Neither had any influence on the outside world. Islands are often forcing houses of culture where small populations, their energies turned inwards, may originate experimental patterns of social organisation, reach high levels of spiritual and artistic creativity; Easter Island and Iceland spring to mind, without considering the megalithic islands of Europe or proto-historic Sardinia. These achievements, most often, have no sequel. Handicapped by poor resources, backward technologies, isolation, in fact by the very insularity that provided the initial stimuli, such cultures have withered and died unnoticed, or been obliterated by conquests, to be discovered centuries and millennia later by archaeologists and historians. It is in no way surprising that Corsica produced unique types of art and political institutions; their particular claim to interest is their astonishingly prophetic content.

4 NIGHT-HUNTERS OF SOULS

Prophetic dreams – spirits of the dead – *mazzeri* – bilocation –
exorcism – Destiny – similar beliefs in Africa – in Australia –
meeting a *mazzere*

EVERY detail of my first visit to Filitosa is deeply engraved in my memory,
for on that day I entered Corsican life and became part of it. Until then I had
felt myself to be a tourist and a stranger; but at Filitosa I underwent what
amounted to an initiation and from then on I thought of Corsica as my home.
True, I was often perplexed and disconcerted by what I found there, but in the
way a distant cousin might be, born abroad and returning to his country of
origin in later years; I was never to suffer the bewilderment of the displaced
person, the unabsorbable alien.

After we had looked at the statue-menhirs Charles-Antoine took us back to
his house, my husband and me, Jean Cesari and his cousin. There we found
the preparations for a large meal well advanced. A huge iron cauldron was
simmering on the open fire, while Françoise, crouched on a low chair – the
dwarf-legged fireside chair of every Corsican peasant home – stirred the contents and threw in tiny quantities of rock salt taken from a sack leaning
against the wall. Her movements were languid and she looked tired; but she
brightened when Charles-Antoine squatted beside her and began clumsily
grating cheese.

'He's a wonderful husband,' Jean whispered to me. 'You see, he does everything for her.' At that moment Charles-Antoine's sister appeared with a
bucket of water on her head. All the water for the household, I was dismayed
to learn, had to be fetched from a spring more than a hundred yards away.

The witch's cauldron was placed on the table beside a loaf of bread and a
bottle of amber-coloured wine; Charles-Antoine shook off his four little children who had been happily climbing all over him and we sat down to the meal.
Or rather I sat down, and the men; Françoise and her sister-in-law remained
standing, serving us and nibbling little snacks in the intervals.

This custom, once general in Corsica and then still surviving in some remote
districts, has invariably shocked foreigners. But for that matter the whole
position of Corsican women – especially of peasant women – has always upset
foreigners very much. Ever since a French officer arriving in Corsica soon after
the conquest of 1769 was moved to chivalrous indignation by the sight of
peasants riding their mules across country with their women trudging on foot
carrying firewood, foreigners have been distressed by the treatment of Corsi-

can wives.[1] They are overworked, oppressed and neglected, so traveller after traveller has complained; they spend their lives in mortifying, unmitigated drudgery. The men go out and amuse themselves, shoot wild boar and each other, talk politics endlessly in the cafés, play cards, gamble away their money, spend it on women and wine; and all this time their wives are shut up at home, year in, year out, carrying wood and water for men who will not even deign to sit with them at meals.

Those who have stayed any length of time in Corsica can add stranger evidence of feminine subservience. A continental French girl I knew became engaged a few years ago to a Corsican of the Sartenais. When she observed that he expected his sisters to wash his feet whenever he returned from a walk she promptly broke off the engagement. A priest who had spent many years in a southern parish spoke to me with grieved amazement of what he regarded as the slave-status of wives. A married woman, he said, would normally refer to her husband as *mio padrone*, 'my master'. When a husband died, the wife would often imprison herself in her house, with the shutters closed, for the rest of her life, never again to leave those walls. Generations of foreigners have raised their voices in outraged protest against such customs, almost as though they themselves were the victims. Why, they ask, do the women put up with this state of affairs? Can they not refuse, rebel?

Such reasoning leaves out of account the fact that nearly all Corsican women, until a few years ago, have wanted above all things to marry, to marry Corsican men with their notorious disadvantages and live with them according to the insular social code. Their lifelong devotion to their husbands can be measured when those men die. Does a Corsican peasant's widow rejoice in her release after forty years of carrying wood and water and serving her man at meals? Travelling about the island I frequently had occasion to lodge in widows' homes. And one and all they told me of their grief, speaking of their husbands with boundless admiration, listing their achievements, praising their characters, displaying their good looks in yellowed photographs, recalling their acts of kindness and their very words with an intense, rather terrifying elation compounded of enthusiasm and tears.

As for those widows, down in the deep Corsican south, who immure themselves for a life in darkened rooms, perhaps they are less enslaved by a sadistic-social convention than – incredibly – by their own choice. 'My mother shut herself up for a year,' the daughter of one of them told me. 'Then I said to her: "Times have changed, widows are no longer expected to behave in this way." So she began going out, but she had no taste for it. I took her to Ajaccio and took her to the cinema, but she had no pleasure. Without my father, you see, she has no pleasure in anything at all.' It is hard for us to credit, let alone appreciate, such intransigent emotions. An English widow who shut herself up for years on end would doubtless be dragged to a psychiatrist. But Corsicans accept such irremediable grief as normal and proper; however badly women are treated, according to our standards, at least their natural, fundamental feelings are respected.

Perhaps they have had less to complain of than foreigners suppose. The most that is ever required of them is to stay at home and work hard. Though seldom harder than the men. According to an immemorial division of labour the men sowed and reaped, herded the flocks and tended the larger livestock; the women looked after the chickens, picked the grapes, gathered the olives and chestnuts and carried in part of the harvests, and the water and the small firewood. The heavier loads were carried by donkeys; the men carried only coffins, so one of them told me with pride. Were the women really despised beasts of burden? Or were not these arrangements designed, in the warring past, so that the men might keep their guns ever ready in hand, unimpeded by bundles, so as to defend themselves if needs be, and also – incidentally – their wives?

Worse than the hard work and the load carrying (the lot of peasant women the world over) seem to me the restrictions imposed on Corsican women in the upper strata of society, the wives and daughters of professional men and country squires. Until very recently they have been completely debarred from public affairs, and even from going out in public at all. When I first went to the island women were frowned on in the cafés, even accompanied by their husbands, and the wives of officials were never invited with their husbands to social functions and ceremonies. Some women of the south were (and still are) virtual prisoners in their homes; I know of a chemist's wife in her seventies who in half a century of marriage has been allowed to leave her house only three times, each time for a funeral (there was a servant to bring in water and supplies). This, however, is an extreme example of what could only happen in the Sartenais, where the Muslim influence still lies like a stain.

Yet the submission of women, here and elsewhere in Corsica, is, I think, more formal than real. Despite all appearances it is the woman, most often, who rules in Corsican marriage, who makes the important decisions, who has the last word. And contrary to what happens in more sophisticated societies, her authority grows with age. A foreigner looking for a partner in a business he wanted to start in Corsica confided to me that every time he found a willing associate the plan was vetoed by a grandmother. Those old Corsican women, who toiled so fearfully in their youth, rule their offspring. Whereas elderly women in more advanced countries tend to be pushed aside, in Corsica to speak lightly of a grandmother amounts to blasphemy; it was a Corsican who gave me the word.

If women often influence material decisions, they rule without question in the spiritual sphere. It is the women, of course, who go to church, taking children and grandchildren, who ensure the continuity of the Catholic religion in their families. And there were many, until very recently, who were also versed in much older, primitive beliefs; they, rather than the men, could foresee, prophesy, avert or invite disaster by techniques inherited from remote unremembered antiquity. The ambivalent relations between the sexes may well derive from this traditional feminine ascendancy. The autocratic behaviour of men to women, I have observed, barely masks a deep, instinctive distrust, a distrust akin to fear. Woman is sly, unfathomable, unpredictable, they will often say; in fact she is felt as dangerous, a constant threat to the male.

The meal served by Charles-Antoine's wife and sister was a large one of many courses: dishes of raw smoked ham and sausages, of tomatoes and onions and hard-boiled eggs, of potatoes and cabbage, of macaroni in a tomato sauce, all swimming in Charles-Antoine's highly flavoured olive oil. He apologised for the absence of meat; if Jean had warned him of our visit, he said, he would have killed a sheep. Corsican hospitality is uncalculating; often one finds oneself, in shepherds' and peasants' homes, sitting down to a Homeric banquet of a whole roast animal, which for these people must represent a real sacrifice, a reduction in the family capital. This meal, even without the sheep, was enormous, and I was as much dazed by the food as the wine when we finally reached the dessert, a soft white cheese known as *brocciu*, made from ewes' cheese-milk boiled with fresh milk; a Corsican delicacy, particularly appetising when eaten, as I ate it then for the first time, with sugar and eau-de-vie, a homemade whitish spirit distilled from wine.

I would probably have fallen asleep on my hard chair had Jean not suggested that we should call on an uncle who lived near by. We almost fell over the uncle taking his siesta under a tree, lying on a pile of sacks with chickens perched on his legs. But when he groaned to his feet he became an imposing figure, his angular frame set off by his traditional costume: a red and brown checked shirt with a wide red cummerbund twisted above dark brown corduroys. He was a fiery old eccentric – past ninety, Jean told me – and he spoke in explosive singsong phrases, spitting between each until the dust around him was watered as though with a spray. This ejaculatory, chanting speech is often affected by the older peasants of the Sartenais; for emphasis, so I discovered, and not necessarily to express indignation.

He led us into his house, into another bare room with guns hanging on the wall. His wife, a wrinkled old woman in a long-skirted black and grey printed cotton dress, greeted us with a toothless smile and then sat in silence opposite her husband by the smoking fire. She was his third wife, Jean explained to us, and more than twenty years younger than he. He had fathered fifteen children by his first two wives, all of whom had died. There must have been a ferocious optimism in this old man when past seventy, twice widowed, his huge progeny untimely buried, he had married this woman in her forties in the hope of yet another heir. And now we were introduced to the heir, child of this last marriage, a young man of about thirty who came into the room carrying his own baby in his arms. He was a very thin young man with the pallor of malaria in his skin. At the time of which I write most people on the coasts suffered from malaria: all the Cesari had had it several times; the father went down with an attack while we were staying in the house, and once when we went to Olmeto to exchange cheese for oil we found the owner of the olive grove shaking in bed with a high fever. Since then the illness has been stamped out by free medical treatment, and the yearly spraying of the coasts with DDT will

44

doubtless prevent its return; but it could have been eliminated generations ago if only the swamps had been drained.

The wife made coffee and served it to us in Japanese porcelain cups – incongruously dainty – with *canistrelli* and eau-de-vie and myrtle-berry liqueur. We spoke with the old couple about the past. Their voices rose to a weird singsong scream as they warmed to the subject: modern civilisation, they said, had damaged the ancestral Corsican customs and virtues and given too little in return. Nearly all the changes they had seen had been for the worse: wars, mobilisations, rising prices, the emptying of the countryside, the neglect of the land. The Corsicans were losing the qualities they had inherited from their forefathers. 'There's no more friendship,' said the man, 'it's always self-interest now.' Old Corsican peasants look back to a golden age before the First World War, when prices were low and hospitality unstinted, when people were not preoccupied with making quick money or getting jobs in the towns and the fields were cultivated and the young men content to stay at home. Such a golden age, I reflected, the Elizabethans saw in the era immediately preceding theirs: Merry England, unambitious, self-sufficing, at peace. Corsica's golden age came only in the mid-nineteenth century and it ended with the First World War.

Later Charles-Antoine came to join us with his father – as ever carrying his gun – and the eating and drinking began again. Then we went back to Charles-Antoine's home for a *casse-croûte* before leaving, which was actually a heavy meal of ham and cheese and bread and cakes and wine. The sun was already low in the sky when we managed to tear ourselves away before Charles-Antoine could fill our glasses with yet another round of eau-de-vie. Whatever the twentieth century may have done to Corsica it has certainly not tarnished the hospitality of this village.

The donkey, eager for home, set off at a canter down the valley of the Taravo where the sun laid level beams across the golden stubble. The sea was a deep peacock blue, the last colour it assumes before the sun drops below the horizon and it turns to green-tinted mother-of-pearl. Darkness was falling as we passed the supposed site of the town destroyed by the Saracens, and the donkey, by then, was plodding wearily.

With the coming of night the scene made an odd impression on me. The trees bending over the track seemed like living creatures menacing our passage; the interplay of light and shadow suggested wandering phantoms. I was irritated by these fancies; even in childhood I had no use for ghosts and a personal pride made me refuse to fear the dark. But rejected feelings have a way of coming back on one in Corsica, and taking hold. The rational consciousness one is so proud of possessing, which one feels so sure of, may suddenly dissolve, leaving one at the mercy of illogical intimations such as have troubled generations of Corsicans. As one moves through the night landscape one may share their age-old apprehensions, shiver with their fears, as I shivered that night while the donkey, as though spurred by the same alarm, quickened its pace down the darkening road. A single light appeared across the water, shining from the Cesari's home, and never was light more welcome than when it became the glow of the open door.

The next day Jean confided to me that he too had felt uneasy during the last lap of our journey. But he knew why. It was there, he explained, that a friend of his great-grandfather's had met his death. Literally met his death, in the form of a woman. One night, Jean told me, the man dreamt that he was riding his mare along that track with his dogs following him. Near a tomb that stood by the wayside he met a woman in white with seven dogs. 'Are your dogs with you?' she said to him. 'Yes', he answered, 'they are all here.' 'Then we will make your dogs fight mine,' she said. And there the dream ended.

A few days later the man received news that a cousin, who lived in the valley of the Taravo, had died. At once he left for the funeral, travelling by night to avoid the heat of the sun. His wife went with him, riding pillion. Towards midnight, as they approached the tomb, the mare stopped dead, refusing to make another step. They dismounted and continued on foot, dragging the mare by the bridle. By the tomb the man saw the white woman of his dream. 'Do you see that woman?' he asked his wife; and when she said 'no' he was afraid, for then he knew that the woman was a spirit. 'Have you your seven dogs?' he called to her. 'Yes,' she cried, 'and I will send them to you.' And she thereupon threw something at him. It struck him like sand, stinging his face and arms. Much troubled, he continued his journey, saying nothing to his wife. Riding home from the funeral he saw no sign of the phantom woman and her dogs. But the next day spots came out on his face and arms, he was taken by a fever, and within a week he died.

This was the first of many stories of prophetic dreams and visions, spirits and phantoms and mysterious deaths, that I heard from the Cesari as we sat round the dining-table after the evening meal. However, we started the conversation, inevitably we were drawn back to this secret realm. The oil lamp, then, illuminating their dusky, intent faces, the wine bottle and the photographs and the framed *Médaille de la Famille Française*, enclosed us in an oasis of familiarity in the huge desolation of the night. Crowded together in the warmly lit room we were always conscious of the darkness that lay around us, of the night that pressed in on us, flooding through the window with the relentless churring and croaking of crickets and frogs, stirring unavowed terrors with the humped black mountain shapes that seemed to threaten our very walls. There was no topic of conversation that could distract us long from the ominous nocturnal world.

The Corsicans have always been aware of a host of immaterial beings surrounding them – ghosts of the dead, nameless spirits – ever present, hovering on the confines of consciousness, manifesting themselves for preference by night. To see them is a terrible misfortune, for they are the harbingers of death. And that no doubt is why some Corsicans still at least half believe in them; people who are neither illiterate nor foolish, nor even particularly imaginative by nature.

It takes more than a village school education to eradicate a traditional

46

curiosity concerning the unseen forces that govern man's existence. Education may explain darkness and light, night and day and many other phenomena, but it does nothing to clarify the mystery of death. According to Jean's story the man riding to the Taravo had been killed by a phantom woman. A doctor would certainly have diagnosed his illness differently; but such a diagnosis would have been of little interest to his relatives. Why should this man in sound health have been struck down by illness at that particular time? Only the encounter with the phantom woman could adequately explain the event.

Jung has observed that 'archaic man' is less interested in events that have ascertainable causes than in exceptional happenings, accidents.[2] This was certainly true of the Corsicans a generation ago and even today there are some who have not entirely given up thinking on these lines. Why does one member of a family live to be ninety and another die of an illness at thirty-five? When two brothers go to a war why is one killed and the other spared? Science ignores such questions; indeed the scientific mind refuses them. The Church, on the other hand, forbids the asking of them: illness and accident and death must be accepted as God's will. Attempts to explain death, to foresee it, to ward it off by other than physical means derive in Corsica (as elsewhere) from very ancient pre-Christian beliefs and practices that have been handed down through the ages.

The spirits of the dead, Jean told me, come to claim the souls of the living. They may appear singly, like the white woman his great-grandfather's friend met on the road by night. But more often they come in bands. They arrive, usually, at the evil hours, that is to say at midday,[3] or in the evening, just after the Angelus, or during that forsaken time between midnight and the first cock's crowing.

'What do the spirits look like?' I asked Jean. 'Can one recognise dead friends among them, or relatives?'

'Sometimes, but not often,' Jean answered. 'At first sight, you see, they look just like ordinary human beings, but when one tries to focus their faces their features flicker and shimmer like the faces in an old, worn-out film. And then sometimes only the upper parts of their bodies can be clearly seen; the rest is like drifting smoke. At least that's what people have told me. No, I've never actually seen them. But I've heard them; of that I can assure you, on the head of my dear mother, as surely as I'm sitting here. I heard them calling a girl; her name was Jeanne. "Jeanne! Jeanne!" they cried. The voices came out of the maquis from every side, it was very strange. They were high thin voices, not like those of human beings. There was no one in sight, mark you; we were out there alone in the maquis rounding up the cattle, the girl's father and her brothers and I, and we all heard the spirits call. No, the girl was not with us; she had stayed at home. But anyhow she probably wouldn't have heard them; the person who is called very seldom hears the spirits. Her father answered them: "Take my best cow!" he cried. Sometimes, you see, the spirits will accept an animal in place of a human being. Then he hurried back to the house to warn his daughter. He told her to go up into the mountain;

the spirits, they say, never follow one uphill. She climbed the mountain, and she was saved. Yes, this happened not so very long ago. I swear I heard the voices; may I lose my eyes! And once I heard the spirits when I was a child; but that was rather different. It was at night, indoors, at home. Their footsteps sounded like a regiment marching by and their voices made a whistling sound like telegraph wires in the wind. That was because they were speaking between themselves. When they call a living person they pronounce his name quite clearly; but when they are talking to each other one can never understand what they say; they gabble in little high thin voices and it's impossible to distinguish the words.'

These flickering gabbling spirits of the dead are known as the *Squadra d'Heroda*, the band of Herod; he who massacred the innocents.[4] They swarm down the village streets, Jean told me, until they come to a halt by the house of which one of the occupants is to die. They surround the house, crowd on to the doorstep, calling the victim by name. But he is the only person in the house who can neither see nor hear them. And from that moment his health begins to fail, and within a year he dies.

The *Squadra* may even perform the funeral rites of the victim while he is still alive. The spirits have often been seen in broad daylight, carrying the coffin to the church. Occasionally the processions take place at night; but then the vision is usually blurred and fleeting, although a few people, gifted as seers, claim to have watched the spirits celebrating the Mass of the Dead from beginning to end in lighted churches.

Generally speaking, the victim is spared the frightful ordeal of seeing his own funeral; but such experiences are not quite unheard of. Jean told me of an old man of a village near Sartène, himself a noted seer, who in daylight met a funeral procession, and approaching the coffin found it uncovered and saw his own corpse lying inside. His death followed soon afterwards. Much later I was to recall this rustic anecdote when I learned that Miguel Manara, the historical Don Juan, born of Corsican parents in Spain, witnessed his own funeral at midnight in a church of Seville, and was thereupon struck down, as though dead, but revived to begin a new and better life like one reborn. But this story must be told later.

'The bravest men fear the spirits,' Jean told me. 'Believe it or not I know some who are really tough, who have shot down enemies in cold blood, but who would be afraid to venture even a short distance in the maquis after dark.' 'Some places are more dangerous than others,' Marie said. 'Cemeteries, isolated tombs; it's imprudent to go near them at night.' 'And there are places where one sees even by day,' Jean said. 'They are usually spots where many things have happened: murders, violent deaths. One is always likely to see the spirits there. I know of one not very far away, on the road that goes from Propriano to Sartène. It's where the bandit Santa-Lucia gouged out his enemy's eyes. And people also see here, in the valley, though I don't know exactly why.'

As I listened to the Cesari plotting this psychic map of the neighbourhood,

48

retailing anecdotes of visions and murders and tragic deaths, I began to have a new idea of the landscape, to envisage it from their point of view. The huge silent air was full of voices for those who could hear; for those who could see the empty acres of the maquis were crowded with the hosts of the dead. Visions would appear if one waited quietly in a spot where a deed of violence had been done, as though it had irreparably torn the veil that separates the physical from the spirit world.

For underlying all these old Corsican beliefs is the concept of a dual universe, composed of the physical, or material world, and the realm of the spirits that lies beyond appearances. When a man dies his soul moves into the spirit realm; in this, of course, Christianity agrees. But whereas Christianity maintains that the soul dwells in the body up to the moment of death, according to Corsican belief it is claimed and taken by the spirits a year or less before. This severing of soul from body – as Jean's stories illustrated – can sometimes be observed: at that dramatic moment the spirits become manifest by breaking through the partition that separates the two worlds. So the subsequent physical death may be foretold. But this death of the body is unimportant; the real death has already occurred.

The dead kill: the dead, it is implied, are jealous of the living; they come back to destroy the living by wrenching their souls from their carnal dwelling. Terror of the dead is expressed in innumerable Corsican customs, though partly disguised as respect and love: in the funeral songs and orations and the elaborate tombs, in the prolonged mourning and excessive displays of grief. The food and wine laid out overnight in peasants' homes on the eve of All Souls' Day,[5] the lighted candles and the chrysanthemums in the cemeteries; all these are offered to placate as well as honour the dead. Christianity, with its more or less comforting promises about the future life has never wholly eradicated this age-old Corsican fear, brooding legacy of the megalithic faith.

This I came to understand by degrees. Sitting in the little lamplit room of the Cesari's home, those dark, scented nights of my first visit to the island, I listened unreflectingly, charmed by the verve and colour of their tales. The concrete details were so vivid, the dramatis personae so sharply defined, that often I had less the feeling of listening to stories than of being a spectator at a play. For Jean was a gifted raconteur, flinging himself into every role with an actor's nervous intensity, his voice ranging from the gruff muttering of old men to the high-pitched cries of the spirits of the dead. Meanwhile the rest of the family would break in from time to time like the chorus of a Greek drama, the brothers and sisters supplying additional details punctuated with exclamations of horror or approval, the father offering the conciliating observations of a well-versed ambassador, until Madame Cesari silenced the interruption with some comment in the Corsican dialect which, to judge by the vigour of her gestures and intonations, was the final word that could ever be uttered on that subject.

There was the story of a girl of their own family, a cousin, who had been called by the spirits many years before. It had happened on the eve of the feast of St John the Baptist, when she and her brothers and friends were leaping over the bonfire which according to tradition is lit that night on the outskirts of the villages. The voice came from the village, and it seemed to be that of the girl's mother. The young men promptly seized their guns and rushed back to her house, fearing that she was threatened by bandits; for those were the days when bandits roamed and might prey on any householder by night. But there were no bandits in the village and the mother had not called her daughter. And exactly a year later, on the eve of the feast of St John, the girl died.

Before this happened her family received another warning. One evening, when the girl and her brothers were bringing in the goats, a drum was heard in the maquis; that is to say the brothers heard it, but not the girl. The beating of a drum, Jean explained to me, is a sure sign of impending death. One can never locate this invisible drum, even when it seems to be very near, in the house, in the next room. When one enters that room the drum is silent; if one hears it in the attic no sooner has one climbed the stairs than the sound shifts to the cellar. Only the victim never hears it, and within a year he dies.

Later, travelling about southern Corsica, I heard many tales of this kind; in fact they are part of the conversational stock of the Sartenais. Often, as I listened to them, sitting by smouldering fires, on stone balconies and terraces, once – on a May morning – under a flowering cherry tree in a hayfield, I had the feeling that I, too, was familiar with such experiences. This was not mere fancy, or an effect of suggestion; I must have heard or read similar stories in childhood. For these intimations of the spirit world are by no means peculiar to Corsica; they are – or were – current in areas geographically very far-away. Phantom funerals are well known in Brittany as the most dreaded of the numerous *intersignes* that give warning of death. And they have been seen within living memory in Scotland, and in Wales.[6] Ethnologists have always assimilated these beliefs with the Celtic legacy; but the theory is inapplicable to Corsica, where the Celts never settled.

The inference to be made is more exciting. These beliefs, surely, must be inherited from the only ancient culture shared by Corsica, Brittany and Wales: that of the megalith builders. Their relevance to a religion based on the veneration of ancestors is clear enough. One may be amazed, but not incredulous, to find remnants of this prehistoric faith lingering on in countries washed by the Mediterranean, the Atlantic and the Irish Sea. The megalithic religion was the most widespread and compulsive in western Europe before Christianity, and it died hard. Not all the proselytising zeal of the churchmen, nor the pressure of rational, scientific thought, has ever quite obliterated the memory of what its colossal stones once stood for. If a menhir of the Rollright circle in Oxfordshire is still thought to nod its head when a flowering branch of an elder, growing beside it, is ceremonially cut on Midsummer Eve, and Breton women, until a few years ago, tapped the cupholes of a megalithic tomb with hammers, by night, to ensure good weather for their men at sea,[7] then it is hardly surprising if images and apprehensions flowing from the same

50

source should have continued to haunt the popular psyche. Christianity hardly touched this secret residue of pagan belief; the Church could prohibit rites much more successfully than visions. It might affect their iconography, but not their meaning: though the phantom funerals have mediaeval overtones, the actors, even when chanting the Mass of the Dead in penitential robes, are wraiths from the prehistoric limbo, bearers of a message that the Church denies.

Of all the areas where the megalithic faith took root, Corsica was probably the least disturbed by later religious influences. The Celtic Druids, it seems, never set foot there; the Graeco-Roman gods never imposed themselves on the mass of the population, no traces of their myths can be detected in local legend. Megalithic veneration – or rather placation – of the dead survived, dark, rank and resistant as the maquis, enlacing and often nearly smothering Christian teaching, right into the present age. Nor is this all. Another complex of beliefs concerning death is current over a large part of the island, un-coloured by Christian ritual and apparently issuing from an even more primitive stratum of culture. This amounts to a veritable 'science of death' which is practised – still, today – by a particular category of people known as *mazzeri*.[8]

Jean often spoke of *mazzeri* in his stories, as seers who more often than ordinary people could discern the phantom funerals, the spirits, the various signs of impending death. If I have avoided mentioning them till now it is only to prevent confusion. Perceiving warnings of death is not, however, their main business: *mazzeri* actually bring death; their name is derived from *ammazzà*, to kill. They are people, Jean explained to me, who have been improperly baptised, at whose christening some words of the ceremony were omitted by the priest or incorrectly repeated by the godparents. Thereafter they live a life apart, linked with the forces of darkness and death. In fact they are intermediaries between death and the living, or what one might describe as 'death's executioners'.

'At night they leave the villages to go hunting,' Jean told me, 'one hears them calling each other in the darkness, and the cry of dogs. They go out into the maquis and kill the first animal they meet; sometimes a wild boar, or sometimes a dog or goat or pig. Yes, they use guns – the men at least – but the women often strike down the animal with a stick. There are very many women *mazzeri*. When they've killed the animal they roll it on to its back, and then they recognise in its face someone belonging to their village. The next morning they tell what they have done, and the person they name always dies within a year.'

'Have you ever seen them kill an animal?' I asked him. 'How could I?' he answered. 'All that passes in dreams. The animal is a dream-phantom.' 'Then they only imagine they go hunting?' 'That's right,' Jean said, 'they dream they're hunting when really they're sleeping in their beds. All the same, I know people who've seen them leaving their homes after dark. A friend of mine who lived with an old woman *mazzere* when he was a child – she was his grandmother – told me he often saw her creeping out of the house at night when she thought he was asleep, and returning just before dawn. He told me that the next morning she seemed at first to have only a vague recollection of how she had spent the night and that she was often surprised to find her clothes torn by the maquis and wet with dew. But after a little time she would remember the person she had killed, and then she would foretell that person's death.'

This matter-of-fact account of the *mazzeri*'s activities only added to my confusion. 'You told me they only dream they go hunting,' I protested, 'and now you say that they've been seen leaving their houses at night.' 'Why yes, that's the doubling of the personality,' Jean said, as though referring to something that should have been self-evident.

And this, I learned, is what many Corsicans believe about the *mazzeri*. A middle-aged wine-producer, Dominique Peretti, told me that in his village, Zevaco, in the central mountains, people have been recognised as *mazzeri* precisely because they were seen wandering about at night when they were known to be in their beds at that very time. The *mazzeri* are generally credited with the power of bilocation; one normally associated with the saints. But other Corsicans have assured me that certain *mazzeri* really do leave their beds to stray in the maquis, as though hypnotised, or walking in their sleep.

For Jean was not the only person to tell me about the *mazzeri*; if so, I might have been tempted to dismiss the whole subject as a figment of his imagination. Many Corsicans, living widely scattered over the island, later spoke to me about them, and what they said agreed substantially with what I had heard from Jean. These people are far from being benighted in rustic superstition. Dominique Peretti, for instance, is not only a prosperous wine-producer but a successful local politician, a role that in Corsica calls for the extremes of disenchanted realism. Peppu Flori, who told me about the *mazzeri* in his home in the Niolo, is a retired high-ranking civil servant as well as a poet in the Corsican dialect; Madame Barbara Benedetti, who revealed to me the existence of *mazzeri*, not long ago, in the beautiful valley of Spelunca that links the west coast with the Niolo, has returned there after some thirty years in Paris working in the Ministry of War.

Caius de Peretti, another of my informants, belongs to a prominent land-owning family of Levie, in the central south. Here the *mazzeri* – very numerous until some thirty years ago – are also known as *culpadori* (from *culpo*, a blow). Often they turned themselves into dogs, he told me, and would terrify people riding by night by leaping on to the back of horse or mule, behind the rider. But they had not been known to kill when so transformed. In the far south-east of Corsica the *mazzeri* are known only as *culpadori*. They are more often women than men, and they kill either with knives, or by tearing the animal to pieces, like dogs, with their teeth. They recognise the person they have killed by the cry the animal makes as it dies. These details were given to me by Charles-André Culioli, a highly intelligent young man now living and working abroad, and they refer to his youth in the remote village of Chera.

52

One would naturally envisage these particularly savage killers as sinister witchlike old hags. But Charles-André remembers some of them as young and handsome. Though greatly feared, they were also respected. The same is true elsewhere in Corsica. Though the *mazzeri* are regarded as outside the pale of the Christian community, people who have never received the purifying sacrament of baptism, their esoteric powers confer on them a privileged status. Theirs is an accepted, time-honoured vocation. They have never, to my knowledge, been the victims of any organised persecution. Only occasionally, when they prophesy untimely deaths, the cause of great grief, the relatives of the deceased will turn on them in fury, strike and manhandle them; but this violence stops short of murder.

The *mazzeri* – and everyone I have questioned agrees in this – are not personally responsible for what they do. They act as though under hypnosis; they are 'called' – as the Corsicans say – by an imperious unseen power. Yet they may develop a taste for their night hunting. 'Some take to it like a vice,' Jean said, 'just as other people take to drugs or alcohol. The addiction increases with solitude and time. The women are the worst. They can become passionate hunters at any age. There was a celebrated one near here; she hunted almost every night. She ended by killing her poor husband; I'll tell you how. They were walking together one evening out in the country; they were devoted to each other, you see. Suddenly the woman said to her husband: "What a fine dog that is! Give me your stick." The husband was not a *mazzere*, but he too saw the dog – perhaps because he was touching her at the time,[9] and he knew that she meant to kill it and that the dog was his own soul. "Don't kill that dog!" he cried, "that dog is me!" But she was driven by an irresistible force and she seized his stick and struck the dog down. Her husband fell ill that very night, and soon afterwards he died.'

The *mazzeri* cannot choose their victims. They are obliged to strike down the first phantom animal they meet, even though they may recognise in it a person dear to them. Conversely, they are unable to harm an enemy by this means. As *mazzeri* they have therefore played no part whatever in vendettas. Nor are they by nature malicious. They have little in common with the witches and sorcerers of European tradition and apart from their night-hunting live normal lives. Often they are very insinuating, Jean told me, and will try by every means to win one's affection. But any intimacy with them is dangerous, for inevitably, and against their own inclinations, they draw one down to the realm of darkness and death. Jean's friend, whose grandmother was a *mazzere*, told him that gradually he became aware of her influence and disturbed by it. Increasingly he had weird dreams, sometimes prophetic and always concerned with death. Finally he became so alarmed that he went to a Franciscan monastery in the neighbourhood and asked to be rebaptised. The monks performed the ceremony, after which the dreams ceased.

They were perhaps not unduly surprised by the boy's extraordinary request. The practices of the *mazzeri* have always been regarded as un-Christian. Though there have been no witch hunts or burnings in Corsica the bishops made many pronouncements against sorcerers which must have included the *mazzeri*.[10]

Mazzeri themselves have been known to repent and seek admission to the Church. Incredible as it may seem, traditional ceremonies for the exorcism of *mazzeri* have been performed within the last forty years. At Chera, the *mazzere* was required to go to the church on Good Friday, stand in front of the altar, facing the congregation, and make a public confession with a phrase that may be translated as: 'Beware of me, I am one who strikes down.' After which he took off his coat and the priest placed it over his head and scattered it with ashes. In the mountains, at Palneca, the priest would shake the dust out of the penitent *mazzere*'s clothes. In the region of Sartène the ceremony was more elaborate. The *mazzere*, going to the church before dawn, knelt in front of the altar; the priest tapped him three times between the shoulder-blades with an axe, then covered his head with his own vestment. A *mazzere* was exorcised in this way in Sartène as short a time ago as 1930.[11]

As little by little I gathered this information, my interest in the *mazzeri* became much more searching and methodical than I could have foreseen during those beguiling initiatory conversations at the Cesari's dining-table. I met people in many other parts of Corsica who confirmed what Jean told me and supplied new details; I discovered that my friend, the archivist Pierre Lamotte, had been making enquiries on the same lines. French archivists do not indulge in romantic speculation; by training they have rigorously rational minds. Yet proceeding objectively, one might say scientifically, Pierre Lamotte had none the less accumulated evidence that corresponded with and added to mine.

He has moreover the good fortune of being acquainted with a penitent, retired *mazzere*. This is an intelligent man in his forties who after some twenty years of night-hunting has found his way back to Christianity. 'I prefer Jesus Christ', is how he defines his position. He was first initiated into the ranks of the *mazzeri*, he explained, by an uncle, a *mazzere* of long standing who 'called' him to go hunting; called him, that is, in a dream. Thereafter he hunted regularly, and with satisfaction, though he sometimes felt a certain unwillingness when he was 'compelled' to kill. He even managed to spare one of his victims, as he related in the following fantastic confession. 'Once I had to kill a goat. I seized it by the leg. Imagine my horror when I realised that the goat was my poor father! I let go of its leg and went home. My poor father broke his leg soon afterwards and he was very ill; but he recovered.'

Pierre Lamotte's evidence particularly emphasises the role of the *mazzeri* in the village communities. They are responsible for all the deaths that take place in their villages, or at least consider themselves to be so. They form a caste, or freemasonry, which is not, however, exclusively hereditary. While certain families may be predisposed to the *mazzere*'s vocation, a *mazzere* may initiate, or 'call', people who are unrelated. *Mazzeri*, as such, treat family ties with an indifference that is altogether astonishing; indeed they form the only human association I know of in Corsica in which family loyalties play no part.

54

The *mazzeri* of a village are known to each other and to the rest of the population; yet nothing in their behaviour distinguishes them by day. Their association operates on an unconscious level, or as the Corsicans say, in dreams. In conscious life they are even inclined to treat each other brusquely: 'Like old friends when they've had too much to drink.' Jean Cesari explained. 'You know how people who are really very close to each other will argue and bicker when they're a little intoxicated, and then behave as friends again when they're sober? That's how the *mazzeri* are.' Ordinary waking life – consciousness – is for them a kind of drunkenness, or dream; the unconscious state, in which they act in cooperation, is for them the true reality.

The *mazzeri* cannot be understood unless one concedes that they, and to some degree the ordinary members of their villages, participate in a collective unconscious life. *Mazzeri* meet and act and communicate with each other on an unconscious level; they may also communicate on this level with the other people in their villages, initiating them into their practices, transmitting to them their visions and affecting their dreams. On the other hand a non-*mazzere* may participate in a *mazzere*'s dream to the extent of seeing him walking about at night when in fact he is sleeping in his bed.[12] The collective unconscious life of a Corsican village is like a deep dark cavern, stretching back into the past, from which some of its members only from time to time, and drowsily, emerge.

Mazzeri are not known of all over the island: they are – or were – mostly to be found in the Sartenais, the mountains of the south and the Niolo. It is tempting to correlate their practices with the megalithic faith which – so far as archaeology shows – was centred in the same regions of the Sartenais and penetrated up and inland to the Niolo, probably by the valley of Spelunca where *mazzeri* were powerful until a short time ago. One would like to think that the *mazzere* who spared his father and repented, the woman who struck down a dog that harboured her husband's soul, are connected, by a tradition reaching through some hundred generations, with the people who raised the dolmens and menhirs, the statues of Filitosa.

A theory inviting, but unproved. Nothing resembling the *mazzeri*'s activities has been reported from other megalithic areas of Europe (nor, for that matter, from elsewhere in Europe at all).[13] Moreover, one has to admit that their practices, closely examined, hardly seem relevant to what is known of the megalithic religion, for they reflect not so much a veneration of dead people as of death itself.

Then again, there are districts in Corsica – such as the Cruzzini and the Fiumorbo – where *mazzeri* are remembered but no megaliths have been found, and others – the Nebbio, Cap Corse, the Balagne – with traces of megalithic occupation and no memory of the *mazzeri*. In Cap Corse and the Balagne types of witchcraft flourished, and techniques of prophecy, that are unknown in the south: in Cap Corse a kind of medical sorcery – such as is still notorious in southern Italy – was current until recent years, with long-drawn duels between good witches and bad; in the Balagne, as in the Niolo, soothsayers, until a generation ago, divined the future by looking at the shoulder-blade of a goat or sheep held up against the sun.[14]

The geographical dispersal of the *mazzeri* may be held to suggest that they were not so much associated with the megalith builders as with the shepherds who through the ages migrated up and down the eastern and western water-sheds of the central mountains. Their science may have existed independently of the megalithic faith, alongside it, or even earlier. One may imagine them as the shamans, or priests, of that aboriginal Neolithic people of whom so little is known.

There is nothing in the *mazzeri*'s science to refute so ancient an origin. By its imagery it suggests a primitive preoccupation with hunting. And this, certainly, was characteristic of the earliest Corsicans, in spite of their herds and their rudimentary agriculture; the great quantities of arrowheads found all over the island point to the importance of hunting in prehistoric economy.[15] No doubt the *mazzeri* also hunted in real life; the women as well as the men, as is still the rule with some very archaic peoples such as the Australian aborigines. In Corsica women's primaeval role as hunters has subsisted only in the dreams of the *mazzeri*;[16] with the development of a patriarchal type of society women were relegated to the drudgery of wood and water carrying while men reserved for themselves the excitement of the chase.

The more attentively one studies the science of the *mazzeri*, the deeper it seems to recede into the night of time. It must date from a period when the people, as a whole, were unable to regard death as a natural happening. Death had to be explained. Certain African tribes, whose culture has remained essentially archaic, still hold this view: a man is never thought of as dying from illness or old age; his end is attributed to the machinations of evil spirits, or magicians. Every death, in fact, is a kind of homicide.[17]

The concept of the relationship between body and soul that underlies the Corsican beliefs about the returning spirits of the dead is present in the *mazzeri*'s practices, but in a rather different form. The spirit – or soul – of a living person may leave his body from time to time to wander about at night; the spirits of the *mazzeri* as hunters (or on occasion as dogs), those of their victims in the shapes of various animals. By striking down the soul-animal the *mazzere* performs the same function as the spirits of the dead when they 'claim' a soul from a living human being: he severs the link between soul and body, after which the body sickens and dies.

The operations of the *mazzeri* and the spirits of the dead are therefore ana-logous, but distinct. *Mazzeri*, one is told, live in constant communication with the spirits; more often than other people they see or hear them when they return to earth to claim the living, to mark the next victim of the dead. But in fact the beliefs connected with the spirits and the *mazzeri* cannot be coordinated, and it seems to me likely that they derive from different layers of culture, the science of the *mazzeri* stemming from the more archaic of the two.

The *mazzeri* differ from the spirits of the dead in that they kill under co-

56

ercion, and without animosity. The spirits – so all my informants have insisted – are spiteful and cunning. Yet they may sometimes be outwitted by appropriate spells and actions: by the recital of certain formulae, or by simply walking uphill. The *mazzeri* are much harder to combat, precisely because their action is unmotivated, involuntary. A *mazzere* is compelled to hunt, compelled to kill the first animal he encounters. Correspondingly, the animal, representing a particular human soul, is compelled to meet the *mazzere*. In this dual compulsion one glimpses an authority dominating both killer and victim, against which man is defenceless. One might think that it resides in the spirits; the Corsicans however invariably refer to it as Destiny. Is Destiny a collective term for the spirits? Or is it not rather the final, overriding, inexorable power, controlling the dead and the living, the spirits and the *mazzeri*, the aboriginal Mediterranean deity, an unpersonalised image of the Terrible Mother Goddess? I am inclined to think so.[18]

Destiny, in Corsican belief, is not directly concerned with physical death. It commands one soul to strike down another; it operates in what the Corsicans call the world of dreams. The *mazzere* known to Pierre Lamotte developed this theme further by explaining that all physical happenings, including such events as revolutions and wars, are enacted in dreams before they take place in material reality. Here, I think, one touches the roots of the peculiar fatalism that still colours the Corsican mind. Man – or rather his conscious part – is less than a marionette in the hands of Destiny; he is a reflexion of a puppet, a performer in a shadow drama, the original of which has already been played, elsewhere. Every one of his actions is predetermined; all that happens to him has happened before.

Far back in Corsican prehistory, before the cult of the hero, evolving from the megalithic veneration of the dead, had upheld the unbounded potential of the individual, before any rebellion against dire Destiny had been envisaged, the *mazzeri*, perhaps, served this dark primordial deity as her slaves. One may imagine them as a priesthood, in which the women, incarnations of the terrible female goddess, outnumbered the men. These dream-hunters of souls are perhaps the last living links with Neolithic Europe; through their eyes we can dimly discern the universe as it appeared to man in the dawn twilight of our civilisation.

Man, then, was humble, fearful of the forces of nature and readily identifying himself with its creatures. The idea that a man's soul may leave his body to inhabit an animal is, according to Frazer, still an article of faith for primitive tribes in Siberia, Melanesia, the New Hebrides and Malaya. Certain peoples of Nigeria, the Gaboon and the Cameroons believe (or did until very recently) that every man has several souls, one of which may dwell in a wild animal and is known as his 'bush soul'. If the animal is killed, the man dies; if wounded, he falls ill.[19]

Yet there is no real parallel between the *mazzeri*'s science and the beliefs of these jungle tribes. The relationships between Africans and their bush souls are played out in real life, on the ordinary level of consciousness, whereas in

Corsica they exist only in the dreams of the *mazzeri*. An African believes that his bush soul resides in a real animal; he may even claim to be able to recognise that particular animal when he is hunting, and so avoid killing it.

Closer to the science of the *mazzeri* is that of the *shamans*[20] of the Murngin aborigines of Australia, known locally, and more accurately, as 'stealers of souls'. They are considered responsible for nearly all deaths. According to Murngin belief (and their own confession) they kidnap living people – usually at night – and subject them to an elaborate surgical operation which leads to the piercing of the heart with a 'killing stick'. At this moment the soul is severed from the body and the 'real' death is thought to occur. The stealer of souls then brings the victim back to consciousness and informs him that he will die within a stated number of days, as invariably occurs. Soul-stealers and victims alike (together with the rest of the population), are convinced that the surgery, the death and provisional resuscitation have actually taken place. The victim remembers nothing of this ghastly experience, because in theory he was unconscious at the time; but the soul-stealers will describe the surgical feats in gruesome detail, not as dream actions, but as material happenings. They are all men; they are initiated into their science by older relatives (fathers or maternal uncles), and they are thought to derive their powers from the dead. Unlike the *mazzeri* they can choose their victims, who are either private enemies or members of hostile clans.[21]

So far as I know, nothing resembling the *mazzeri*'s activities is known of elsewhere in Europe. It is in the last primitive pockets of the world, among the tribesmen of the African jungles, the Australian bush, that one can detect beliefs in any way similar. But the resemblances are partial, or superficial; viewed as a whole the *mazzeri*'s science of death appears unique, as original as Corsica's prehistoric monuments. That it should have survived into the twentieth century so close to civilised centres of Europe is very strange.

It may be difficult for anyone unacquainted with Corsica to believe that *mazzeri* still exist there, and practise their dark calling. They do, though they are not nearly so numerous as twenty years ago and most of them are old. But although I heard many tales of the *mazzeri*, a long time went by after those evening conversations in the Cesari's home before I actually met one. People who were ready enough to talk to me about them were unwilling to bring me face to face with the last adepts in a science which they tended to regard as uncivilised and shameful.

I had despaired of ever meeting a practising *mazzere*; I was living in Ajaccio, writing about other aspects of Corsica; Jean had gone to Turkey. Then, one day in late November, he telephoned to me from the south. He had come home; would I join him immediately? I did. 'Tomorrow we will go to see a *mazzere*,' he announced, just as several years before, on my first visit to the island, he had announced that he would show me the statues of Filitosa.

The *mazzere* was an old woman, he explained; he had known her all his life; she lived in a neighbouring village. 'Are you sure she's still alive?' I asked him. 'We will enquire,' Jean said. By good fortune the young schoolmistress of the *mazzere*'s village was staying, on holiday, in the village where I had joined Jean. 'She's alive and at home,' the girl told us. 'I don't know her,' she added, 'I never speak to her; she makes me afraid.'

We drove away into the country on the mild grey winter's afternoon. 'D'you think she'll tell us anything?' I asked Jean. 'I think so,' he answered, 'she's fond of me, I've always been kind to her. And she's been badly treated by the people of her village. Once she prophesied that two coffins would leave a certain house, together, within eight days. And it happened; a week later two men, brothers, both died within a few hours. Their relatives were mad with anger; they thought her responsible. They dragged her down into the valley and ducked her in a pool; she might have drowned, but somehow she fought herself free. They say, too, that she foretold her own husband's death; that's to say she killed him, to their way of thinking. Everyone avoids her; she must be very lonely.'

We had turned into a rough track, climbing slowly uphill through monotonous maquis. The *mazzere*'s village stood on a mountain spur; half a dozen houses facing each other across a patch of bare earth where the track ended. No gardens, no trees; only a skinny dog and a few women around. The women bolted on our arrival, slamming shutters and doors. As they fled I caught glimpses of haggard faces and matted hair dangling under black kerchiefs. They might have belonged to some wild tribe of the Atlas; one was wearing a kind of turban. 'You see,' I said, 'she won't speak to us.' 'Yes she will,' said Jean, 'she's outside, over there.'

He pointed to her, standing alone, behind the houses, near the edge of the escarpment dropping to the valley. She was not as I had expected her to be. An old woman *mazzere* had conjured in my mind the picture of a huddled, crunched-up hag. This woman was certainly old – in her seventies I should say – and she was wearing black rags and she was scarecrow thin. But she was erect, imposing as a statue. She came towards us with a springing tread; and then I saw her face. A black kerchief covered her hair, falling almost to her eyebrows, and she held one end of it across the lower part of her face with her teeth, so that her mouth was covered. It made a frame for her high-bridged nose and huge, amazing eyes. She unclenched the kerchief to greet us, then swept it back into position between her teeth with a gesture at once regal and barbaric. 'She wears it like that to make her gaze more formidable,' Jean later explained to me.

Yet this woman was not only intimidating; she fascinated. Her eyes, immense and deep sunken, were a clear sky blue; young girl's eyes, ageless, unveined, and brilliant as though lit from within. They looked at me without the shrewd scrutiny of the average Corsican peasant woman; they looked through me, as though fixed on some private vision. She knew their power. A white tape, to which was attached a little gold ear-ring, circled her brow beneath the headscarf. 'It's to ward off evil spells on the eyes,' she told us, fingering the ear-ring; 'I have need of my eyes.' Those seer's eyes which can perceive the spirits of the dead and the animal souls of the doomed living, so

I now realised, are the essential instrument of the *mazzeri*. They see beyond appearances; they magnetise. Primitive man knew by experience what science is only now beginning to rediscover: that the eye can affect what it looks on; according to recent Russian research it emits a measurable electro-magnetic ray.

Contrary to what I had expected, the *mazzere* told us about herself, without prompting or questioning. What she said amounted to a spontaneous confession. Do *mazzeri* habitually speak of their activities, fearlessly, sustained by the authority of their calling? Or was she so communicative because she was meeting Jean, whom she was fond of, after a lapse of years? No sooner had she embraced him, and greeted me – without any sign of distrust – than she began to speak of her life-work.

At that time I could understand a good deal of the Corsican dialect provided it was spoken slowly, and without an excess of the harsh, guttural accent sometimes assumed by the country people. The *mazzere* was easy to understand because her accent was unusually pure. Moreover, her speech was a form of chanting. By her voice and delivery she compelled one to grasp her meaning; she spoke in magic intonations, like a great actress, or as the sibyls must have uttered their oracles. After we left her Jean and I stopped in the maquis to record her words, which I reproduce here. Some of her statements, cryptic, cast in trenchant images, require amplification, which I give in parentheses.

'It still happens to me that I go out by night,' she began, 'over there, on that mountainside!' (She was pointing across the valley.) 'I tear my flesh and my clothes.' (Her clothes were indeed torn, and there was clotted blood on her legs and hands.) 'It is stronger than I' (the need to hunt), 'the blood wills it so. I have rendered my daughter exactly as I am' (I have made her into a *mazzere*). 'Often we see the night complete its span and day come without closing our eyes, (because we are hunting). 'I have lost my wits and I remember nothing' (of the ordinary events of life); 'but there are things one can never forget' (the experiences of a *mazzere*). 'The first time it happened to me I was young' (the first time I went hunting). 'When my master' (my husband) 'was taken by something in the night' (was taken ill), 'he did nothing but cry aloud. The others' (the villagers) 'wanted to fetch a doctor. I opposed them, saying that what God has destined those madmen and liars' (the doctors) 'can do nothing to prevent. They took him away to the Continent, but before they put him in a boat he died. He came back in a closed coffin and I never saw him again.'

'They' (the villagers) 'have harmed me. But nevertheless what God has written, when man is born on the sheepskin, that is marked down, and none can avoid it.' (In these primitive districts sheepskins until recently served as blankets.) 'It is better to die in my way than like those they cut down in the wars.'

She had been speaking, almost without pause, in melodious, rhythmic phrases, verging on music; now she passed naturally into song. In that high thin poignant voice in which Corsican women mourn the dead, she began to chant, her hands clutched together, her eyes turned to the dark sky, repeating: 'May the blessed mercy hold me as witness, I spoke only what was written, what was written!' We were standing, then, on the extreme edge of the cliff; her black vibrating figure, silhouetted against the vast backdrop of mountains and sky, was spellbinding. This was an authentic prophetess, proud of her calling. Clearly she had never thought of herself as a killer, but as a world-crier of the unseen powers; of God, for she had no difficulty in reconciling Christian belief with her calling: for her God and Destiny were one. I sensed no evil in her, but extraordinary gifts. She belonged to that category of human beings who in modern society must be poets, and in the Graeco-Roman world, more numerous and respected, were also seers and oracles.

She had reached the apotheosis of her monologue. She was telling Jean where she hunted on the mountain slope, pointing across the grey chasm of the valley with a magnificent hieratic gesture. Then, abruptly, she disappeared. With the dynamic vitality that characterised all her movements she suddenly strode away, out of sight, into the maquis. 'I think she's gone hunting,' Jean said. 'You saw how tense and restless she was, and how she was hovering on the edge of the village when we arrived. I think she's been called.' So, by an incredible accident of fortune, I was privileged to hear the confession of a *mazzere* at the very moment when she was about to execute her mission.

5 ARISTOCRACY AND HONOUR

Living from the land – Sinucello della Rocca – Vincentello d'Istria – Olmeto and Propriano – the Evil Eye – a murder-honour of women – marriage

OUR stay with the Cesari lasted longer than we had intended; longer, indeed, than was prudent in view of the ground I planned to cover after my husband left for England. It would be inexact to say that we were happy in the Cesari's home; the word happy has sentimental connotations quite irrelevant to what we experienced. In London I had not taken the true measure of our deprivations. I had not understood how far my daily load of anxiety was a craving for the things every peasant knows: space, silence, and food that is not stale. Blindly, automatically, like released circus animals rediscovering their natural environment, we slipped into a routine of bathing from the empty beach, eating huge meals and listening to Jean's stories after dark. Almost at once we grew accustomed to sitting on hard chairs and living in a house without running water or drains. In fact the body seemed to rejoice in such conditions, as though all the money one had ever spent on making it comfortable had been thrown away. A persistent headache disappeared: I slept the sleep that seems like falling back into a dark lost paradise every night.

We envied the Cesari. They had leisure, and we had not had any for several years. The farm work seldom needed more than two of the brothers at a time; the sisters got through the household chores in a couple of hours of the day. In the long intervals between work François shot hare in the maquis which Antoinette cooked in a pot on the open fire with olive oil and whole cloves of garlic; Antoine and Jean-Baptiste repainted the living-room, experimenting with pale Etruscan red framing several shades of blue and grey; Marie embroidered sheets with intricate patterns of roses; Pierrette studied a book on the geography of the world. Meanwhile Madame Cesari decided and presided, marketed the cheeses and made the household purchases, walking to Propriano and back balancing a basket on her head as grandly as a queen wearing her crown.

There were hours, too, when no one did anything; when brothers and sisters and parents sat on the little terrace overlooking the bay, hardly speaking, glad to be together, glad to be there. Working a little, resting a little, doing a little of everything, inexpertly, but just well enough: this is how Corsican peasants, in favourable circumstances, have always spent their time.

62

And it is a way of life that has always irritated foreigners extremely. Why, one hears, don't the Corsicans work harder, clear more of the maquis, produce more food? How dare they sit about on walls and stones doing nothing at all? The sight of Corsicans of all ages sitting about doing nothing is positively outraging to many visitors. So are the answers to their questions (though seldom given): that the Corsicans see no reason to work any harder, to grow more food, when they already have enough to eat, and that if they did they would have great difficulty in selling their surpluses. Moreover (and this, I suspect, is what most infuriates office employees on holiday), there is no one to make them work all day: their land belongs to them, as does their time. Leisure or laziness – call it which you will – is their one luxury, tenaciously preserved in the absence of all others; a luxury so inaccessible even to the prosperous tourist that he is likely to regard it as a sin.

Yet this was men's birthright, the world over, before landowners and employers got control of them and forced them, by threat of hunger, to labour all day long. Red Indians and other so-called savages lived like this before the Europeans took them in hand. The Corsicans may have missed many of the benefits of civilisation, but they have also escaped its inhuman servitudes. And they are proud of the achievement. One evening, as a change from tales of phantoms and *mazzeri*, my husband was giving character-sketches of the different races of Europe. 'The Dutch', he said, 'spend their lives working as hard as possible.' 'Then they must be barbarians!' the Cesari chorused, in genuine dismay.

Working intermittently, the Cesari were none the less almost self-sufficing on their eighteen-acre farm. The father grazed his long-legged sheep on the rough pasture verging into maquis above the house; Madame Cesari and Marie made the ewes' milk cheeses that were the main source of revenue. There was a vineyard that provided enough wine and eau-de-vie for the year, and a vegetable garden, and bees and chickens and pigs. Some extra land was regularly rented from a neighbouring landowner in the marshy valley and paid for according to a time-honoured arrangement with a half-share of the produce. There barley and wheat and maize were grown, with tomatoes and melons between the lines of the maize. The Cesari told us that during the war, when supplies from the outside were practically cut off, they could procure for themselves everything they really needed except coffee and sugar. Cousins in the mountains gave them chestnut flour to eke out their rather meagre crops of cereals; they could exchange their cheeses for oil with the olive-grove owners of Olmeto (as they still did); salt could be bought straight from the producers at Porto-Vecchio. As for sugar, honey did almost as well, while Marie made a brew from the acorns of evergreen oak which served (rather less well) for coffee. 'We might have come to like it,' she told me, 'if the war had lasted longer.' I remembered, as she spoke, the passive pasty-faced London hordes queueing for Iceland cod, the gnawing fear that 'rations' would be cut yet again; and I thought I was right in envying the Cesari.

As I later came to realise I was seeing Corsican peasant life at its very best.

63

The Cesari are unusually lucky in owning a farm with a good water supply where they can pasture sheep all through the rainless summer, instead of taking them up into the high mountains, as most shepherds must do. They also have an invaluable vegetable garden close to their house, productive all the year round. More often in Corsica the only spot with enough water for growing summer vegetables is half an hour's ride away, or more. One may come on these tiny green patches far from anywhere, in the beds of rocky gorges, which the owner must visit daily, creeping mile after mile over the huge savage landscape on his donkey to tend a few onions and beans. The same man may possess chestnut trees at a higher altitude, an olive grove and a vineyard at a lower, so that he spends his time continually climbing up and down the mountains as though living on a ladder joining peaks and sea.

Peasant is in fact a misleading word to apply to the Corsicans. The nomadic pastoral life, dating back to the earliest times, has marked the people as a whole. Corsican farmers have not the characteristics of peasants in other countries: they are not stingy or laborious, they have no real love of the soil. More than a thousand families still live according to the primaeval trans-humant system, migrating twice yearly with their flocks between two fixed points, at around five thousand feet and near the coast. Others became sedentary only a generation or two ago: the forbears of the Cesari were mountaineers who had driven their flocks up and down the Taravo until the parents of the old couple we were staying with bought the property by the gulf of Valinco. There they had prospered; the little house with its eight small rooms and good beds and tables and chairs was built in the interwar years to replace a typical shepherds' one-storeyed cabin.[1]

Although I hardly appreciated, on this first visit, how exceptionally favoured the Cesari were, I was fascinated by the ordering of their lives. Security, which no war or slump or inflation or political upheaval could really damage; free time, absence of worry, rush and strain: none of my friends, even the wealthy ones, enjoyed such blessings. The Cesari were privileged people, and they behaved as such. They all shared an aristocratic serenity such as is seldom seen today. Their gentle, attentive, ungushing manners, their unassertive self-assurance, were qualities I had observed only in a few upper-class Spaniards and Chinese.

Little by little we came to know them as individuals: Blanche and François, who were almost unnaturally silent – Blanche seemed to float through the days on the stream of some secret personal felicity – Antoinette, lively, vivacious, an inspired cook; Pierrette, who loathed housework but was meticulous in her appearance and choice of words; once I caught her studying an old-fashioned book on etiquette. Marie, the eldest sister, had a more spontaneous nature with germs of old peasant women's wisdom. Much of her conversation was cast in anthropomorphic imagery. 'The sea is worried; look it is wrinkling its brow!' 'The mountains are moody, they have hidden their faces in clouds.'

The Cesari became and remained friends. This was something more uncommon in Corsica than I at first understood. Corsican hospitality can be very misleading to foreigners. Never has one met a people who welcome one so warmly to their homes. It is quite a long time before one comes to realise that this kindness and generosity is given to strangers precisely because strangers they really are. A visitor, a foreigner, is sheltered and entertained because he is thought of as being at a disadvantage, a displaced person, outside the structure of insular society. He is; and he is likely to remain so. A Corsican satisfies all his need for intimate human relationships in his family circle, a self-sufficient unit that encompasses its members in unfailing affection and excludes any possibility of loneliness. The cult of friends may even seem to him frivolous and artificial.

All the same, friendships are sometimes engendered between unrelated Corsicans, or between Corsicans and foreigners, and are the more scrupulously handled because they are felt to be contrary to the normal pattern of behaviour. The Cesari became our friends. I knew this when I received a Christmas card from them, that shrivelling winter of my return to London, and read the message which only a very sensitive sympathy could have prompted: 'This is to wish you good health, and the realisation of all your desires, always provided those desires are realisable.' Several years passed before I found my way back to their home; years riddled with shocks and disappointments, of which, however, I had told them nothing. But Marie greeted me as though she had been aware of these vicissitudes by clairvoyance. 'Now I see you in good health and unchanged,' she said, 'I have no more anxieties about you; I have laid them down at last like heavy suitcases.'

When I returned after this unhappy interval the gulf of Valinco had become a bathing resort with several new hotels near the shore. But on the summer of this first visit tourists had not yet discovered the place; the beaches were empty, the coastline unimpaired. In the countryside, mostly pathless and uninhabited, the landmarks were natural features, or spots that had been the scenes of strange and stirring happenings, now crystallised in popular tradition and legend.

Over towards Olmeto, a shaggy peak rises steeply from the valley, its summit crowned with vertical boulders like the bastions of some great Gothic castle. In fact a mediaeval stronghold once really stood there (some walls remain), and the most celebrated of its owners is remembered. Hunchbacked, hideous and poor, he loved Sibilla, it is said, a widow of great beauty, owner of the castle of Istria on a neighbouring mountain-top. He sought her hand in marriage, threatened to abduct her unless she consented. Sibilla, who despised him, invited him to her castle, had him seized by her guards and imprisoned in an underground dungeon in an iron cage. To complete his humiliation she went daily down to the dungeon and there paraded herself in front of him, in all her loveliness, stark naked.

His revenge was swift and appropriate. Bribing her guards, he freed himself, took possession of the castle, imprisoned Sibilla in the cage, transported it to the neighbouring mountain pass of Celaccia and there forcibly prostituted her to passing travellers until she died of exhaustion and shame. 'Of course for him it was a matter of honour', I was told, and left to ponder on this curious point of view.

Later I read a more explicit version of the story in a Corsican mediaeval chronicle. The hero, or anti-hero, was none other than Sinucello della Rocca, neither hunchbacked nor poor, but the first of the historic noblemen of the house of Cinarca who attempted to rule Corsica as an autonomous principality. Born in the thirteenth century, when Corsica was a bone of contention between Genoese and Pisans, he became vassal of Pisa, where he won fame in arms before returning to Corsica to claim his domains, recently occupied by a pro-Genoese kinsman. The castle of Istria, on the border of his speedily reconquered properties, had been built by a Genoese seigneur; it was then in the hands of his widow, Savilla da Franchi. Sinucello was the more anxious to make this expedient marriage because she was very beautiful. Savilla invited him to Istria and there imprisoned him, as the popular story goes; Sinucello escaped, seized her and her castle, and in the prim, cryptic words of the chronicler: 'To avenge himself of the affront he had received he put Savilla in a place that was less than honest.'

What later happened to him was a marvellously apt sequel. After years of fighting rival Corsican seigneurs, while opposing or conciliating Pisa and Genoa as circumstances demanded, he eventually came to control the whole island. Like all the Cinarchesi leaders – and perhaps more than any other – he had a sense of the art of government. Supporting the people against the greedy insular nobility he imposed himself by his impartial administration of justice, and so earned the name of Giudice, judge. In 1264 he was powerful enough to summon seigneurs and chieftains to a national assembly and proclaim what amounted to a primitive constitution. But war was soon resumed, with the Genoese backing the disgruntled nobility; their crushing defeat of Pisa in 1284 robbed him of his best ally; his illegitimate sons abandoned him. Past ninety, driven down to his original domains in the south-west, he had almost lost his eyesight as a result of a venereal disease contracted in his youth. Salnese, bastard son commanding the castle of Istria, had no hesitation in laying hands on the blind old warrior and turning him over to the Genoese. Shipped to the mainland, he was left to die of a slow fever in a common prison.[2]

Alas that there has been no Corsican writer to transform this story into art! With its interplay of sensuality and sadism, ambition and revenge, its dramatic reversals of fortune, determined, always by the psychological make-up of the characters, it is the raw material from which a great tragedy could have been written. One cannot know Corsican history without regretting that Shakespeare never heard its tales. So many of its episodes seem made for his genius to work on; the quality of Corsican passions is paralleled in his plays. The landscape, too, recalls his magic settings, as Sir Gilbert Elliot, British Viceroy in the eighteenth century, did not fail to observe.[3] Indeed I have often wondered if the reason why so many British people have felt at home in

Corsica is not that they recognise there the elements of Shakespeare's imaginative world.

The ambition to free and rule Corsica was not extinguished in the Cinarchesi by Sinucello's wretched end. On the contrary they struggled to realise it, on and off, for some two hundred years. While a popular party in the north dethroned the local nobles around 1359 and welcomed the Genoese colonial regime, the Cinarchesi continued to reign, undefeated, over nearly all the west and south. Their territory corresponded, broadly speaking, with a natural division of the island made by the granitic mountain range that walls it across from north-west to south-east. Ethnic differences probably distinguish the two areas, known in history as the *Diqua* and *Dila dai Monti*; at all events the cultural cleavage between them dates back to prehistoric times. The north-eastern region, the *Diqua dai Monti*, less rugged (the mountains are mainly of schist, not granite), and easily accessible from Italy, just out of sight across the Tyrrhenian sea, early on became the more prosperous, populated and civilised; the *Dila*, granite land of the megalithic warriors, remained archaic, introverted, impermeable to foreign ways.

There the Cinarchesi, from the thirteenth century to the sixteenth, ruled like petty sovereigns from their roughly-built castles, spectacular clusters of square towers erected amid natural boulders on the mountain peaks. If serfdom seems to have been unknown, they judged and taxed their subjects and raised armies with which to make constant war on the Genoese and each other. Sixteen of them at different times controlled the island with the title of Count of Corsica. Prodigious fighters, rich in lands and men, they might well have defeated Genoa for good and established a reigning dynasty had they been able to agree between themselves. But they were never able to agree for long. Each warlord was a ruthless individualist, out to crush and if needs be betray all rivals, close kinsmen included.[4]

They were a treacherous, unidealistic lot; yet one can hardly remain unmoved by their breakneck valour, their disastrous destinies. For one and all the Cinarchesi leaders ended badly: ruined, defeated, exiled, executed, or massacred by the Genoese with guile, in ambush (as happened, according to the chroniclers, to forty-five of them in the fifteenth century within a few years). Fighting a desperate cause – the independence of Corsica – backing losing sides – Pisa and Aragon against Genoa – the Cinarchesi were condemned to fail. Moreover, some predisposition to tragedy, that seems inherent in the Corsican character, led them to aggravate their difficulties by their private feuds, their arrogance and their excesses. Like Shakespeare's tragic heroes they carried in themselves the seeds of their own destruction.

One who best succeeded before he ran into disaster was a direct descendant of the iniquitous Salnese, Vincentello d'Istria, who in the early fifteenth century championed the cause of Aragon, with a rare constancy, during some twenty-eight turbulent years. There were good reasons why Aragon should have found staunch supporters among the Cinarchesi. Aragon was further away than Genoa, and its monarchs, if ever they came to rule the island, might therefore be counted on to leave the Corsican seigneurs a free hand. Moreover, the authority of the kings of Aragon was limited by a code of rights and privileges that allowed considerable independence to their subjects. The Aragonese nobility had been forged in the national crusade against the Moors; its members, proud and valorous, were attached to their king as to a leader rather than a sovereign. Their oath of allegiance would certainly have appealed to the Cinarchesi: 'We, who are as good as you, swear to you, who are not better than we, to accept you as our king and sovereign lord, provided that you observe all our liberties and laws; but if not, then not.'[5] Such a regime, at once liberal and aristocratic, was much more in keeping with the spirit of the Cinarchesi (and indeed of the Corsican people as a whole) than Genoa's mean commercial imperialism.

Yet the kings of Aragon were unwilling to risk their armies in Corsica, shrewdly preferring to leave the Cinarchesi to fight out the issue with Genoa while supplying them with occasional aid, usually less and later than promised. Vincentello obtained little from King Pedro except a flattering reception at his court. He had to conquer almost all Corsica before Alfonso V (the sole Aragonese monarch ever to set foot on the island) arrived at the head of a fleet and army in 1420, only to abandon him at the siege of Bonifacio, the last fortress faithful to Genoa. That Vincentello continued to rule the greater part of Corsica as Viceroy for the next fourteen years was due to his exceptional gifts as statesman and soldier. Florence, and the Pope, acknowledged his sovereignty; Genoa was obliged to accept it; no other rebel leader before Pasquale Paoli came so close to giving Corsica an autonomous status.

The traditional vices of his family, rather than Genoese arms, brought about his fall. An incomparable warrior, Vincentello was also arrogant and vindictive, and his passionate sensuality was in no way curbed by his sinister physique. He was tall and well built, writes a chronicler, with fine black eyes; but his arms were deformed, and his face, wrinkled like that of an old woman', was disfigured by an enormous wart that appeared, at first sight, like an eye hanging out of its socket.[6] Such was the demoniacal warlord who seduced so many wives and virgins. If his personal magnetism failed, he used force. When he raped a girl of noble family, already betrothed, and at the same time increased taxation, his supporters turned on him. Captured by the Genoese, he was publicly beheaded in 1434 on the steps of the doge's palace in Genoa. With his death any serious prospect of making Corsica an Aragonese protectorate came to an end.

The Istria, however, managed to keep control of their domains, and steering clear of later uprisings almost alone among the Cinarchesi weathered the Genoese regime. By the sixteenth century they had deserted their peak-perched castle and moved into a fortified house at Sollacaro, at the foot of the mountain, near Filitosa. The gaunt granite mansion with forbidding machicolations is still inhabited by their descendants, who welcomed me and showed me their family tree. There Boswell stayed (in the absence of the owners) when visiting Paoli, and later, Alexandre Dumas, who was entertained by the family while he found local colour for his romantic but rather unconvincing novel, *Les Frères Corses*.

Living with the Cesari, I came to know this country as intimately as one only can when constantly moving about on foot. Since they had no car, and the donkey was often needed for farm work, walking filled a great part of their lives. Towards evening my husband and I would accompany Antoinette to Olmeto on what I came to think of as mediaeval shopping expeditions. The shopping consisted in a series of visits, to buy oil or smoked sausages, or to exchange such things for cheeses. The homes we called at were flats in the tall stone houses, with high-ceilinged rooms and large windows framing, most often, squares of maquis, like tapestries, on distant mountainsides. The parlours were cosily furnished with Louis-Philippe walnut or mahogany couches, oleographs of Lake Como or the Sacred Heart, bright coloured satin cushions embroidered with camels and exotic birds, as was natural enough seeing that they belonged to well-off landowners. Yet it was never without a shock of surprise that I entered one of those well-garnished interiors, for the streets had prepared me for the very abyss of squalor. Washed by the rain of centuries, the paved alleys are rough as the beds of mountain torrents, and their pits and crevasses are resting-places for accumulated rusted tins, old shoes and whitened bones.

The visits always lasted a very long time; discussions about oil and cheeses and sausages, discreetly conducted in dialect, seemed interminable. When a deal was concluded gifts were added to whatever was bought or exchanged: a melon, perhaps, or clusters of cherries, just picked, with their leaves. Such usages belong to a traditional scheme of life in which every action – the daily chores no less than great events – are enshrined in ceremony, integrated in a pattern of personal relationships.

However dilatory the proceedings, I always enjoyed Olmeto; the village has a mellow, peaceful air. But this serenity is recent, and perhaps superficial; for in the past the inhabitants were much given to murderous vendettas. The Franciscans of the monastery on the outskirts of the village, now ruined and smothered in ivy, made it their special business to appease hostilities. But the local character was not, for that, changed; a man in his sixties I met not long ago told me he had known twenty people killed in Olmeto before he left home to go to school on the mainland at the age of ten.

Propriano, our other shopping centre (where one could buy most things in little stores stuffed with heterogeneous objects, cartridges alongside sardines), was a good deal less mellow and even more rubbish-cluttered. A port hardly more than a century old, it still has a raw, unfinished look. The houses straggle along the endless main street as in some unhappy Irish village, concealing for much of its length the superb expanse of the bay. The people, I thought, had something villainous about them; lounging in doorways and cafés they looked lethargic but unquiet, as though permanently premeditating ugly deeds. The Cesari seemed to regard them in the same light; it was Madame Cesari, not the daughters who did the family marketing there, as though she thought it an unsuitable place for them to visit. As I later came to learn, her precautions were as well grounded as my impressions. In Olmeto one is unlikely to run into trouble if one behaves according to the established code; but Propriano is a place where almost anything may happen. An apparently harmless old man was deliberately shot in the back in May 1958 during the celebrations that marked de Gaulle's return to power; a continental Frenchman was found murdered in a car; the corpse of a girl – a visitor – was discovered in a thicket; a young man killed a coastguard who had convicted him for fishing with dynamite and was recently sentenced to ten years' imprisonment; this is only a selection from the crime-chronicle of this ill-starred village during recent years.

Jean Cesari, the emancipated cousin, was however not discouraged from going there, and my husband and I sometimes slipped out of the family routine to join him in sampling what we imagined to be its more sophisticated pleasures. We drank pastis in the ramshackle cafés of the port where one could dance in dark back rooms to Gramophones, ate huge meals of fish and langouste in a restaurant built on piles over the harbour, its roof thatched with rushes, like the dives one sees in films about Indo-China. Nothing, however, seemed to go on there except eating, and in fact there were few amusements in Propriano at that time before the building of the holiday camps and hotels.

But one could never be bored in Jean's company. It was in Propriano that he first introduced me to a *signadore*. *Signadori* are clairvoyants and healers, women who cure illnesses, physical and psychological, ward off misfortunes and foretell the future. They, and they alone, can wrestle with the Evil Eye, author of illness in man and beast, of accident, fire, madness and sudden death. The Evil Eye is the ultimate cause of all catastrophes: more powerful than the *mazzeri* or the spirits of the dead, omniscient and omnipresent, it symbolises the negative, lethal aspect of Destiny. Referred to, often, simply as 'the Eye', or 'the Eyes', it must surely represent an unconscious memory of the salient attribute of the Earth Goddess, the Terrible Mother, that primordial deity of the underworld who devoured the life she created.

The intervention of the *signadori* generally takes the same form: the *incantesimo*, a simple but apparently efficacious rite. The *signadore* pours cold water into a soup plate, makes the sign of the cross over it three times, then throws into the water nine drops of hot olive oil, usually taken from one of the old metal lamps (in form similar to the earthenware lamps of the Romans) kept at hand for the purpose. Meanwhile she repeats inaudible, secret spells, that can be learnt only from another *signadore* on Christmas Eve. The pattern the oil makes in the water reveals the patient's condition: his physical and mental health, his immediate prospects, and whether or not he is afflicted by the Eye. The Eye manifests itself when the oil disperses in little blobs and refuses to coalesce, in spite of the coaxing of the *signadore*'s finger. On these occasions she will make the experiment over and over again until it flows into a compact mass, thus exorcising the forces of evil – so she maintains – by the

70

repeated sign of the cross. But this Christian formula is merely an accretion on a pagan rite of deep antiquity; the method of divination with oil and water, widespread in the Mediterranean, is said to date back to the Chaldeans.

When first I came to hear of the *signadori* I thought of them as white witches, the counterparts of the *mazzeri*, and their enemies. But this was a naïve view. Though some *signadori* use their occult powers solely to heal and protect, others, so I learned with astonishment, may heal by day and destroy by night. In fact there is no hard-and-fast distinction between *signadore* and *mazzere*, between white magic and black. Access to the secret forces of the universe confers powers which may be used for good or for evil, often by the same person, but which are always felt to be dangerous, and in spite of the evident piety of the *signadori* are generally regarded as un-Christian.[7]

There is however a vital distinction between the harmful and helpful practices: the latter are learnt, voluntarily, from older initiates, and are performed by the conscious will; those of the *mazzeri* are imposed by unseen forces beyond human control. Here one has to do with the fundamental Corsican belief that man – his conscious self – is by nature good; when he does harm he is acting under the compulsion of Destiny or the Evil Eye. The conviction must surely date back to prehistory, to the period of the Filitosa statues, at least, when emerged, in monumental form, the essential humanism of this godless race which conceived the supernatural forces as essentially evil, and all goodness and glory to reside in man.[8]

The Eye, it is true, operates through human agency, but not necessarily that of vindictive or spiteful individuals; anyone, however well meaning, may inadvertently 'cast the Eye'. For the Eye is always present, ever seeking to destroy human health and well being. To express admiration of another person is particularly dangerous, for the words will attract the Eye's attention to his beauty, his health or happiness, and these the Eye will instantly destroy. The Eye battens on babies and little children; any such compliment as 'What a pretty baby you have', must immediately be followed by some such phrase as: 'May God bless it', otherwise the child will sicken and die. It is unwise, too, to announce any agreeable plan or happy coming event – a journey, a christening or wedding, a purchase of property – without adding the words: 'If it pleases God.' What little satisfaction can be squeezed from life must be placed under God's protection – the Christian God, nearly always referred to as 'the Good God' – and carefully concealed from the ever-watchful Eye.

The Good God may be invoked against misfortune, but in really crucial situations many people have more confidence in the *signadori*, expert in combating the pitiless Eye. Though fear of the spirits and the *mazzeri* is fast disappearing in Corsica, dread of the Eye, at least among simple people, is still real enough. Today the *signadori* have been practically ousted from the medical profession (doctors are everywhere held in high esteem); but they are still resorted to for psychosomatic troubles, to which the Corsicans are curiously prone. Sometimes a *signadore* is consulted at the same time as a doctor; the doctor is then thought of as treating the symptoms of the illness while the *signadore* attacks its root cause.

I was neither ill nor distressed when Jean first took me to a *signadore* in Propriano; merely curious. The experience was mainly interesting because there was nothing uncanny about it. The *signadore*, who lived in a clean, pleasantly furnished flat, was a neat, middle-aged woman who reminded me of an old-fashioned governess. I have never been able to believe that she was also a *mazzere*. 'You would like me to sign you?' she said briskly. 'You believe in God of course?' She lit an old brass oil lamp on the mantelshelf, took a soup plate from the dresser. The experiment was satisfactory. 'Your oil is clear,' she said, 'there's no sign of the Eye.' As is invariable with those of her calling, she refused payment. 'Come back to me if you are ever in trouble,' she said. (I did, years later, and felt the better for her spells.)

That evening, as we were walking home along the sea, we heard shots in the village behind us. 'It's nothing,' Jean said. My husband and I concurred. We had been long enough in Corsica to be unsurprised by gunfire. All the men had guns, and usually revolvers as well (as is still so); although it was the close season for game everyone went shooting in the maquis, hare, partridge, almost any small bird; little boys practised shooting at tree trunks; the sound of firing had become an accepted accompaniment to our otherwise quiet lives. During the two days following our visit to Propriano the Cesari girls succeeded in keeping us at home: Pierrette wanted help in translating a passage from her English textbook; Marie asked my husband to design her an embroidery pattern of roses. We stayed with them willingly enough, for the heat had become extreme.

Afterwards Jean told us that a man had been killed by the shots we had heard in Propriano, and another seriously wounded. The reason was as follows. A widow in her forties had been having a secret love affair with a married man, the father of several children. Her brother, at least ten years younger than she, had discovered their liaison. He ordered the man to divorce his wife and marry his sister immediately. The man refused: Corsican husbands, even when in love with another woman, even when threatened with death, will hardly ever leave their wives (those wives whom from our standpoint they treat with such scant consideration). The two men met in the street. They fired on each other: the husband was killed and the woman's brother dangerously wounded. At the funeral, Jean told me, the dead man's widow had shrieked and wailed and cursed her husband's murderer while her eldest son, a boy of eight or nine, his hands stained with his father's blood, had publicly vowed revenge.

According to the traditional code this murder would be the starting-point of a vendetta. In times past the widow's son would have grown up with the obligation to murder his father's murderer, or one of his near relatives if the man had died, and the war between the families might have lasted for generations, or until all the men on both sides had been killed. In fact only the young age of the widow's son offers a chance that no vengeance will ensue.

72

For today the vendetta is on the way out; but at the time of this murder it was still a possibility.

I would have given much to have seen that funeral, though I was bound to respect the feelings that prompted the Cesari to conceal it from us. For them it was not so much an exhibition of regrettable primitive violence as a disclosure of intimate matters that a foreigner would be likely to misinterpret. They were right. I was unable, then, to understand the murderer's motive. I was baffled because the Cesari, like everyone else I spoke to, considered that the brother had no choice but to kill. To me it seemed absurd that this young man should feel compelled to interfere in the private life of his sister, who could hardly have hoped to marry her lover and had successfully kept their liaison from public knowledge.

I had yet to fathom the passionate puritanism of the Corsicans, especially where women are concerned. According to the traditional code no allowances are made, no degrees of guilt admitted, no extenuating circumstances; sex, outside marriage, is sin. Sin may mean death for a man, but not dishonour; to seduce a woman is to take a manly sporting risk. But for a woman sin, if discovered, means irreversible social ostracism: she is a *putana*, a prostitute. And seeing that in Corsican society a woman is the property of her husband, father and brothers, her shame is also theirs. Self-respect demands that they either kill the lover or get her married to him immediately. This young man of Propriano was not thinking of his sister's private life, for in his eyes she had none, nor of her happiness, which he probably wrecked, nor even of morality in the abstract (Corsicans are disinclined to abstract thinking); he was saving himself and his family from public humiliation.

'Surely you understand, he had the family honour at heart,' Jean said to me, 'he sacrificed himself for that.' 'She had disgraced herself,' said Antoine. 'If he did nothing people would say she was only good for a macaroni.' Corsicans despise the Italians – the *macaroni* – not only on account of those historical scapegoats, the Genoese, but also because the only Italians many of them have met were either poor migrant labourers or the detested occupying troops of the Second World War. An Italian is just good enough for a fallen woman. 'A Corsican brother always protects his sister,' Antoinette said with satisfaction, 'her honour is precious to him.' One after another they laboured to persuade me of the absolute necessity of killing a sister's lover. The conversation was brought to an end by one of Marie's fine downright phrases: 'Honour is like ink,' she said. 'Once it has been spilt the stain can never be erased.'

Honour: in Corsica one is always hearing the word. It has been used to justify all the violence and intransigence of local life: forced marriage, banditry, killing, vengeance, vendettas. But what exactly does it mean? 'What is honour? Air,' Falstaff exclaimed in understandable exasperation. The idea of honour is immemorial, but its content has altered through the ages. In England today it means little more than keeping one's word and paying one's bills. But in the past it was more glorious: in the age of chivalry, as in

73

Homeric times, honour meant reputation won by deeds of valour. Honour, clearly, has no constant attributes; it began as warlike prowess and has dwindled to passive respectability. For its mainspring is not an ideal, but the individual's awareness of his own worth, and what that worth consists in depends on the ethos of the society to which he belongs. Only the very strongest can be convinced of his own value unless it is reflected back to him in the opinion of others: honour is at once what the individual thinks of himself and what others think him to be.

The Corsicans have their own, traditional notions of honour, and these have little or no reference to the modern world. For centuries back Corsican honour has been out of step with European civilisation. One may understand that to run away with, or make love to, a wife or daughter is to inflict a mortal injury on her reputation, and with a proud, uncompromising people can lead to murder; such behaviour strikes one merely as extremist and old-fashioned. It is harder to sympathise with the view that still decreed, after the Second World War (and in some southern villages, and in Sartène, today), that a girl's honour is damaged if she is seen speaking to an unrelated man, and lost if she goes for a walk with him.

And what is one to think of the *attacar*, which was a principal cause of murders and vendettas well into the present century? The *attacar* was a public gesture – no more – whereby a man was held to have taken possession of a woman. Once she had been subjected to it, even if unwilling and resisting, she was dishonoured and no other man would marry her. The gesture might be a kiss, and here one can begin to appreciate the feelings involved; but to touch a woman's face or hands, or worse still, to pull off her headscarf, was just as serious. Cries of *disonorata!* accompanied the act, which was performed for preference in some crowded place; on the church steps, most often, just as the congregation was leaving Mass.[9] Either the man married the girl immediately or else a vendetta was declared. The latter was by far the more common result. If a man inflicted this public humiliation on a girl it was unlikely (unless he was trying to catch an heiress) that he had any intention of marrying her; the act was an incident in a feud already existing, designed to discredit the girl and her family.

Foreign observers and official records agree that the *attacar* caused more violent deaths in the eighteenth century than any other circumstance, including, it seems, war. The Genoese, Pasquale Paoli, even dense-witted King Theodor legislated against it; prison and even execution might be the penalty for the culprit; yet the offences continued and were much more often punished by the girl's relatives, by murder.[10] Such irrational, implacable, instinctive reactions are not to be explained by a regard for Christian morality. The Corsican sexual code, as applied to women, always exceeded the already high demands of Christian teaching; the attitude of the Church was liberal by comparison. A girl, to be marriageable in Corsican eyes, had to be not only a virgin, but untouched by any man.

The pollution implied by the *attacar* can hardly be explained except on the

74

supposition that these gestures had some symbolic meaning to the Corsicans, unconnected with Christian precepts. And that is just what insular custom suggests. A traditional form of marriage actually existed in Corsica, and was practised until about twenty years ago, which took no account of ecclesiastical or civil rulings. There is a wealth of written evidence to show that the Corsicans, until quite recently, preferred this 'customary' form of marriage to that blessed by the Church or prescribed by law. The authority that sanctioned it was the head of the family, a figure who has always wielded greater power in Corsica than either magistrate or priest. Marriages were arranged by fathers. When a match was decided on, and the amount of the girl's dowry fixed, the young couple met in the house of the girl's parents and there kissed each other in the presence of their assembled relatives. The girl's mother then handed the bride a plate of *fritelli* (fritters, usually of chestnut flour); the bride offered it to the bridegroom, and following his example the rest of the company each ate a *fritelle*, thus sealing the union by the ritual sharing of food. The marriage was consummated immediately afterwards, in the girl's room. A religious or civil ceremony followed, if at all, only after the birth of a child.

This wedding ceremony (described by a Corsican specialist on the subject as a 'symbolic choreography')[11] must surely derive from remote, pre-Christian times. In fact the Church laid down no hard-and-fast regulations for the solemnisation of marriages before the sixteenth century, when the Council of Trent decreed that marriages must be solemnised by a priest before witnesses. But the Corsicans, ignoring its edicts, remained deeply attached to their own ancestral form of marriage. Exhortations, excommunications, orders for fines and public penances issued in spate by the clergy all through the seventeenth and eighteenth centuries went almost unheeded; parents, especially in out-of-the-way districts, continued to marry their children according to time-honoured tradition. Bishops might condemn these marriages as invalid and immoral, but the Corsicans persisted in believing that the ritual kiss and partaking of *fritelli* were sufficient to solemnise the union.[12]

In the light of this custom the enormity of the *attacar* becomes more understandable. The gestures of kissing and touching were associated with the very form and ritual of the accepted wedding ceremony; performed by force they amounted to a public mockery of marriage. The bridegroom, presumably, would remove the bride's headscarf as the first gesture of intimacy when they retired together to her room; if, therefore, a man tore off a girl's headscarf in public he as good as proclaimed his right to possess her. But the right had not been sanctioned by paternal authority or established ceremonial, so that in fact the man declared the girl to be his mistress, a loose woman to be had for the taking. Her reputation could only be rehabilitated if he immediately married her in earnest.

Yet there is something in the superstitious horror surrounding the *attacar* that still eludes one, and may well lie hidden in primitive beliefs long ago forgotten by the Corsicans themselves. One knows that Corsican ideas about marriage, however it was celebrated, were bound up with obscure notions of magic. The sexual union was thought to ward off the Devil (in other words the forces of evil, the Eye), and, as the bishops complained, was habitually performed in advance of the church ceremony for this purpose.[13] The same precaution is shown in customary marriage by the consummation immediately following the ritual kiss. The removal of a headscarf may have been connected with similar fears. In archaic societies the head was universally regarded as the sacred member of the body, the abode of the individual's essential worth or 'honour', as is reflected in the traditional gestures and ceremonies of crowning, veiling, adorning, touching, covering and uncovering the head, as well as in the acts destructive of that worth, such as scalping and beheading. The veil was commonly thought to protect this precious quality in women, to guard it against evil influences, malignant spirits.[14] One can understand, then, that if a girl's headscarf (an emblematic, vestigial veil) were removed without an accompanying purifying ritual, she might be considered as exposed to the contamination of evil; in fact accursed.

When customary marriage went out of fashion in the present century it was not because the Corsicans were becoming more obedient to the clergy (on the contrary), but because the immemorial social structure was breaking down. More and more young men were going abroad for a living; the authority of parents, as of village opinion, was losing force. A father could never be sure that the son-in-law who planned a career in the colonies would respect the vow he had tacitly made when he kissed his bride in her parents' home. And if he defaulted, it might be no easy matter to find and murder him. For the obligations of customary marriage, being unrecognised in law, could only be enforced by parental authority, and in the last resort by killing. When customary marriage died out the *attacar* also disappeared from Corsican life, complementary facet of the same social complex.

Nevertheless, until the interwar years, marriages, however celebrated, were nearly always the outcome of long, careful negotiations between fathers. The children were rarely consulted. The ruling motive in matchmaking was not so much money, which was extremely scarce in Corsica, as the power and prestige of the families concerned. A good match was one that brought an alliance with a large number of males of fighting age; a girl with half a dozen stalwart brothers was sought after like an heiress. The possession of land might also be taken into consideration; the girl's dowry was often a slice of the family property that might be advantageously joined to a neighbouring plot belonging to the bridegroom, who was very often a cousin; Corsican marriage is by tradition endogamous.[15] But the main advantage sought was aggrandisement of the family in terms of numbers of men: 'rich in men' is an expression one often finds in Corsican documents. Marriages thus had the character of dynastic alliances; as a Corsican authority puts it, every shepherd thought of himself as the sovereign of his little kingdom.[16]

Personal inclinations had of course no place in this concept of marriage; girls and young men were constantly called upon to sacrifice their feelings in

76

the interests of state. But in fact few were even tempted to rebel.[17] Children grew up to think of themselves, not as individuals with preferences and passions, but as members of the family group to which total devotion was due. Corsican arranged marriage on the whole worked out as well as either party expected; that is to say, well enough. All the same there were some terrible exceptions, such as that of the girl, forcibly married a generation ago to a man of inferior social position, who bore her husband three children but never, to her death, addressed him a single word.

If one occasionally meets victims of the system, hard-drinking husbands and shrewish wives embittered by a lifetime of unchosen cohabitation, examples of romantic love, that love which braves every law, convention, danger and disgrace to achieve union with the loved one, are strikingly absent. The best Corsican marriages repose on a loyal, loving, constant friendship. Until very recently the Corsicans have had little awareness of love as sung by the poets and extolled in the women's magazines. One may look in vain for any parallel to Tristan and Iseult or Romeo and Juliet in the mass of folk tales and semihistorical legends.[18]

But it was impossible for this French province to remain permanently immune to the ideas of love and marriage current on the other side of some hundred and twenty miles of sea. Foreign ideas began to seep into the island after the First World War, and poured in with the Second, during which insular conventions lapsed: in the towns there were simply not enough Corsican fathers and brothers left at home to murder the troops who consorted with Corsican girls. By the time I arrived in Corsica the traditional code had been seriously undermined. Yet in the impermeable south, at least, some of the old prohibitions were still enforced. A girl was still compromised if seen talking or walking with a man (as is still in some places true); a private rendezvous, if discovered, might still bring the man up against the alternatives of marriage or sudden death.

The Cesari were very well aware of this. None of the daughters had ever been out with a man, and the sons never stopped to speak to the girls we met in the streets of Propriano and Olmeto. These taboos certainly limited social pleasures; but they put an edge on village life. Always one was conscious of the tension between the sexes, a highly-charged current sparking off in *sotto voce* exchanges, sign language gestures, glances heavy with significance. The Corsican boys and girls had made a fine art of almost invisible, almost inaudible communication, as though engaged in a concerted resistance movement against their elders.

For secretly they were in revolt, especially the girls. They were claiming the right to get to know each other before marriage, to choose their life-partners. Extreme cunning was used (and still is) to contrive lovers' meetings, by fountains and cemeteries outside the villages, under archways at nightfall. The prize was a foretaste of love; the penalty might be death for the man, and for the girl scandal, disgrace, or the death of father or brother. Yet their parents, too, were beginning to doubt the old system, and there was always the chance that they might prefer even an unsuitable marriage to murder. So courageous young couples, by arranging to be seen together, could sometimes override parental opposition. A scheming girl, too, might catch an unwilling husband by such means. She had only to be seen talking to the man of her choice and her parents would hasten to force through the marriage, regardless of the man's feelings. If, on the other hand, the girl was already tired of the man she had been flirting with, and her parents disapproved of the match anyhow, her honour might be saved if the man publicly demonstrated his willingness to marry her.

Jean Cesari told me of the consternation of a couple of Swiss tourists who not so very long ago found themselves in a southern village on the day of a wedding. The ceremony, they thought, would make a good subject for their movie cameras. It did. As the two groups – the bride and her relatives, the bridegroom and his – converged on the Town Hall, they noticed that all the men were carrying guns. These were however left in the porch, and the ceremony followed its usual course until the bride was asked if she would take the man as her husband. 'No!' she hissed, and spat in his face. The men rushed for their guns, followed by the tourists with their cameras; but the rejected bridegroom managed to make peace before any shots were fired. 'It had all been arranged beforehand,' Jean explained, 'the man had agreed to take the girl in front of the mayor so as to redeem her honour and get rid of her. But of course her parents were not at all sure how he and his family would react when it came to the point. It was a delicate situation, you understand, so the men of both families went armed, just to be on the safe side.' That Corsican way of being on the safe side which has led to innumerable deaths!

Fake marriages of this kind were (and still are) by no means uncommon. Sometimes a couple will go through with the ceremony and separate immediately afterwards, preparatory to divorce. A fanciful case was related to me by a priest of a southern parish: a girl, compromised by a married man, accepted in restitution of her honour marriage with one of his uncles, a very old bachelor whom she divorced immediately.

These manœuvres amount to cheating with a code that has lost its validity. In the past, shot-gun marriages were at least real marriages; the girl paid for her recuperated honour with a lifetime of the heavy duties of a Corsican wife, and the man, of course, for his recklessness by the heavy responsibilities of a father. Today divorce has become a convenient means of evading the rigours of the code while using it to save face. Not alone among the immemorial Corsican institutions the complex of feminine honour, marriage, sex relationships, is being caricatured. Two world wars, cars, television, and air travel that brings the island within thirty-five minutes of Nice cannot but crack the staunchest traditions.

6 LAW OF THE OUTLAWS

Unwritten law – code of the vendetta – domestic animals –
archaic honour – appeasing the dead – church versus vendetta
– law versus vendetta – funeral rites – bandits of honour –
the death of honour

HISTORIANS, when speaking of the Corsican vendetta, invariably describe
it as a barbarous custom that was brought to the island with the invasions of
the early Middle Ages, took root in a period of anarchy and was perpetuated
by Genoese misrule. For centuries, they argue, the Corsicans were badly
governed, barely governed at all; lacking any impartial authority to administer justice they administered it, each man for himself, a life for a life, in
accordance with 'natural' or talionic law. The thesis has been so often repeated
and with so much conviction, that no one has been inclined to question it. Nor
was I, until I came to realise how little it matches the facts.

To look upon the vendetta as a form of bloody barbarism into which men
automatically fall in times of disturbance is to misunderstand its nature. On
the contrary, the vendetta is a method – one of the methods – by which
primitive societies keep order between their members: a kind of unwritten
law. Our assumption that governments can be relied on to punish such
offences as murder, theft or rape, belongs to civilisation. In archaic, preliterate
societies the central authority, if any, is likely to be weak, and the defence of
life and property is left, most often, to individuals and their kin. Murder is one
of the sanctions they may use.

In European history state law came to supplant private vengeance by a
slow process of evolution. Blood vengeance came to an end in Greece, as an
authorised institution, in the seventh century B.C. with Draco's code, which
decreed death or voluntary exile for the murderer.[1] The Romans, who likewise imposed the death penalty for homicide, spread their law over Europe in
the wake of the victorious legions. As a novelty; the people they came up
against still countenanced the blood feud. Tacitus relates that the Germans
held tribal gatherings in which crimes were punished that affected the tribe
as a whole, such as desertion in battle; but that the blood feud was an
approved means of settling private quarrels. Hostilities could however be
brought to end by customary payments; even homicide could be atoned for
by the payment of a fixed number of cattle or sheep to the injured family.[2]

This, one may suppose, was the type of blood feud practised by the Germanic tribes that temporarily controlled Corsica after the fall of Rome: the

79

Vandals, the Ostrogoths, the Lombards. The Lombards, who civilised themselves fairly rapidly, codified their tribal usages in a body of written law that tolerated private vengeance and allowed for payments to be made in compensation for murders, one part going to the injured family, the other to the king. Their customs had an enduring influence in northern Italy;[3] but can the same be said of Corsica? The Lombard domination lasted only fifty years, and like that of the Vandals (which was not effective for much longer), has left no visible traces in the island whatsoever. As for the Ostrogoths, they came and went within the space of three years. Is it really likely that an institution so deeprooted as the Corsican vendetta, so intimately bound up with the social structure, values and passions of a people always hostile to outside influences, could have been introduced by these unwelcome foreign overlords during their brief periods of incomplete rule?

If this were so, then one would at least expect the type of vendetta current in Corsica to conform to theirs. But no. Blood money – *wergeld* – essential to the Germanic blood-feud systems, has always been abhorrent to the Corsicans, a point of view summed up in their immemorial axiom: 'Blood is not for sale.' The vendetta was more destructive in Corsica than in other European countries where it survived into the Middle Ages (such as Italy) precisely because payments could hardly ever serve to make peace. If peace ever was concluded between the warring families the offending family might pay a dowry to a girl of the offended; but this was either accessory to her marriage with the murderer or one of his close kin, or was given to help her find a husband, to replace, in her family, the man who had been killed.[4] The compensation was not in money, but in male lives. Nothing, in Corsican eyes, was so valuable as a human life; and if this conviction seems to stem from a philosophic concept that one can detect in the statues of Filitosa, it has also corresponded with the persistently archaic pattern of Corsican society. The operative value in Corsica, until very recently, was not property or money, but the status a family could acquire by its sheer strength in numbers and physical fighting force.

The Corsican vendetta has its own code, which may owe little or nothing to the Germanic invaders. Nor to the Arabs, among whom blood money was, and still is, an accepted means of ending feuds. It is quite possible that the vendetta was a primaeval indigenous institution. Diodorus Siculus gives a handsome description of the Corsicans as the Greeks and Romans found them, at the dawn of their history. They were pastoralists, he writes, who lived on meat, milk and honey, and among themselves they lived 'lives of honour and justice, to a degree surpassing practically all other barbarians'. A deposit of wild honey belonged to whoever found it, and no one disputed his claim; the herds, each distinguished by its owner's mark, could wander unguarded and their owners suffered no loss, 'and in their other ways of living one and all it is astonishing how they revere uprightness before everything else'.

This picture of the Corsicans in the shining light of Rousseau's state of nature has often been quoted by Corsican historians to show that the vendetta was introduced from abroad, in later, historic times. But the passage is open to a contrary interpretation. If the Corsicans so respected justice, surely they had some method of enforcing it. And this, as in many primitive societies, may well have been the vendetta. Perhaps sheep and cattle could be left unguarded, then as later, precisely because theft incurred murder and the extermination of families. Other classical writers had a very different opinion of the Corsicans: Strabo and Seneca describe them as ferocious. And so they may well have been, on occasion.[5] It is permissible to suppose that when the Romans conquered the island the vendetta was an already established institution, and that it persisted in defiance of their administration, as it persisted through the four centuries of the Genoese ascendancy and under French rule almost to this day.

The blood feud is by no means inevitable in archaic societies; but there are sound reasons why it should have been so in Corsica. Among some very primitive peoples sanctions other than murder suffice to keep order: mockery, house-burning, ostracism. Or killing may be only one in a graded scale of penalties: among the Murngin Australian aborigines, if a wife is seduced, a fight takes place that rarely leads to death; but if she is stolen a *maringo* ensues, a night attack on the camp of the abductor's clan by all the males of the husband's clan that usually ends in wholesale slaughter.[6]

Social anthropologists have observed that the blood feud is characteristic of societies based on lineage, societies, that is, in which the kinship group, composed of persons descended from a common ancestor, usually in the male line, constitutes the paramount social unit.[7] Respect for governments, chiefs, the state, is altogether alien to such peoples; each family, or rather lineage group, fends for itself, ready to make war on every other and rejecting all exterior control. Traditional Corsican society certainly functioned in this spirit; but it was organised differently. The Corsican kinship system (as is the rule in Europe) is bilateral, with an emphasis on the patrilineal side; children recognise and respect their mother's relatives and ancestors but attach rather less importance to them than to their father's. The kinship group is therefore larger in Corsica than in purely unilineal societies, and its loyalties wider: an injury to a member of a wife's family may be avenged by her husband, her sons and her brothers-in-law as well as by her own father, her uncles and her brothers and their sons. This extended kinship group is cemented by a rather unusual characteristic that has given powerful encouragement to the vendetta. By tradition Corsican marriage is endogamous: that is to say cousins – second and third cousins, but sometimes first cousins, in the lines both of the father and of the mother – have constantly been chosen as marriage partners. As a result, if a man happened to be killed who had no brothers or sons to avenge him, the feud, most often, was automatically taken up by a brother-in-law, who was one of his own kin, having the same grand- or great-grandparents.[8] The Corsican kinship group, folded in on itself in a tightly knit web of blood relationships, acted as a forcing ground for the vendetta. The vendetta is in fact exactly what one would expect to find in Corsica; the conditions it thrives on are united there.

A distinction is usually made between the vendetta and the blood feud. The principle of the blood feud is talionic compensation: once a murder has been revenged by another murder institutions come into play to make peace between the warring families, usually accompanied by a payment. The vendetta, on the contrary, implies total war, without rules or restriction or possibility of composition; the two families continue killing each other until one or both are exterminated.

The Corsican vendetta almost fits this definition; but not quite. In periods for which there are records (since the fifteenth century), the principle of a life for a life has been on the whole observed, or, according to an eighteenth-century writer, two lives for a very valuable life: the murder of a priest or the head of a family had to be revenged by two murders; their lives, in fact, counted double.[9] I have found no record or memory of any custom resembling the terrible Murngin *maringo*.

The duty of avenging a murder – for duty it was – fell on the nearest able-bodied male relative of the victim. For preference he killed the murderer, or one of his close kin. Not all blood relations could be drawn into a vendetta; in theory its obligations extended no further than to second or third cousins.[10] Often it was the female head of the family, a mother or grandmother, who undertook to charge the victim's next of kin with his solemn mission of executing vengeance; as is the rule in Sicily (a legacy, surely, of women's primaeval ascendancy in the Mediterranean world). Women have always played a vital role in the Corsican vendetta, but in the psychological sphere: with justice they have been called its priestesses. It was they who performed the funeral ceremonies for the murdered man, designed to whet the rancour of the surviving males. But they were not, in theory, killed, or expected to kill. Old men, monks (but not parish priests) and children of both sexes were likewise, in theory, treated as non-combatants.

But in fact these rules were all too easily forgotten in the intensity of passion unleashed by a vendetta. Once hostilities had been declared there was a total mobilisation of both groups, and all their members went in fear of their lives. Women were sometimes killed, and several achieved celebrity by themselves executing vengeance in the absence of male relatives. Sometimes even children were murdered; boys who were certain to become enemies as soon as they could handle a gun.[11] Family loyalty allowed for no distinction between the innocent and the guilty. The cousin of a murderer (who had perhaps taken no part whatever in the crime), might be killed by a second cousin of the victim (who had perhaps hardly known him); the inhuman 'transversal vendetta', as this vengeance system is called, though thunderingly condemned by governments, continued into the present century. No one felt it to be unjust. If one member of a family killed or raped or stole, the others accepted the consequences: brothers and cousins and uncles and fathers and children suffered and triumphed together. From their total solidarity they derived an extraordinary force and fortitude; like patriots in time of war they became ruthless, heroic, surpassed their normal selves.

82

The vendetta has so often run to excesses as to obscure its character as an institution. Yet beneath the frightful sequences of killings, the extermination of generations, and the atrocities of banditry (which was its offshoot), one can detect its original function. It cannot be regarded as a survival of primitive intertribal war. Bloody disputes between communities are on record; but the institutionalised vendetta was usually between families living in the same village. A few villages are composed of a single family, which may, however, expand so far as to split into two distinct groups; but most are made up of three or four families, sometimes distantly related by marriage but none the less thinking of themselves as separate units. The vendetta was a primitive instrument for punishing offences perpetuated by one family group against another.

As a deterrent, it worked. The high standards of honesty and of sexual morality (at least in appearance) that traditionally prevailed in rural Corsica were certainly to a great extent due to the vendetta. 'Better occasional murders than frequent adulteries', Boswell wrote, in praise of the Corsican system. Bandits might sometimes take to robbery; but they were outlaws, excluded from the social structure; in the villages theft was relatively rare. When I first arrived in Corsica one might still leave a handbag containing three hundred pounds in notes on the beach and have it returned the next day by a stranger who refused any reward, as happened to me when staying with the Cesari. The vendetta achieved its object, by substituting itself for nearly all other kinds of wrongdoing.

It was of course a sledge-hammer method of enforcing good behaviour. The talionic law of compensation – a life for a life – operated only after a vendetta was under way; the first murder, which precipitated the rest, might be a life for a woman's honour, but equally well for a cow, a dog, a tree. The vendetta can hardly be called a form of justice; rather it was a barbarous substitute for justice in which any and every offence was punishable by death.

For anyone but a Corsican the motives behind the first murders in many vendettas may seem trivial, if not sordid. The last full-scale vendetta in Corsica was instigated by a donkey straying into a garden. And it was the owner of the erring donkey, Jules Giuly, who killed Joseph Susini, the offended owner of the garden, not vice versa. Susini merely complained of the damage the donkey had caused. In so doing he fell short of the alacrity the vendetta system demands; for if the injured person expostulates, instead of killing at once, he may well become the victim of the offender.

This murder occurred on Armistice Day 1954 at Moca Croce, a village south-east of Ajaccio. Jules Giuly, the murderer, was arrested and condemned to five years' imprisonment. He served only eighteen months, and on his release prudently went to live in continental France where he died a natural death in September 1958. Most of the village joined in the funeral procession at Moca Croce where his corpse, according to custom, had been returned for burial; except, that is, a brother-in-law of the man he had murdered, and a couple of cousins, the Guiderdoni brothers. They sat outside a café and hurled insults at the Giuly family as they passed by at the head of the funeral cortège on the way to the cemetery. When the mourners returned the insults began again, and by then the Guiderdoni brothers had armed themselves. Someone fired; the shooting became general; Dominique Guiderdoni was wounded, and five of the mourners, including three Giulys, one of whom died. The police arrived to find twenty spent cartridges on the site but no sign of the Guiderdoni.

They remained invisible until Ange-François Guiderdoni gave himself up at the end of seven months. While awaiting his trial in prison he fell into a state of melancholia and hanged himself. In January 1962, on the day before his funeral back in the tragedy-stricken village, Dominique Guiderdoni also surrendered to the police. He was condemned to a ten years' prison sentence in December 1964. Here ends (perhaps) a modern vendetta. Murder, street-fighting, wounds and death, life in hiding, suicide, life in prison; all these catastrophes were brought about by a straying donkey.[12]

But when a vendetta concerns property, as often happens, the value of the property at stake is never even considered. Seventeen men were killed in the early years of this century in a dispute about the ownership of a chestnut tree growing out of a wall dividing two families' land. The opponents were surely not thinking of the chestnuts (which no one, most likely, bothered to gather); their reactions were as maniacal, in our eyes, as those of the shepherds involved in an eighteenth-century vendetta in the Niolo that was started by the wounding of a sheep and led to the death of thirty-six men.

In Corsica the killing or maiming of domestic animals has been liable to stir up passions as violent, and as incomprehensible to the modern mind, as those excited by the *attacar*. Savage vendettas have been triggered off by the killing of neighbours' dogs within living memory. It was certainly not love of man's dumb friends that set the families at war; Corsicans, though not wilfully cruel to animals, waste few sentiments on them. Nor was their value at issue; dogs are over-numerous in Corsica. The killing of the animals was felt as a personal injury, something only a little less serious than a physical assault on their owners. Here one has to do with an attitude to property alien to the modern mind, and which might be described as pre-economic. For a Corsican a possession is not a commodity with an ascertainable market value, but a part of himself, an extension of his being. Women, until very recently, came under this heading, along with dogs and sheep and trees. The feelings aroused by the tearing off of a daughter's headscarf and the laming of a sheep were equal in violence and the same in kind.

The Corsicans describe all such feelings as 'honour'; and indeed, in the light of their concept of honour their reactions to damage of property become quite understandable. Property, in Corsican eyes, is an aspect of personal worth; a man's sense of his own value is reflected back to him by his domestic animals, his land, his women. And what is that worth, that value, if not his honour? To appreciate the kind of honour that propels the vendetta one must look back to its origins, in prehistory. One must envisage an era when consciousness of man's worth had the force of a religious creed; when veneration of the nameless head became veneration of the individual dead hero and so led to the Nietzschean conviction that every man was a potential divinity. The warriors of Filitosa can be regarded as prototypes of the Corsican man of honour.

What is surprising about Corsican honour is that it should have kept this violent, intransigent, exceedingly archaic character. In other societies the concept of honour has evolved with the centuries. Most notably, of course, in the upper classes; educated Englishmen no longer challenge each other to duels, though dockers and seamen may come to blows or even killing in quarrels about women and personal prestige. The primitive Greek Sarakatsan shepherds still kill for honour; the bourgeois Greeks do not. Thorstein Veblen, in his *Theory of the Leisure Class*,[13] shows how the honour of the ruling classes, at first warlike and predatory, is gradually tamed, transformed by the progressive accumulation of wealth. The barbarian warrior becomes the feudal knight, the gentleman; honour won by prepotence and predatory exploit gives way to honour asserted by the display of wealth, by all that cultural superstructure that he includes under the heading of 'conspicuous consumption'.

In Corsica this development was frustrated from the start. A society made up of self-sufficing shepherds and subsistence farmers is alien to the class system. Differences in wealth and status, in Corsica, have always been narrow and fluctuating; every man was a potential warrior; warlord and shepherd, political leader and peasant shared the same craving for prepotence, the same criteria of personal dignity and worth. Few people were obliged, or willing, to sell their labour, with the result that the surplus wealth was never created which elsewhere in Europe generated the successive transformations, through history, of barbarian warrior into chivalrous knight, merchant prince, princely landowner, factory owner and company director.

The population, as a whole, remained warlike and poor; killing continued as the paramount proof of honour right up to the present day. Money and privilege were hard to win, and harder to keep. The Cinarchesi, it is true, controlled vast territories, proclaimed their honour with armies; yet they were never secure enough in their status to conceive of honour outside war. Later, during the last two centuries, a class of big landowners came into being in the Sartenais, self-styled nobles who lived indolent, arrogant lives. Yet they were badly off compared with landed gentry elsewhere in Europe; labour was scarce, the shepherds recalcitrant, money scarce. Political eminence was their one means of demonstrating their worth, their honour, with constant invitations to quarrels and vendettas. And so it happened that these ill-served gentlemen, who lived for honour but were deprived of the means of satisfying it available to their equals elsewhere, became the most aggressive of Corsicans. The spectacular vendettas of the last century – those that fired Mérimée's imagination – were not between backward shepherds, but country gentlemen of the Sartenais. With all their acres, and their large stone mansions, they found their fulfilment in hunting each other like wild animals in

85

the maquis, and their women in performing antique ritual chants over the corpses of the slain.

Religious beliefs, the more compulsive because largely submerged below consciousness, enshrined this brutal, primitive code. Veneration of the dead, correlative with the cult of kinship solidarity, not only incited blood vengeance but sanctified it. When a society spontaneously substitutes state law for private vengeance the motive behind the change is likely to be religious. Murder is thought of as an offence against the gods, and is believed to bring down their anger in famine, pestilence or defeat. Mosaic law was determined by the wrath of Jehovah. The cult of Apollo, Olympian enemy of barbarism, antedates Draco's code; according to the Apollonian doctrine of pollution the murderer was accursed and a danger to his people so long as he stayed in his native land.

The Corsicans, apparently, had no such gods: they dreaded Destiny and revered the dead. Destiny is non-moral, strikes blindly, irrespective of merit; the dead, on the other hand, may demand blood vengeance as their due. For in Corsica they are thought to value their honour, like the living, but more fiercely, because all their passions are darkened by envy. The dead are vindictive, and none more so than those who have been struck down in their prime. Murder must be atoned by murder to appease the spirit of the murdered man. If not, he may return to claim his defaulting kinsmen; at the evil hours, at midday, at sunset, between midnight and the first cock's crowing. The living must kill if they hope to keep alive.

The Christian Church, of course, was, and is, resolutely hostile to the vendetta. But the Corsicans had accepted Christian beliefs uncritically, without altogether discarding their own. The Catholic Church has always known how to dispose of pagan divinities, by attaching their cults, hardly altered, to Christian saints; but the dead were much harder to deal with. They were always present, their bones disintegrating into the Corsican dust, their spirits haunting their tombs. Each family derived from them its sense of identity and continuation, its pride of being, as a people may draw strength from a national religion. And the dead accumulated, were renewed with each passing generation. The Church could never deny them, since personal immortality is essential to its creed. As a result the Corsicans merely transposed the duty of avenging the dead into a Christian framework of belief. 'Of course one would be afraid of meeting the murdered man in the next world if one had failed in one's duty to him here on earth,' a middle-aged landowner recently explained to me. With the whole population ostentatiously professing Christianity, outwardly very pious and much given to ceremonies and processions, the old religion has lingered on, a cavern creature of the Corsican psyche, exacting its victims at its hours.[14]

In its long struggle against the vendetta the Catholic Church was wrestling with an active survival of paganism, pitting one religion against another. And though the clergy never succeeded in eradicating the custom they did more for peace than the repressive legislation of governments. Persuading, exhort-

86

ing, preaching brotherhood and forgiveness, they could touch feelings as fundamental as those that impelled the vendetta, and though contrary, of the same order. The French government made use of their cooperation until quite recent times. Formal treaties of peace negotiated by the government authorities were signed in the village churches, before or after a religious service in which the men of the opposing families took part. The latest I have seen was concluded in 1904, in the heretics' village, god-forsaken Carbini.[15]

The people who engaged in these desolating feuds were not, of course, inclined to think of themselves as barbarian pagans. A vendetta, for a Corsican, is a 'misfortune' (imposed by Destiny), its execution a sacred duty to his kindred, living, dead and unborn. During the Genoese regime the Corsicans habitually vindicated the vendetta by reference to its original function as an instrument of justice. Understandably, for though the Corsican code of law was fair enough, the Genoese application of it was deplorable.[16] Magistrates were corrupt, from the Governor downwards. Certain provisions in the constitution positively encouraged abuses. One may imagine those that resulted from the procedure known as *ex informata conscientia*, which allowed the governor to condemn to death without trial or appeal. 'An Italian republic held certain islanders in subjection; but its political and civil law in relation to them was vicious,' Montesquieu wrote, in a barely disguised allusion.[17] The governor also had the right to quash prosecutions without giving his reasons, by the simple formula of *non procedatur*. In effect this meant that men involved in vendettas could buy acquittals, not only for murders they had committed but for those they intended to commit in the future; in short, purchase licences to kill. The bandits, who in the early eighteenth century numbered no less than two thousand, took full advantage of the arrangement: a 'horrible market in human blood', in the words of the author of the *Giustificazione* of the national rebellion. Towards the end of the Genoese regime the vendetta had assumed hardly credible proportions: the official records show that 28,715 people were killed between 1683 and 1715, over 900 a year in a population that barely exceeded 120,000.[18]

Though the Church was the one influence that made for peace, priests themselves sometimes took part in vendettas, being dragged into hostilities by their families. A French officer stationed in the island in the 1740s was horrified to see priests celebrating Mass with a couple of pistols on the altar, closely surrounded by their relatives, all armed.[19] (Such situations were repeated up till recent years and have been described to me by elderly eyewitnesses.) The same writer notes that enemies, apparently reconciled, might receive the sacraments side by side at the altar, but no sooner had they left the church than one would set on the other, shooting or stabbing him to death in the street. There was worse. A Corsican contrived, if possible, to assassinate his enemy when he was in a state of mortal sin, so as to be sure of sending his soul to eternal damnation. A man who was known to have a mistress, for instance, would be killed just as he was leaving her house. The killer, of course, deliberately, by the same act, condemned his own soul; he was prepared to endure irrevocable torments provided his enemy suffered them as well.

During the national rebellion the vendetta was a worse enemy to the Corsicans than Genoese or foreign armies; time and again victory was sabotaged by internal feuds. All the national governments enacted repressive legislation, sometimes more drastic than any devised by the Genoese. A pre-Paoli government decreed the death penalty for wounding, even if the victim recovered. King Theodor condemned those guilty of the 'transversal vendetta' to be tortured to death, their bodies quartered and exhibited in public. Paoli, with his finer intelligence, struck at the heart of the problem by attempting to change the Corsican concept of honour. A murderer, with his kinsmen, was to suffer national disgrace, the loss of titles and distinctions; his house was to be razed and a 'pillar of infamy' erected on the site inscribed with the record of his crime. Paoli's reign was too short to show whether he could have modified convictions consecrated by immemorial custom; that the vendetta did decline was probably rather due to his ruthlessly impartial application of the law (he executed one of his own relatives guilty of murder).

At all events there was a recrudescence of violence after his defeat, resistants to the French conquest joining forces with the bandits in the maquis. The French introduced the torture of breaking on the wheel; with disappointing results: the Corsicans, so a French officer observed, remained silent under torture and went to their horrible deaths uttering one word, *patienza*, the word they still pronounce in distressing circumstances, the profession of faith of insular stoicism.[20] Napoleon, never indulgent to his countrymen, suspended the French constitution in Corsica in outright contradiction to the Rights of Man. Under his administrators repression of the vendetta reached the extreme limit of rigour: General Morand decreed that if a murderer was not captured four of his close kinsmen were to be arrested and executed within two hours.

Executions, however, did little to check murder, and logically enough, for a man who engages in a vendetta is prepared every day to die. 'It's a form of suicide,' a Corsican recently told me, but without disapproval. During the nineteenth century the murder rate dropped, it is true, to just over eighty a year between 1825 and 1857, and to just over forty-seven between 1858 and 1891; but it was still fantastically high for a population that crept up slowly during this period from 180,000 to 280,000.[21]

The incidence of violence fluctuated with the political situation; electoral rivalries, easily turning into vendettas, had become the main interest of a people who, theoretically at peace, lacked outlets for their energies and ambitions. Murderous disputes between Bonapartists and Bourbonists ushered in the century; the revolutions of 1830 and 1848 brought fresh disturbances; a period of relative calm followed under the severe but quite constructive government of Napoleon III; the Third Republic was greeted with a new outbreak of killing. Frightful atrocities occurred as late as the 1890s, when the bandit Colombani, who had taken to the maquis after a village election quarrel, captured a supposed spy, blinded him, and cut off his nose and tongue; later, after a pitched battle with a rival gang in which three men were killed, a Colombani carried a wounded enemy to a charcoal burner's furnace, stuffed him in head downwards and so finished him off. Such incidents are the more shocking because the Corsicans are not normally a brutal people; sadistic murders (outside vendettas), are not heard of, nor is physical cruelty to children and the old. And always I have been struck by the delicate gentleness of the elderly shepherds and peasants, men who witnessed the atrocities of the vendetta and perhaps took part in them.

By the nineteenth century the vendetta had become a fantastic anachronism, a primitive survival that set the Corsicans apart as Frenchmen and Europeans. Visitors observed and studied it, commented on it in books, reports and articles, horrified or fascinated according to temperament. Most were deeply attracted by what is courageous and disinterested in the custom: the fortitude and tenacity of the opponents, their willingness to sacrifice their tranquillity, their prosperity and their very lives to the abstract idea of honour. That people could feel strongly about anything other than money seemed in itself admirable to visitors from a Balzacian France; the violence of Corsican passions offered an exhilarating affirmation of the human scale. To writers Corsica was a revelation: the travellers Valéry, Mérimée, Alexandre Dumas, Flaubert, the German globetrotter Gregorovius, Guy de Maupassant, all responded to its romantic appeal. The landscape – marvellous discovery – was in keeping with the tragic climate of local life; grand and mournful, studded with ruins: in Corsica the dreams of the romantic age came true.

The Corsican code decrees that strangers shall never be molested in a vendetta, even if they are the guests of a family at war. Travellers could therefore witness these savage dramas at close quarters without risk to themselves. Accidental pioneers in ethnology, they noted the sombre ritual of the vendetta, inherited from remote ages and unchanged by time. There was the formal declaration of hostilities; then the solemn vow to avenge the injury, pronounced in the presence of the assembled family. If the injury was murder, a shirt or handkerchief stained with the victim's blood was exhibited in the house until vengeance was achieved. In the meantime the men would let grow their beards, as a sign, understood by all, that they had accepted the obligation of revenge. Windows would be kept shuttered, and were sometimes blocked with bricks and stones; this was not only a security measure but a gesture of respect to the deceased. The family lived in darkness until his death had been atoned.

But in fact from the moment hostilities were opened it was incumbent on both families to protect themselves. The conventions of the vendetta include no rules of chivalry where killing is concerned. Killing by ambush has been the rule. The murderer might wait for hours, for days and nights even, hidden in the maquis near a spot where he knew his enemy was sooner or later likely to pass by, to shoot him, cold-bloodedly, when he at last appeared.

Constantly threatened, a family 'in vendetta' would curtail its activities to a minimum. The men, of course, never left home unarmed. Work on the land was limited to providing the bare necessities; only holdings close to the house were tilled. The children, most often, were kept from school; little Corsican boys can handle firearms from an early age. The men of the warring families even avoided meeting each other in church; according to an old saying of Sartène, where the vendetta literally controlled daily life, the men of the town never entered the church between their baptism and their funeral. Waiting, spying, scheming, taut with resolution and dread, the warring families lived side by side, each knowing that one of its members must kill and one or more must die. This state of affairs might last for years, for decades, for generations.

When a murder took place (climax of a tension flesh and blood could no longer bear), a truly terrifying ritual ceremony was enacted in the house of the deceased. This centred round the *voceru*, sung by women over the victim's corpse. Until very recently Corsican women habitually mourned the dead, including those who had died peacefully, by chanting improvised verses over their corpses and tearing their faces and hair. The custom, which is paralleled in many countries (including Crete and the Mani), certainly derives from a primaeval cult of the dead. The song, which was a kind of poetic funeral oration in praise of the deceased, the frantic gestures and the wailing, were all designed to placate his unquiet spirit.

Though the displays of grief were unbridled and terrible to see, the *voceri* were never disorderly outpourings of words. The verses, sung to simple, traditional, hypnotising airs, were improvised in four- or six-lined rhyming stanzas. Formerly nearly all women could compose them; but those particularly gifted would make it their business to perform *voceri* for the dead of relatives and friends. A *voceratrice* had a privileged status in a Corsican village, like the men, natural artists too, who improvised sung verses on topical events, or in honour of local heroes.

Improvisers are still to be found in Corsica, and I have spent some unforgettable hours in their company. Most are men, for their type of singing, which has the character of an entertainment, has better withstood the onslaught of civilised notions than the sombre, ritualistic *voceru*. All the same, I have been privileged to meet two *voceratrici* (one still practising her vocation), and to hear them perform again the songs they improvised for peaceful deaths. Spontaneously conceived under the impact of a poignant emotion, they were intensely moving, though mild, no doubt, in comparison with the demoniacal *voceri* of revenge.[22]

These, most likely, will never be created again; the last of them must have been improvised forty or fifty years ago. A few have been recorded, by travellers and enthnologists of the last century, who noted down some of those most celebrated in popular memory. It would of course be unreasonable to judge these verses by the standards normally applied to poetry; a *voceru* was a histrionic performance that depended as much on the voice and delivery of the *voceratrice* as on the words. Even so, as written works they have their own

90

Barbara Benedetti, one of the last of the *voceratrici* who mourn the dead in improvised verse and song. (*Dorothy Carrington*)

weird appeal. The deceased may be likened to any and every object the bereaved considers beautiful, or of value. So a woman mourning her husband exlaims: 'O my tufted cypress! My muscat grape! My sugared cake! My good and sweet mana' . . . 'You were my column! You were my support! You were my grandeur! You were my brother! My oriental pearl! My finest treasure!' The apotheosis of these metaphors is 'You were my brother!' for to the Corsicans, closer and deeper than the bond between husband and wife is the blood-tie between brother and sister. An elderly Corsican once told me that the highest tribute a husband can pay his wife is to address her as 'sister', thus conferring on her what he holds most precious, his blood.

When the death is by violence praise of the deceased is followed by an account of the murder, leading to a torrent of invective against the murderer and appeals to the men of the family to take revenge. The verses, when read, often make a disconcertingly uneven impression, for the causes of the quarrel, baldly stated, may seem absurdly trivial in relation to their consequences. So a woman will announce that a cow has been killed, a tree cut down, that her husband has been murdered and she longs to eat the murderer's entrails. To appreciate the true flavour of a *voceru* one must imagine its context: the corpse laid out, according to custom, on the dining-table; the bloodstained garment exposed to view; the dishevelled, shrieking women tearing their faces and hair, smearing the victim's garment again and again with the blood of his open wound; the men crowded in the background drumming the floor with the butt ends of their guns, while the *voceratrice* intoned the cruel words in a high thin penetrating impersonal voice, like a medium speaking for the dead.

This, indeed, was her role; one surely inherited from the megalithic age. Sometimes, before she began to improvise, she would speak in the dead man's ear, lay her own ear to his mouth; by this mime she symbolised her function of transmitting his will to the living. As her chant proceeded she would gradually work herself into a state of trance, to collapse into semiconsciousness when she reached the climax of her performance. The succession of declaratory phrases, piling insult on insult, would culminate in a paroxysm of vituperation that tore the spectators' emotions by the roots. In a celebrated *voceru* on the deaths of two cousins, the sister of one of the victims execrates a priest who, being a kinsman of the murderer, had refused to toll the funeral bell for the slain: 'May I see in a basket/The entrails of the priest!/May I tear them with my teeth/And rub them with my hands./In the house of the priest/ One hears the Devil!/Infamous priest, excommunicated!/ Dog, eater of the sacraments!/May you die in anguish!/In spasms and in torments!'[23]

A *voceru* was an incantation for the most bloodthirsty instincts of the men; it battered any pacific notions into submission. No one could stand up against those inspired tragediennes who drove their men to murder – the weakest, the most irresolute or reasonable – by an overwhelming force of suggestion. There was even a dance associated with these barbaric funeral rites: the frenzied, ghastly *caracolu*, in which the mourners linked hands and gambolled round the corpse. Though energetically forbidden by the clergy it was still to be seen in the last century, a survival, without doubt, from pagan times.[24]

All through Corsican history women were the instigators of the vendetta, supplied its psychological ammunition. Always they stimulated and glorified the cult of 'honour', by a hideous paradox sending to their deaths those husbands and brothers and sons they loved so excessively. If all the available men in a family had been exterminated they never rested until they had summoned relatives home from abroad to assume the awful obligation to the dead.

Not only the venom of the women, but the scorn of neighbours operated against any chance of making peace. A man who shirked his duty of avenging a murder was disgraced, ostracised. The contemptuous comments and glances to which he was subjected were not to be endured; either he had to kill or leave the island. There is a word in the Corsican dialect for this kind of taunt: *rimbeccu*. The *rimbeccu* was always a principal cause of murders, and in the eighteenth century was classed as a crime in law. In modern times murders so provoked have always been very leniently judged, the French having understood that to be publicly humiliated in this way is for a Corsican utterly insupportable.

In Corsican eyes, to accept forgiveness is as humiliating as to offer it. I have even heard of an occasion when the offending family gave the *rimbeccu* to the family of the victim, thereby inviting revenge. The incident occurred towards the end of the last century, in a southern village, after the vendetta had been in abeyance for many years. The last victim had been a woman, who was shot with a baby in her arms. Her relatives had been so stricken by the tragedy that they determined the feud should end. For some thirty years her sons had lived in the village without attempting any reprisals on the enemy family, which remained none the less implacably hostile.

One Christmas Eve, when snow had fallen, as they were leaving their home with their wives and children to attend Midnight Mass, they saw, in front of the door, a life-sized snow-figure of a woman, with a child in her arms. They thought the village children had made an image of the Virgin and the infant Christ until they caught sight of the red stain on the woman's breast, where their mother had been fatally wounded. The enemy family had built the statue to remind them of the injury unavenged.

They broke down the snow-figure and went to Mass according to their intention; but the men all took their pistols, and the wife of the head of the family stuck a stiletto into her stocking, which impeded her genuflexions, so she afterwards complained. With exceptional self-restraint they ignored the provocation and in time stifled the feud.

When I first heard this story, from the continental-born widow of a man of the injured family,[25] I could only explain it by attributing to the offenders some masochistic perversion. A deep compulsion, I supposed, impelled them to complete the cycle of destruction; they were obsessed by the death-wish. But a Corsican of that same district I spoke to saw the incident in quite another light. 'You're too romantic,' he told me. 'It was all a question of pride. The people who made the snow-woman were issuing a challenge, a sneering sort of challenge, of course, as much to say: "Come on and attack us if you dare, but you daren't because you're a pack of cowards." You don't appreciate,' he concluded, 'the immeasurable pride of a Corsican.' Pride, antique hubris; the worst part of honour. A foreigner is always liable to underestimate this trait in the Corsican character because he is simply unable to believe that pride in such dimensions can exist.

Pride was the mainstay – and often the undoing – of those victims and heroes of the vendetta system known as *bandits d'honneur*. The term was coined in the last century to distinguish Corsican bandits from common highwaymen and brigands. The latter had not been unknown in the island; in fact under the Genoese regime they were a notorious menace to travellers. But by the nineteenth century they had been practically eliminated by French law, together with the gangs of political malcontents who formerly roamed the maquis. Only outlaws of the peculiar insular category remained: men who had taken to the maquis in the course of vendettas, to evade their enemies or the police. There, in the great wilderness of rocks and jungle vegetation, penetrable only to those who knew its hidden paths, they could hide for years, for a lifetime. They did not, in theory, rob or steal. Their families supplied them with food and ammunition; they could count on shelter and protection from the whole population except their personal enemies.

So they wandered, with a gun and faithful dog, or with a 'guide' (an aide-de-camp, a non-bandit who had taken to this life for the sake of adventure), or sometimes in small bands. They set up temporary homes in caves and ruins, or knocked at the doors of shepherds' huts to ask for hospitality, which was never refused. Far from being miserable outcasts they were respected figures, local heroes; every Corsican admired a man who had murdered to vindicate his honour and preserved his independence in defiance of the law. The people of Ciamannace went so far, in 1885, as to vote a pension of 1400 francs a year (a large sum then) to their mayor, Frattini, who had taken to the maquis after committing a murder but none the less kept his office.[26] For the Corsicans, a bandit was the embodiment of the insular virtues, of their ideal of themselves. As French civilisation gradually closed down on the island the bandits came to represent a kind of psychological resistance movement, a last assertion of Corsican separateness.

Travellers went out of their way to meet them and were seldom disappointed. There was nothing rough or sordid in their bearing; they were aristocratic in manner, eloquent and dignified; they passed their lonely hours composing songs. Flaubert, visiting the Laurelli, notables of the wild Fiumorbo, was introduced to a nephew who had taken to the maquis three years before. 'He was handsome,' wrote Flaubert, 'all his person had something naïve and ardent, his black eyes shone with a brilliance full of tenderness at the sight of men holding out their hands to him. . . . Great and valiant heart that beats alone in freedom in the woods . . . purer and nobler, no doubt, than most

93

respectable people in France, from the meanest provincial grocer to the king.'[27]

The nobility of the bandits was certainly exaggerated, by travellers and by the Corsicans themselves; they were guilty of horrible brutalities to each other, to enemies and spies. Yet the legend was not quite without foundation. These men were not by nature criminals; some, according to insular standards, were well educated and gently bred. Charles-Camille Nicolai was the son of big landowners of Carbini; his role as a bandit (in the 1880s) was forced on him by an outrageous injury. His brother had abducted a girl, who loved him, but whose parents were opposed to their marriage. The girl's father brought a suit against the seducer which led to his imprisonment, took his daughter home, locked her up and beat her. Not content with this vengeance, he shot the seducer when he came out of prison and set fire to his corpse. Charles-Camille arrived on the scene just in time to see his brother burn. The murderer was arrested, tried and acquitted.

Faced with this miscarriage of justice Charles-Camille had no choice but to kill him and take to the maquis. As a bandit he suffered exceedingly, and composed a *lamento* which is among the most rending of its kind. Indeed the hardships of the maquis were so uncongenial to him that he preferred the risks of living in Ajaccio in disguise. There, got up as a Spanish tourist, he stopped the Préfet in the street to question him about his own exploits. An American lady staying at the Grand Hotel proposed to carry him off in her yacht; but Charles-Camille, not for nothing known as the most honourable of the bandits of honour, thought twice about reducing himself to the rank of *cavaliere servante* in the New World. While he was hesitating he met his tragic-comic end. The police surprised him at a wedding party, dressed up as a woman, and promptly shot him dead.

The Bellacoscia brothers, who lived in the mountains near Bocognano from 1848 for nearly half a century,[28] were of tougher material, but they had great social success. Their name, meaning 'beautiful thighs' was inherited from their father (in reality a Bonelli), who had earned it on account of his three concubines, sisters who lived amicably together in his home and between them bore him eighteen children. Two of them, Antoine and Jacques became bandits, following an attempted murder and a kidnapping. They lorded it over the family property, Pentica, situated in a remote rugged gorge, which in fact became a rebel enclave on French soil. Raids by the *gendarmerie* (including a large-scale expedition in 1888 authorised by the Minister of War) invariably failed; the brothers, always warned in time by the conniving population, shot their way back into the rocks and disappeared into the impassable landscape. In the intervals of guerrilla war they entertained celebrities and high-ranking officials: a Princess of Mecklemburg, Prince Roland Bonaparte, a Préfet of Corsica, and Emmanuel Arène, deputy for Corsica and writer, who noted that their fortress-home was full of expensive gifts from their guests.

Antoine, four times condemned to death by default for murder and armed rebellion, gave himself up in his old age, in 1892. He was acquitted by the jury of the Court of Assizes at Bastia, according to the local press 'in a thunder of applause'.[29] In the course of the nineteenth century the Corsicans had so well succeeded in deforming French justice as to make it an instrument of their own customs. Juries habitually echoed popular or partisan opinion; trials were merely prolongations of vendettas in which the witnesses systematically perjured themselves to condemn their enemies and acquit their friends.

Jacques Bellacoscia remained an outlaw to the end. When he died, of pneumonia, in 1897, his friends dammed a river, buried his body in its bed, and then released the water, so as to respect the last of his arrogant commands: that no man should ever walk over his grave.

The Bellacoscia brothers certainly had a flair for grand gestures, an Elizabethan bravura; but this tendency to extreme behaviour was shared in some degree by nearly all bandits. Hunted and in hiding, destitute and parasitical, they none the less achieved the Corsican ideal of freedom; their mere existence was a denial of the law and of contemporary civilisation as a whole. When they took to the maquis they were even liberated from the archaic code that had driven them there: having made this supreme sacrifice to their families they were absolved from further obligations; thereafter their families served them. In the emptiness of the savage countryside they expanded, as individuals, sounded the limits of their possibilities. Some ran amok, took to drink, motiveless murder, rape, and having broken every rudimentary rule of human coexistence ended mercilessly slaughtered by the population. Others became Robin Hood characters, protected the people from less scrupulous bandits, kept peace among local outlaws and sometimes even cooperated with the police.

A few became ascetics, mystics and visionaries. One, by the name of Franceschino, who roamed the country near Filitosa in the reign of Louis-Philippe, declared himself a prophet. In a grandiloquent letter he informed the Préfet that on 6 August 1835 'a new sun' would appear on the horizon which would 'astonish the universe', and that on the following 8 September the dead would rise from their graves. He begged the Préfet to warn the sovereign of these coming events. Should they not materialise, he was willing to surrender to the law and suffer its penalties. The letter is signed: 'Your brother in Jesus Christ, the Divine Prophet, François.'

The local clergy, at least, were impressed. The parish priest of Calvese (a hamlet of Sollacaro), having observed that on 6 August 'the sun was not the same as usual', sang Mass in honour of the bandit and preached a sermon to the effect that he should receive 'the honours due to a saint'. A *gendarme* in the congregation sent a report to the Préfet. On 8 September, the day when the dead should rise, a great concourse of people, including several priests, assembled at Sollacaro. The incident was reported to the Minister of War; the priests fell under suspicion and the Préfet complained to the bishop. The bishop defended his ministers. No one, he replied, who had seen the unfortunate bandit could doubt the sincerity of his repentance. The priest of Calvese had merely meant that it was impossible not to regard him as a saint 'in view

95

of the air of mortification and saintliness that emanates from his person'.

Reading this correspondence I was inclined to sympathise with the Préfet. But in fact, as priests and bishops insisted, Franceschino must have been a true repentant sinner. A laconic pencil note at the end of his file in the archives records that he died 'in odour of sanctity' in a monastery in Rome.[30]

The bandits were extraordinary men, and I think that many of them must have been well worth knowing. Unfortunately I arrived in Corsica too late to meet an authentic 'bandit of honour'. During the last thirty years changes that nobody foresaw have brought banditry, with the vendetta, to an end. Briefly, the Corsicans have become familiar with money; and money has superseded honour as a symbol of worth and prestige. The shift in outlook began with the First World War. Mobilisation took the Corsicans abroad and kept them there long enough to learn about a civilisation that offers satisfactions other than the arid cult of abstract honour; satisfactions money can buy. They saw, and occasionally enjoyed, some of the pleasures of an affluent society. Though not the most elevated; the outstanding result of their wartime experiences was the introduction to Corsica of the methods of the French underworld.

Thereafter bandits were less inclined to eke out their days on irregular food parcels. They used their privileged position to racket their more prosperous countrymen, and so transformed the bandit's life from a tragic duty into a profitable career. The population gave them the name of *bandits percepteurs*, tax-gathering bandits, to distinguish them from the bandits of tradition; and indeed few if any of them had taken to the maquis for reasons justified by the ancestral code; they had simply chosen to live outside the law.

They carved out spheres of influence: Romanetti, Caviglioli, Spada and Perfettini to the north of Ajaccio; Bartoli and Bornea in the south. There they reigned through the 1920s, imposing themselves on the public by menaces and violence, personal magnetism and the prestige of their calling. They drew tribute from hotel keepers, bus services, wood merchants, well-off peasants; they wrote grandiloquent threatening letters to the press; they gave interviews to film producers and journalists, were entertained by election candidates, the enormous meals being accompanied by suitable bribes. Women loved them, used and were used by them: prostitutes, foreign ladies, and shrewd shepherds' daughters who piled up small fortunes as their associates. Sportsmen and adventurous tourists joined in their revels, when they feasted on *bouillabaisse* with fishermen on deserted shores or chanted ballads in all-night drinking bouts in isolated inns. The excitement and crude poetry of their desperate way of life were irresistible to those who felt stifled by a respectable routine.

But excitement often turned to horror, and menaces were put into hideous execution, as when Spada murdered a bus driver and a couple of *gendarmes* he was transporting, set fire to the vehicle and threw their bodies into the flames. The population served them with increasing fear and resentment, so that when a special expeditionary police force was sent against them in the winter of 1931, for the first time in the history of Corsican banditry people were found willing to cooperate with the law. All the bandits were eventually captured or killed, most often by private enemies protected by the police.[31] Bornea is now one of the few survivors; he has served his term and lives in irreproachable obscurity. I spent one Christmas Day with him, as I shall later tell.

The tax-gathering bandits were thus exterminated; but one bandit of the old school held to the maquis, on and off, till 1952; Muzarettu, bandit of honour, who survived in the caves of far south until he crept into a Franciscan monastery to die. That same year a man of a very different stamp returned from the maquis: a man, too, of the south, but wealthy and in the prime of life, who eighteen months before had killed a cousin in pursuance of an old vendetta between two branches of his family. After the murder, he had kept to his own estates (he was the son of big landowners), and lived exclusively on his relatives. He was given a four years' prison sentence and served only two. Taking to the maquis was for him less a precaution than a matter of honour; the kind of gesture gentlemen are prone to make to a dying code.

By then traditional ideas of honour had ebbed to the extremities of the social scale: to the country gentry, and to the underworld, the *milieu*, where the law of a life for a life still holds sway. In 1954 a mysterious but much publicised quarrel about a contraband cargo of cigarettes, smuggled across the Mediterranean in a boat called the *Combinatie*, exploded in a series of vengeance-killings in Corsica, where the cargo had been deposited. The code of the vendetta and the code of the *milieu* both came into play, interacted and fused: according to police records thirty-two Corsicans were murdered in the island and in mainland France.[32] Not all were gangsters; some were merely related to men who were. The mayor of a village in the Sartenais was machine-gunned in the legs (in fact his legs were almost shot off); he went abroad, acquired artificial limbs, and returned to his village where he is still mayor and has donated a reinforced concrete campanile to his village church. I knew him; but not so well as an altogether charming café proprietor in Ajaccio who was apparently mixed up in the affair. Heading for his place one night I arrived just in time to hear firing and a car speeding away into the dark. He had been shot dead at his bar by enemies aiming through the bamboo curtain that hung in the doorway. Today the vendetta is becoming the prerogative of professional gangsters.

It is finished as a popular institution. The law, at long last, has won a grudging respect; judgments are as fair as can be hoped for in a country where family or underworld solidarity prevent most witnesses from speaking the truth, and often from speaking at all. Official justice has imposed itself, finally, by tolerance: no murderers have been condemned to the guillotine since the bandit Spada, in 1935, and few to sentences exceeding five years. If this lenience hardly discourages killing it has bred a feeling – more valuable for keeping order – that state justice is not an inhuman institution, at all costs to be disregarded and opposed.

Murders do still occur, but much fewer than ever before: about half a dozen a year, instead of ten to twenty as in the period immediately following the Second World War.[33] Café brawls (the Corsicans are less sober than of old), sexual jealousy and election disputes are the chief causes outside the underworld; especially election disputes: two newly elected mayors were shot at in the Easter week of 1961.

But murders no longer lead to *voceri*, vows of vengeance, counter-murders and the maquis; the compulsions inherent in the vendetta have withered. Honour and fear of the dead have no place in the modern world. Technical civilisation, coming to the island with the tourist industry within the last few years, has overthrown the old Corsican way of life, its traditional principles, code and beliefs, together with its economy. True, the island is still far from rich and barely prosperous; but there is enough money in circulation to discredit traditional notions of honour. A Corsican no longer respects himself, or is respected, for killing a neighbour because of a straying donkey or even because that neighbour killed his second cousin; personal worth now consists in new clothes, large cars. At the same time civilisation has taken the meaning out of the cult of the dead as the Church, in centuries, failed to do. With the efficiency of the bulldozer, which in Corsica has become its symbol, it is breaking down, uprooting, ironing flat the whole indigenous culture the Corsicans have lived by, through the millennia, until today.

PENITENTS AND BANDITS

Aftermath of a murder – storm and illness – the gentry of
Sartène – vendetta and violence – death of a bandit –
Franciscans – a penitential procession

T H E murder at Propriano broke the spell that held us to the Cesari's home.
It made me realise that with all their willingness to tell us about their country,
to confide in us matters as intimate as visions and dreams, there were others
they would always try to conceal. Though they remained as friendly, even
affectionate, as before, I suddenly felt myself a stranger among them. They
were absorbed, now, by feelings I was unable to share. For them the murder
was an inescapable tragedy, like a mortal illness or accident which serves to
remind that life and well being are always precarious. It rent the atmosphere
of security which had seemed to envelope their lives. In spite of their house
and sheep and land and the regular produce of their toil, the Cesari, I now
came to understand, lived in a world where any deviation from a rigorous
code could smash the edifice built with the labour of generations. In Propriano
a man and a woman had loved, and two families had been ruined: the woman
was dishonoured, her brother wounded and apparently dying; the lover had
been killed; a desperate vindictive widow was left with three young children
to provide for; a little boy had dedicated himself to revenge. The Cesari looked
on, appalled; their own morals were irreproachable, yet they were too well
aware of human frailty not to feel concerned.

The village, of course, was heavily overshadowed by the event. Few people
were seen in the streets, and those few stood about in little groups, muttering,
and fell silent as I drew near. To add to the prevailing oppression the heat had
become excessive. The summer had been closing down on us in the gulf of
Valinco. It had come by stealth, almost imperceptibly. Until then the sea
breeze, constant as an electric fan, had been shot through with streams of
cooler air; I had welcomed their freshness when out walking, often I had the
sensation of being carried along by them, like a fish in ocean currents. But on
the evening of the murder the wind died. The heat at once grew opaque, unmitigated. Storm threatened. The following days a bank of cloud appeared
edging its way above the mountains, making an upper, darker range.

'You see, the clouds are trying to prevent your leaving,' Marie observed. In
fact I knew that it was high time for my husband and me to leave; but we
lacked energy for the move. Corsican lethargy, so shocking to hurried visitors,

is perfectly understandable to anyone who has spent a summer in the island. The temperature, wandering in the eighties and nineties, is no doubt lower than in the tropics, but I can only say that central Africa never affected me in the same way. There are days in Corsica when one cannot do anything; not for money or convenience or good opinion; not even to avoid looking ridiculous.

Everything stops in this weather: men give up working and women do as little as possible; the birds no longer sing, even the sea barely stirs. The Cesari's dogs lay on the tiles like corpses while flies crawled over them; the sheep huddled under the low boughs of the lentisk bushes, the ewes all squatting, only the ram standing, immobile, the weary guardian male. Bathing was hardly pleasant; the sand made one itch and the sea felt like warm melted butter. Long past the siesta hour we lay inert on our beds waiting for the merciful deliverance when the sun dropped to the horizon of the sea. That was the magic hour of release, rebirth; with the failing of light the world revived, dew restored scent to the maquis, animals rose and stretched themselves, as we did too; a few birds began to sing.

One morning we woke up without the cruel sunbeams piercing the shutters. The clouds had spread all over the sky so that we seemed to be enclosed in a low grey stifling tent. The sea looked like oil and had a similar consistency; sandflies pricked us viciously on the beach. In the maquis a few birds squawked, loudly, as though in alarm. We dragged ourselves back to the terrace of the house and waited with nature and the Cesari for the imminent cataclysm. It came with the midday meal. There was a crashing and rumbling as though all the sky were collapsing like a bombed cupola, lightning danced across the mountains in shining triangles, and then water came pouring down in a dead straight deluge. Mountains and sea and sky were engulfed in a uniform grey primal mass; we could see nothing out of the windows.

A bang on the door completed the drama. A boy rushed in, drenched, with a telegram. An unexpected telegram is never welcome in a home of this kind; the Cesari greeted it with the matter-of-fact calm that Corsicans automatically assume in distressing circumstances. Madame Cesari gave the boy a chair by the fire, Marie silently took the coffee pot from the tripod and filled his cup, François added a shot of eau-de-vie. Jean read the telegram, then drew Madame Cesari and her husband into a little scullery at the back of the house. Their conversation was brief; the sons were already out in the rain looking for the donkey before the telegraph boy had left. Few words were exchanged, and those in dialect. 'Françoise is very ill,' Jean eventually explained to us. 'You know that Charles-Antoine has taken her up to Zicavo in the mountains for a change of air; she's been unwell ever since the birth of her last child. But now she's fallen seriously ill, my uncle and aunt must go to her immediately.'

There were several means by which they could have travelled to Zicavo. They could have gone by bus; but this would have meant waiting for the bus to Ajaccio the following morning and taking another on to Zicavo in the afternoon; a time lapse, in fact, of over twenty-four hours. Or they could have hired a car in Propriano. But this too would have involved delay in leaving. Perhaps, moreover, the expense was really beyond their means; or perhaps in a crisis they felt more sure of themselves when acting in a traditional way. At any rate they did as they had always done in such situations: the father harnessed the donkey to the little cart, Madame Cesari tied a cheese and some bread and sausage and a bottle of wine in a cloth and stowed it under the seat, and before my coffee was cold they were aboard and away in the driving rain, Madame Cesari sheltering them both under a huge dark blue green-bordered umbrella, such as shepherds use. This was the last I saw of them for several years.

The rest of the day was spent telephoning from the post office in Propriano while the rain sloshed into the sea. My husband and I and Jean had decided to leave. By evening – a glowering evening without a sunset – our plans were made. The family to which Comte Peraldi had recommended me in Sartène could receive me the following day; there was a boat sailing from Ajaccio to Marseilles which my husband and Jean could take that same night. We would all three leave in the morning, my husband and Jean stopping the bus going to Ajaccio, I, an hour or so later, stopping the one bound south for Sartène.

The day dawned clear and brilliant; one of those miraculous shining scented days which in Corsica follow rain. The sky was stainless, the maquis glittered as though newly washed with gilded varnish. Its perfume was overwhelming, a transmutation of the air. All the essence of the earth, it seemed, was steaming up to fill the sky; the aroma was at once innocent and violent and it made me think of the creation of the world.

Coffee and eau-de-vie, *canistrelli* and myrtle-berry liqueur appeared for early breakfast; we were sitting at the circular dining-table, saying good-bye. I felt I had spent a lifetime with the Cesari, a happy one. The morning's freshness held against the mounting heat of the sun; even Propriano looked less sullen that day. The journey on to Sartène was short; less than ten miles. Turning inland, the road followed the river Rizzanese upstream through a wide, richly wooded valley, hardly inhabited, magnificently green. The mountains, though not really high, seemed greater than they were because of the audacity of their characteristic, repetitive form. Each mass rose in a gentle concave slope to about two-thirds of its height, then shot up almost vertically with perpendicular rocks thrusting through the maquis to end in turret shapes. It was as though one drove through an avenue of mighty castles set on green pedestals.

A bend in the road brought Sartène into view, ahead and above, its very tall houses ranged along a mountain crest in two and three tiers. I had been prepared, from descriptions, for a mediaeval fortress town; but this had no resemblance to any European stronghold. Rather it recalled engravings of mysterious sacred Lhasa; the superimposed skyscraper façades fronted the valley with an inscrutable, hallucinating stare.

Six to eight storeys high, these stark mansions belong, mostly, to the last two centuries; but their architecture is timeless, the expression of a permanent

101

condition, a cast of mind. The so-called mediaeval part of the town became visible only later, as we drove under a tower and remnants of ramparts joined to houses built of enormous blocks of stone. These fortifications, too, are more recent than they appear: Sartène was founded by the Genoese in the early sixteenth century after the defeat of Rinuccio della Rocca, the last of the Cinarchesi warlords, to protect the inhabitants of the surrounding country from Barbary pirate raids. But the Moors were undeterred: in 1583 Hassan Pasha, Dey of Algiers, landing in the gulf of Valinco, captured Sartène in spite of its defences and carried off four hundred of the inhabitants as slaves.

Entering the granite-bound streets I had a strange impression of blackness and sadness: all the men were apparently dressed for a funeral; the women were all widows, and toiling widows too, trudging in black boots with buckets of water and bundles of firewood balanced on their black-swathed heads. All the shutters of the windows, from ground floor to roof, were closed.

My host was waiting for me at the bus stop; a tall, willowy young man with a pale, thin, elongated face. Refinement of physique is general among Corsicans (the result perhaps of inbreeding, or of freedom from brutalising industrial servitudes), and with those whose families have done no manual work for several generations it may run to extremes. This young man belonged to one of the patrician families of Sartène, a place where the distinction between landed gentry and landowning peasant – often uncertain in Corsica – is much more marked than elsewhere. 'My mother would have come to meet you,' he said, 'but she was retained in the shop by business. We have a shop, you see; that is how we have saved our material situation. We belong to a class that has always been too proud to work; our ancestors lived by renting their land. Of course today that would be quite insufficient. We have acres and acres of land, down in the south-west; there are plenty of rocks on it, and possibly some dolmens and menhirs and certainly a great amount of maquis. Even if one could afford to put it under cultivation one would hardly know how to sell the produce. Most of the old families of Sartène are in the same position. Some have reacted energetically; others have slid down.'

He took me to the family house in an adjoining street; one of the enormous stark mansions where he lived with his wife and children and his widowed mother in flats on the upper floors. The interior was quite out of keeping with the forbidding stone façade. The room where his mother – a charming, much occupied woman – received me, was a lighthearted nineteenth-century drawing-room, all decorated in yellows and reds. Louis-Philippe chairs and settees covered in red plush were dotted about a Turkey carpet; crimson and gold embroidered Chinese silks hung on a yellow moiré wallpaper; a canary-coloured porcelain mandarin stood by a gilded lyre. It was a thoroughly irresponsible décor, and successful; the Eastern elements, my hostess explained, had been brought home by an ancestor associated with the building of the Suez Canal.[1]

'My mother is a Parisian,' the son told me, 'I hope you like French cooking.' I said I liked both French cooking and Corsican. 'Corsican food is rough and indigestible,' his mother said. 'I contrive to eat in the continental manner even though it's not always easy to procure what one needs here.' 'The market is a miserable affair,' said the son's wife, 'none of the peasants bother to grow vegetables.' 'They live on enormous quantities of smoked sausage and strong cheese,' said her mother-in-law, 'one wonders how they can support such a diet.'

After the carefully cooked un-Corsican lunch I wandered alone into the town. Though the black-kerchiefed gnarled-faced women, now sitting on small hard chairs on their doorsteps, seemed to belong to some archaic village, the main square had an urban allure (with some four thousand inhabitants Sartène is in fact the fourth town of Corsica, and the seat of a *Sous-Préfecture*). Substantial glass-fronted cafés, a solemn large old granite church, a fortress-like Town Hall (once the residence of the Genoese Lieutenant-Governor), fill three sides; the fourth is open to a view of the maquis. Most of the Corsican towns and larger villages have a square laid out in this way, and the views, seen as through a window, are sometimes superb. So designed, the square has the appearance of a stage where dramas may be played before an empty auditorium of the mountains or the sea. Appropriately enough, for this is exactly what happens. The main square of a Corsican town or village is the place where political action is planned, where mayors and councillors, deputies and senators are made and ruined; the place, too, where men and women can see each other and marriages or perilous love affairs are conceived.

The people of Sartène, I observed, were thoroughly engrossed in their dramas: gentlemen in dark suits, peasants in near-black corduroys and wide-brimmed black felt hats conversed earnestly at café tables, promenaded muttering in pairs. The social climate of Sartène is typically Corsican: tense, conspiratorial. In Ajaccio, where foreigners and Italian labourers settle, there is hailing and greeting and gesticulating in the streets as elsewhere in the Mediterranean, and the banter of housewives calling from window to window; but in this mountain capital of the south silence and secrecy prevail.

A vaulted passage, cutting through the Town Hall, led me into the old part of the town. Here the proximity of stone was overwhelming. The houses, stacked close on the hillside, are built of huge roughly hewn blocks of granite of a grain so coarse that the walls, seen always at close quarters, seem to scowl and snarl. Arches, springing from different levels, span the alleys like giant creepers; outside staircases slant from arch to arch and floor to floor. This stone jungle almost obscures the sky, and it seems that little rain can reach street level for in the lower angles of the walls I found the largest and thickest cobwebs I have ever seen. Most of the houses resemble fortresses, growing wider towards their foundations; their ground-floor windows are crisscrossed with pike-thick iron bars. Veritable boulders are incorporated into the lower walls, and large upstanding living rocks; to storm Sartène, in times past, must have been like storming the mountain itself.

Now, in the siesta hour, no living thing was to be seen except an occasional red geranium in a pot set like a lamp in an embrasure of an upper window.

These beacon flowers were all that relieved the ubiquitous harsh granite; for when I caught sight of the outer world – under an archway, at the end of an alley – there too was rock: the embattled cones of the valley of the Rizzanese, and inland, the distant Aiguilles de Bavella, a string of peaks less suggestive of needles than a jawful of monster's teeth.

Sartène could hardly be called a wealthy town today; but it is the centre of a good wine-producing district and the home of various big landowners. Known as the *sgio* (abbreviation of *signori*) they descend from offshoots of the Cinarchesi, or from influential notables who succeeded in piecing together large properties during the last four hundred years. The French monarchy recognised their titles to nobility, even though most, at that time, were ignorant and poor: of the fifty *sgio* of Sartène who swore fidelity to Louis XVI, fourteen were unable to sign their names.[2]

But during the nineteenth century the fortunes of the *sgio* improved. The nineteenth century was a good period for Corsica. Oil and wine and corn, briar pipes and charcoal, could be exported with profit; the French administration offered opportunities for advancement; Napoleon III went out of his way to bestow official posts on upper-class Corsicans. In these conditions the landowners of Sartène prospered, came to form an exclusive, arrogant ruling caste. Some acquired political influence in a national sphere; the Pietri produced a succession of eminent public men; Chiappe, the dynamic Chief of Police of the 1930s, originated here.

I found the houses of the gentry on the upper edge of the town, aligned rather sadly along a road. The largest of them enclosed three sides of a paved courtyard. The wings were designed with open arcades, in the Italian style, but the house, being built of grey granite, managed to look Nordic and dour. Though planned on a large scale it hardly suggested an elegant style of living, and now, abandoned to caretakers or poor tenants, it was backsliding to the farmyard state that constantly threatens all houses in Corsica. Dung covered the steps; the arcades were littered with straw and chicken houses and chickens; a loggia was garlanded with strings of onions and many of the doors were patched with rough boards.

This dilapidated mansion was in keeping with its setting; the one next to it, well-cared-for, would have been out of place almost anywhere except on the French Riviera. Decorated with fancy Ionic pilasters and stucco work in the Moorish style, it had a flight of marble steps leading to a garden full of cacti and urns. While I was taking in all this the owner came strolling down the steps. He was an elderly gentleman with bicycle-bar moustaches, a Homburg hat, high stiff-winged collar, bow tie and cane. I might have been looking at a photograph album of some sixty years ago.

I found myself wondering where he was going, and why. To pay calls, I supposed, for what else could one do so elaborately dressed on a summer afternoon in Sartène? I was wrong. Gentlemen do not pay calls in Corsica; ladies do not, cannot, receive impromptu visits from men. He was going to sit in a café with other local notables, and talk local politics. And under that tight black Edwardian jacket he carried (so I was later told) a loaded pistol; for politics, in Sartène, is a very dangerous sport.

In fact politics is the only kind of sport a Corsican country gentleman can really enjoy. Not for him the satisfying round of hunting, shooting and fishing, horse shows and point-to-points. He lives in a village or town and leaves it as seldom as possible. And in a way, no wonder. Wealth, in Corsica, is more envied than respected, and only a few unskilful unfortunates are willing to work on the land for a wage. A Corsican gentleman usually rents his land and lives in underserviced isolation on the proceeds. If he wants to shoot on his estate he must tramp through the maquis like any peasant in search of birds that have already been trapped by his tenants; he must fish streams where the trout have already been netted by poachers and come home to an unheated house and a wife or mother who complains that her soup is already cold on the table. It probably is.

Things were better, I have been told, in the last century; in those days, it is said, the gentry shot and rode and entertained with the panache of their kind elsewhere. But I am not convinced. Servants and game may have been more plentiful; but in Sartène, at any rate, local vendettas must have put a damper on any kind of social life. I can hardly believe that the Corsican country gentleman has ever been other than an isolated, insecure figure, surrounded by hostile equals and jealous inferiors, obliged to rent his lands and haggle for payment, and left with no way of asserting his superiority except controlling elections in a black suit bulging over a pistol. The peasants and shepherds and fishermen, even the bandits, have always seemed to me better adapted to local conditions than he.

If the lot of the well-off gentry seems unsatisfactory to anyone acquainted with English country house pleasures and privileges, that of the impoverished can only be described as appalling. There are *sgio* in Sartène too proud to work, or too old, who are virtually drawing-room prisoners between their faded Second Empire wallpapers. Some have not left the town for years: while they cannot afford to buy or even hire a car, to be seen taking the bus would be unbearably humiliating. The sensible example of my hosts has not been followed, even though there is money enough to be made in Sartène on those lines. The inhabitants – *sgio* or otherwise – have a high contempt for the petty ways of commerce. I once wanted to peel an apple in a café in the main square. I asked for a knife; there was no knife in the establishment. Finally the owner, with grave courtesy, lent me his stiletto.

At sunset I was back in the old town, on the edge of the fortifications built into the natural rock escarpment. Below, in the valley, I could see peasants riding home on their donkeys and mules, heading towards the town from many directions like marionettes drawn by invisible threads. As the sun dropped the view became a study in grisaille: the dark grey of the near-by slopes in shadow, the silver grey of the further mountains veiled in the gauzy evening light, the pearl grey of the distant sea. The only patch of colour was an emerald-green garden plot immediately below, with a stone hut from

105

which a thread of woodsmoke rose vertically into the sky. A bearded patriarch was still at work in this tiny oasis in the maquis.

In the main square I found the evening promenade in full swing, with luscious tangos pouring from the café radios. Girls had joined the crowd, pacing in couples, self-assured and serene as mannequins. Indeed they might have been mannequins; most of them – daughters, no doubt, of the more prosperous *sgio* – were handsome and wonderfully well dressed. If there was any criticism to be made of their sober, expensive clothes it was that they seemed more suited to Paris than Sartène.

Up and down, round and round they stalked on their high heels; every step, it seemed, was calculated. The men drinking in the cafés (where respectable women might not go), sat staring at them intently, but without evident reactions. Occasionally, when a couple of strolling men passed a couple of girls, I observed a quick, furtive communication: a word or two exchanged, but without any slowing down of walking pace, a gesture of head or hand. The scene was taut with hidden purpose; all the actors, it seemed, were bent on watching each other, meeting or avoiding each other; their conventional movements covered a network of urgent concealed motives. After a while my increasing awareness of these submerged currents began to press on my nerves. I longed to escape into the maquis that beckoned, empty and impersonal, through the open window of the square. This was to be my reaction every time I visited Sartène. The town fascinates and intrigues me, there is nowhere else quite like it; all the same I have never wanted to stay there very long.

But Sartène must be banal now compared with what it was in its heyday of violence. In the early nineteenth century the town was divided by a desperate feud between two leading families of *sgio* and their supporters. The ostensible pretext was political: the Roccaserra, living in the upper part of the town, known as Santa Anna, were the 'Whites', or supporters of the Bourbons; the Ortoli and Pietri in the lower quarter – known as Borgo – were the 'Reds' or liberals. With the 1830 revolution that dethroned the Bourbons open hostilities broke out. The Ortoli formed a National Guard in defiance of the mayor, a Roccaserra; the guard marched through the streets to be greeted by volleys of gunfire from the windows of Santa Anna. The commander, Sebastien Pietri, was killed, with one of his men; five others were wounded. The following day crowds of supporters of both sides moved into town; wild men from the mountains, more than a thousand of them, according to the traveller Valéry. The French authorities looked on helplessly and acquitted everyone concerned.

Three years later the enemy families came face to face in the valley of the Rizzanese. It was never known exactly what took place except that Alexandre and Camille Pietri, brothers of the murdered commander, were killed, and Jérôme Roccaserra, brother of the mayor, was severely wounded in the arm. He was acquitted for lack of evidence. The following year two other members of the Borgo faction were ambushed and killed at Propriano. The French authorities then intervened to put an end to what amounted to a local civil war. A formal treaty of peace was negotiated by the military governor, General Baron Lallemand, a man much respected as a mediator in vendettas. At that same time he pacified a particularly bloodthirsty vendetta at Fozzano.

His peacemaking role in Corsica was the unlikely conclusion to a lifetime of fighting, usually for desperate causes. Lallemand was an adventurer of quality, an idealist according to his lights, a man of action in the style of the romantic age. General in Napoleon's army, baron of the Empire, he had been one of Napoleon's most ardent supporters. He had fought for him from the Egyptian campaign to his final defeat; he was only prevented from accompanying him to St Helena by order of the British, who judged that his presence there would be dangerous. Exiled from France, he emigrated to the United States, to Texas, where he founded the ill-starred Champ d'Asile, a colony for the survivors of the Imperial armies, and worked on a scheme to rescue Napoleon from St Helena with the aid of a French pirate fleet. Rehabilitated by Louis-Philippe, he was appointed military governor of Corsica, where he remained till his death in 1839. It is curious that his last years should have been spent bringing peace to these remote villages; the most constructive work, perhaps, in all his turbulent career.

The peace of Sartène was signed in the parish church in December 1834 by the surviving men of both factions after they had attended Mass together and solemnly vowed, before the high altar, to live in brotherhood. Among them was an elderly priest, uncle of the three murdered Pietri brothers. He had been particularly afflicted by their deaths; they were orphans, and he had regarded them as his sons. Being unable, as a priest, to execute vengeance, he had gone into deepest mourning, blocked the windows of his house with bricks and shut himself up there with the avowed intention of never again leaving its walls. The treaty, to which he subscribed from a sense of duty, did nothing to appease his grief; he remained immured in his darkened home, continued to wear black and leave his beard unshaved as a sign that the offence remained unavenged.

In spite of the official peace, feelings in Sartène still ran high. Valéry noted, appalled, that in Borgo most of the windows were still blocked with bricks, while young men were posted, armed, at a street corner of Santa Anna. It was hardly conceivable, he exclaimed, that such a state of affairs could exist under French law; the French had ruled half Europe but they were powerless against Corsican passions.

But it was not so much Corsican passions that precipitated the last act in the vendetta as the indiscretion of a French Inspector of Historic Monuments. The climax of Prosper Mérimée's novel, *Colomba*, is the moment when the hero, ambushed by a couple of enemies, wounded in the arm, shoots them both dead. Mérimée, while principally inspired by the contemporary vendetta of Fozzano, had derived this particular incident from the feat of Jérôme Roccaserra; indeed he had heard it from his own lips when Roccaserra had entertained him in superb style in his house in Sartène. Fearing the incredulity of his readers, Mérimée could not resist adding a footnote to the effect that anyone who doubted the possibility of such a performance could go to Sartène and learn for himself how 'one of the most distinguished and agreeable citizens' had 'saved himself' in similar circumstances.

The words were sufficient to condemn his distinguished and agreeable host. The book fell into the hands of the Abbé Pietri. For him it had only one interest, and not a literary one; it proved that Jérôme Roccaserra, after being forgiven by his enemies, had committed the monstrous injury of boasting of his crime. In 1843 he was killed on the road to Propriano; by bandits, acting, it was generally assumed, on behalf of the priest. Vengeance had been accomplished. On the day of the funeral, it is said, the Abbé Pietri shaved his beard and opened the windows of his house. It overlooked the entrance to the church. Breathing the light of day for the first time in nearly ten years, he waited at a window to see the coffin pass by. But his enemies, rather than allow him this satisfaction, took another route to the church, broke open a lateral wall, and so carried in the coffin, unseen.[3]

Such was the climate of Sartène just over a century ago. It changed very little until after the First World War. 'There was one way of settling every problem: with a gun,' my host explained to me. We were drinking after-dinner coffee in the gay red and yellow drawing-room with his mother and wife. 'Take the case of my grandfather,' he continued, 'he was a great spender and of course he had no idea of working; he let out his land and mortgaged it heavily. When he failed to pay any of the interest over a period of years the bank in Paris that had made the loan sent a representative to Sartène with instructions to collect the overdue payments or arrange for a sale of the land. My grandfather didn't give him much of a reception, as you may imagine. In fact the wretched man was so scared that he left that same night for Ajaccio by the stage-coach. But my grandfather hadn't done with him, oh no! When he heard of his flight he saddled his best horse, took his pistol and gun, and rode after the coach. By taking a short cut he managed to intercept it near Olmeto. He held it up, just like a highwayman, so that he could tell the bank employee exactly what he thought of him. His words and appearance were so terrible that the bank never again tried to enforce the terms of the loan.'

This is a typical story of Sartène in the near past; but a mild one compared with others that are told. Some fifty years ago two young men were drinking together at a café in the main square. They had been close friends since childhood. They were discussing the relative merits of the guitar and the mandolin. They disagreed. They simultaneously pulled out their pistols and shot each other dead.

Another anecdote of our evening's conversation was legendary. Long ago, my hostess told me, a monk and a nun of Sartène fell in love. On Good Friday night, when everyone in Sartène was following the yearly penitential procession, they slipped away unnoticed to a rendezvous in the valley of the Rizzanese. But before they could consummate their guilty love they were turned to stone. And there they can still be seen; a pair of menhirs standing close together by the roadside.

Woman of the Sartenais. (*Merle W. Moore*)

A shepherd. (*Jean Bailet*)

The Good Friday night procession was what interested me most in this tale. It was a representation of the Calvary, my host explained to me, enacted every year on the night of Good Friday; it was known as the procession of the *Catenacciu*, 'the chained one', because the chief penitent, who represents Jesus Christ, drags a chain. Shrouded in a red hood, barefoot, the chain attached to his right leg, he carries a huge heavy cross through the streets, followed by other penitents, all barefoot and hooded, and almost the whole population of the town. His role is a highly regarded privilege; a man may play it only once in his lifetime; applications are booked for as long as ten and twelve years in advance. The penitent is unrecognisable; his identity is known only to the priest, and to the Franciscan monks established on the outskirts of the town to whom he makes his confession beforehand. In the past, I was told, he was often a bandit who would come in from the maquis, remain hidden with the monks until the time of the procession and then slip away afterwards at dead of night. The monks never thought of betraying him; that would have been contrary to their principles as well as to Corsican tradition. 'Of course it's different now,' my host said to me, 'there are practically no bandits left. The chief penitent may be anyone.' 'But there are plenty of people here who have sins on their consciences without being bandits,' said his mother. 'There are still men who have killed, or are prepared to kill,' said his wife, 'we have not basically changed.'

The words, thrown casually from one plush settee to another, stirred my imagination. Such a procession, in which real penitents expiated real sins, would be very different, I thought, from the theatrical Easter pageantry of Spain. I promised myself to spend an Easter in Sartène.

Several years passed before I could do so. During that time banditry in Corsica came to an end. The last of the bandits, known as Muzarettu, repented – but not at the *Catenacciu* – and died in the Franciscan monastery. I heard his story when I arrived at Sartène for Easter a few weeks after the event.[4]

Muzarettu belongs to a type of human being once very familiar in Corsica, but which is unlikely to be seen there again. The last – almost – of the bandits of honour, he lived in the maquis, on and off, for some twenty years after the rest of the bandits had surrendered or been killed. It was an argument with a nephew in 1932 – no more – that launched him on his terrible career. The dispute culminated when the nephew slapped Muzarettu in the face. This slap in the face determined the rest of his life. It rankled, assumed fearful proportions in his mind; it drove him to ambush and kill his nephew that same night. Perhaps even murder was insufficient to wash out the offence; possibly he continued to brood on the injury until he had projected it into physical form: Muzarettu died of cancer of the face.

The tragic sequence none the less developed slowly; as often happens when a man has engaged on a disastrous course, the consequences were not immediately apparent; there was a lull, a false remission, and for a time he seemed to be saved. Muzarettu was arrested three months after the murder and acquitted the following year. But his life had been fatally dislocated. Menaces from his nephew's relatives forced him to leave his village, to sell his land. Moreover, he himself had changed. He found lodging in a cellar in a small seaside village, lived there in ramshackle, Bohemian style. Fishermen from Ajaccio who made a habit of visiting him have told me astonishing tales of all-night drinking bouts in his dank home.

This life of wild pleasures came to an end with the Second World War, when Muzarettu was ordered out of his cellar to make way for Italian troops. He retaliated by murdering the secretary of the mayor who had evicted him. The family of the victim then bribed a young man of Olmeto to murder Muzarettu. Muzarettu got wind of the deal and killed him, waiting behind a rock overlooking the road between Propriano and Sartène.

This time Muzarettu had no thought of surrendering to the law; he took to the maquis, where he made himself feared. But he none the less fell into a trap soon afterwards, when he was arrested in an undignified, almost ridiculous way. On a lonely beach he ran into some people who looked like tourists and accepted their invitation to share their *bouillabaisse*. While he was picnicking with them they seized him, policemen in disguise, and carried him off to prison.

Muzarettu's story is by turns brutal, sordid, grotesque and heroic. He was seventy-seven at the time of this second imprisonment and already suffering from cancer of the face. Yet the old man managed to escape from the hospital in Ajaccio, to which he had been transferred from prison, and find his way back to the maquis. There he spent the rest of his life – more than ten years – scorning the hardships, the police (he fired on and wounded more than one *gendarme*), his enemies, his poverty, and even his illness, which increased appallingly. Down on the desolate south-west coast he took possession of a cave; the fishermen of Ajaccio still visited him, brought him futile patent medicines which accumulated until the place smelt, so they told me, like a chemist's laboratory.

He was dying when he accepted an invitation from the Franciscan monks to end his days in their monastery at Sartène. Muzarettu was not a religious man; he was a notorious blasphemer, scorning God as he scorned the law. He was merely acting in accordance with an ancient Corsican tradition, for until the French conquest the monasteries had the right to give asylum to outlaws and criminals.[5] This privilege was revived for Muzarettu: the monks obtained assurance of his immunity from the police; the commander of the local *gendarmerie*, I was told, went so far as to visit him on his sickbed.

Even so he was at first a far from easy patient. He planned suicide, yelled for his revolver, tried to poison himself with a tube of strychnine he kept hidden in his wallet. Only at the very end could the fierce old man come to terms with God. The dying bandit, so one of the monks told me, lay quite still, monstrously disfigured, past speech, silently and repeatedly making the sign of the cross.

The Franciscans must have many such acts of humanity to their credit in Corsica. Though they were not the first monks to establish communities in the island, they came early, during the lifetime of their founder. They arrived to teach the Christian ethos to a violent and primitive people. And they were well attuned to the task, for these men who had vowed to live in poverty, in imitation of Christ and His disciples, generally had to do, in Corsica, with a people as poor as themselves. There was little to choose between the Franciscans' robe and the *pelone*, the rough goat's hair cloak worn by the Corsican shepherds until a generation ago.

Between Franciscans and Corsicans poverty constituted a fundamental bond. The Corsicans trusted the Franciscans because they were poor; the Franciscans must have felt towards the Corsicans a particular sense of obligation: St Francis loved, above all, poor men. Corsica became one of their special fields of endeavour. Followers of that spiritual revolutionary who sought and found God in the forests and fields, they surely recognised their proper environment as they adventured into the untamed Corsican landscape.

The population willingly gave them food; Franciscans, like Corsican shepherds, could walk all day on a handful of dried figs. Wealthy people bestowed on them considerable gifts: two of the Cinarchesi warlords – Gian' Paolo da Leca and Rinuccio della Rocca – endowed monasteries; Rinuccio and others gave them paintings and statues, so that their churches gradually assumed a luxuriousness oddly out of keeping with their bare monastic buildings and the simplicity of their lives. But they owned no land, except their gardens which they tended skilfully, so that today, after a century and a half of neglect, these walled green peaceful spots where unkempt fruit trees dangle over stagnant pools suggest the earthly paradise, abandoned and in decay.

They were respected as holy men. Burial in their churches was a privilege thought to confer blessedness on the spirits of the dead; lying-space under their baroque vaults became the ultimate goal of a people who attach extreme importance to their tombs. Sinners preferred to make confession to the Franciscans than to the parish priests and – mistakenly from the Catholic standpoint – valued their absolution more. The bandit-penitents of the *Catenacciu* confided themselves only to the monks.

Their order, the most popular in Corsica, became by far the most influential; at the end of the thirteenth century they had eight monasteries in the island, by the eighteenth no less than sixty-four. Of the eleven hundred monks then in Corsica a thousand were Franciscans. Champions of the people, and ardent patriots, they backed the national rebellion against the Genoese. Rebel assemblies and councils of war were held in their monasteries; national constitutions, considerably in advance of the time, were hammered out and adopted there. In one Theodor von Neuhof was crowned constitutional monarch; in another, more usefully, Pasquale Paoli was elected head of state.

These large buildings also served as guest-houses in the absence of inns; travellers of mark, including Boswell, enjoyed their hospitality. The Franciscan foundations were in fact oases of civilisation in a rough, dangerous country. The French, however, when they conquered Corsica, considered them far too numerous, an inadmissible drain on the island's resources. One French ecclesiastic calculated that their upkeep cost the people nearly five

III

times the sum they paid in the tax on revenue to the French crown. The monks, he complained, had established a begging tariff of a loaf of bread per household, thus turning alms into tribute.[6] No doubt their original austerity had by then declined; undeniably they lived as parasites on a poor people. Yet the Corsicans, who have always reacted ferociously to exploitation, never thought of getting rid of them until the French Revolution made the matter a political issue. For centuries the monks were willingly supported, as though their presence, however costly, was an indispensable luxury.

With the Revolution they were pressed out of their monasteries, which were subsequently put up to auction. Some have become private houses, hostels, schools; but most have fallen into ruin, romantic piles of ivy-covered masonry with crumbling vaults and gaping tombs surpassing the dreams of Monk Lewis. In recent years a handful of Franciscans have trickled back to Corsica. They render useful services by relieving overworked parish priests (many of whom have to minister to several villages); and they perform other good works, some intimately related to insular tradition: they rebaptised a boy who feared the powers of a *mazzere*; they rescued Muzarettu from the maquis and helped him to end his terrible life in peace.

I arrived to spend Easter in Sartène a few weeks after he died. That evening the streets of Sartène were lit with candles and oil lamps set in all the windows. The effect must have been even better in the days before electricity made a rival illumination, but it was still very moving. The homely lights cast a warm glow on the fierce masonry, and each little group of them quivering in an embrasure seemed a humble expression of man's hope of redemption. All the surrounding villages were similarly lit; when I walked to the edge of the town I could see their lights burning in the black mountains, and those of isolated houses deep in the maquis. The cafés were empty and the streets silent as I walked back to the house of my hosts; only a few dark figures were to be seen entering and leaving the church, which was kept open through the night for prayer.

In the morning I found the priest, a fragile old man sitting by a smouldering fire. 'What you will see is not so much a procession as a representation of the Cavalry,' he told me. 'I hope you'll not be shocked; the people push and shout and the children scream and cry. But perhaps all this is not really out of place; no doubt the historical Calvary was just as disorderly.'

That evening I found a dense crowd gathered in the main square, waiting for the penitents to come out of the church. Muffled cries arose as they appeared on the steps: the chief penitent, carrying a huge black cross on his shoulder, robed in scarlet, wore a conical hood like those of the Ku Klux Klan, or the penitents of Seville, but without a point, the top being gathered and sewn down in a lump. There was something particularly humiliating about this nobbly, crunched up ending to the hood where one expected a tapering peak; this was really the dress of mortification. Behind him, bearing the shaft of the cross, was Simon of Cyrene, hooded and robed in white, walking in a crouching position, his hands almost touching the ground. Priests, monks and choir followed, and the members of the parish fraternity, unhooded, in white, with scarlet capes, carrying lighted tapers. Then came eight penitents hooded and robed in black; four carried a bier on which an effigy of Christ taken down from the cross lay on a white shroud sprinkled with pale flowers; the others upheld a black palanquin over the bier. These figures are said, rather implausibly, to represent the Jews; but to me they suggested, rather, the dreaded *squadra d'arozza*, the company of the spirits of the dead.

The procession wound round the church into a narrow street; the townspeople, hundreds strong, pressed behind. As I had been warned, they pushed and thrust and shouted and exclaimed, so loud, often, as to drown the chanting of the choir. These people who go about their daily affairs with the solemnity due to a religious rite become boisterous, even aggressive, when engaged in the sacred ceremony of Good Friday. What they conveyed was not a religious emotion, in the accepted meaning of the words, but a release of violent primitive energy. They would be terrifying and irresistible I thought, when acting in unison. But perhaps they are never so united as in this yearly procession; they become aware of their brotherhood only in their shared sense of guilt.

The crowd forced its way behind the penitents like a river in spate. Spectators leaned out of windows, crowded on steps and balconies; the street had become a seething mass of humanity from paving-stones to roofs. Word was passed from mouth to mouth: the chief penitent had fallen; for according to tradition he must fall three times in the course of the procession, as Christ fell on the road to Golgotha. A stranger, a young man, grabbed my shoulder: 'Come this way quick and we'll get to the front,' he hissed. I followed him darting through the stepped alleys of the old town until we cut into the head of the procession moving back towards the square. The slow scrape of the chain heralded the dogged progress of the chief penitent; as he passed I could see that his naked feet, bending over the paving-stones, were already cut and bruised. But he was beyond the reach of sympathy. The disguises made the penitents inhuman, abstract figures, so that one was surprised to see their eyes flickering inside their hoods.

'I know who he is!' the young man told me, pointing at the chief penitent. 'He's come back from Indo-China, he was there thirty years.' Not a bandit; but one, perhaps, who had laid considerable burdens on his conscience. In times past, my companion told me, the crowd would pelt the penitent with refuse and stones, batter him with staves; but now the procession was more decorous. 'In those days the penitents were all murderers,' he said. 'Of course things are different now; we've become civilised. All the same there are still some who take part in the procession with good reason. You see that short, thick-set man?' He pointed to one chanting in the fraternity. 'He killed not so very long ago, in self-defence.' It had often happened, he said, that mortal enemies found themselves side by side in the procession; but no vengeances were ever taken; for the duration of the ceremony a general truce was observed.

113

The *Catenacciu*, I thought, must always have operated as an indispensable antidote to the tensions of Sartène. On this one night of the year enemies joined together to seek the forgiveness they could never offer each other, nor accept from any man; as chief penitent a murderer, or a bandit, was reintegrated into the Christian community. He would suffer indignities that he would never otherwise tolerate; he would humble himself, perhaps for the only time in his life; but victimised, he none the less personified the Son of God. The Church never succeeded in eradicating the Corsicans' code of vengeance; but it did implant in this headstrong people the concepts of sin and redemption, so that while they still killed, faithful to honour and their dead, they at the same time, in so doing, suffered their own guilt. Christ came to Corsica, but bringing the sword.

The crowd converged under the great arch of the Town Hall, then fanned out over the square, where the penitent fell again. With Simon of Cyrene bearing the head of the cross the procession began to climb a street leading up and out of the town. Here the scene had a pictorial quality, for one looked at a rising vista of windows and arches and balconies all crowded with spectators. The indoor lighting made a shining ground for the motionless figures staring, as in mediaeval paintings, from the windows that framed them; a girl with fair hair falling over a blue dressing-gown had the grave loveliness of a quattrocento madonna. But on the arches and balconies men were leaning and twisting in extravagant poses, with the lamps and candles on the window ledges accentuating the vertical lines of their weatherworn faces, so that these groups, in which gestures and expression had been arrested and fixed by eager concentration, called to mind the canvases of Caravaggio.

By now the long walk had almost silenced the crowd and the singing could be clearly heard. '*Perdonnu mio Dio, Mio Dio perdonnu, Perdonnu mio Dio, Perdonnu pieta:*' the refrain was taken up by the crowd between each stanza of the chant, sung to an old sad Corsican air. This reiteration, accompanied by the rhythmic scraping of the penitent's chain that now marked the slow measure of our steps, was hypnotic. I began to lose track of time, to forget that I had joined the procession as a visitor and observer; I was living rather than watching it as I plodded uphill with a very old woman clutching my arm.

Only one episode in the latter part of the procession stands clearly in my memory, when the chief penitent and Simon of Cyrene entered a little chapel near the upper edge of the town to rest and pray. A wooden figure of the dead Christ lay on a white-draped bier below the altar, surrounded by bowls of young corn, grown indoors for the occasion, and still very pale. A statue of the Virgin knelt beside him, a very ordinary figure, draped in black like any peasant woman mourning her murdered son. Irises stood stiffly in cheap vases on the altar and all the saints' statues were hidden in black shrouds. This picture of the dead god surrounded by mourners, lying among the spring vegetation from which he was soon to rise, stirred and satisfied some primordial instinct quite outside the scope of piety.

The resurrection was commemorated the following midnight. I had been warned that shots would be fired in the square in accordance with a tradition that has often allowed for the murderous settling of feuds. During the service I took up my position by the church door; as the serene mediaeval ceremony drew to its close I saw the young men beside me already fiddling with their revolvers. The priest was gliding about the nave, lighting the many candles, switching on the electric lights that garlanded the side altars and lifting the black shrouds from the saints' statues. The nude bulbs and the plaster statues were vulgar enough, but this simultaneous lighting and unveiling none the less made its effect. Then the church bells pealed, a siren, installed by American troops during the war, howled into the night; the young men rushed into the square and fired off their revolvers, and for the next few minutes the town resounded with shots echoing from the encircling ranges. No quarrels were taken up; no one was accidentally hit; the yearly period of mourning ended in an explosion of light and sound; Christ had risen from the corn.

8 VIOLENCE AND PIETY

The empty south – Corsican renegades – Mérimée's Colomba –
the real Colomba – sea-borne Virgins – Pisan churches –
warlord and art patron

M Y first visit to Sartène was brief. I realised that whatever I failed to learn
about that weird town in a day or two would still be obscure in a week, a
month, a year. Meanwhile I was eager to move on to Bonifacio, by all accounts
a place of spectacular beauty, full of antiquities.

The obvious route was by the road running south through the barely inhabited country stretching to the straits of Bonifacio, the strip of sea, barely
eight miles wide, that separates Corsica from Sardinia. Sartène is a frontier
town of this desolate region, offering the last chance on the way to Bonifacio
to buy petrol, repair a car. In those reaches of maquis and bare hills rolling
towards the sea few villages are seen, few houses, even, except one-storeyed
shepherds' cabins hardly distinguishable at a distance from the natural rocks.
Man's imprint, in some areas, is negligible save for the broken lines of menhirs,
or the isolated dolmens rising above the maquis, the most skilful feats in
building for many, many miles. The inhabitants still follow a primaeval
pastoral routine, and it is not uncommon to see whole families, trunks on
heads, babies in arms, tramping across country to hail the bus on the main
road, their lifeline to the twentieth-century world.

It would have been easy enough for me to take the bus which covers that
road daily; but I had planned a roundabout journey through more populated
districts, rich in historical associations. I wanted to visit Fozzano, the setting
of Mérimée's *Colomba*, and neighbouring Santa-Maria-Figaniella, site of a
Pisan church; to see, also, Sainte-Lucie-de-Tallano, where Rinuccio della
Rocca endowed a Franciscan monastery, before going on to Bonifacio via
Carbini, the village of the heretics and the improbable Hotel des Nations.

The bus timetables were unaccommodating, so I decided to hire a car. A
taxi-owner proposed a reasonable price because he wanted to visit some
cousins at Sainte-Lucie-de-Tallano, after which he would take me on to
Carbini. 'Though personally I don't advise you to go there,' he added, 'I warn
you, you'll find nowhere to stay. There's nothing in Carbini; its a place of
barbarians. Why, until a few years back they didn't even have a road,' he
concluded, as though this were an unanswerable reason for not going there
now. I told him there was a Hotel des Nations with private baths for every

116

room; he told me that I would find out for myself that the hotel was an illusion. Early in the afternoon my hosts bade me a provisional farewell, the sort of farewell very common in Corsica: 'Good-bye till tonight or next time you pass this way. Bon voyage.'

We swung downhill from Sartène through a landscape of maquis and vineyards. Heat dimmed its colours and blurred its outlines, so that it appeared as though in an amateurish photograph, faint and fuzzy. In the valley we struck an upper reach of the Rizzanese, hidden between alders and poplars. A humpbacked Genoese bridge leaping the river with a single high arch stood out dramatically in the indefinite, intricate scene. It was a very handsome bridge, I observed, flanked by triangular bastions and surmounted by a parapet making an obtuse angle. Its surface, wide enough to allow riders to pass each other, was paved with large rectangular stones, and this paving was prolonged on either side into the wild maquis.

The Genoese wasted little of their artistic accomplishment on Corsica. One may look in vain for any counterparts to the stately *palazzi* and sumptuous baroque churches of the metropolis, with façades loaded with giant caryatids and gesturing marble statues, *trompe-l'œil* painting and polychrome or embossed stonework. The houses in the Corsican–Genoese towns are bleak apartment blocks; the churches hardly rival those of the small Ligurian villages except in the occasional beauty of their sites. It is as constructional engineers that the Genoese displayed their quality in this colonial territory, with their forts and bridges and walled citadels, solidly built in bold lines and noble proportions. These are the works of pioneers and conquerors, charged with purpose and power.

We had stopped by the bridge; I was observing how its paving-stones seemed to be deliberately ridged laterally, across their centre, to allow purchase for the hooves of horses and mules. 'One can say it's quite well conceived,' my morose driver commented.

A short distance upstream we crossed the river by a modern bridge, then climbed the opposite range. Sartène, far behind us on its mountainside, looked more than ever like Lhasa. Over the top of the range we came to a little village called Arbellara which arrested my attention by a high square tower isolated on a knoll. Its single-pitched roof and casement windows gave it more the look of an elongated house than a fortress, an *avant-garde* house, the work of some rustic Le Corbusier. In fact (as my driver explained) it was built by the villagers as a defence against pirate raids. Later I learned that they had twice been attacked the same year that Sartène fell to Hassan Pasha. The raids were ably led by a local Corsican, one Filippo, who had himself been taken prisoner and then abjured his faith and joined the Moors. Crowded in the tower, the inhabitants successfully resisted the first onslaught; but during the second they accidentally set fire to their ammunition and to escape death by burning flung themselves out of the windows onto the heads of the assailants.

Such renegade Corsicans were by no means uncommon, and often ensured the deadly efficacy of the Moorish raids. By the sixteenth century piracy had become an organised business in the Barbary states, the main source of revenue for those half-desert lands. Thousands of Christians were captured yearly, to be held as slaves for ransom; in idleness, for there was no possible occupation for this huge labour force. By adopting the religion of their masters they could free themselves, as many did, and then used their abilities to organise and lead the pirate expeditions. Indeed North African piracy flourished at this period precisely because it was largely run by Europeans. Corsicans, as always on the lookout for profitable openings overseas, readily took to this career: of the ten thousand renegades engaged in piracy in Algiers in the mid-sixteenth century, no less than six thousand were Corsicans.[1] One, known as Mammi Pasha, was the terror of Cap Corse, where he successfully plundered his birthplace. Two actually became Deys, or kings of Algiers: Piero Paolo Tavera, known as Hassan Corso, elected by the janissaries in 1556, and a certain Lazaro of Bastia, both of whom reigned rather briefly before being deposed and murdered by their subjects. Yet another Corsican renegade is said to have been so stricken with remorse, when commanding a naval attack on Bastia, that he jumped overboard and drowned himself within sight of the town. Such crises of conscience must have been rare; the Corsican pirates were probably as little troubled by moral scruples as their present-day compatriots who discard the severe precepts of their upbringing to make good in the underworld of Marseilles.

Arbellara, a cluster of old stone houses at the base of the tower, looked as grim, I thought, as though it were anticipating another assault from the Moors. The single street was empty and every shutter closed. Each Corsican village has its individual character, and that of Arbellara is dour and comfortless.

I was expecting Fozzano, a couple of miles away, to be even more forbidding, for I had read and heard too much about this village not to have formed a precise picture of it in my mind. Mérimée recreated Fozzano, gave it that supernormal life which a writer of talent may confer on a locality, so that it must thereafter appear to those who know his work in the light of his vision. Just as travellers may see the Malay archipelago in the thundery gleam of Conrad's imagination, and Dublin as a reflection of Joyce's *Ulysses*, so Fozzano has come to represent, for visitors, what Mérimée discerned there over a century ago: the essence of fierce and sombre Corsican tradition.

From motives of discretion Mérimée called the village of his book Pietranera, and placed it in the north of the island. But as was soon discovered, his novel was based on contemporary events at Fozzano and named after a real woman he met during his journey: Colomba Bartoli, born Carabelli. Visitors who have subsequently made the pilgrimage to her tomb have unconsciously imposed on Fozzano Mérimée's setting for his tale of death and revenge. Their descriptions always insist on the warlike aspect of the people and their fortress-homes, in one of which Colomba Carabelli was born.

Mérimée's account of a village 'in vendetta' is certainly spellbinding, the product of a very close and penetrating observation of Corsican life. A murder

118

has been committed, outcome of an ancient feud between the two leading families of the village; with great skill Mérimée relates the accumulation of small frictions and provocations that relentlessly build up a situation in which a second murder is inevitable. The obligation of performing it falls on the victim's only son, Orso, a young army officer returning to Corsica after a lapse of years. When he reaches Pietranera the whole population is waiting: the enemy family is waiting to be attacked; his sister is waiting for him to kill at least one of his enemies; shepherds, supporting each side, are spoiling for battle; the neutral members of the community are an impatient audience waiting for the curtain to rise on the next act of the drama. 'I smell gun-powder in the air,' one of them remarks with satisfaction as the young man enters his home. Most writers of vendetta stories have been preoccupied by their violent aspects; Mérimée was particularly sensitive to the ominous climate prevailing between murders.

Coming down to breakfast on the day after his arrival, Orso finds his sister casting bullets in the kitchen. Colomba has one aim, and one only: to induce her easygoing brother, denatured by European civilisation, to execute revenge. The war of nerves between the hostile families is insignificant compared with that waged against the unfortunate Orso by his sister and her supporters. The basic conflict in Mérimée's novel is not between two families, but two ways of life, two codes. As might be expected in nineteenth-century Corsica, the forces of the primitive world triumph. If Colomba fails to incite her brother to commit coldblooded murder she is only too successful with his enemies. The two sons of the opposing family ambush him in the maquis; wounded in the arm, like Jérôme Roccaserra of Sartène he shoots them both dead.

As a portrait of a Corsican woman of the traditional type, inexorable, single-minded, exquisitely cunning and possessed of an uncanny power to make men act according to her will, Mérimée's Colomba is superb. She is ruthless, and not above petty deceits; but she has undeniable grandeur. Mérimée also makes her attractive on a more accessible level: she is young and pure and beautiful; in her devotion to father and brother ardour is tempered with tenderness and submission. Colomba fascinated the French public. In literary circles she represented a variation on the theme of *la belle dame sans merci*, the cold, cruel heroine dear to the romantics. For the average reader she became the image of Corsica, of that virile, uncorrupted island, that late-acquired province of France which so few Frenchmen had visited.[2]

The real Colomba Bartoli was just as ruthless and less attractive. She was a widow in her late fifties at the time of the drama that inspired Mérimée, a masterful woman, fanatically vindictive. She gave Mérimée her lovely, inappropriate name and the idea of a new type of heroine; but he never attempted to portray her character, not even transposed into the figure of a young girl. In the same way he derived the idea of his story from the vendetta of Fozzano, but without reproducing its events. They engage less sympathy than those he relates.

For the best part of a century Fozzano had been divided by political antag-
onisms originating in the Corsican national rebellion. The village was split
into two hostile groups: the Durazzo and Paoli in the upper half against the
Carabelli, Bartoli and Bernadini in the lower. All these people were *sgio*,
gentlemen landowners. In 1830, that disturbing year of national revolution,
the old quarrel flared up again on the feast day of the Holy Trinity. A member
of the Durazzo-Paoli clan had transferred his allegiance to the opposing
group: an unpardonable treachery; the expected violence broke out after
Vespers as the enemies were leaving church. 'Why are you looking at me, you
madman?' one said to the other. 'Because you're a fine man,' was the reply.
These words were a declaration of war. The two men fell on each other then
and there with swordstick and stiletto; partisans rushed to join in the battle;
shots were fired. Three were killed that day: a Durazzo, and two of the opposing clan, including the renegade. A year later men of the enemy families met
in the maquis; they fired on each other, and yet another Carabelli, a nephew
of Colomba's, died.

The members of the Bartoli–Bernadini–Carabelli clan now had a heavy
account to settle with their enemies, and with their own dead. In 1833 they
determined to take action, at the instigation of Colomba, so it is said. One
afternoon in late December the Durazzo were seen leading in a horse from
the maquis; by this sign it was known that they intended to ride down to
their lands near Propriano the following day. That evening Colomba's son,
Francesco, and three of his kinsmen, posted themselves behind a wall bordering a path which the Durazzo would be bound to take. After an all-night wait
they were able to fire pointblank on their enemies. The Durazzo fired back;
two on each side were killed, including Colomba's son.

Baron Lallemand intervened to make peace the following year; the treaty
was signed in the church of Sartène just before a similar ceremony put an end
– in theory – to the vendetta of that town. This peace treaty of Fozzano is a
vivid historical document; the solemn rhetoric of its opening phrases allows
one to appreciate the appalling effects of a vendetta in a small village. 'The
hostilities of Fozzano date back to the most distant times; born in war, the
generations destroy each other unceasingly. Innumerable are the victims who
have paid to the vendetta the tribute of a regrettable prejudice. . . . Shut up
and barricaded in their homes, the inhabitants never go out without risking
their lives. For nearly a century humanity bewails the blindness that destroys
the finest youth. Whole years go by without the celebration of a single marriage; soon one will meet in Fozzano only widows and orphans.'[3]

As in Sartène, formal peace could do little to change old habits of hate and
fear. 'The warlike aspect of the village was wretched and frightful,' observed
the traveller Valéry, writing a year or more after the peace treaty, 'the peasants walked about armed, the houses were crenellated and barricaded, the
windows blocked with large red bricks. About a quarter of the population is
involved in hostilities. . . . The members of the warring families are consigned
to their homes; even the children cannot go to school, for they would not be

spared; it is true that these rustic urchins know very well how to handle a pistol.' The tension must have persisted; Mérimée's searing account of Pietra-nera is undoubtedly based on what he saw at Fozzano in 1839.

I was expecting to find the village still overshadowed by those tragic times. In Corsica such memories linger on. Sartène was officially pacified the same year as Fozzano, yet it bears the impress of its sinister past today. I was prepared for something similar at Fozzano. But what I found was an exceptionally pretty village, well-cared-for, and apparently serene. The old stone houses overgrown with climbing plants clung to terraces green with fig trees and mimosa. There, sure enough, were the celebrated towers of the enemy families: the Carabelli tower, where Colomba was born, built of huge blocks of granite, equipped with massive machicolations, and higher in the village, a similar tower belonging to the Durazzo. One of its windows, surmounted by an enormous semicircular lintel, was blocked halfway up with bricks; pre-sumably it belongs to a room which has remained unused since the family lived there in a state of siege. But now, with wistaria cascading over a balcony and fruit trees pressing to the walls, the old fortress looked as innocuous as the leaf-shaded, creeper-grown castles one sees in Victorian sketchbooks.[4] (All the same, as I later learned, the old feud is still not quite extinct.)

Some men, sitting smoking on a wall, rose to meet me, smiling and affable. 'You're a stranger here? You're looking for something?' I was almost em-barrassed to tell them that I was looking for the house where Colomba lived after her marriage, and the tomb where she is buried with her son. But they seemed in no way put out. 'It's down at the bottom of the village,' they explained. 'No one lives there now; if you find the door unlocked you can go inside.'

It stands, charmingly, on a grassy terrace overlooking the long valley stretching to Baracci and the sea. A vine interlaces a flight of steps leading to the upper storey. The tomb is placed only a yard or two away, a whitewashed building large enough for a summerhouse, or guestroom; as often happens in Corsica the dead and the living dwell side by side. The door of the house was unlocked, as foreseen; in the ground-floor room I found a jumble of debris, including a pathetically bad oil painting of the Last Supper. Here Colomba plotted the ambush of the Durazzo; on a balcony of the upper floor (according to local memory) she waited, on the day of the slaughter, heard the shots in the valley below. But news came first to the Durazzo who, hurrying to the valley to collect their dead, passed close by Colomba's home. 'There's fresh meat for you down there!' she cried. 'And for you too!' they retorted, and by these words she knew that her son had died.

Mérimée recoiled from the real Colomba; to use this belligerent old woman as the heroine of a novel called for a talent of a different kind. Though he never idealises the conduct of the vendetta, he deliberately detracts from the brutality of his story by giving grace and beauty to his heroine, and by inventing a foreign-educated hero with chivalrous principles. He also introduces a prosy, hesitant Préfet, a blimpish Irish colonel and his warm-

121

hearted daughter; slightly foolish figures, but essentially civilised. *Colomba* is an admirable novel which diverts as much as it disturbs; but it left room for another about the Corsican vendetta; one which would present it in all its harsh unmitigated Elizabethan anguish.

That book has never been written. *Colomba* had great success but no noteworthy succession. Alexandre Dumas, it is true, hurried to Corsica soon after its publication and there had the privilege – invaluable to a writer – of staying in the Istria fortress-mansion at Sollacaro, a village almost as much impregnated with sombre Corsican tradition as was Fozzano. But he bungles his opportunities in *Les Frères Corses* by laying on local colour as crudely as in a picture postcard. There are better accounts of Corsican bandits and vendetta situations in Seton Merriman's forgotten tale, *The Isle of Unrest*. Maupassant's journey to Corsica gave rise to some beautiful descriptions in *Une Vie* (where he uses Corsica as the setting for a honeymoon), besides a couple of slight, stylised stories of vendettas, more remarkable for their scenic than their human content. Alphonse Daudet's cruel little tales of lonely Corsican lighthouse keepers and seaworn coastguards are among the best in *Lettres de mon moulin*, stripped clean of the sugary sentimentality that overlays his treatment of Provence. But these are mere sketches that never match, nor attempt to match, the sources that gave them life.

Stories of bandits and vendettas were also produced by Corsican men of letters in the nineteenth century, and since; but they suffer, most often, either from a pedantic insistence on local customs or else from the contrary fault of excessive emotion. Whereas non-Corsican writers have been inclined to back away from the fantastically rich and powerful material Corsica offers, local novelists have been overwhelmed by it. What has been lacking is any writer of a genius fit to stand up to the imaginative stimulus of the Corsican world. Flaubert, who toured the island in his youth, alone might have done justice to the country which he describes, in a letter to his friend Ernest Chevalier, as 'grave and ardent, all black and all red'. His travel journal has a magical quality. On his return to the mainland he planned a more ambitious work, a drama based on the tragedy of Sampiero Corso and his wife, whom he killed. It is a story intense and rending as *Othello*, one of those episodes in Corsican history that resemble art, that call for the hand to complete the transformation towards which they tend. Flaubert wrote to Chevalier, then a magistrate in Ajaccio, asking for further information about Sampiero and his times; Chevalier failed to supply it. Many of Corsica's misfortunes have been due to negligence and this is not among the least.[5]

Some well-mannered little boys, descendants, perhaps, of those who could never be trusted not to shoot each other at school, showed me the way from Colomba's house to the parish church. I had been told of a miraculous Virgin kept there, a wooden statue found long ago by fishermen in the gulf of Valinco, floating on the waves. The statue, it is said, was so heavy that they were unable to lift it from the water; nor could any of the people who thronged to see it, until two old men, coming down from Fozzano, raised it without effort onto their shoulders and carried it back to the village. And there the Virgin has remained, the author of many miracles.[6]

She is one of several miracle-working statues said to have been found on the Corsican shores; by fishermen, who in all these tales play a privileged role, in the image of Christ's disciples. Another Virgin, of white marble, was washed up, it is said, on the east coast sands, and she too was mysteriously conveyed into the mountains where she is still venerated today by the people of Cervione. The recurring tale, which calls to mind the myth of Venus rising from the waves, is a Christian variation on a fundamental religious theme. The symbolism is archetypal, the sea being the unconscious realm, the origin of all things, and she who rises from it the universal mother, author of life; a parable of genesis at once more poetic and closer to scientific truth than the megalithic concept of the clay-clotted Earth Goddess procreating and devouring in the underworld.

Mary, mother of Jesus, inherited the sea attributes of Aphrodite, and also, perhaps, of Isis, patroness of mariners, so that in Roman Catholic liturgy she is hailed as Star of the Sea, although her marine associations are unsupported by any biblical authority. Aphrodite was descended from the star-goddesses Syrian Astarte, Akkadian Ishtar, Sumerian Innana; and mother of them all was Tiamat of the Babylonian Epic of Creation, the saltwater deity who before the beginning of time, before the creation of heaven and earth and gods and men, coexisted, mingled and confounded with her freshwater spouse, Apsu.

The Corsican sea-virgins must be among the very last inheritors of this formidable mythical tradition, for both belong to the seventeenth century. A miraculous statue borne on the ocean suggests something numinous and arcane, washed to unearthly ivory tints by the tides. But the figure I saw in the candlelight of the church of Fozzano was mundane and conventional, a plump-faced Virgin posed in the baroque manner with the weight of the body thrown onto one foot and the folds of her cloak draped from the hip. Her garments were gaily painted red and blue and dotted with gilded flowers.

Her legend, like that of her marble counterpart of Cervione, is a product of the Counter-Reformation, unlinked with the local pagan heritage. The ancient lore of Corsica ignores the sea; from the earliest times, it seems, the inhabitants of the island turned their backs on the element surrounding it. They rejected, too, the concept of the sacred mother: when Christianity reached the island the Earth Goddess had long ago been discarded; no memory of her survived to be carried over into the veneration of the Virgin, as is said to have happened in Italy and Spain. The mother of God was introduced to a society wholly dedicated to male heroism, and she gained ground only gradually. Though many mediaeval churches (including two of the Pisan cathedrals) bear her name, the sculpture of the Pisan churches speaks, for preference, of erring Eve.[7] It was the Franciscans, patiently labouring against the harshness of island life, who were her champions. Through their influence her image gradually came to invade the churches: inscrutable in local wood carving; serene, hieratic, in many anonymous altarpieces; sometimes young and lovely but more often matronly in the numberless baroque statues of marble, and wood painted and gilt.

By the seventeenth century her cult had conquered the population; in the eighteenth it assumed a national significance when the rebel leaders, having declared the island independent, solemnly placed the newborn state under the protection of the Immaculate Conception. The Virgin, in fact, was acknowledged queen; her figure was embroidered on the patriots' banners and the *Dio vi Salvi Regina* became the national anthem, or battle song, which can still be heard on ceremonial occasions, its solemn, stirring strains floating above the Corsican crowds.[8] Even the Virgin was never quite dissociated, in the Corsican mind, from war; yet her elevation was one of the great triumphs of the clergy. It consecrated a feminine archetype alien to a people who while insisting on the sexual purity of women also assigned to them the occult, death-dealing powers of *voceratrice* and *mazzere*. And so it is appropriate that she should be portrayed, in local legend, as a merciful stranger come from across the sea.

Fozzano has been given international celebrity by *Colomba*; but the village's claim to distinction once resided in the antithetical figure of the seaborne Virgin. During a plague she was carried to a neighbouring mountain peak, and there, focus for the prayers of the population, she miraculously brought it to an end. Rather surprisingly, the ecclesiastical records suggest that the people of Fozzano were extremely pious, and until the national rebellion split them into two opposing groups, peaceful enough. No murders occurred among them in the first half of the seventeenth century, and only a few in the second, that black period when some nine hundred Corsicans were being killed in vendettas every year.[9]

No doubt they continued to revere their Virgin, to honour her altar with costly gifts, after they became divided by a murderous feud. Corsicans have always managed to reconcile the vendetta with a respect for their religion; piety and violence are among their outstanding characteristics, and these extremes coexist in their nature with only occasional conflicts. Mérimée is true to Corsican psychology when he describes Colomba praying for the rest of her murdered father's soul just before she exhibits his bloodstained shirt to her brother with passionate exhortations to avenge his death. The real Colomba took pride in building a mortuary chapel for her son; perhaps she planned the slaughter of the Durazzo in the presence of the poor little painting of the Last Supper I found in her home. The men of Sartène who dared not go to Mass for fear of meeting their unforgiving, unforgiven enemies probably thought of themselves as good Christians, unfairly victimised. Murder was wrong, as a sin against God; but it might also be a sacred duty to the family. A man with an injury to avenge was therefore obliged to sin, and in so doing he was less guilty than unfortunate.

The clergy opposed this casuistry; in theory always, in practice when they were not compelled by it themselves. If some parish priests were drawn into vendettas, the monks, at least, and the higher ecclesiastics, were earnest propagandists of brotherhood and forgiveness. However badly the Genoese governed Corsica, their bishops certainly laboured conscientiously for the welfare of the people, according to their lights. They varied, of course, in quality; moreover, the Catholic Church had its ups and downs in Corsica as elsewhere, lapses into negligence and worldliness being followed by renewals of effort. The Pisans in the twelfth century, the Franciscans in the thirteenth, lifted the country from near-barbarism; the fourteenth century was a time of crisis and confusion in the Corsican Church, corresponding with heretical movements abroad. But after the Council of Trent, and all through the seventeenth century, the Counter-Reformation made itself felt and did much to offset the defects of the Genoese administration.

Political conflicts put an end to this influence; during the national rebellion the Corsican clergy, having repudiated the Genoese bishops, became less a religious institution than an association of militant patriots. The French, after they conquered Corsica, shocked by the ignorance of the priests, the parasitism of the Franciscans, and irritated by their hostility, did little to improve the quality of the clergy, which after the Revolution fell perhaps to its lowest point of spiritual apathy. But in the 1830s a regeneration was set in motion by the bishop Casanelli d'Istria, a genuinely enlightened Corsican who tirelessly travelled the island on foot and mule to collaborate as peacemaker with Baron Lallemand. Thereafter the Corsican Church settled into respect-worthy ways; the inspiration of a few, the comfort of many, the standby of oppressed women and widows, the last resource of guilt-stricken bandits, the provider of much-loved ceremonies, spectacles, and processions; an abiding but not domineering feature of local life, as it has remained, with its many buildings, ruined, neglected or falling into decrepitude with their ageing congregations.

Too large and far too many for the presentday faithful, the crumbling Corsican churches are monuments of the forceful phases of insular catholicism: the Pisan ascendancy, the Counter-Reformation (there are no Gothic churches in Corsica outside Bonifacio, the transition was straight from Romanesque to baroque). Though they have long since become part of the landscape, so that one can hardly imagine it without them, they all, even the humblest, make a dramatic contrast to the rough stone dwellings of indigenous tradition. Designed in foreign architectural styles – Pisan Romanesque, northern Italian baroque – the work, often, of Italian architects or craftsmen, they are a visual demonstration of the fact that Christianity was a gift from abroad, the only one that had any considerable influence on island life before the bulldozing technology of today.

The parish churches are often products of the Counter-Reformation; like that of Fozzano, a modest example of what one might call 'village baroque'. Vaulted within, severe without, it is redeemed by a recurring felicitous feature of these buildings: a slender detached campanile pierced by superimposed arches and topped with a little domed lantern. The inhabitants subscribed to erect it in the seventeenth century; until then they had depended on the neighbouring Pisan church, Santa-Maria-Assunta of Figaniella, the head church of the district and for a long time the only one.

The Pisans tackled their ecclesiastical mission in Corsica with a vast building programme covering practically the whole island. They proceeded methodically. First they built cathedrals in the towns, or rather in the ruins of the old Roman cities on the coasts. The cities, plagued by malaria and exposed to pirate raids, never recovered. But two of the Pisan edifices have survived: the so-called Canonica, consecrated in 1119, an austere, perfectly proportioned monument stranded in a desolate plain on the site of Roman Mariana, and the cathedral of Nebbio, elegant in pale limestone with its elaborate, enigmatic sculpture, placed in a pastoral setting near the little holiday resort of Saint-Florent.

Later the Pisans sent their skilled craftsmen inland, and a church was built for each of the *pievi*, ecclesiastical administrative units roughly corresponding with the modern 'cantons'. The churches were placed at key points accessible to the scattered rural communities: in the centre of valleys, at the intersection of mule tracks. Most, now, are isolated in the empty countryside on a network of communications long ago superseded; many are pitiable ruins. Eventually, churches were built for individual communities; but many of these, too, have been abandoned with the villages they once served.[10]

Santa-Maria-Assunta of Figaniella is an exception; here a community has grown up round the head church of a *pieve* and survived the centuries. I was luckier than I realised in being able to see a Pisan church, for the first time, by simply driving to its door. Most are far from any road; and I have some acute memories of my searches for them, pushing for hours through cist and myrtle and a broom with vicious thorns, slithering over rocks and stones that danced like boiling water in the heat haze, to be spurred through the last lap of the walk by the sight of my objective rising in insolent serenity above the wicked maquis.

The changes that left these buildings useless and abandoned took place, mainly, in the sixteenth century. Genoese reprisals against the Cinarchesi, and the great rebellions instigated by Sampiero Corso and the French, destroyed hundreds of villages; Barbary pirates wiped out others and depopulated large tracts of the coasts. The inhabitants moved inland, took to living in larger, more compact communities, hill-villages easier to defend. The latter part of the sixteenth century was a time of wholesale rebuilding and reorganisation under the reinstated rule of Genoa, a regime that few welcomed but most were willing to accept. New churches went up to suit the new communities in the contemporary Genoese style; their domes and many-storeyed campanili rose like hothouse plants above the rooftops and the Corsican scene assumed the appearance it has kept to this day.

The rediscovery of the lost Pisan churches meant more to me than locating some neglected mediaeval antiquities: these ruins testify to a forgotten era in Corsica, one more idealistic than the Genoese ascendancy. Only a driving force as vital as mediaeval Christianity could have produced them. However small and remote the parish there was never any skimping of quality. Where only a handful of peasants or shepherds lived, in some rock-girt valley or hidden bay, the church may be no more than a cell-like chapel; yet the construction is always admirable, a *tour de force* in stone.

Though the sites of the churches were chosen for practical reasons, their builders, within a given area, selected spots that would show them to advantage; in a very modest way these unpretentious monuments share with the Greek temples the quality of being harmoniously placed in relation to their setting. Santa-Maria-Assunta of Figaniella stands alone, on a saddle between a craggy eminence and the village, stacked against the adjoining mountainside. It riveted my attention as an object perfectly made. In Corsica one grows accustomed to an extreme roughness in the works of man: houses built of irregular lumps of stone, so that their walls look like vertical crazy pavements; fortifications built into cliffs; shepherds' cabins formed by a single wall blocking the entrance to a rock shelter or cave. Everywhere there is stone, extravagant piles and expanses of stone, and man has struggled to use it without ever quite subjecting it to his will. But here was stone, mastered, transformed: the rectangular slabs of yellowish granite that faced the walls were beautifully shaped and dressed, and meticulously fitted together, edge to edge.

The beauty of the Corsican Pisan churches resides above all in this: the superb, mathematical precision of their masonry. To describe them as Pisan is not to imply any jewel-like richness of design such as radiates from the *Duomo* of the metropolis; in relation to that glittering masterpiece they are paupers. Their builders (in obedience, perhaps, to some official ruling) conformed to a standard utilitarian model, derived from the Roman basilica, which was repeated all over the island almost without variation. These simple buildings had the merit of durability; their massive walls, faced inside and out with ashlar masonry, still stand after some eight centuries, when every house, often, of the near-by communities has gone to earth, leaving no trace.

Yet though the Pisans brought to Corsica only the essentials of their architecture, they were at pains to bestow on even the smallest of them some particles of the imaginative stock of Romanesque art. The decoration is always unostentatious, and related to the structure: bas-reliefs in the semicircular tympanums above doors, on lintels, or archivolts, or framing windows. And nearly always dwarf blind arcades follow the lines of roof and pediment, falling on to small square consoles that are intricately carved. Compact, secretive and highly stylised, this work belongs to the authentic Romanesque tradition.

At Santa-Maria-Assunta of Figaniella the sculpture of the consoles on close inspection proved enchanting. As I moved from one to another to find each little square filled with a design unrelated to its neighbour I had the sensation of turning the pages of an illustrated book. There I saw arrangements of geometric forms – bars and squares and triangles, animal shapes – rams' heads and twisted serpents, as well as human heads, flat, masklike, Mongolian. I was later to meet many such strange faces staring down at me from
127

the eaves of the Corsican–Pisan churches, remote and alien as the ghosts of Asian chieftains turned to stone.

With the Pisans the oriental currents of mediaeval art percolated all over Corsica. Squeezed into corbels and archivolts, the sacred beasts of the ancient middle-eastern civilisations are juxtaposed with the geometric designs of Islam. The exotic imagery that came to Europe even before the Crusades, with the invaders from the steppes, with the Arabs, from Persia and Babylon by way of the Armenian and Byzantine churches, is fixed pell-mell in the Corsican granite. Recurring motifs have distant origins: the pairs of birds and beasts, confronted and back to back, derive from Sassanian Persia, the lions and horses and galloping quadrupeds from the bas-reliefs of the old Mesopotamian kingdoms; a cubistic tree, with its branches pointing at right angles, has its prototype in the Assyrian tree of life. Most if not all, had a symbolic significance in mediaeval Christianity based on interpretations of the Scriptures or the fanciful natural history of the bestiaries;[11] and these allusions cover others, pertaining to the ancient eastern mythologies. Such things and creatures speak not one, but several sign-languages, barely intelligible today; yet it is a vague awareness, surely, of the density of meaning inherent in those forms of reptile and bird, beast and plant, that gives them so disturbing a fascination.

The Corsicans set little store by their antiquities at the time of my first visits to the island. On the whole they are a people more sensitive to words and music than to the visual arts; their appreciation of buildings and objects is, by tradition, functional. A saint's statue, an altarpiece, is valued (like an ikon) for the holiness inherent in it rather than for any aesthetic quality; a church is simply a building used by the population. Paoli himself baffled Johnson and Boswell by his dogmatic assertion of this view at a London dinner party. 'We then fell into a disquisition whether there is any beauty independent of utility,' writes Boswell, 'The General [Paoli] maintained that there was not.'[12]

My driver was obviously chafing to leave while I lingered at the church of Santa-Maria-Figaniella, absorbed in the bewitched world of its sculpture; a world where plant and man and beast and geometric form interpenetrate each other, mask and disguise each other and exchange identities. I tried to interest him. 'I'll admit it's very well finished,' was all he could find to say.

Hastening on to his cousins at Sainte-Lucie-de-Tallano he rushed me back through smiling Fozzano, sullen Arbellara, down into the rampant maquis and over the bridge of the Rizzanese. A few miles inland up the river valley Sainte-Lucie and its satellite hamlets appeared, each clumped on a foothill of a wooded mountainside. The main village dominates these scattered communities; a compact, defensible village that has withstood wars and invasions; in the fifteenth century it was a place of consequence as one of the chief seats of Rinuccio della Rocca. The houses, I observed, were of the type I had grown accustomed to, and fond of: built of huge uneven blocks of granite and roofed with humped, earth-coloured tiles. The square where my driver left me was a

Sainte-Lucie-de-Tallano, seat of Rinuccio della Rocce, who in the fifteenth century fought to free Corsica from Genoese rule. (*Jean Bianchetti*)

The twelfth-century church San Giovanni Battista and its belfry, at Carbini. Two hundred years later the church became the meeting place of a revolutionary sect. (*Louis Bianchetti*)

platform or stage, like that of Sartène; but more spectacular, for the side open to nature – the proscenium – looked out over the tree-tops of a deep, deep valley to a higher mountain range where crimson rock escarpments emerged, perpendicular, from the forests. Nothing in the square was stirring save a fountain; no one was to be seen except a few old men lying fast asleep on stone benches under the planes.

A café proprietor, dozing in a broken wicker armchair, told me that the monastery was locked; in my search for the key I wandered about the silent streets and square vainly questioning drowsy old men until I came to fancy that the entire population had succumbed to a sleeping sickness wafted in from the maquis. Finally, providentially, I ran into a young man, home on holiday from the Continent and thoroughly awake, a descendant of the noble house of Rocca and himself an artist, who promptly produced the key from the parish church. There he showed me a marble bas-relief commissioned – according to an inscription – in 1498, by his ancestor, Rinuccio della Rocca; in Florence, to judge by its style. A Virgin with the soft, unawakened face of a child, looks down through lowered lids, as though dreaming, at the infant Christ lying across her sturdy knees, who seems like a little brother only a few years younger than she. This lovely sculpture was Rinuccio's gift to the Franciscan monastery he had endowed at Sainte-Lucie six years before.[13]

The last of the Cinarchesi rebels, Rinuccio stands out as a hypnotic figure in the turgid annals of his age. Though not a great man, nor even admirable, he was moulded on a scale that disarms criticism. Warrior, aristocrat and courtier, sincerely devout and an enlightened patron of the arts, he lived boldly, pursued large ambitions; he died, like so many Corsican leaders, alone, rejected, a failure.

Possessed of a vast domain that covered most of the south of the island, at first he was an ally of the Genoese, married into one of their leading families, the Catanei, and aided them in crushing the formidable rebellion of his cousin, Gian' Paolo da Leca. But in 1502, after Gian' Paolo had been defeated and exiled, he turned on his protectors, fired by the recurrent ill-fated dream of the Cinarchesi: to rule Corsica as an autonomous principality. The war lasted, on and off, through nearly a decade. Three times Rinuccio was worsted and forced to leave the island: he had to accept terms, to withdraw to Genoa; he travelled to Sardinia and Spain in unsuccessful quest of reinforcements (Aragon was no longer prepared to back Corsican revolts); he lost his eldest son and two cousins, who were coldly executed by the Genoese. Only the personal intervention of Louis XII of France, who as temporary ruler of Genoa granted him an amnesty, rescued him from the consequences of his third, unsuccessful rebellion.

One might think that having been spared – almost miraculously spared – prison or the scaffold, Rinuccio would have resigned himself to an honourable retirement. By then his partisans had been massacred or exiled by the Genoese, scattered and ruined; Andrea Doria, later admiral of international renown, had earned advancement by his scorched-earth tactics in the Sartenais:

'what is left of this region barely allows one to think it was once inhabited', he reported to his superiors. Yet in 1510 Rinuccio landed once again in Corsica; he had appealed for support to 'nearly all the princes of Christendom'; but only eight men had been found to join him in the mad venture. His vassals, one reads in a contemporary chronicle, received him 'with tears of joy'; but none were willing to take up arms for him. Genoese troops were sent in search of him; this time a humiliatingly small force of fifty men. Entirely abandoned, Rinuccio was hunted 'like a wild animal' through the maquis. Peasants, exasperated by Genoese brutalities, killed him: according to the chronicler he defended himself to the end with all the valour of which he had given proof during his life.[14]

So fell the last of the Cinarchesi heroes, a victim not so much of Genoese tyranny as of his own disproportionate ambitions, suicidal ambitions such as often possess the descendants of very old and illustrious families, born too late and conscious of being the last of their kind. With his death the power of the Cinarchesi was crushed for good. The role of national liberator thereafter fell to men of less exalted origin: the shepherd's son Sampiero Corso a generation later; in the eighteenth century Giacinto and Pasquale Paoli, among other notables of the north.

The monastery Rinuccio donated to the Franciscans stands on a grassy platform above the village. The church is still intact; but the monastic buildings are sadly dilapidated and deformed, their high-arched cloisters blocked with crude masonry and rough patched farmyard doors.

'One feels so despairing!' my companion, Rinuccio's descendant, exclaimed. 'Everything in Corsica goes to ruin and no one cares.' We had paused under the elm tree in front of the church door. Seen from above Sainte-Lucie looked like a densely inhabited island, the surrounding maquis a dark rough sea. Other, smaller villages appeared on distant mountainsides, like rocks where sea birds rest or ships labouring through the waves.

Inside, the church was derelict. Blinded by the gloom I stumbled over worm-eaten planks, broken glass and the tatters of paper flowers. Damp had eaten into the walls like a gangrene; only the high altar, a billowing Genoese production in polychrome inlaid marble with angels' heads as caryatids, had resisted decay. It is of a type much favoured by the Franciscans; incongruously, I have always felt, though one knows that they took pride in the luxury of their churches while continuing to live in bare poverty. But now these opulent decoration pieces, forgotten in mouldering buildings and ruins, seem an object lesson in the vanity of worldly goods, even those acquired in a spirit of renunciation.

Grumbling, my companion guided me through the debris, showed me the finely carved choir stalls, sacristy cupboard and lectern, all smothered in dust and rubble. 'But this is even more disgraceful,' he said, pointing to a side-chapel. I found myself looking at a beautiful and compelling face; pale, elongated, marked with vertical furrows like so many Corsican faces, and framed in long black hair. It was the face of St John, in a painting of the Crucifixion

130

with the Virgin and Mary Magdalene grouped beside the cross. Behind them stretched a deep landscape with bushy little trees dotted on hills, a castle flying brave red flags, a river where ducks swam; this lively rustic scene cruelly emphasised the tragedy of the mourners isolated on a bare hillside in their pain. Propped against another rotting wall was a second picture, in the same manner, a complete altarpiece in which an austere, pensive Virgin, surrounded by lean-faced saints, sat regally enthroned with her child beneath a scarlet canopy upheld by angels in flight.

Though pitiably damaged by damp these paintings had an enchantment that transcended their degradation. But who had painted them, and when? Where had they come from, and how had they reached this obscure mountain village? In their pictorial conventions and general feeling they appeared Spanish rather than Italian, with Flemish inflexions in the background landscapes. Their style was transitional: gestures were restrained, expressions withdrawn, set in a tender dreaming melancholy; the figures, neither symbols nor yet fully incarnated human beings, hovered on the confines between the mediaeval and Renaissance worlds.

My curiosity about their origin was later to involve me in a quest as intricate and stormy as any I undertook in Corsica, though in the end the most rewarding. It sent me to Spain; it lured me through art histories and monographs. It sent me to Sardinia, encouraged by some lines in an Italian guidebook which attributed the pictures to one Master of Castle Sardo, a Spanish painter (in all probability) who emigrated to Sardinia towards the end of the fifteenth century and worked for the Franciscans in the town that gave him his name.

This attribution proved correct: the paintings of Sainte-Lucie are undoubtedly the work of the Master, or rather of his workshop; for the altarpiece at Sainte-Lucie is by the same hand as a Virgin and Child (now in the Sassari museum), by one of his pupils; the two Virgins are in fact almost identical. The Italian art historian Carlo Aru dates this panel to the first years of the sixteenth century: precisely the period when Rinuccio della Rocca was visiting Sardinia in search of reinforcements. Advised, perhaps, by the Franciscans of Sainte-Lucie, he must have taken time off from his war diplomacy to commission this pair of paintings for the monastic church; the Crucifixion, superior to the altarpiece in quality, is probably by the Master himself.[15]

During these researches I had often had the sensation of conjuring two linked figures out of the fifteenth century: the anonymous Hispano-Sardinian painter of Castel Sardo (resuscitated by Aru as an artist and a man), and Rinuccio himself, whom I now came to see in a new light. The tempestuous Corsican warlord, I realised, was a true prince of the Renaissance, a discriminating lover of the arts. In this he was untypical: soldiers, statesmen and adventurers, churchmen and monks and ascetics and occasionally saints, the Corsicans have hardly explored the realm of manmade beauty that lies between the poles of violence and abnegation. Rinuccio was an exception; the only noteworthy art patron before Fesch and the Bonaparte. He can now be remembered as such; for after much writing of articles and letters and many urgent appeals to the authorities I eventually, against all hope, had the satisfaction of seeing the two paintings expertly restored under the supervision of Jean Leblanc. When they were hung, for a time, in the Fesch museum, they serenely held their own beside accepted masterpieces.

This sequel was of course quite unforeseen as I stood in wonder before the forgotten panels with Rinuccio's artist descendant, grieving for their neglect. When we left the church the magical sunset hour was near. Old men were resting in the deep porch of a side entrance smoking their pipes; others were stabling their donkeys in the ruined cloisters. Down in the village the inhabitants, risen from their interminable siesta, were sitting on the parapet along the open side of the square, watching the mountains being transformed by the alchemy of the setting sun. The escarpments of the opposite range had assumed a new, three-dimensional magnificence; their crimson rocks glowed brighter, rifted by blue shadows. The forested valley had become a golden pool; a pink roof, formerly unnoticeable, gleamed like a treasure in its depths. It belonged, I learned, to the Pisan church of St Jean-Baptiste, the head church of the *pieve*, placed in this isolated spot to be equidistant to the many scattered villages.[16] But this was not the moment to visit it, for my taxi driver had already found me and was pressing me to leave.

'You'd better hurry,' he said, 'or we won't get back to Sartène in time for supper.' I told him again that I was staying in Carbini. He chuckled. 'That hotel's a joke, I keep telling you. They're barbarians over there.' Then suddenly, to my relief, he jumped into the car and started the engine. 'No matter!' he cried with fatalistic glee as I hurried in beside him, 'we can but see!' And he stamped on the accelerator and shot up and out of the village.

9 HERETICS AND REVOLUTIONARIES

The desolate interior – the Giovannali – a Franciscan heresy –
a Corsican revolution – village welfare states – Carbini in
decay

THE drive to Carbini took me, for the first time, into the deep interior, showed me the magnitude of its desolation. Above Sainte-Lucie-de-Tallano the scenery was breathtaking. Thick maquis and holm oak covered all the valley running parallel with the road, and the mountains beyond that rose tier above tier to the south, as though drawn by an imaginative child who piles outline above outline until he has filled the paper to the top. I stared; the driver commented: 'The soil's good enough but the people don't bother to cultivate it. Why should they? There's no one to buy anything they grow.'

I could understand their discouragement. Any but the stoutest pioneer, I thought, might well be defeated by such a country. Extravagantly virile, and huge in scale, it looked hostile to human effort. The very sun, now sinking at the valley's end, had a threatening quality; its light was so densely golden as to seem charged with fire. The sea was lost behind crowded peaks; I felt dwarfed, engulfed, as though penetrating a continent as yet barely explored. Even later, when the Corsican interior became familiar to me, I never quite overcame this sensation of being swallowed by the landscape, nor failed to feel relief when I glimpsed between mountain masses the distant, familiar sea. It brought me the kind of reassurance experienced by ships' passengers when they first sight shore.

We skirted Levie, an improbably large village, gaunt in the wilderness, then branched on to the new road to Carbini; new only by local standards for it badly needed repair. Headlong we plunged into the darkening valley; mountain oak surged overhead, the air was chill and dank as in a cavern. The sun had set as we began to grind up the further slope. 'What a road!' cried the driver, crashing over potholes. 'No one uses it! Why should anyone want to go to Carbini? You won't want to stay there; that I can guarantee.'

We were swerving at sharp angles between walls of high maquis. I was beginning to imagine Carbini as an African village, a cluster of huts in a jungle, when abruptly we emerged into a cropped, boulderstrewn pasture, pale in the wan light that lasts, here, so short a time between the blaze of sun and moon. A church and campanile jutted out of the earth, stark and flawless; a perfect little Pisan church and a three-storeyed campanile, so well preserved

133

that they looked like an architect's models accidentally dropped on to this barren heath from a plane. They stood close together to one side of the road; on the other a magnified pile of boulders or small rock mountain shot into the sky with a cross on its topmost crag. This was the church where the heretics – the Giovannali – are said to have celebrated their unholy rites, where at night, the candles extinguished, they took part in unbridled orgies without regard for the distinctions of sex. 'They did everything,' the driver said with dark disapproval, 'but they paid for it. You see that peak, with the cross? That's where they died. They defended themselves there against the army of the Pope until they were all killed in the rocks, every one of them, the women and children too.' It was easy to believe the popular tale in the face of this harsh, pitiless scene.

Between belfry and peak lay the village, low and mean; a double row of rough stone cabins facing a street strewn with loose stones. My belief in the Hotel des Nations withered. 'You see!' said the driver. 'Nevertheless, we will enquire.'

He slowed down as we jolted over the littered road. Peasants, all old, the women in black, the men bearded, stared at us, silent and motionless, from their doors. Most of the men were carrying guns.

Before we could make any enquiries a young man in unsuitable town clothes sprang on to the running board and thrust his head through the window. 'Where are you going?' he hissed. 'To the Hotel des Nations,' I answered. 'There's no hotel here,' he declared. 'There must be,' I said. 'I've reserved a room.' 'You're wasting your time,' he retorted, 'the hotel no longer exists. It closed today.' 'I'll go all the same,' I told him, 'will you please tell me where it is?' 'At the other end of the village, that's where it was!' he ungraciously answered. 'Drive on,' I said to the driver. 'We will continue!' he cried, and accelerated so suddenly as to jerk the young man off the car. 'Remember, you can count on me,' he added, with unexpected chivalry.

We banged ahead over the stones; dogs barked, chickens and children fled; old, old men stared, expressionless, armed. We were nearly out of the village and my driver was again saying 'You see!' when one of the very last houses caught my eye. It was a three-storeyed house built in the style of a fairly rich man's villa on the French Riviera some fifty years ago. The Hotel des Nations, without a doubt. We drew up by a wrought-iron gate with oriental porcelain lions on the gate posts. An elderly man, scarecrow thin, wearing a Chinese cotton jacket and coolie hat scurried out to meet us. He gripped my hand with a hand that was all bones. 'Thank God you've come,' he said.

Nimble as a bird he seized my suitcases and darted indoors. The driver and I followed him into a dark hall, where, skipping between luggage and furniture, he was lighting a candle. 'The electricity! Ah the electricity!' he muttered. 'Smashed! Wrecked! The glasses broken! The pillows thrown into the maquis! But never fear, with willpower we shall succeed!' And without further explanation he scampered upstairs, a suitcase in either hand. I followed, followed by the driver. We found ourselves in a bedroom full of new veneered furniture brightly lit by a naked overhead bulb. 'Ah here it works!' the old man cried, switching the light on and off till my eyes dazzled. 'And here too, just as it should!' He had slipped into the adjoining bathroom, white tiled, equipped with chromium-plated gadgets. In the bath lay a very old felt hat. 'All new! Perfectly new!' he announced, and turned the shower full on so that I cowered against the wall to escape a wetting. 'There's been money spent here,' the chauffeur mumbled. 'Come, let us have a drink, my friends,' said our host.

The electricity was inoperative in the sitting-room downstairs, and it was by the glow of candlelight that I first came to know its contents. There were many things to look at; enough to convince one for good of the undesirability of laying up treasure on earth. There was a very large incense burner: a brass sphere poised on the head of an agonising brass dragon with other dragons clinging to its scales, while yet another straddled the sphere, ridden by an emaciated demon. There was an old upright piano and a new glass-fronted cabinet. On the piano-top stood a white china figure of a girl wearing only a ballet skirt, and, for some reason, boxing gloves. In the cabinet was a white porcelain cat and a Chinese sage, a herd of soapstone elephants and a large Chinese junk carved in horn.

Our host disappeared to fetch the drinks. The driver lowered himself gingerly into one of the armchairs upholstered in railway-carriage plush. 'I'm bound to say it's fairly clean,' he said.

The drink was Black and White whisky; something rare in Corsican villages at that time. 'I had it sent from Ajaccio, twelve cases of it, enough for all the tourists who'll be coming this summer,' the old man explained. 'It's quite nice,' said the driver, and then, as though unable to cope with the situation another minute, without warning he rose to leave. As I paid him he slipped me an envelope. 'That's my address. Remember, if you need me I'll always come,' he said in a stage whisper.

My host had left me to supervise dinner. Clearly I was the only guest. The silence was oppressive, and as my eyes travelled from the red and beige cubistic wallpaper hung with landscapes of Indo-China painted almost entirely in black and orange to the elephants and dragons and the half-naked girl with boxing gloves, and then to the black patches of the uncurtained windows opening on to an invisible landscape, I longed for some sound to break a tension that was becoming unbearable. It came: the roar of a human voice. Or rather it was the sound a human being may make when he has lost consciousness of his humanity and has forgotten that other human beings may hear him. The sound was without words, a howl of naked emotion and blind distress. For a moment it ceased, during which the silence was as startling as the sound had been; then it came again, nearer, louder, rose to a shriek of pain, sunk to a hopeless groan and reverted to the original full-throated bellowing. Evidently someone was being murdered; not neatly shot with one of those guns I had seen on the way to the hotel, but tortured to death slowly.

During a lull in the howling my host appeared. 'Dinner is served,' he said in a fair imitation of butler English. I felt I would be spoiling his act by referring to the drama outside, so I followed him into the dining-room without comment. Two young girls with wholesome country faces were standing to attention at the candlelit mahogany banqueting table. They served me an elaborate meal accompanied by harassed instructions from my host. 'No! Not that soup bowl! That's the common kitchen bowl. The salt! It must be served in the silver salt cellar, I have a beautiful one, it's not possible they've taken that too! No no! Take the plate back and warm it; chicken must be served on a hot plate.' Frantically he intercepted one of the girls with a loaf of bread in her hand. 'Stop! stop!' he entreated her, 'the bread must be served, sliced, in the little breadbasket. What, it's not there! My little breadbasket! Did they dare throw it away?' He seemed really stricken.

The story came out while he was looking for the breadbasket. He had only recently come back from Indo-China, the girls told me; he was a very successful man. The house had been built before his return, for his retirement. But the architect had exceeded his specifications and so he had decided to turn it into a hotel. The house was large enough, there were at least six rooms with bathrooms, the girls told me in awed tones, but there was no one in the village who could work for him, or at least no one who knew how to work 'his way'. So he had engaged a waiter and a cook from Ajaccio. There had been discussions, disputes, from the first; and then the day before I, the first guest, was due to arrive, the two of them had broken the glasses, fused the lights, thrown the pillows – and apparently the breadbasket – into the maquis and walked out. But they were still in the village; the bus passed only twice a week and they had no other means of getting away. The girls had come in to help; they were sisters; their parents owned a café.

I suggested that the young man who had boarded the car might be one of the ex-servants. 'Why yes, that would be the younger one,' they agreed. We were discussing the matter when the old man returned, without the breadbasket. 'Ah yes! It's the cook!' he said. 'You see what they're capable of! Thieves! Gangsters!' His voice rose in hysteria. 'But I'm better off without them. They might have poisoned me! Killed me!' 'Yes, that's possible,' the girls chorused, undismayed. 'Gangsters!' he shouted, then smiled. 'But they've not stolen the coffee. I found it just now. I'll make you coffee immediately; it will be excellent, it comes from Indo-China.'

The howling, which had been a background noise to our conversation, had come closer. It was interspersed, now, by a battering on shutters and doors; our shutters, our doors. Was it the cook, waging a war of nerves on his former employer? Or a victim of that disreputable pair? Or was a longstanding local vengeance being horribly, abominably consummated? I had had as much as I could stand. 'What is it? Who is it? What's happening? You must explain!' I cried, stupidly getting to my feet.

'Oh that!' one of the girls answered negligently. 'That's our drunkard.' 'An unfortunate,' muttered my host, and left the room. 'He does it almost every night,' the other girl explained, 'he starts soon after sunset.' 'He goes round banging on the shutters and doors,' said her sister, smiling indulgently, 'we all know him, we laugh at him and calm him down when he gets too excited.
136

He's very nice really.' 'And very cultured,' the other girl added, 'and quite handsome, although of course now he is losing his intelligence and his looks.'

'But need he drink like that?' I asked. I was aghast at this baldly stated tragedy.

'It's because of his pension,' she replied. 'He was in the army, that was his profession. But he was discharged because he was ill; an affair of the lungs. The army pays him the maximum disability pension. He touches a considerable monthly sum.'

'But need he drink?' I insisted. 'What else can he do?' she said. 'He needn't work, and we've no distractions here; no cinema, nothing but the café. He can't sit all day long in the café and not drink.'

'We would be very unhappy if we stayed here all the time,' the other girl told me. 'We only come home for holidays. The rest of the year we are studying in Sartène. When we pass our exams we shall become schoolteachers.' 'We are specialising in science,' her sister explained, 'that's the subject that interests us most.'

I felt badly let down. Ever since my arrival in Carbini I had been aware of a sinister tension; loaded with tragedy, so I thought. But here was no tragedy: an elderly retired colonial was having servant trouble, a discharged soldier was blind drunk, a couple of schoolgirls were chattering about their exams. I was suddenly aware of an immense fatigue. The drunkard was still at large, howling intermittently and banging on windows and doors, when despite the strong black coffee and the absence of pillows I fell asleep in my brand new bed.

When I woke up Carbini seemed far from sinister. Before I opened my eyes I was conscious of the gurgling of streams and the pure keen nip of the mountain air; then I saw brilliant sunlight piercing the shutters. From the window at the back of the house I looked down on a grassy valley, interlaced with sparkling brooks, dotted with fruit trees, patched with plots of bright green maize and beans. On the opposite slope chestnut trees shaded golden bracken.

After breakfast – which took a long time to come – my host offered to show me the church. Together we paced down the stony street in the hard sunlight. He had discarded his oriental clothes for an expensive businessman's suit. The walk, I realised, was a gesture of defiance to the hotel-wreckers, perhaps to the village as a whole. I felt glad I had put on a clean dress.

Despite the anticlimax of the previous night I was again aware of an ominous ambience in this village. People came out of every house to watch us pass: old men in worn corduroys, old women in black cotton, a few younger men in shabby jerseys and slacks. The average age seemed very high, the population wretchedly poor. The houses were not of the tall fortress type I had seen elsewhere in the Sartenais, but low hovels; their doors opened straight into rooms more than usually bare. A few people – but not the majority – came up to shake hands. The rest just stared. With all eyes fixed on me I felt like a prisoner being led to public execution.

The village petered out in a clutter of pigsties at the foot of the rocks where the Giovannali had been killed. Church and campanile rose in magnificent contrast from a ground littered with stone crosses and stones. Beyond, vistas of maquis-covered mountains rolled mile on mile to the soaring peaks of Bavella.

Silhouetted against this tremendous backdrop the campanile was something one would go far to see. A square tower, very slender for its height, it is pierced by three storeys of twin arches, the bottom storey being placed more than half way up, so that it seems like a fabulous plant with a very long stem, thrusting towards the sky. The church, of unusually dark granite, is impeccable in its finish and proportions.[1]

My host showed me the foundations of another, rather smaller church, a yard or two away. As I already knew from Prosper Mérimée (who saw it when its walls were still standing), it was known as San Quilico and had been built in the same style. 'They say that's where the Giovannali met for their shameful rites,' my host told me. 'You know, of course, what they did; they used to extinguish the candles and take part in the most outrageous orgies. Men with women, women with women, men with men! After they were defeated and killed the church was left to fall into ruin. No one would go near it; it had been irremediably profaned! Or that's what I've heard. But they also say the heretics met in the other church, St Jean – San Giovanni – and that's why they're called the Giovannali. But if so, why was St Quilico abandoned and St Jean preserved? Ah, there's so much we shall never know! There are practically no records of the heresy, and can you wonder? It was the most disgraceful episode in all our tragic history. By the grace of God the heretics were destroyed; nothing of the kind has been heard of here since then, of that I can assure you. But even so, the people are very far from being good Christians. Look at those tombs! All neglected! No enclosure! Anyone can walk over the dead. We need a priest, but we've only one who comes from Levie to say Mass from time to time. It's a disgrace to leave us without a priest! This used to be an important place, the head village of the *pieve*. But now we're entirely abandoned! No one cares what becomes of us! We live and die and no one cares!'

His voice was tinged with hysteria, as always happened, I had noticed, when he reached a climax of his emotions. With a gesture of despairing helplessness he squatted on a stone. I sat on another beside him; a cloud of blue butterflies, the only carefree creatures I had seen in Carbini, fluttered above the graves. I reflected that when St Quilico was still standing this group of Pisan buildings must have looked superb. But why, I wondered, had two churches been built here, close together, in a village which must always have been small, even though it was the capital of a *pieve*? It was hardly likely that one of them had been built by the notorious Giovannali, for the heresy had lasted only a few years in the mid-fourteenth century and the churches were surely considerably older. The contradictory local traditions retailed by my excitable host only added to my confusion.

I questioned him; he repeated what he knew about the Giovannali; but he

138

had nothing to add to what I had already gathered from the taxi-driver and the guide book. And that in fact represented the sum of current information on the subject at this time. It was derived from local tradition and a passage in a chronicle written more than a century after the events. The chronicler describes the Giovannali as members of a sect formed in Carbini around 1354, open to both women and men. They held their possessions in common, women and children included; they practised peculiar penances; they assembled in the church at night to take part in superstitious rites and 'disgusting' orgies. Their leaders were a pair of noblemen. Polo and Arrigo, illegitimate brothers of the local seigneur of Attalla (Tallano). Thwarted in their political ambitions they took command of the sect, which spread rapidly, not only in the south of the island but beyond the mountains to the north and east. The Pope (then in Avignon) excommunicated the heretics and sent troops to destroy them. Corsicans hostile to their movement joined the crusade; the Giovannali were attacked and defeated at Alesani, in the north-east of the island, the survivors hunted to death in the maquis.[2]

Even then the story struck me as unconvincing, and certainly incomplete. The accusation of sexual orgies told one little about heresy; such accusations have been made at all periods against heretics of all kinds. And how had this vigorous movement originated in remote Carbini? And why had the heretics entrenched themselves at Alesani, at the other end of the island?

These questions chafed my mind whenever I thought of the Giovannali; yet I hardly hoped to find out much more about them. No one in Corsica was inclined to study the heresy, and such matters are strange to me. Moreover there are few documents referring to Corsica in the fourteenth century. None the less, by examining the few that are available (notably those relating to the excommunication of the sect, preserved in the episcopal archives of Pisa), and by following up the clues they provided, I did come to learn something about the Giovannali. The total picture, assembled from various sources,[3] was certainly still incomplete; but it was sufficient to enable one to understand that the movement was no irresponsible local outbreak, but was closely linked with contemporary social and religious conflicts in Europe and with a revolution that decided the history of the island.

The heresy was not peculiar to Corsica; nor did it spring up spontaneously in Carbini. The Giovannali were no more and no less than members of the Third Order of St Francis. Their fraternity was founded in Carbini by a certain Ristoro, a Corsican, with the authorisation of two members of the Third Order living in Marseilles, his superiors in the hierarchy of the organisation. They were called Iohannis, and Iohanne; the name Giovannali may have been derived from that of either of these two men.

The Third Order was a popular and extremely influential creation of the outstandingly humane genius of St Francis. It was open (as it still is) to all men and women, married or single, who were attracted to his ideals. They took no vows, but engaged themselves to observe certain moral and religious disciplines. By this institution the saint's teaching rapidly spread outside the monastic communities to permeate the mass of the people. When Ristoro founded the fraternity of Carbini the Third Order no doubt already counted many adherents in Corsica (as is still true today).

The Franciscans had by then nine monasteries in the island, founded in the first wave of enthusiasm for their Order during and just after the lifetime of the saint. Two were at Bonifacio, the remaining six in the north; there were as yet none in the Sartenais. Carbini must have appealed to Ristoro as a place where a fraternity would be welcome to the Franciscan authorities but which was none the less remote enough to escape close supervision. The village had a traditional importance in Corsican religious life. According to the researches of Geneviève Moracchini-Mazel the second Pisan church, St Quilico, was a baptistry; one of several built in the interior in the course of the Pisan evangelising campaign. The creation of a Franciscan fraternity in this old missionary centre evidently met with official approval. The Bishop of Aléria (in whose diocese Carbini was situated), himself attended the inaugural meeting. A historian of Corsica states that a third of the inhabitants joined the fraternity: sixty women and forty men.[4]

But they soon gave rise to scandal. For this congregation was dedicated to a peculiar, heretical creed. From the documents of Pisa one learns that in 1353 the Bishop of Aléria excommunicated the fraternity, that Ristoro appealed to the Archbishop of Pisa, that the Archbishop upheld his protest and ordered the Bishop of Aléria to lift the sentence. But Ristoro was excommunicated by both the Pope and the Franciscan Order that same year. Most regrettably, the documents never describe the heresy of which he was accused. The much-tried Bishop of Aléria refers to him as 'the pestiferous Ristoro', 'corrupter of the people', fulminates against his 'monstrous and superstitious conventicle', but without ever indicating what these superstitions were.

Fortunately there are other sources from which one can infer the nature of the heresy. Ristoro had formed the fraternity of Carbini with the backing of a prominent member of the Third Order in Marseilles; the project it seems, had taken shape when he was himself in that town. Now the contemporary inquisitor Bernard Gui tells one that at precisely this period a heresy had developed in the Third Order of St Francis in Provence. The heretics were known as the Beguins, and styled themselves Poor Brothers of Penitence. Between 1318 and 1352 more than a hundred of their members were condemned by the Inquisition and burnt to death. One may imagine that Ristoro moved to Corsica to avoid persecution; at all events there can be no doubt that his fraternity at Carbini owed allegiance to the same ideas.

These were certainly calculated to incur the wrath of the ecclesiastical establishment. The creed of the Beguins was based on the apparently blameless cult of 'absolute', 'evangelical' poverty: since Christ and His disciples had renounced possessions, to own nothing, either individually or in common, was the true Christian life, the path to salvation. With this doctrine they were merely repeating the teaching of St Francis in all its pristine rigour.

140

But the Church of the day, with its wealthy, worldly prelates, its ample landed property and sumptuous buildings, and above all its immense political power, was very far from following the Franciscan ideal. In the opinion of the Poor Brothers of Penitence the Church was the Whore of Babylon, the Pope the Anti-Christ, a ravening beast of the forest, hungry for the blood of the poor. Their beliefs included an interpretation of the Apocalypse according to which the 'carnal Church', the 'great prostitute', would shortly be destroyed in a cataclysmic war. Nearly all the men of Christendom would perish, except a body of the elect, which would include themselves. On them would descend the light of the Holy Spirit, and they would establish the true, humble, spiritual Church on earth. Such, in broad outline, were the ideas of the Beguins, who lived together in 'houses of poverty', condemned manual labour and supported themselves mainly by begging.

Their heresy was a vigorous, popular offshoot of an extremely important religious movement that rent the Franciscan Order (and indeed the whole Christian world) for some two centuries after the death of the saint. St Francis, with the supreme fearlessness of a revolutionary, had put into practice his ideal of 'evangelical poverty', in his own life, and in the communities he founded. But after his death the Order split into two parties: the Spirituals, who upheld his tenets in their original severity, and the Conventuals, who sought to mitigate the austerity of the rule. The Spirituals defended their views with extreme selfless heroism; but they were outnumbered. It is very saddening to learn how these men who were guilty of nothing worse than voluntary destitution were hounded and persecuted, chained in dungeons for years on end, tortured and burnt at the stake before crowds of jeering friars of their own Order. Their original resistance centres were Tuscany and Provence; but their movement was broken in Provence by 1318 when four of their leaders were sent to the stake in Marseilles. Their ideas were however kept alive in this area, in vulgarised form, by the Beguins of the Third Order, ignorant violent people who inherited all their zeal with little of their enlightenment. But they too were heroic and died for their beliefs.

Throughout their persecutions Spirituals and Beguins derived great support and courage from the prophetic writings of Joachim da Fiore, a Cistercian abbot of Calabria who died in 1202, when St Francis was still in search of his vocation. Joachim, whom Dante places in the second circle of glorified souls in Paradise, has been described as a visionary upon whose fantastic and elaborate speculations men based their hopes of a new and better age.[5] He believed that the history of the world was divided into three periods: first the Age of the Father, or of the Old Testament, the time of servitude and fear; secondly the Age of the Son, or of the New Testament, a time of partial enlightenment, and thirdly and lastly the Age of the Holy Spirit, which would come into being after the destruction of the Anti-Christ. In this final period of the world love and peace would everywhere prevail, and a spiritual understanding of the Scriptures would be given to all men by the preaching of an order of barefooted monks.

Not unnaturally the Franciscans, and in particular the Spirituals, were tempted to identify themselves with the barefooted monks destined to save mankind. Joachim's prophecies seemed to the victimised Spirituals a promise of imminent victory over their adversaries. To the unlettered, aggressive Beguins his vision was nothing less than intoxicating. He had provided them with a theory of the predetermined course of history charged with a revolutionary message beside which that of Karl Marx seems pale.

From the first the Franciscan doctrine had struck hard blows at the feudal system. Wealthy noblemen had given their possessions to the poor and joined the austere Franciscan communities. The Third Order, which affected a far greater proportion of the population, challenged, directly, the authority of the feudal lords, for the Tertiaries – first conscientious objectors – undertook to refuse to make vows of allegiance or to accept military service. In fact the Franciscan rule of life amounted to a formidable passive rebellion, sanctioned by divine guidance, against wealth and worldliness, class distinctions, privilege, war. The heretical Spirituals and their even more extreme disciples, the Beguins, represented the revolutionary left wing of the movement. By their ideas, their writings and the conduct of their lives they indicted not only the contemporary Church, but the very foundations, the essential values of European society.

In Corsica, as nowhere else, the forces of revolution triumphed, though at the cost of their spiritual content. The ideas of the Beguins, introduced with the fraternity Ristoro founded at Carbini, rapidly gained support. One can understand why. The cult of poverty would naturally appeal to a people which was by condition poor; the doctrine of equality and community of possessions corresponded with immemorial insular custom. Diodorus Siculus describes the Corsicans as shepherds and food-gatherers who owned their livestock individually but used the resources of their land in common. This arrangement persisted, evolved. The chronicler Giovanni della Grossa speaks of self-administrating communities, from the eleventh century, existing alongside the seigneurial domains. They were organised according to a 'popular and communal system', what he terms 'the popular regime'. The system seems to have been based on very ancient usage; probably it represented the basic Corsican social pattern. Most of the seigneurs had in fact been lifted to power by the communities, elected as chiefs or magistrates by popular vote. Once elected, they endeavoured to make their office permanent and hereditary. But their position was always insecure. The chronicler relates how time and again seigneurs who abused their authority were dethroned by their own subject, who thereupon reinstituted the 'popular regime'. The Corsican seigneurial system was in fact merely a product, or rather a deformation, of a primordial egalitarian collective organisation of society which the people never lost sight of and were always ready to resume.[6]

Something on these lines must have been attempted by the Giovannali of Carbini; their movement implied social as well as religious upheaval. According to the chronicler they held their possessions in common: by this is meant, presumably, their livestock and the land, although the land lay within the domains of the seigneur of Attalla (Tallano). When the two illegitimate brothers of the lord of Attalla took command of the sect their action amounted to a rebellion, political no less than religious. The accusation of sexual orgies can be dismissed. The work of della Grossa was revised by two later chroniclers, in which form it has been published in French translation. An earlier, unrevised text makes no mention of such excesses; this lurid tale is a sixteenth-century interpolation to be attributed to a chronicler who was a member of the clergy.[7]

The rest of the story can be pieced together from other sources. Armed and militant, the Giovannali advanced northwards across the island, attracting recruits as they went. At Alesani, in 1354, they stormed and seized a monastery. The attack was directed against the orthodox Franciscans who were their immediate superiors, the monastery of Alesani being then the only Franciscan foundation in the large, sprawling diocese of Aléria. Two monks, who prayed earnestly for the preservation of the monastery, were killed; they are honoured in Corsican religious history as martyrs. The Giovannali remained in possession of the monastery till 1362, when Pope Urban V organised the crusade that destroyed them. During those eight years they had time to spread their doctrines all over the surrounding country.[8]

The importance of their campaign becomes clear when one knows that at precisely this period a popular revolution broke out in the same area, a revolution that determined the pattern of Corsican history and society. According to Giovanni della Grossa, around 1358 the inhabitants of the *Diqua dai Monti* elected as their chief one Sambocuccio d'Alando, a man of the people but 'full of valour'. Under his leadership they took to arms 'with such impetuosity and resolution' that they swept the country, defeated the seigneurs and seized and destroyed their castles. These events were taking place at exactly the same period when the Giovannali were triumphantly installed at Alesani, besides other points in the *Diqua dai Monti*, preaching community of possessions and the equality of men.

The revolution was a crisis of mounting resentment against seigneurial tyranny. Corsica had not, it is true, experienced the full weight of the feudal system as operating in continental Europe. Serfdom, and the various restraints of the manorial system, seem to have been unknown. The traditional independent spirit of the village communities, with constant threats of uprisings and a return to the 'popular regime', had acted as checks on abuses of power. Menaced from below, the seigneurs were also, at different times, controlled from above; by the government of the Pisans, and of Sinucello della Rocca.

But the early fourteenth century was, precisely, a period when superior control was in abeyance. The Pisans had retired after their defeat by Genoa in 1284; Sinucello had died in a Genoese prison. Claimed by rival foreign overlords, the island belonged to none. The kings of Aragon had done little to assert their rights; when, around 1347 the Genoese sent an expedition to

Corsica to impose their sovereignty it was frustrated by the Black Death and they had to content themselves with holding Calvi and Bonifacio. Meanwhile the country was ruled by its warring seigneurs, all competing for supremacy, and they soon showed what they were capable of when left to themselves. They progressively increased taxation: in the words of the chronicler they 'so oppressed the unfortunate populations as hardly to allow them to breathe.'[9]

Sambocuccio's revolution and the campaign of the Giovannali were simultaneous explosions of popular indignation. There can be no doubt that they were associated, though whether the Giovannali actually joined Sambocuccio's angry people's army or merely provided ideological encouragement remains obscure. Until today historians have failed to correlate the two movements, with the outstanding exception of Napoleon in his *Lettres sur la Corse*.[10] Ignoring the whole religious aspect of the Giovannali he boldly proclaims their leaders, the Attalla brothers, as the regenerators of their country: 'They saw that the debris of the feudal regime, combined with laws instituted by prejudice, dictated, for the most part, according to circumstances, and alloyed with Roman [Catholic] superstition, presented only a disgusting concoction fit to prolong anarchy. . . . They made use of the strongest methods; they preached the most daring truths, the great dogmas of equality, the sovereignty of the people, the imposture of all authority not emanating from it.'

According to Napoleon, Sambocuccio and the Attalla brothers acted in concert; but his sources are unknown. The chronicler merely tells one that Sambocuccio, victorious over the seigneurs but unsure of being able to consolidate his position, appealed to Genoa for protection. The Genoese responded with alacrity and in 1359 sent a brother of the reigning doge to Corsica as governor, followed by others, on Sambocuccio's repeated requests. The new regime was however only really operative in the *Diqua dai Monti*; the Cinarchesi, overriding Sambocuccio and the Genoese, kept control of the south and west until the death of Rinuccio della Rocca some hundred and fifty years later.

In the meantime the Giovannali were liquidated. The Pope sent troops; Corsicans hostile to the heresy joined his army; the Giovannali were defeated at Alesani and elsewhere, their corpses publicly burnt on enormous funeral pyres. The survivors were hunted to death so mercilessly that the phrase 'wiped out like the Giovannali' became proverbial in Corsica when referring to any brutal massacre. All the same some of these convinced heretics managed to hold out in the maquis for at least forty years after the holocaust of 1362, swelling the ranks of the bandits; the Franciscan Order and the Holy See sent missions to convert them at intervals until the end of the century.[11]

As a religious sect the Giovannali failed lamentably. These men who had inherited the ideals of pacifism and humility turned into an armed mob, spread violence and destruction, were defeated, slaughtered and dispersed; they are remembered as the murderers of two good monks and as shameless debauchees. Yet indirectly they did achieve something of lasting value, some-

144

thing in line with their original ideal: they contributed to the success of a revolution that freed about half Corsica, centuries before other European countries, from seigneurial domination, and made possible a democratic system of local government with collective exploitation of the land. From then on Corsican social history deviated from that of the rest of Europe.

The liberated area, which included all the *Diqua dai Monti* except Cap Corse (and contained a larger population than the *Dila dai Monti*), was known thenceforth as the *terra del comune* and was incorporated into the Genoese Republic. The stifling vexations of Genoese colonial rule were of course not foreseen by Samboccucio and his supporters. The Genoese themselves had recently gone through a social upheaval that had brought the popular, Ghibelline, party to power. The first Governors of Corsica dealt drastically with the defeated seigneurs; an agreement, according to the chronicler, was made between Genoese and the Corsican leaders setting a permanent low limit to taxation.

Though the Genoese later made light of this undertaking, proved themselves corrupt and grasping rulers, apart from collecting taxes they interfered little in rural life. Settled in their coastal fortresses, they never attempted to colonise the interior. The village communities were left to run themselves under their elected podestas and 'fathers of the commune', who acted as trustees of collectively owned property. The system, though it sometimes slipped into disorder, stimulated a development of local self-government unique in the history of the European rural communes. This experience of democratic organisation became the directing force of the eighteenth-century rebellion and under Paoli served as basis for a liberal type of national government. The uprisings of Sambocuccio and the Giovannali marked a turning point in the long, slow Corsican evolution from primaeval to modern democracy.

The importance of the achievement can be judged by the failure of contemporary revolutionary movements elsewhere. The fourteenth century was a period of antifeudal revolts. In northern Italy, from 1300, the peasants were rioting, encouraged and inspired – just as in Corsica – by extreme interpretations of the Franciscan doctrine: the cult of absolute, evangelical poverty. The movement, condemned as heretical, was crushed by force of arms. All over Europe itinerant preachers, simple exalted men speaking of the golden age of Eden, gave hope to a proletariat exasperated by the pressure of the ruling classes and the economic crisis following on the Black Death. Rural populations plotted, preached, proclaimed, prayed, marched, killed and burned, presented demands and were promptly re-subjugated. In France the Jacquerie, outbreak of peasant violence exactly contemporary with the Corsican rising, was savagely repressed; later, in England, the better organised Peasants' Revolt was tricked into submission. Partial successes were obtained only in mountainous, outlying regions, like the Briançonnais, where fifty-one villages managed to commute their traditional obligations to their overlords.[12]

But in northern and eastern Corsica the victory was total and lasting. The rural communities, free of the crippling taxation of the seigneurs and their recurrent calls to arms, were able to operate their traditional collective economy in security, by traditional democratic procedure. Notarial acts of the sixteenth century, recently studied, reveal the complex organisations that had been elaborated by the villages of the *terra del comune* during the two hundred years following Sambocuccio's revolution. Local affairs were decided by the vote of the full village assembly, which in certain villages, such as Belgodere in the Balagne, included the women. The first preoccupation was the exploitation of the common lands, then very extensive, which included arable areas as well as pastures and forests. In orderly discussions the assembled population decided which lands should be cultivated each year; the available area was divided into portions of more or less equal value and assigned to the cultivators – the heads of families – by the drawing of lots. Wardens were elected, and paid in kind, to prevent livestock from straying into sown fields.

Food production was not the only concern of these assemblies. In numerous villages, miniature welfare states, a form of health service operated that has no parallel, so far as I know, before our time. The community made a contract with a doctor, chosen by public vote; every householder guaranteed him a yearly remuneration in the form of cereals. Patients were treated free of charge but had to pay for their medicines; the prescribed 'remedies and syrups'. Other public employees were the notary and the blacksmith. The latter, most valued of specialists in agricultural communities, received a yearly tribute of cereals about twice as large as that accorded to doctor and notary; moreover, each tool had to be paid for separately with about two litres of wine.[13]

The parish churches, symbols of village unity, were the meeting-places of these little parliaments; undertakings for public services were sworn with the gospels in hand, facing the altar. The parish priest was himself a kind of public employee, and his role was that of ministering to all non-material needs. The religious fraternities, too, had their part to play. Their feast-day ceremonies and processions were an uplifting break in the hard routine of the land. They also performed funeral rites, paid for in advance by regular subscriptions; every member of these Corsican communities was cared for from the cradle to the grave.

The Franciscans, settled in their large mansions just outside the villages, certainly shed an influence on local life. In a curious parallel to the campaign of the Giovannali, during the fourteenth century a number of Spiritual monks – known as Fraticelli – found shelter in the island, refugees from a persecuted religious underground in Italy. They occupied two of the oldest monasteries, at Calvi, and at Nonza, in Cap Corse.[14] There, on the wild Corsican shores, while the Franciscan conflict still raged in Europe, they were able to follow the rule of their founder in its primitive unimpaired rigour until they were finally converted or dispersed in the following century. Corsica was probably one of the areas of Europe that was most affected by the doctrine of the Spirituals: their belief that man, stripped clean of possessions, might accede to the brotherhood of men and the communion of men with God. With the turbulent Giovannali and the ascetic Fraticelli it was a living influence in the island for the best part of a hundred years. And the Franciscan ideal was to remain preponderant in insular Christianity, long after the Fraticelli had been forgotten and the Giovannali had become a bad memory.

Meanwhile the village welfare states went the usual way of enlightened institutions: they degenerated. From the start the communities of the *terra del comune* had to deal with a new type of potential oppressor, the so-called *caporali*, who first came to the fore as defenders of popular liberties and soon moulded themselves into an hereditary class of domineering notables. As time went on the collective system was increasingly challenged by private ownership of land; first in the north, later in the south, where the villages became independent after the death of Rinnucio della Rocca. In the Balagne, in the Sartenais, local leaders carved out large estates, most often by appropriating common lands. By the seventeenth century the *sgio*, making up a new class of rural notables, were in the ascendant. In many communities they controlled elections, monopolised public office. Leaders of rival groups, they broke up village cooperation; the vendetta often took the place of democratic consultation. At the same time the Genoese government, impoverished and corrupt, had become an interfering factor in rural affairs.[15]

Yet the village system never quite broke down under the impact of these disruptive forces, never wholly repudiated the principle of collective responsibility. If it failed to nip the growth of class distinctions and self-abrogated privileges, it did ensure a tolerable minimum standard of living for all. It lasted. In political crises and civil wars it provided a framework of social order (at times the only one); it was the mainspring of the national assemblies of the eighteenth-century rebellion, and of Paoli's parliament; under the smothering French monarchical regime it kept democratic traditions alive. The administrative innovations of the French Revolution and subsequent governments were less significant than the persistence of local custom. Great tracts of land in the nineteenth century were still village communal property; and the proportion is still 24 per cent of the whole today, as opposed to 9 per cent in mainland France. Until the First World War cracked the immemorial subsistence economy many of the collective customs and services were maintained. I have spoken to several elderly people who remember the yearly visits of the village doctor, when after the harvest he rode from house to house to collect his tribute of grain. Most look back to those days as a time of deep contentment; and there are still villages, tranquil and mellow, which seem permeated by the well-being of that ancestral way of life.

Carbini is not one of them. After the defeat of the Giovannali the village, depopulated perhaps by their massacre, and later, certainly, by pirate raids, dropped out of history, to reappear in modern times as the scene of particularly atrocious vendettas. It was the home of Charles-Camille Nicolai, he who found his brother's burning corpse and murdered his brother's murderer and suffered and wrote poetry in the maquis before he himself was killed. This happened in the last quarter of the nineteenth century when such dramas were common in the Sartenais. But Carbini remained lawless for years to come. In 1904, at the close of an election during which the entire population was in arms, shooting broke out between the Giuseppi and Nicolai, causing a death on either side. The victim in the Nicolai family was a young priest, who while he was bleeding to death wrote a message that has become celebrated in local memory: 'I forgive.' A treaty of peace was subsequently signed in the church of St Jean; so far as I know the last of its kind.

My host was telling me of these tragic events as we walked back to the hotel in the midday sun. 'It was abominable! Unspeakable! A crime against God!' Hysteria was again creeping into his tones. I reflected that he was old enough to have witnessed what he described, as were many others in the village. I understood, now, their watchful stare, and why they carried their guns. I was experiencing, at a greater distance in time, something of what so impressed Mérimée and Valéry in Fozzano and Sartène: the aftermath of a vendetta. 'It's a terrible spot!' my host lamented. 'Those poor people! Who will save them? They live in ignorance and wretchedness!'

As though to confirm his words we were stopped in the street by a man wearing the raggedest of rags. Tall and lean, with a straggling beard and a little beret perched on his long, silky hair, he had the wide innocent eyes and demented smile one associates with the holy idiot of Russian literature. But for that matter Carbini as a whole resembled some despairing village of the steppe.

He signed to me that he wanted a cigarette (he was apparently dumb). When I gave him one he immediately squatted in the middle of the road and smoked it with an expression of ecstasy. A toothless old hag came hobbling up. 'What are you doing, my poor friend?' she screamed at him. 'It'll kill you, that cigarette! You're as good as dead! You're finished! Done for!'

For a moment I feared I had given the cigarette to someone in an advanced state of consumption; to the drunkard, perhaps. But my host reassured me. 'No, this is our other unfortunate,' he explained, 'our idiot.' 'I talk like that to tease him,' the old woman cackled. 'We all tease him, he's so funny. You must make him dance for you, it makes one laugh. Get up and dance for the visitor!' she screeched. 'On to your feet you lazy good for nothing!' But the idiot, bowing and smiling with sweetly dotty decorum, merely made signs for another cigarette. I gave him two. He smiled rapturously, lit them both, and holding the three between the fingers of one hand smoked them in turn as though playing the pipes of Pan. 'He's the happiest in the village,' my host said to me as we moved away.

The idiot was with me again when towards evening I left the hotel. My host had told me that the sunset was particularly fine when seen from the heights of the pinnacle where the Giovannali had been killed. On my way I stopped at the café in the hope of shedding my mad companion. It was the very

148

smallest café I had ever seen: a stone box planted on a lump of rock just above the road. There was no one inside but the schoolgirl sisters, serenely reading. 'There'll be plenty of company in an hour or so when the men come in from work,' one of them said.

Some were in fact already returning from their flocks and fields, plodding along the street, singly, with their guns slung on their shoulders. One was a veritable giant, well over six feet tall, with a straggling beard and long white hair streaming from under his very wide-brimmed black felt hat. Striding firmly, he supported himself with a shoulder-high forked stick, his cavernous eyes fixed straight ahead as though on some celestial goal. He made me think of the Old Testament prophets, those who were for ever predicting calamity and woe, and I could easily imagine him as a spokesman of the Giovannali invoking apocalyptic destruction on the Carnal Church, the Whore of Babylon. 'He's over ninety,' one of the sisters explained, 'but he's by no means the oldest in the village. There are several here who must be over a hundred because their births are not recorded and the register was started about a hundred years ago. They don't know how old they are, you see. There's a woman; she's supposed to be the oldest of them all, well over a hundred, they say.' 'But she's still healthy and in good heart,' the other girl told me, 'she stays in bed and lives mainly on sugar dipped in eau-de-vie. Of course she has no teeth left at all.'

The sun was sinking as I toiled up the pinnacle. The idiot soon gave up following me, for with its jagged spikes of granite shooting out at all angles it was quite difficult to climb. It would have made a formidable fortress, I thought, in the hands of a desperate crowd. From the summit I could see rocks and maquis rolling away to all the horizons: to the peaks of Bavella, to the mountain ranges rising in many tiers; and to the west to a little triangle of quicksilver, the distant, untormented sea. The view was circular and without sign of human occupation, so that Carbini no longer seemed a back-of-the-beyond village but the centre of a newly created world. And now all this world was being flooded with golden light, a light so laden with glittering particles that I felt it must surely lie heavy in my hand. Yet it was not a mist, confusing outlines; on the contrary its action was to clarify. Things far off appeared in startling detail; every crease and wrinkle and projection of the myriad rocks manifested itself with a supernormal intensity. The maquis, which all day long had looked tediously uniform, was now fragmented into gleaming tufts of vegetation growing from wells of shade; bushes assumed the dignity of forest trees. Colours, too, were transformed: grey rock turned pink and orange, slashed with deep sea blue; the stately peaks of Bavella, suddenly close at hand, soared, crimson, between vertical violet chasms. All that was normally dull and indefinite had become sharp, brilliant and solid; the change was not only of colour but of consistency. The transfiguration lasted some twenty minutes, perhaps half an hour; then the colours began to fade; the outlines blurred; only the peaks of Bavella remained clothed in their power and glory a while longer.

Whispering voices jerked my attention back to my immediate surroundings. Startled, I made an abrupt movement, dislodging a stone. At once the whispering ceased, and as I stood up I caught sight of a girl and a man cowering in the rocks. Lovers in hiding; they must have been a very daring pair, I thought, for the penalties of discovery in this village would surely be drastic.

In the last light I reached the village street and made my way back towards the hotel under the disquieting scrutiny of staring eyes. Yet I was reluctant to face the incense burner and the jazz wallpaper and my despairing host; the café, I thought, could hardly fail to be less depressing. Also it occurred to me that I might meet the drunkard there and that he might be interesting.

The little room was now packed with men playing cards. The mayor, who rose to greet me, was wearing a dark town suit; the rest were dressed in a rustic Bohemian style. The sisters, those two enormously self-possessed young women, were busy serving drinks to the shipwrecked-looking crowd. Their mother, a thin haggard creature, was holding a baby which I took to be a grandchild until she told me it was her youngest son. Youth is short and life is long in Carbini, so that old age may last, here, some fifty or sixty years. While I was admiring the child her husband came in and stood his gun against the wall. He too was prematurely aged, and his eyes had the fixed, obsessed expression I had so often seen in this village.

The drunkard was unmistakable when he arrived. His movements were slow and imprecise, as though he were walking on the bottom of the sea. Obviously he had already drunk a good deal. His face, long and white, once handsome, was framed in dangling pale hair. The tweed jacket peeling off him in spectacular rags must have been an expensive one.

He smiled when he caught sight of me, approached and shook hands; his voice had cultured inflexions. 'I think you like Corsica!' I said I liked Corsica and the Corsicans very much. 'We are strange, no? Serve me a drink!' he called.

'Corsica is poor,' said one of the card players. 'Yes, we are poor,' said the drunkard as he gulped his *pastis*. 'Our houses are ruins, our fields are deserts, our clothes are rags! Look!' He waved the eighteen-inch tatters of a sleeve. 'Sometimes our stomachs are empty, sometimes we have no bread! But we are free,' he continued, 'that's important. Look at me! I have no master, I belong to no one. Why sometimes I don't even belong to myself!' 'But you belong to God,' said a card player, without lifting his eyes from the table. 'That's true,' the drunkard said, 'we all belong to God.'

This man, I thought, was the degenerate spiritual descendant of the Giovannali, those religious anarchists who refused the ways of society to seek the light of the Holy Spirit unhampered by possessions. The people of Carbini, for all their lamentable appearance, were not really primitive; in the tradition of their heretic ancestors they were undisciplined metaphysicians, given to speculating on their place in the universe and their relation to their Maker. Probably they were not even, by necessity, poor; after all they had their flocks, their lands; even the drunkard touched his considerable monthly sum. They simply set no store by comfortable houses and good clothes; like the Giovannali they took pride in their destitution. Where the present is empty the past lingers; little had happened in Carbini since the fourteenth century and the shadow of the Giovannali still hovered there.

The girls' father told me that the bus going south to Bonifacio was not due till the day after the next; but I could go to Zonza the following morning by a truck coming up from the south which stopped to collect passengers. I decided to take the truck, even though this meant missing the uninhabited country to the south of Carbini, covered, so I had heard, with remnants of the primaeval forest of mountain oak that once spread over all the lower part of the island. Theophrastus marvelled at its luxuriance, and later, when I travelled that road, I was able to share his wonder, for the trees, which have miraculously escaped cutting and fire, black, close-growing and immensely high, must be just like those seen by the amazed travellers of antiquity [16]

But all this I was prepared to forgo if I could avoid staying in Carbini another twenty-four hours. Not that I wanted to leave; on the contrary I was afraid that if I stopped there another day I might be tempted to stay on indefinitely. The place was dangerously fascinating. Under the microscope of passionate curiosity it might come to represent the world. The physical world would be reduced to its single street, the campanile, the church, the ruins and pigsties, the peak on which the Giovannali had been killed. The surrounding mountains would be prison walls, and I would come to know every fold in their surface, every tone of light that passed over them from sunrise to sunset as accurately as I knew my own face in a mirror. The human world would dwindle to the handful of village inhabitants, and I would note each of their words and gestures with the concentration due to a great work of art. To understand their aims and feelings and interrelationships would seem equivalent to learning all the secrets of the human psyche. And perhaps some such understanding would really ensue, but at the expense of everything else in life.

I was downstairs before dawn the following day; but my host had preceded me. Breakfast seemed to take even longer to prepare than the day before, and as he pampered me with small courtesies and attentions I realised that he was unwilling to see me go. To make sure of not missing the truck I finished my boiled egg in the street. My host's intentions became obvious when the truck arrived. 'Wait a little! I have another egg for you,' he begged me. 'Come back indoors, there's no need to hurry. The driver always stops here some minutes; twenty minutes at least, half an hour. Come inside and I'll make you ham and eggs, or an omelette with *brocciu* and wild mint,' he entreated me, offering one of the Corsican delicacies. But the driver was already shoving my luggage onto the truck and seemed in no mood to wait. It was an old businesslike truck packed with peasants sitting high up on benches laid across it laterally. Nearly all had guns, held upright; they were a party of countrymen on their way to a boar hunt, but they looked like a guerrilla detachment.

'Allez op!' they shouted at me. My host had vanished into the house and I thought I had really taken leave of him when, just as I had got a foothold on the mudguard, he came darting back.

'Wait wait!' he beseeched me. 'You must stay now! See what I've found! My little breadbasket! Come back and we'll have breakfast together, correctly served!' And there it was in his shaking hand; a little breadbasket with some potato peelings, it is true, in the bottom, but also three slices of freshly cut bread.

I was already half on the truck. 'No no!' I cried, as though dismissing an extreme temptation, 'it's impossible! I must leave!'

Strong arms hauled me onto a bench; I found myself squeezed between a couple of guns with a hairy dog under my knees. 'Come back! Come back!' cried my host. 'Yes yes, I'll try!' I shouted as the truck jerked forward. I waved my hand; he waved his, still holding the breadbasket; and that was the last time I saw him, waving the little breadbasket in the street of Carbini in the dawn.

When I returned to Corsica some years later I learnt that he had died. As for the hotel, brave pioneer symbol of the values of modern civilisation, it had closed, and it has never been reopened. Carbini has not become the tourists' playground its builder imagined. All the same the village, distantly affected by an economic evolution that is now transforming all Corsica, has become much more prosperous and cheerful, and memories of the Giovannali have receded almost out of mind.

10 THE OUTPOST

Alpine Zonza – spires of Bavella – forest of Ospedale – gulf of
Porto-Vecchio – Bonifacio – the Laestrygonians – a historic
siege – a Renaissance citadel – baroque processions

I DROVE away from Carbini with the sensation of waking out of a dream;
one of those dense, disquieting dreams, charged with obscure menaces. It
began to lift when I lost sight of the village as the truck roared down into the
valley still dank with prolonged shades of night; it was dissipated, as though
exorcised, by the time we reached Levie, in the sunlight, on the opposite
mountain slope. Here was an ordinary village, beginning an ordinary day:
dogs barked, cocks crowed, smoke rose from freshly kindled fires. My mind
felt suddenly light and vacant as the upland air, and I rode on to Zonza in a
holiday mood, watching the maquis give way to chestnut trees, sweet
meadows and groves of pines, and the rising sun tinting red the peaks of
Bavella which now appeared clustered together in a baroque pyramid. The
landscape was bold and opulent, broken into vistas of open heath; the chestnuts, decked with sprays of catkins, golden against their rich green leaves,
had a texture like that of tapestry.

Zonza, a village happy without a history, caters for tourists, the old-
fashioned kind who are content with mountain walks and views. A fellow
passenger directed me to a café owned – so he told me – by a man from mainland France who made delicious cakes to sell at village festivals. In fact he
was making some that very day. The whole place smelt of cakes; a couple of
Arabs in tall white caps were dashing in and out of the kitchen like musical
comedy chefs with platters piled high with cakes; another was stirring a luscious
creamy mixture in a copper cauldron. Delicious cream cakes are a rarity in
Corsica, so I promptly ate several, feeling frivolous and thankful to be so.

The bus to Porto-Vecchio, stopping-place on the way to Bonifacio, called
at Zonza, I was told, in the early afternoon. I had time to spare. 'Why don't
you take a look at the pass of Bavella?' one of the Arabs suggested. 'I've a
friend with a taxi who'll take you right away.' The friend turned up in a
matter of minutes, a Corsican with the same type of features as the Arab, and
handsome enough until he opened his mouth to reveal only three teeth,
broken and black. 'Just give me the price of the petrol,' he said, 'I've nothing
better to do.'

We swung uphill through pine woods; the peaks, now at eye-level, seen

153

through the tree-trunks, seemed to be advancing on us, menacing, as their jagged structure was exposed every instant in ever more intricate detail. We met no cars, only a caravan of mules stepping delicately under their great burdens of planks and piercing the air with their jangling bells. A meagre little man followed on foot, holding a whip in a hand small as a child's. My driver stopped with a greeting. 'We were together in the Resistance,' he explained,' he's a hero.' A hero: one of those Corsican guerrillas who in all periods have unnerved better-armed invaders; like the partisans of Rinuccio della Rocca who drove Andrea Doria to barbarities, or the little brown men described by a French officer, more resembling bears than men, who held up the proud army of Louis XV for the best part of a year, darting out of the woods and rocks in scattered formation 'like a covey of partridges' and disappearing as suddenly, to attack again from an unexpected quarter.[1]

The final upthrust of the road took us on to the level corridor of the pass, with the naked peaks towering immediately above. It was a place that seemed haunted by catastrophe. Ancient, stout-boled pines growing between granite outcrops, flattened and deformed by the winds, recalled the Chanson de Roland, though identified in my mind not so much with the pines of Roncevals as with Roland and his knights, making their last, doomed stand. We had stopped by the roadside. 'Go to the edge and see for yourself,' said my companion.

The edge – the eastern limit of the pass – came suddenly. I found myself looking down into a valley, or well, of immense and uncertain depth, for blue mist obscured all its lower zone. Perpendicular mountains enclosed it, and they were crimson, except where they had cast blue shadows into their own recesses; clusters of crimson peaks spired out of it, like icebergs or islands. Strands of mist swam in the middle air, wrapped themselves round these floating columns, hung in their clefts and dusted their pinnacles. I could fancy I were looking at an experiment in creation, an early, eccentric episode of Genesis. Here mountains had been thrown up pell-mell in an unbridled surge of primal energy. Only vertical shapes had been attempted, and only three colours, strong and unalloyed: crimson for rock, blue for mist and air and shadow, and dark green for vegetation, and the only vegetation was pines. These had been placed in spots where trees would never again be called upon to grow: on the edges of shafts of rock and their uppermost extremities, like ornaments capriciously disposed. The Creator had made this, His first work, for His pleasure; He had seen that it was good, but extravagant, unpractical; thereafter He had adopted tamer colours and designs.

The vapours shifted, drooped and wandered, allowing new vistas of peak and canyon to sail majestically into view. Then a volume of mist blotted out the vision, a vision so improbable that it could hardly be remembered. I stood there staring, insanely trying to conjure up what I had half forgotten. As though to mock my pretensions a woman came out of the clouds, carrying firewood. 'D'you live here?' I asked her, foolishly incredulous. 'But yes,' she said, 'I'll show you, come with me.'

154

The road dropped sharply over the escarpment. Immediately below the pass was a group of stone huts set close together on little terraces. They were primitive one-storeyed cabins with wooden roofs, making a settlement where women sat in doorways and children played in the rocks and goats and pigs and chickens nibbled and rootled and pecked the turf. The cries of children and the yapping of dogs sounded tragically feeble in the vastness of the air.

'We come up here every summer,' she told me. And so I learned that this was a peasants' holiday resort, that the cabins belonged to the inhabitants of the subtropical east coast plains who moved up here with their children and livestock during the hottest months of the year. While we were talking a truck came grinding out of the abyss. 'You see, there's a new lot arriving, they all come from the same village,' the woman explained. They were so crowded in the truck that they were all standing, the women carrying their babies and the men their guns, and as they arrived they were all cheering. The Corsicans, I thought, might not be a gay people, but they had their own deep fantastic pleasures.

The mist was now clearing, revealing a huge oval amphitheatre shelving towards the east where a spiked crimson obelisk seemed to block the only possible exit. But the lower regions were still invisible, for there the mist is almost permanent. It is the landscape of the Epic of Gilgamesh, the green mountain where dwelt Humbaba, whose name was 'hugeness': 'The forest stretches ten thousand leagues in every direction; who would willingly go down to explore its depths? As for Humbaba, when he roars it is like the torrent of the storm.' On a subsequent journey I in fact went down into the forest, following the road into the depths of the nearly-perpetual clouds, and there, like Gilgamesh, I found green glades, and shade 'beautiful, full of comfort'; but when the mist disperses and one looks above those empty hidden pastures, then one sees the rock walls rising sheer on every side, diminishing the sky to a well-head and, one may feel, threatening to topple down on the intruder. So dreamed Gilgamesh: 'We stood in a deep gorge of the mountain, and suddenly the mountain fell, and beside it we two were like the smallest of swamp flies.'

But now I was bound for the east coast by a more southerly route, through another haunted forest, known as the Forêt de l'Ospedale. Delayed by a breakdown, the bus arrived at Zonza three hours behind schedule; but I was rewarded for this exasperating wait by seeing the forest in its rich, dense splendour of late afternoon. It is a savage, unvisited forest, growing unevenly between colossal outcrops of silvery granite. There are areas where the tall trees stand in close formation, so that the only vistas are of bracken and undergrowth, and the hot, contained air stifles with the scent of pines. But we also passed through stretches devastated by reckless cutting and storm and fire, where saplings sprang haphazard from charred and rotting trunks and mournful brackish pools lay open to the sky. I glimpsed cataclysmic arenas, enclosed by naked piled boulders and rock mountains, arenas where Titans,

I fancied, might have played tragic masterpieces – the Ring, perhaps – and wrecked the décor by their own clumsiness or the sheer violence of their performance. The evening sunlight, brilliant as stage illumination, magnified the demented rocks which cast dramatic shadows on to their own surfaces.

Granite masses reared up all over the forest, even where the trees grew thickest, bare walls seen between tree-trunks which at first sight one might take for houses. But the forest seemed uninhabited, and we met no one, except, unaccountably, a smiling Indo-Chinese boy who stopped the bus and boarded it without comment. The sun was coming sideways through the branches, lighting the red in the withered bracken, before we emerged on to the eastern watershed above the sea.

Here the panorama was enormous and contrasting; one of those that make travelling in Corsica a succession of bewildering surprises. Far-away and below, beyond the maquis-covered foothills, the great sprawling gulf of Porto-Vecchio, almost landlocked, lay shimmering in the gold-powdered sunset haze. The town, at first a white blur on a promontory, gained substance as we looped downhill, split into pink roofs and white walls; the intricacies of the gulf became concrete, with its tree-fringed beaches, its numberless bays and creeks and wooded peninsulas and little tufted islands, while the water took on the delicate pearly tints peculiar to this eastern coast where the setting sun is obscured by high ranges.

Down in the plain we entered a forest of another kind: of cork oak, growing from knee-high grass. The trunks, struck horizontally by the sun's rays, were blood red, purple or violet according to when the bark had last been harvested. Fat cattle browsing among wild flowers, voluminous briar-tangled hedges, reminded me of the English countryside until I caught a gust of the heavy, exotic scents carried on the hothouse air.

By the time we reached Porto-Vecchio (stopping, disappointingly, in an ugly street of featureless stone houses), the connecting bus to Bonifacio had of course long since left. I was the only passenger who wanted to go on there; but I was given no time to complain. A hefty brown-faced girl, a total stranger, seized my luggage, hailed a passing truck, stopped it, pushed me and my suitcases on to the back platform and stood waving in the street as I was sped away. 'Don't sit down!' yelled the driver, thrusting a curly head through his window, 'we're carrying ice!' 'Don't smoke either!' shouted his companion, 'we're carrying petrol too!' So I stood braced against the hood while we bounded along a straight, level, but exceedingly bad road, down a shallow valley, out of sight of the sea. It was a weird place, littered with rocks, rocks of all shapes and sizes, including many cracked spheres and ovals hollowed by some action of the weather so that they looked like nothing so much as monstrous broken eggshells. They belonged, I thought, to science fiction; one could imagine the valley as the nesting-ground of some monstrous astral blood.

The vision was as brief as improbable; within a few miles the landscape abruptly changed; the eggshell caverns disappeared; the rock became chalk, phantom white in this twilit hour. We were driving through a gorge with high chalk walls, like a railway cutting; and then Bonifacio appeared, as astonishing as anything I had seen in the course of that day.

A wide channel, dead calm, flowed like a river between limestone cliffs, winding out of sight towards the invisible sea. It made a square-headed harbour where many weathered boats rode at anchor. A line of tall old houses overlooked a wide paved quay littered with *langouste* baskets, ropes and nets. Lights shone from their many storeys; the notes of a guitar drifted across the water. But this picture of an ancient, thriving Mediterranean fishing port was only the foreground for another, more surprising; for directly above the quayside houses rose a cliff, and on its summit was a second town, hidden by intimidating walls and bastions, above which only the top of a campanile showed.

'You'll be staying in the port, no?' the truck driver said to me, 'we're going up to the citadel.' I agreed, bewildered. Ever since leaving Ajaccio – half a lifetime ago, I felt – I had seen only rough stone houses, manmade extensions of the rocks on which they stood. This double town, with its fine harbour, houses and citadel, was so alien to the country as to seem unreal. Here, at the southernmost extremity of the island, beyond the wastes of maquis and rock and mountain and forest, a civilised enclave had been created, far back in time, and had survived, forgotten and hardly changed.

Several of the quayside houses were hotels; through their ground-floor windows I could see tourists cheerfully crowded round dinner-tables. Yes, I could have a room; I could have dinner; would I like red wine or white? The meal consisted mainly of *langouste*, so I chose white and relaxed, as into sleep, into a way of living remote but familiar. 'It's a marvellous place,' the French couple at the next table told me, 'we have *langouste* for every meal. The fishermen take any quantity; they go out in all weathers. But then they're not Corsicans; mostly Neapolitans and Sardes; the Corsicans have always been poor seamen. And anyhow Bonifacio isn't really Corsica; the people in the upper town are Genoese by descent and speak a special dialect and the fishermen make up a mixed race of their own. They're a splendid crowd. They take one out all day in their boats and resolutely refuse payment. The sea here literally teems with fish. When we've caught enough they make us a *bouillabaisse* on the rocks somewhere along the coast. What a life! One ought to be a fisherman; it's inexcusable not to be. In the evenings one can hear them sing in the cafés; some have good voices. Why don't you come along?'

The café was a vaulted tunnel full of fishermen with sharp, prematurely aged faces which suggested that their lives were less idyllic than a visitor might suppose. A wizened little man was crouching over his guitar while a youth flung out a *lamento* in a strong, untrained tenor. Though new to me, it was one of the songs current in the Corsican parts; laments of love, in which the burning accents of the insular tradition are muted, translated into a soft velvet melancholy. I could not be initiated, at Bonifacio, into the harsh heartbreaking indigenous music of the shepherds; the airs I heard were gentler, more melodious, and strongly influenced by Italy. Yet they were convincing enough in their setting. *Frederi*, a fishermen's ballad, may, as is said, be of Sicilian origin, but it has gone the rounds of the Mediterranean ports, an exhilarating song with a gusty refrain made for groups of friends, home from the sea, huddled shoulder to shoulder at café tables. Here too I first heard the lovely lullaby, *Sotta lu Ponte*, quite recently composed, but in its grave remoteness true to Corsican tradition.[2] The fishermen – as promised – had good voices; but it was their zest that gave quality to their performance: they sang as though singing were the satisfaction of some basic human appetite. In the intervals they made conversation with the tourists, treating them as guests. Dazed and exhausted I left late at night with confused impressions of a red-bearded young man describing fantastic sea-caves and urging me to visit them the following day.

I found him in the morning, staring at the harbour's still green surface. 'We'd better leave at once,' he said, 'one can't get into the caves except in good weather.' Fair-sized ships can sail right up to the quay of Bonifacio, and sometimes do; but the channel, that day, was empty. The fisherman's boat seemed microscopic as we crept down this majestic waterway, the sound of its engine as insignificant as the twittering of a bird. Our slow, solitary progress seawards revealed new perspectives of white rocks with every bend of the winding passage, flights of incredible fortifications. Walls and towers and bastions, concealing the city, rose and fell according to the accidents of the site; only once the walls, curving to a glacis near the water's edge, allowed us to glimpse a stack of gaunt, yellow-green houses, rotted by age.

A rush of salt air, foam swirling round a lighthouse, heralded the open sea. The city was now far up in the sky, for here the promontory rises to great heights. At its point it overhangs the water like the hull of a huge liner. The sea has eaten away the soft limestone to make a lofty, shallow cave, a triumphal arch upholding the town where we circled, scaring seabirds from its ledges.

Then we veered into the glittering ocean spray; our boat, always too small for the setting, became a mere nutshell bouncing on the waves. The new dimensions were geographical: to the west, the coastline of Corsica slanted away out of sight; southwards, Sardinia was faintly visible with a seaboard town shining white in ghostly blue hills. I realised, now, that the flat calm of the harbour had been deceptive, and as we tumbled in the clutch of the blue breakers I looked back longingly at the entrance to the channel, and the pale, still water lying within its walls.

This amazing harbour must have been used by the earliest Mediterranean navigators, a safe refuge from the notoriously rough seas of the straits. Certain scholars contend that it is mentioned in the *Odyssey*, in the episode of the Laestrygonians.[3] If one subscribes to the belief that the landfalls of Odysseus represent real places, visited by Mycenaean seamen, the theory is almost unanswerable, for Homer's precise description of the home of the Laestrygonians undeniably matches Bonifacio better than any other spot in the western

Bonifacio, Genoese mediaeval stronghold, built on cliffs facing Sardinia. (*Louis Bianchetti*)

Mediterranean. Odysseus and his men had rowed away from the floating isle of Aeolia – identified as one of the Lipari isles – during six days and nights, a time in which they might reasonably be expected to reach Corsica. On the seventh day they came to 'an excellent harbour, closed in on all sides by an unbroken ring of precipitous cliffs, with two bold headlands facing each other at the mouth so as to leave only a narrow channel in between'. All the ships, except that of the wily Odysseus, entered the channel. It was a place 'never exposed to a heavy, or even a moderate sea',⁴ or according to another translation: 'no wave, great or small, ever arises there; it was a white calm'.⁵

The adventures of the Greeks in this inviting haven were nothing short of appalling. Climbing to a cliff-top, Odysseus had a discouraging view of the hinterland: 'No ploughed fields or other signs of human activities were to be seen: all we caught sight of was a wisp of smoke rising up from the country-side.' The description still applies, today. Three men were then sent to make contact with the inhabitants. They found their way to the abode of the Laestrygonian chieftain who gave them a 'murderous reception', and prompt-ly pounced on one of them with the intention of eating him for supper. At the call of their chief the Laestrygonians came running in their thousands, 'huge fellows, more like giants than men'. From the top of the cliffs they pelted down lumps of rock on the Grecian ships, destroying all except one and killing their crews; after which 'they harpooned their prey like fish and so carried them off to make their loathsome meal'. Only Odysseus and his crew escaped: 'with a sigh of relief we shot out to sea and left those frowning cliffs behind.'

A specialist in the geography of the *Odyssey* points out that Corsica lay within the orbit of Mycenaean trade, as is indicated by the weapons on the statues of Filitosa; but that the island, only occasionally visited, must have remained on the whole savage. The story of the giant rock-throwing cannibal Laestrygonians is thought to be based on travellers' tales of a stone age tribe installed at Bonifacio, where in fact quantities of Neolithic artifacts have been found.⁶

After reading this thesis I was fascinated to discover that an artist of an-tiquity, depicting this episode of the *Odyssey*, gave it a setting that most startlingly resembles Bonifacio. A Roman *topia*, a garden painting found on the wall of a portico in Rome, shows the Greeks landing below pale overhang-ing cliffs sprinkled with meagre vegetation and hollowed by the arched en-trances to marine caves. The Laestrygonians' stronghold is represented by a group of towers on a cliff-top extremely similar to the site of the present town.⁷ Is this an imaginative interpretation of Homer's tale? Or was there not, perhaps, a living tradition that identified the home of the Laestrygonians with Bonifacio, a place that is known to have been occupied by the Romans?⁸

Even without considering the Laestrygonians, the coastline of Bonifacio evokes the *Odyssey*. This is the seascape of the great mythical voyages: one-eyed Polyphemus in his cave overhung by laurels, spellbinding Circe, Calypso singing and spinning amid the fragrant cypresses, all, here, are credible. The hidden beaches call to mind those where Odysseus and his companions –

piratical explorers – feasted on stolen sheep and wine; the rock islets, sculptured by wind and wave, seem animate, menacing as Scylla and Charybdis.
The sea caves I saw with the red-bearded fisherman might be haunted by the
ancient divinities; the Bain de Venus – aptly named – by sea nymphs, the
Sdragonatu by a luxurious, treacherous ocean god.

The Bain de Venus is a small, ravishing grotto near the harbour's mouth,
its floor a rippling pool that casts flashes of vibrating light on to the natural
rococo carving of the limestone vaults and walls. But the fisherman barely
gave me time to dive into its shining waters before setting off along the coast
to the Sdragonatu, a cave entered by an archway in the cliffs, curtained by
stalactites and passable only in fair weather. We swooped through this portal
in the trough of a wave to reach a kind of antechamber preceding a second,
lower arch; the water, here, was of a turquoise so brilliant that one felt it must
take its colour from the light of a submarine sun. Then we glided through the
inner entry, and I found myself floating in a circular hall, a sea cathedral
rising the whole height of the cliffs and open to the sky. Pines border this
overhead window, and pigeons roost in their branches, fluttering down into
the cave in flocks. They serve to remind one of the familiar world, for nothing
here resembles what one has ever seen before. The rock walls, streaked ochre
and green by the chemistry of the sea, enclose a lake all scintillating with
facets of bright colour; like an oriental carpet, said the fisherman, or like a
stained-glass window, or a mosaic of jewels. For below the surface of the
water lies a litter of peaks and plateaux and chasms, and these submerged
rocks are encrusted with weeds sumptuously tinted pink and green and lilac
and regal purple and gold. Never had I so strongly felt that bathing is a
luxury as when I lay on couches that felt like silk and looked like amethyst
with gold inlays, plunged into shadowy depths where the water was an
opaque violet substance, or floated in sandy shallows where it shone, trans-
parent aquamarine, lending its lustre to one's limbs.

But the fisherman was uneasy. 'We'd do well to leave at once if we want to
avoid a disagreeable experience,' he said. When we passed through the inner
archway I understood what he meant; the sea was heaving close to the stalactites of the outer arch, scouring its walls and sucking in and out of the passage
with a gruesome animal sound. I had hardly time to wonder if we were trapped,
if my delectable bathing-place was about to turn into a seething cauldron, and
if so, whether we could climb to a safe ledge on its slimy walls. 'Lie flat!'
shouted the fisherman, and from the bottom of the boat I watched his expressionless face with terrified admiration as we bashed our way through the
outer arch with the waves crashing in on us from either side.

After that I had no more dread of the open sea. Fatalistically I allowed
myself to be tossed round the peninsula and into the straits. I was rewarded
by a view of Bonifacio that sums up all the daring and isolation of its history.
The southern side of the citadel, facing Sardinia, is unwalled, its great height
being sufficient protection, and here the houses are perched on the extreme
edge of the cliffs; 'like the nests of wild birds', Guy de Maupassant observed.

Some actually stand on platforms jutting over the void. Far below, slabs of rock torn from the cliffs lie about like wrecked ships, rimmed with foam.

A marvellous natural stronghold, Bonifacio must have been continuously inhabited from the earliest times. Neolithic tribesmen were eventually succeeded by the Romans; their town had disappeared by the early Middle Ages, but around 828 the crusading Count Bonifacio, returning victorious from an expedition against the Saracens at Carthage, built a castle on the peninsula to which he gave his name. During the twelfth century Pisa and Genoa disputed the site until it finally fell to the Genoese, who massacred the inhabitants and replaced them with their own colonists. Thenceforth Bonifacio was a self-governing city, inhabited almost entirely by people of Genoese origin, with their own laws, constitution and privileges.[9]

At first few volunteers could be found to settle in this forlorn spot; but the Genoese overcame the difficulty by sending two hundred and fifty serfs from the mainland, with their families, who received incomes from the Republic as long as they stayed there. Later the privileges accorded to the town proved sufficient to keep the population up to strength: the inhabitants were exempted from taxes to Genoa and customs dues in the Genoese ports, and they were licensed to supplement trade with piracy. Though producing little themselves they did exceedingly well from the carrying trade, importing cheeses, wines and hides from Sardinia, and selling them in Leghorn and all the Genoese ports. Their arid promontory became a rich warehouse, replenished by intrepid voyages; in the tradition of their countrymen they constantly braved the seas. Hardly less hazardous was the cultivation of the land assigned to them by the Genoese government in savage southern Corsica, where the shepherds waged an unremitting war against the intruders, plundering their crops, and murdering the men and raping the women who went to work there.

The Genoese, in their period of mercantile glory, are not a people who inspire much sympathy. But undeniably they were courageous. The history of Bonifacio records how some twelve hundred to eight thousand expatriates not only kept alive on this barren ridge,[10] but made themselves prosperous, built handsome houses and churches, preserved their standard of living and their culture, though separated from any semblance of civilisation by rough, pirate-ridden seas and acres and acres of maquis inhabited by primitive, hostile strangers. Frequently attacked – by Corsicans, Aragonese, French, Turks and Moors – invariably resisting, they remained loyal to Genoa until the French conquest, even though the Republic gave them minimal assistance in their various trials. Twice the colony was only saved, it seemed, by a miracle; in 1528 when plague reduced its numbers to seven hundred, and in the memorable winter of 1420, when it was besieged by the King of Aragon.

Corsica was then controlled by the leader of the pro-Aragonese faction, Vincentello d'Istria; Calvi and Bonifacio had alone kept faith with Genoa. When Alfonso V of Aragon appeared with his fleet and troops Calvi immediately surrendered. He was then a dynamic young man of twenty-six, with large ambitions. If he could take Bonifacio (so the chronicler Pietro Cirneo repeatedly insists), he would be master of Corsica, as he already was of Sicily and Sardinia; the conquest of the Genoese Republic would follow, perhaps of all Italy. To Alfonso it seemed that only a handful of men in this remote outpost stood between him and the possession of a great Mediterranean empire.

On an unlucky thirteenth of August he advanced on the city by land and sea, sailed his eighty ships into the harbour, destroyed the warehouse in the port, breached the walls and set fire to the municipal granary. The attack was held thanks to the presence of mind of Margherita Bobbia, one of the heroic women to whom the Bonifaciens, time and again, were to owe their salvation. Meanwhile the Aragonese had set up cannon on the mainland plateaux, with which they bombarded the city day and night. They were also using muskets, an innovation that spread panic among the townspeople, who were without firearms. No Genoese troops were then stationed in the town; Bonifacio resisted for nearly five months with a citizen army, fighting some of the most seasoned troops in Europe.

Pietro Cirneo, with a true historian's concern for facts, took the trouble to visit Bonifacio, sixty years after the siege, when the memory of it must still have been very much alive. He describes how the citizens defended themselves with bows and arrows, javelins, spears, poles on which they had fixed hooks and harpoons; how they flung down stones on the enemy, boiling water and oil, ingots of lead, wooden beams: reading of these improvised weapons one has the impression that almost everything movable in the town was hurled over its walls in the effort to save it. One reads of towers collapsing under the Aragonese cannon-balls with a deafening crashing and rolling of masonry; of the outnumbered defenders running, shouting, from one danger spot to another; of women and children repairing the fortifications and manning them; of priests and monks armed with torches dipped in sulphur and pots of powdered lime swarming on to the broken walls to blind and suffocate the assailants.

By the third month the population was starving, eating the bark of the few remaining trees. A truce was arranged: the Bonifaciens gave the Aragonese thirty-two child hostages and guaranteed to surrender at the end of forty days if no help from Genoa came. A ship was built to carry a message to the mainland and lowered over the cliff into the straits; the townspeople walked in procession from church to church, praying for relief. At last one night in December the messengers returned with the glad news that a Genoese fleet was on its way. But delayed by contrary winds it had not arrived by the fateful fortieth day. King Alfonso sent for the city keys; the Bonifaciens bargained for a delay till dawn; there was talk of surrender, or of mass suicide.

But that night at the fourth watch the Aragonese heard shouting in the town and all the church bells ringing. The Bonifaciens had decided on a last-card policy of bluff. At dawn troops were seen marching round the ramparts, led by a standard-bearer, their lances glittering in the sun. All the surviving men took part in this parade, and all the women, now much more numerous, dressed in the dead men's armour. The Aragonese concluded that reinforcements had somehow reached the town; the fighting began again.

'It was Christmas day', notes the chronicler, 'when the wind changed.' Soon afterwards, with the famished women still resisting, seven Genoese ships appeared. They bore full sail against the Aragonese defences that barred the entrance to the harbour; the townspeople came to their aid with their usual resourcefulness; young men let themselves down the cliffs on ropes to join in the fighting, now hand to hand on the decks of the grappled ships, others rained down rocks, like the Laestrygonians in the *Odyssey*. At the end of seven hours' carnage the Aragonese gave way and the Genoese were able to land some desperately needed supplies.

Five days later they forced their way out through the enemy fleet with the aid of a fireship and set sail for home. Little, really, had been achieved by their ferocious intervention. The supplies, as one of their captains pointed out, could have been hauled up the southern cliffs by ropes; the Aragonese remained almost as powerful as before. But the balance of psychological factors had changed. The Genoese had left covered in glory; the Bonifaciens felt victorious; the Aragonese felt defeated. Had they continued the siege they might well have ended by taking the city; but they had lost heart. Moreover, news had come that the inhabitants of Calvi had massacred their Spanish garrison. At this moment, too, Alphonso V received a message from Joanna, Queen of Naples, in which she offered to make him her heir in return for his protection. Fascinated by this new prospect, and thoroughly discouraged by Corsica, he sailed away with his troops and the thirty-two child hostages. This happened on 5 January 1421.

Bonifacio was saved, and Aragonese prospects in Corsica were at an end. Though Vincentello d'Istria managed to hang on as Viceroy for fourteen years, he never attempted to capture the city, nor Calvi. Meanwhile the Genoese, secure behind their fortress walls, waited their chance to dethrone him. When it came the King of Aragon did nothing to rescue him or reassert his own rights.

For the Corsicans, the consequences of the Aragonese withdrawal are debatable. The island might for a time have been more peaceful and prosperous under the distant protection of the Spanish monarchs than it became during the fifteenth and sixteenth centuries, torn by wars between Corsicans and Genoese and the French. But in the long run Spanish rule, by its very stability, might have proved even worse than the Genoese. Corsica would have been subjected to the bigoted Spanish type of Catholicism, with the Inquisition, which brought such misery to Sicily. And as in Sicily, the Spaniards would have supported the local nobility; the superb, arrogant, irresponsible Cinarchesi would have ruled unchecked. Sambocuccio's revolution in the north would no doubt have been reversed, and the local democratic institutions crushed.

For the rest of Europe, the defence of Bonifacio was probably providential. When the Aragonese sailed out of the harbour they threw away a unique opportunity: they never again came so close to defeating Genoa; they never laid hands on northern Italy. Had they done so, would the Renaissance have flowered there quite as it did?

The way to the citadel is up a broad cobbled ramp – stepped for horsemen, not pedestrians – leading to an ancient gateway in the city walls. The draw-bridge is still intact with its formidable mechanism of chains and wheels, and its immense wooden doors, studded with square-headed nails. This gateway, in spite of its appearance of dour mediaeval antiquity, is of Renaissance design, and was built (according to an inscription) as late as 1598. Little, if anything, remains of the original fortifications; it is impossible to recognise the gates and towers mentioned by Pietro Cirneo in those that exist today. The defence system of Bonifacio has been repeatedly restored and altered; the French, in particular, made important modifications in the sixteenth century after they temporarily captured the city in alliance with Corsicans and Turks. Bonifacio, as it now stands, is less a mediaeval fortress than a Renaissance fortified town.

All the same, as one walks through the gateway, which is Z-shaped and vaulted, so that one passes through a succession of tunnels, the sensation of reverting to the past is so acute as to seem the prelude to an experience in time. So I felt when I entered the city on the afternoon of my first day there. The streets were empty, the houses apparently deserted: built to accommo-date several thousands, Bonifacio then had a population of barely eight hundred. The life of the city-state came to a standstill two centuries ago, when it was incorporated into France; the merchants drifted away, monks and priests were driven out by the Revolution, churches and houses and monas-teries fell into ruin. Though the buildings present a jumble of styles dating from the foundation of the city to the eighteenth century, almost none has been added since. The streets have kept their cramped mediaeval dimensions, the original chessboard plan of the city is unchanged. The oldest houses have retained fragments of their mediaeval architecture: bands of closed arcades with pointed arches and twin arched windows separated by little columns such as one can still see in the old port of Genoa. There is nothing else like these houses in Corsica, for the other mediaeval towns have either been unrecognis-ably altered or entirely destroyed.

These are details one comes to notice gradually; the first impact of Boni-facio is an overwhelming, generalised impression of age. Here, for more than five and a half centuries, a tough, crowded, ambitious population of merchants, seamen, farmers, monks and priests and artisans, fought, worked, walked in procession and prayed. The setting they created is so complete and un-challenged that one half expects to meet them: armed horsemen clattering over the paving-stones, files of chanting monks, the municipal officers – the *podesta* and *anziani* – Margherita Bobbia and her stalwart feminine contem-poraries. Every street is marked by memories and monuments and legends: the house, its doorway ornamented with a flamboyantly carved marble lintel, where in 1541 Philip Cattacciolo entertained the Emperor Charles V, stormbound on his way to his disastrous attack on Algiers;[11] the *podesta's* palace, with remnants of a thirteenth-century colonnade; the parish church of Sainte-Marie where news of imminent relief was announced to the starving beleaguered citizens during the Aragonese siege.

Built and rebuilt with Gothic features between the twelfth and fifteenth centuries, it is a hybrid product;[12] but its architecture, though curious, hardly arrests attention, for the church is so integrated into its setting as to have lost individual character. Like a forest plant enlacing neighbouring trees, it reaches across the narrow alleys to the enclosing houses with flying buttresses that carried rain from the roofs to an underground cistern, the invaluable summer water supply of the town. The front façade is masked by a vast loggia, where *podesta* and *anziani* regularly held public audience, proceeding there from the *podesta*'s palace a yard or two away.

In the dark interior, matrix of the community, I found a tottering old priest who offered to show me the church's treasure, though he was hardly reassured when I said I was a writer. 'I beg you not to mention where it's kept,' he said, 'one must always beware of thieves.'

The nucleus of the treasure is a much-valued relic of the True Cross, one of those scattered about the Mediterranean by St Helena, mother of Constantine, she who exhumed the cross on Golgotha. Tradition includes her in the sequence of celebrated visitors who sought refuge in the harbour, along with St Francis[13] and the Emperor Charles V; escaping shipwreck in the straits by miracle, she gave the relic as an ex-voto to the town. It retained its power to still the elements, and during storms, those storms that could bring hunger and mourning to Bonifacio, was carried in procession to a spot on the brink of the citadel overlooking the raging waters of the straits.

My interest in these tales had allayed the old priest's wariness; careless, now, of risks of indiscretion and theft he ordered a little boy to show me the interior of another historic church, St Dominique. Together we walked the length of an empty, paved shadowy alley, past high worn houses, some of them bearing marble escutcheons above their doorways with the arms of noble Genoese families: the Serafini, the Salinieri, the lustrous Doria. An archway led us out of the city on to an open plateau of dazzling white limestone, naked to the sun. The white waste was full of relics, like driftwood on a beach: empty barracks, built by the French, facing each other across a parade ground strewn with lumps of chalk; abandoned windmills and blockhouses; entrances to mysterious tunnels choked with rubble and tangles of barbed wire. St Dominic dominates the wreckage, flawless: a Gothic church of pale limestone, austere, devoid of sculpture, with a bold octagonal crenellated campanile spearing the huge sky.

Tradition, always rife in Bonifacio, insists that it was built by the Templars on their return from the Fourth Crusade. I have found no proof of this but on the contrary there is good evidence that it was built by the Dominicans in the mid-thirteenth century and belonged to an adjoining monastery.[14] The monastery was a wealthy one that owned house property and land; no doubt the church was once richly furnished with mediaeval works of art, but these have long since been replaced by Genoese baroque decorations. Their worldliness assumes a quality of heroism in this desolate site; the extravagant attitudes of saints and angels are gestures of defiance, postures of combat in the struggle of civilisation against barbarism. One cannot but feel a tenderness, as for exotic flowers, for the ornate altar of many coloured marbles, the tabernacle, a folly of green and gold carved wood, the gilded angels in peplum and buskins, like figures in a masque by Inigo Jones, holding gilded cornucopia as candelabra. A series of little paintings of the life of Christ, in their original baroque frames, are light and airy in faint imitation of Tiepolo; Roman soldiers wearing fanciful helmets swagger in oratorical poses; Christ leaps like a ballet dancer from his tomb.[15]

Since the French Revolution the church has been only occasionally used; in consequence it is unblemished by the hideousness of modern plaster statues and artificial flowers. Here everything belongs to a period when grace informed the very meanest works of man. So I observed with a pang of delight when I came upon notices pasted above the organ stops, inscribed in a delicate handwriting some two centuries old. They completed the enchantment of the organ, a blue and yellow domed pavilion.

Spurred on by the recurring pleasure of each small discovery, I wandered from aisles to organ loft and into the sacristy, a small room full of immense cupboards, splendidly carved. As I dragged at the heavy drawers and doors piles of musty vestments, embroidered and brocaded, fell into my arms, and a flutter of mildewed engravings of saints in the costumes of the court of Versailles. But the best surprise was in a homely hanging cupboard, where I found two life-size Virgins with identical young, pure, almost boyish faces. One wore a black peasant woman's dress, the other, like a twin sister attired for a fortunate marriage, a sky-blue gown sprinkled with tiny white flowers. My child companion told me that they are brought into the church in Easter week, the black Virgin on Good Friday, the blue on Easter Day. The rest of the year they remain imprisoned, side by side, their hands touching, staring at the cupboard door.

I would have liked to stay longer rummaging in that sacristy; but the little boy was tugging at my arm, begging me to look at St Barthelémy. 'He weighs eight hundred kilos,' he kept saying. What he had to show me were two great groups of baroque statuary, tableaux vivant in painted wood. One represents the three Marys swooning at the foot of the cross; the other is a spirited portrayal of the flaying of St Bartholomew. The saint is bound to a stake, bleeding, surrounded by ferocious Moorish-looking executioners; a butcherly pair in turbans advance on him with enormous knives; another holds an eager little dog straining to catch the peeling flesh; their leader, adorned as an Arab potentate, gesticulates from his horse.

These groups, which belong to the religious fraternities of St Barthelémy and Sainte-Marie-Madeleine; are the pride of the town; the days when they are carried in procession count as the chief festive occasions of the year. The fraternities of St Jean-Baptiste and Sainte-Croix have analogous groups: a

cruelly realistic representation of St John bowed at the feet of his executioners, with Salome and Herodias gloating on their triumph; a stately portrait
of St Helena kneeling before the freshly excavated cross with her six companions.[16]

When we left St Dominic evening was near. Beyond the deserted barracks
the views became enormous and forlorn. The harbour was a dark fissure in the
earth separating the black promontory from the bleaker maquis, rolling mile
on uninhabited mile into the mountainous interior. To the south lay the open
sea, ever pressing on one's consciousness, even when temporarily out of sight,
by the unremitting washing of its waves. Sardinia was a ghost on the horizon,
a mirage, a cloud. Who could live here without the anguish of melancholia,
self-doubt, despair? Only ascetics, hermits, mystics, like the monks of Athos,
fixed on visions of eternity. Yet the Genoese colonists were hardheaded
materialists who viewed their religion as a safeguard rather than a path to
enlightenment.

The church of the ruined Franciscan monastery[17], crouching on the extremity of the peninsula, white walled, cubistic, might seem a fortress but for
its slender campanile, unbearably poignant, pierced by arches enclosing slits
of sky. Every object of value has long ago been removed except a marble
effigy of Rafael Spinola, a fifteenth-century bishop, and this is sadly damaged,
though for reasons that would have pleased him. He asked, it is said, to be
buried in the nave, so that his body might continually be trodden on by men;
a dying wish diametrically opposed to the bandit Jacques Bellacoscia's
arrogant demand that no man should ever walk over his grave. The bishop's
self-obliteration has been almost accomplished, for the passage of feet has
nearly effaced the carving of the head, leaving only the eye-sockets in a featureless mask.

An iron gate, half open by the ruined monastic buildings, tempted my
curiosity. I pushed through a mass of pink climbing geraniums to find myself
in the cemetery, a miniature city of the dead. The family tombs, arranged in
streets and crescents and squares, were more elaborate than any family
home; microscopic palaces with domes and broken pediments and Corinthian
columns and pilasters, statues and urns and double-curving stairways. Every
frivolity of architecture has been attempted here, as though to compensate
the dead for the harsh struggle of their lives: red and yellow tiled Moorish
cupolas surmount Grecian porticoes, Gothic spires top Renaissance doorways,
one baroque façade carries Egyptian heads at the angles of its cornice. But
most of these fanciful mausoleums were far gone in decay; everywhere white
plaster had fallen into the white earth; poppies sprang from the dust in the
untrodden streets and neglected peristyles, putting to shame the rusted
wreaths of metal funeral flowers. Abandoned by the living, the place seemed
also free of the dead; their bones, surely, had fallen out of their mouldering
coffins and collapsing tombs, become indistinguishable from the chalk and
plaster, bleached and purified by the tireless winds and the daily visit of the
sun.

We paused to watch the sun setting before returning to the town, to see it drop to the horizon, straight ahead beyond the point of the peninsula, and lay its beams across the sea now streaming in between the islands like a celestial golden river. Phantom Sardinia was fading into a gentle lilac haze; but Corsica, with the relief of its rugged landscape accentuated by shadows, black on the pale soil, remained concrete and baleful.

When I reached the town dusk veiled its buildings in a timeless antiquity. Yet the streets were full of movement, for this is the hour when the peasants return from their land. Sitting sideways on their diminutive donkeys above baskets of onions and tomatoes, bundles of hay and maize, they came tripping in single file over the paving-stones, old men mostly, directing their animals in a secret muttered language evolved between them in the intimacy of the years. All along the alleys donkeys were being unloaded and pushed into stables, dark holes in the old merchants' houses; as the doors were closed for the night the air was rent by the sound of their braying behind carved and escutcheoned arches.

The donkeys may occupy grander quarters than in the past; but the routine of the peasants' homecoming must be almost the same as could be seen any evening over the past seven hundred years. Little has changed in Bonifacio since the French took over the city, except that the rich have gone away, and with them the colour and glamour of their lives. The peasants trot out at dawn on their donkeys and home again at sunset like the ghosts of their ancestors, and now there is practically no one else in the town.

Yet once I saw Bonifacio alive and glittering with the pageantry which must have been current in the days of its autonomy. It was Good Friday night, when the four fraternities carry their sculptured groups to the church of Sainte-Marie to receive the blessing of the relic of the cross. There was no hint of the tragic, almost savage feeling that permeates the Good Friday ceremonies of Sartène. The streets were brightly lit, crowded with people in a holiday mood; swarms of children were lighting candles with gaily coloured paper shades. The members of the fraternities – the *confrères* – those of St Barthelémy robed in white and scarlet, those of Sainte-Marie-Madeleine in blue and green – packed the cafés, fortifying themselves for their coming exertions.

The group of St Barthelémy had been decked for the occasion: the executioners' turbans flaunted crimson ostrich plumes, the wicked little dog had been given a crimson satin lead. Half a dozen hefty young *confrères* heaved it onto their shoulders; but they could only support the weight by moving at a coolie's shuffling run. Their companions hurried behind them with cries of warning and encouragement, followed by scampering children with their lanterns bobbing up and down. The magnificent unwieldy statuary swayed between the houses, the plumes brushing the first-storey windows; the bearers lowered and raised it with the sharp, urgent cries of acrobats while the wooden angels fluttering round the saint's head scraped the masonry of the arches spanning the alleys.

The *confrères* of St Barthelémy were too anxious to give more than apology for singing; but advancing by another street, those of St Jean-Baptiste, old men but sturdy, carrying a less cumbersome group, struck up a swelling Stabat Mater to a liturgical air with variations in the longdrawn wailing manner of the mountain bards. This music was all that recalled Corsica in a ceremony incandescent with light and colour and Italianate bravura.

11 THE DISINHERITED

Isles of the straits – a Roman quarry – shepherds – the bard of
Chera – cave-dwellings – banquets – a bleak Christmas –
hero-bandits – a retired bandit of today

WHY are remote places so fascinating? What drives one to backward and
primitive pockets of the world? According to the ethnologist Levi-Strauss, not
to evade civilisation, but to rediscover it as it once was: something rare and
precious, diversified and colourful. 'There is nothing else to be done,' he concludes, 'civilisation is no longer that delicate flower that one cherished, that
one cultivated with great difficulty in a few sheltered corners of a land rich
in wild species, menacing, no doubt, by their vitality, but which could be
used to vary and invigorate the seed beds. Humanity has adopted the system
of monoculture; men are preparing to mass produce civilisation, like beetroot.
Their daily fare will be this sole food.'[1]

Bonifacio is a place where civilisation still manifests its pristine quality of
exoticism. Here, if anywhere, it appears a marvellous plant, acclimatised in
defiance of environment. Many towns are more beautiful in their architecture; Bonifacio is magical simply because it has been created and has
survived. Every arch and campanile, doorway and moulding, acquires a
supernormal intensity of existence by reference to its setting. One notes such
details and delights in them; they remained engraved on one's memory
when the masterpieces of the great historic cities have receded into the lumber
of the mind.

So I thought as I walked down towards the port in the twilight. This view,
I knew, would stay with me: the honey-coloured bastions confronting the
white cliffs of Corsica's wilderness; in the distance, beyond the harbour, a
rambling mansion at the head of a green valley; and close beside me, plumb
above the darkening creek, a column, roughly shaped, hewn from a single
block of granite. It is the war memorial, the only inspiring one I have seen in
Corsica (or for that matter anywhere else), and it was brought here, so reads
an inscription, from 'the lost islet of San Baïnzo'. The house in the valley is
something that has overflowed from the city, a Franciscan monastery planted
just outside its walls;[2] the column was gathered in, relic of an earlier phase of
civilisation, the product of a Roman quarry on an island in the straits.

The islands lie about an hour's voyage by fishing boat off the south-eastern
extremity of Corsica. Known to few people except coastguards and fisher-

men, they are shrouded in almost perpetual wind and storm. Many ships have foundered on their reefs, including the *Sémillante*, wrecked on the southern-most, Lavezzi, when transporting French troops to the Crimean War. All the seven hundred and fifty men aboard, soldiers and crew, without exception were drowned.[3] In the course of the following weeks hundreds of their bodies were washed ashore, mostly naked, and so horribly mangled that only a single one could be identified. In the face of this tragedy the sole inhabitant of the island, an old shepherd, lost his wits. He was a leper, writes Daudet, who found him there some years later, 'three quarters idiot', with blubber lips, 'horrible to see'. Lifting his diseased upper lip with his finger, so as to articulate, the crazed eye-witness could just stutter out the frightful tale. The corpses are buried, each marked with a little iron cross, in a graveyard where Daudet and his coastguard companions paused to pray: 'Enormous seagulls, sole guardians of the cemetery, circled above our heads and mingled their harsh cries with the lamentations of the sea.'[4]

Lavezzi is still the preserve of sea-birds, though lighthouse keepers are now installed on the island and cattle graze near the tombs. When the bull is taken to the herd from the mainland he is dragged through the sea with his horns tied to the stern of a boat, for there is none at Bonifacio large enough to hold him. Early spring is the season of this yearly ritual voyage, reminiscent of the myths of antiquity. From time to time parties of friends camp on the island, fishing for most of their food. They are distinguished, on their return, by their Robinson Crusoe beards no less than by their habit of shouting at each other, the only means of conversing in the howling winds of the straits.

Cavallo, with the adjoining islet, San Baïnzo, were exploited as quarries by the Romans, but for centuries now have served only as a refuge for fishermen. Rumours of hundreds of columns stacked on their barren shores, and huge heads carved in the living rock, sent me there one autumn with Jean and Laurence Jehasse, classical archaeologists working at Aléria. The sea, as usual, was rough. The fishermen, encased in oilskins and sou'westers, had prudently decked their little boat; we stowed our cameras below and crouched on the boards at water level, as on a raft. The waves washed over us continually; my terror during that crossing was transformed into an acute, sensual awareness of the elements as I lay sandwiched between the tearing wind and the pounding body of the sea.

Cavallo first appeared as a shimmering phantom such as featured in mariners' tales, for its low coastline was entirely veiled by spray. But when the fishermen had threaded through the outer shoals we had a vision of a whole spawn of sculptures in the manner of Henry Moore, feminine forms which the ocean had scooped and rounded from the silvery fine-grained granite so valued by the Romans. We anchored in a bay ringed by these massive marine goddesses; one of many secret harbours, for the island twists like a skein of snakes, so that walking there, at every turn one meets the sea. Sparse maquis, richly scented, grows from its thin soil, but no trees.

We landed on the columns themselves; monoliths, twenty feet long and more, rectangular, with waving surfaces like giants' cheese straws. They are piled haphazard at the water's edge where they were rolled preparatory to embarkation; others lie scattered on the granite slopes that fall in ramps to the beaches. The Romans evidently evacuated the islands in haste, leaving their wealth in stone behind them. Strangely enough no remains of these granite colossi have been found in the ruins of their Corsican towns, where the columns are made of segments of brick, faced with stucco. Cavallo and San Baïnzo must have supplied their half-finished products exclusively to the home market.

A few yards inland we came to a quarry; its face, perfectly smooth, is scored with a deep horizontal groove to mark the width of the next column to be cut away. I could hardly believe that the Romans had left some fifteen hundred years ago; workers and overseers, I thought, had merely broken off for a midday rest, and at any moment I might stumble over a slave, dozing in the shade of a rock.

The slaves' quarters, close to the only well, are located by a multitude of broken bricks and tiles, and pottery which – as elsewhere on the islands – is no older than the third and fourth centuries A.D. Apparently the Romans occupied Cavallo and Baïnzo only towards the end of their reign in Corsica (neither is mentioned in Ptolemy's second-century geographical description); their output must have been intended for the ambitious building schemes of the later emperors. Monolithic columns were an architectural luxury, reserved for grandiose monuments; these remote islands must have been ransacked in a final search for raw materials to satisfy the tastes of Rome's decadent baroque age.

Nothing remains of the workers' settlement except – most poignant of relics – a rustic shrine to Hercules Saxanus, patron of human toil. His bust is crudely carved on a boulder, with his mace engraved alongside. The head is brutal, thick-cheeked, heavy-jawed, probably bearded; the unskilful work of slaves, clumsy tribute to their divine protector. A somewhat similar bust, again carved in a living boulder, according to Jean Jehasse is an image of the emperor, proprietor of all mines and quarries in the Roman world.[5]

There are ruined cities on the Corsican mainland that give a much better idea of the refinement of Roman civilisation: Aléria, where vast quantities of elaborately decorated Arezzo ware have been found, besides elegant small objects in ivory, glass and bronze; or Mariana, site of a palaeo-Christian basilica and baptistry with beautiful naturalistic mosaic pavements, recently uncovered by Geneviève Moracchini-Mazel.[6] But nowhere is one so impressed by Roman might and vigour as on this desert islet littered with the uncouth relics of an imperial industry. The enormous, embryonic columns, the powerful, rudimentary bas-reliefs, bear the stamp of a master race.

One may speculate on the Roman withdrawal from Cavallo. One can imagine the quarry-workers slogging through their routine in growing uncertainty and dejection, alarmed by ugly rumours, waiting for overdue transport vessels, accumulating merchandise, until the shattering news comes home to them,

The Roman quarry on the island of Cavallo. The groove in the face of the rock marks the width of a column to be cut away. (*Syndication International*)

brought, perhaps, by a panicked refugee from the Corsican mainland: the Vandals from Africa have landed, killing, burning, looting, raping the women and cutting the children in two. There is no choice but to take to the boats, to fly; but where? Italy too is being overrun.

Something like this may have happened; yet the quarries were not permanently abandoned with the fall of Rome. Many of the bricks on Cavallo are post-Roman, and a large slab of granite is carved with mouldings alien to classical convention. The islands must have been exploited again in the early Middle Ages; perhaps they remained productive until the coming of the Saracens who, according to local tradition, used Cavallo and Lavezzi as bases for their fleets.

The Roman towns went down under these invasions: burned and battered by the Vandals, deserted, reoccupied, perhaps, and again destroyed by the Saracens, most of the ports mentioned by Ptolemy on the southern coast of Corsica were wiped off the map. They never recovered. Malaria took hold of the low-lying lands; Barbary pirates succeeded the Saracens; the chain-sequence of disasters emptied the coast of its inhabitants. Even today, with no risk of malaria and the tourist business spreading like a rash along the island's seaboard, one can still, here, swim from cape to cape, to discover, as one rounds each tongue of rock, yet another arc of untenanted, flawless sand.

Many of these beaches are inaccessible by road; one comes to them on footpaths worn by fishermen, meandering through the rocks and lentisk to coves where a single boat is moored at a rotting jetty and pines and juniper grow to the water's edge. Or one may glimpse a little bay from afar, a blue triangle between headlands, as I remember when walking all one summer's day through the maquis with Jean Cesari in search of menhirs, to reach it after sundown, exhausted, perspiring, feet bruised, legs bleeding, so that the plunge into the lunar-pale water was an allegory of entering paradise, or of release from a troubled dream.

Other gulfs and bays, exploding into sight suddenly, in their totality, give a taste of the incomparable sensations that must from time to time reward an explorer. Santa Manza, only four miles east of Bonifacio, a gulf large and deep enough to hold a navy, was practically uninhabited the first time I saw it: immaculate, encased in luxuriant vegetation, bounded by red cliffs and pink beaches, with a white limestone bluff clashing with the red and blue of rocks and sea. I knew, then, the evil joy of violation, of crashing through the untrammelled branches, digging my feet into the virgin sand, of smashing and splintering the peerless glass of the sea, and then, as overwhelmingly, the contrary need for self-immolation, to be dissolved into those serene waters, pulverised into the grains of sand on which I lay.

'Bring only bread and wine, the rest we shall find on the spot,' said my Corsican friend with whom I picnicked there daily, walking over the vacant white tableland from Bonifacio. And he showed me how to fish with a snorkel for the sea-urchins, large as oranges, covered, like hedgehogs, with spikes, lilac and yellow and brown, that lie massed in the crevasses of the submarine rocks. We dived, too, for the giant shell-fish, locally known as *nacres*, which when one first glimpses them from the surface seem more like the relics of some wrecked ship or submerged city than any living thing, for they stand, incredibly, upright on the seabed, a foot or more high, balancing on the pointed ends of their shells. The outer surface of the shells is rough and greyish, giving the illusion of stone; but inside they are a shining blood red, turning, towards their tips, to shining mother-of-pearl. Philippe Diolé aptly describes this large mollusc, the *pinna nobilis*, as 'one of the great prizes of the modern diver'. It grips the seabed with barely visible filaments of great strength which in the Middle Ages were highly prized 'to spin fine stuffs for princes and prelates'; until the eighteenth century the Italians used this tough gossamer for making stockings and gloves. Diolé adds, dubiously, that the flesh of the *pinna nobilis* is said to be edible.[7] Personally I would describe it as a neglected delicacy of the sea. Eaten raw it tastes like lobster, but sweeter.

After this rare hors-d'œuvre the shells became luxurious platters for our bread and sea-urchins – another much underrated sea-food – and some wild figs we had picked near the shore. Later we found some small sweet brownish grapes in an abandoned vineyard before fishing for supper in the pearl-pink evening sea. Days spent like this awake insistent cravings. Why work? Why not live by fishing sea-urchins and *pinna nobilis*, picking figs and grapes? In early autumn the meadows are white with mushrooms, and several varieties of brown and orange boletus are found under the cistus bushes, and in the mountains, at the roots of the beeches and pines. By November the chestnuts are falling that no one bothers to gather, and then the olives, while the arbutus bushes produce millions of berries to ripen and rot among clusters of their own flowers. There is a wild lettuce, too, and a wild carrot and cabbage, and various small green plants that make soups and salads; and the bulbs of the asphodels are edible, those asphodels that light acres and acres of the land in the spring. One could keep alive all the year round by gathering food no one else wants or needs. It tastes well enough; but the overpowering satisfaction is the finding of it; a herd of untamed instincts one has always ignored, strain and bay and clamour for this life, the first known to man.

For the Corsicans the tradition is unbroken through the millennia; the country people still know how to gather what nature provides. Their age-old poverty is a subject of pride and grievance; life was certainly hard and bare; yet their country has always offered food on easy terms. How far is Corsican austerity a choice, or a necessity? Or is not rather correlative with a semi-nomadic routine? Today the shepherds are prosperous (in fact more so than the small landowners); the sheep-breeders have middle-class incomes, thanks to the Roquefort Company which buys their winter milk, and the high prices they can get for their summer cheeses.[8] Yet their homes could hardly be more primitive. Leading their flocks up and down the mountains from sea to Alpine level, pasturing them far from the towns and villages and roads, they have consecrated a traditional way of life, enshrined it in a philosophy. Shepherds must travel light; usually nothing can be taken to their cabins too large to

174

load on a mule. Deprived of possessions, they despise them, and the values possessions entail: life is a passage from birth to death and one should hope for no more than to eat sufficiently and remain one's own master. Civilisation is a toy for degenerates; their pride is to refuse its ways.

One sees them all over the island, the aboriginal type of Corsican: moving across the maquis, dwarfed and hardly visible in their earth-brown corduroys; reclining like effigies on boulders from which they survey their flocks; crouching under huge striped umbrellas in the rain; holding up traffic as they guide their flocks along country roads at the time of the transhumance; emerging, like troglodytes, from their *bergeries*, cabins lower than the surrounding rocks. In some districts, like the Niolo, they still predominate; and south of Sartène and Carbini one meets hardly anyone else until one comes to the recent, raw little villages near the straits. Their homes are dotted about the forlorn landscape, singly, or two or three together, often one-roomed and windowless, with a hearth without a chimney, the *fucone*, which floods all the interior with woodsmoke. The better-off shepherds of the Sartenais have walnut bedsteads which were transported there piecemeal, on the heads of women, the backs of mules; but these are a fairly recent luxury superseding stone or wooden platforms. The rest of their furniture consists of a rough homemade table, benches and stools; an *objet trouvé* may serve as a chair, a root that provides a seat and back; the guns hanging on the unplastered granite walls are often the only well-made things they own. Yet the heterogeneous, makeshift contents of their homes acquire beauty and harmony with the years, for the woodsmoke gives to all these objects a shining black patina, as of lacquer.

Outside, where the maquis has been trampled to lay bare the dust, there is seldom a plant or flower; only a dead tree or two, stuck upright in the ground. These are functional, and indispensable, for sheep's skins, milk pails and mules' harness are hung on their branches out of the reach of wandering animals. The branches, sawn off short, by long use become grey, spiky and polished as antlers. Sometimes cows' or goats' horns have been fitted to their tips as though their owners recognised their decorative quality; and in fact these intricate skeleton forms often have the personality of abstract sculptures. They dominate, with their gaunt presences, the space where one might expect flowers to grow; an impossible luxury here (even if the shepherds cared for flowers), for nearly all the *bergeries* are built at some distance from water, on high dry ground, usually up against granite outcrops where the natural rock-shelters are used as kraals. No doubt the shepherds once shared these caverns with their flocks, like one-eyed Polyphemus in the *Odyssey*.

How stark these houses appear, yet in their context how reassuring! During those weeks I spent fishing sea-urchins alone on the southern coasts in bays where no footprint but my own marked the sand, I learned to value them, those archetypal dwellings, when the shepherds, dismayed by an existence only a little more rudimentary than theirs (and which I had eagerly chosen), invited me to their homes. The tables were laid with piles of tomatoes, whole hams and golden brown cheeses smoked over the *fucone*. I crossed a threshold into a grotto-cool room; a woman said, 'This is your place,' pointing to a bench, as though she had known me always. Yet she had never seen me before, and she never asked me my name. The shepherds' hospitality is impersonal, offered to anyone – bandit, camper or archaeologist – who happens to be passing by. And surely it is nobler to receive the stranger because he may be tired and hungry, than to invite a friend so as to enjoy his company?

It was another woman who crystallised, in a concise image of great beauty, the shepherds' profound awareness of the human condition. I was up in the high mountains above the beech forests, in the midsummer pastures of the southern shepherds, and I had come to a settlement of people so old and haggard, so used by years of exposure, that they seemed to carry in their knobbly, twisted bodies the accumulated weight of man's struggle. Few could speak French; living, winter as summer, away from the villages, they must have been passed over in the round-ups for military service, mobilisations and compulsory school.[9] Language was however less of a barrier than the gulf that lay between us of experience unshared: the battered, toothless faces, the eyes that looked through and beyond me as though immersed in another dimension, belonged to men and women with whom I had no more and no less in common than membership of the same species. A woman, rather younger than the rest, invited me, in French, to her cabin, and unspeaking, unsmiling, poured me a cup of coffee. I thanked her: 'It's natural, people are not mountains,' she replied.

Yet the shepherds are far from saintly. Every year they set fire to acres of maquis and forest, to obtain fresh grass for grazing at the cost of degrading the island's vegetation, and in the long run its climate. They have a reputation for watering milk and overcharging for cheeses; their sharp practice in business dealings is proverbial. All through Corsican history they have been at loggerheads with the sedentary population. Convinced, by immemorial tradition, that the land of Corsica belongs equally to all Corsicans, that they are entitled to pasture their flocks wherever they will, they have always despised and opposed the landowners, regarding them as usurpers of their birthright. Their livestock strays into sown fields and gardens, tramples and consumes crops; they haggle over rents to be paid for pasture, cheat, default, abscond; or so the landowners have constantly complained in this perennial conflict, often waged by the shepherds with intransigent ferocity. Even today the shepherds may settle accounts by violence; those gentlemanly hosts keep their guns loaded. Their resentment of the landowner springs from motives even deeper than greed: not only the occupation of acres of maquis is at stake, but their primordial status as free men, living outside the organised communities, beyond the reach of police, tax-collector or even priest; the shepherds tend to identify their religion with talismans and ritual and they have been the guardians of the secrets of *signadore* and *mazzere*.[10]

Many hold to their primal independence in a spirit of stubborn negation; others have used their money to buy land, 'so as not to have to bend and bow

A goatherd. (*H.-L. de la Grange*)

before the *sgio'*, as Charles-Antoine explained to me. Having acquired it, they often become themselves sedentary, take to mixed farming; but the ways of the pastoral life – its austerity and hospitality – are likely to linger through more than one generation. And since this process has been going on for centuries, Corsican society has been constantly irrigated by a vigorous stream welling up from its most archaic level which has determined the climate of the whole. All the specific characteristics of the Corsicans are derived from this substratum of pastoral culture, and their one, authentic, original art: indifferent craftsmen, uninterested in visual beauty, they have inherited from the shepherds a marvellous form of expression as poet-musicians.

I came to know it gradually, from a song heard here and there by accident, at long intervals, in remote, deprived places (for it is uncongenial to modern civilisation), and then in an overwhelming burst of experience in a little semi-pastoral village in the far south-east. The day had been spent with a Corsican woman journalist walking through an oracular landscape of cavernous rocks and ancient olive groves. We had seen several castle sites and Pisan chapels; towards evening our guides introduced us to the bard of Chera.

I recognised him at sight as we came to the rough stone hamlet; few poets or singers can be blessed with a physique so appropriate to their calling. With his aquiline features and flowing, reddish beard, he is Michelangelo's Almighty of the Sistine Chapel but for the cunning sparkle of his greenish eyes. 'How old are you?' asked the journalist. He roared with laughter: 'I must be seventy since I was born in February, work it out for yourself!'

Without prompting he began to sing, there in the street, while neighbours listened at open windows and doors. The sound came like a war-cry, a challenge to instincts long submerged below consciousness; Corsican music is a voice from the depths of time. It is modal, and oriental; one can detect a connection with Arab music, and a more precise relationship with the liturgical chants of the Middle Ages. But these influences probably overlie even older traditions that may go back to the very sources of Mediterranean song.[11] Many Corsican airs have a quality of primaeval magic, fit to conjure demons; the Christian accents mask those of other rituals, more violent; often one seems to catch the sound of untamed pagan voices piercing the solemn tones of the Gregorian chant.

The bard took us into his house, where guns hung on the smoke-blackened walls, improvising, meanwhile, a song in honour of our arrival. The words poured out to a buoyant air, verse after verse, without hesitation or apparent effort; we were witnessing a spontaneous act of creation. Jean-André Culioli, the bard of Chera, belongs to the élite of the Corsican singers: those who simultaneously improvise words and music. All the Corsican songs began as improvisations; but their music is usually better remembered than their unrecorded words, so that poet-singers are inclined to fit new verses to a limited stock of immemorial airs, sometimes regardless of their suitability. Culioli is one of the few who knows how to harmonise music and words; though the influence of mediaeval liturgical chants is uppermost in his songs, he handles rhythm and tempo with virtuosity to produce airs that are lyrical, lilting or melancholy according to his subject.

A selection of his previous compositions followed. There were songs for every mood: a ballad set to an engaging skipping rhythm about a 'valorous' goat called Stellina, bought cheap at twenty years old who lived many years longer and provided *brocciu* for the whole family; a malicious dialogue between two squabbling women, Checca and Sagra, who accused each other of stealing some washing. There was a mock lament concerning a village election, when the party that had held municipal office for twenty-five years was defeated. The mayor's scarf, insignia of his office, was personified as a woman, married all this time to one man, then wooed and won by another. But her seducer, the new mayor, was a customs' officer overseas (Corsican absentee mayors are numerous); alone and neglected, she bewailed her mistake. There were real laments, too: the bitter lament of the bandit in prison; the tender lament of the old wooden and earthenware untensils, discarded for aluminium pots and pans, of the old stone bread oven, unused since bread had been delivered from the towns.

Domestic subjects of this kind are much favoured by the Corsican poets, who manage to handle them without falling into querulous sentimentality.[12] On the other hand they respond, on the whole, very little to nature. Culioli's originality appears in his close, loving observation of rocks and trees, shadow and light, the forms of the mountains, the moods of the sea. If his verse is occasionally overloaded with the anthropomorphic metaphor which is an established convention of the improvisors, sometimes he strikes out a memorable image, the true matter of poetry. So in his song about the peaks of Bavella he speaks of their shadows, cast on the eastern sea at sunset to make 'an altar for the fishes', and of the pines up on the pass, like church candles, praying that they may be spared axe and storm.

All his life-experience has contributed to his art. Two of his favourite songs refer to his adventures in the First World War: a sombre prayer, like an incantation, recalling the first time he mounted guard on the western front, and a gleeful ditty relating his encounter with a certain Madeleine after months of enforced celibacy in the lines.

Evening raced into night as I listened to him with my companions, alternately stirred and – a more unusual reaction to Corsican songs – amused. Poet and musician, Culioli is also a born actor. Whereas most Corsicans sing in hard, expressionless voices, as though performing some rite of obscure significance, Culioli uses all the resources of his person to communicate with his audience. He can be caressing, mocking, mournful or passionate; he can mime; he can reproduce the spiteful or mincing tones of bickering women as convincingly as the stricken accents of the captive bandit or the gusty banter of a couple of shepherds bargaining over a goat. By vocation he is a public entertainer; a figure as essential in an archaic Corsican community as *voceratrice, signadore* or *mazzere*, and perhaps inheriting a function as old, in local tradition, as theirs.

One of his most moving songs was composed in honour of the fourteen members of his family whose names are inscribed on the village war memorial. It bears no others. Chera belongs to the Culioli, shepherds, so they believe, who came down from the mountains about four generations ago to build a village on this site, which may have been the centre of their winter grazing grounds.

I was struck, in this song, by the repetition of a word unknown to me: *oriu*. When I asked the bard its meaning he was amazed. 'The *oriu*!' he exclaimed, 'why there it is! Everybody knows the *oriu*!' And he took me to the door, pointed to a high smooth lump of rock on the edge of the village, larger and higher than the houses. Like so many rocks in this district it is concave; but a wall has been built to fill the space below the overhang, leaving a square aperture a few feet from the ground. I must have been thoroughly bewitched by the bard's singing not to have noticed, on arriving, this weird combination of the work of nature and man. An iron cross, bent and twisted, stood on its summit. The bard's poem, so I came to understand, honours the *oriu* as much as the Culioli, heroes of the wars. It is the '*oriu* of the Culioli', personified as the guardian spirit of Chera, which has known the family for two hundred years, has heard the lullabies sung by the children's cradles and has watched over the village, at night, in silent prayer.

But what exactly was it, I asked him, this monument and cave which also, apparently, symbolised the life-force and continuity of the family, of the village community? Originally it had been the dwelling of the ancestors of the Culioli, the bard told me; now it was used as a communal village storehouse for grain and hay. A cross had always stood on its summit; a religious procession was made to the *oriu* every year on the second day of Rogation.

The answer was clear enough, but hardly explanatory. It left me questing on the frontiers of that mysterious world, ever immanent in the Sartenais, from which issued the bard's own music, the cult of the dead and the science of the *mazzeri* (who here, at Chera, are the terrible *culpadori* who tear their prey to death with their teeth like hounds). After this evening with the bard I kept my eyes open for *orii*, and was rewarded; for I found a number in the Sartenais (though they are unknown in the rest of the island, as is their name). I saw *orii* that looked like hurricane breakers and cumulus clouds and shells suspended above the ground; the *orii* are one of the very strangest Corsican phenomena, so strange that one is constantly tempted to credit them with some magical, arcane significance, as the dwellings of barbaric deities or *mana*-harbouring shrines. One can hardly believe that these phantasmagoric rock formations were used for nothing more exceptional than sheltering men or grain or hay, as in fact seems to be so.

An *oriu* is a natural cave, not a tunnel in an escarpment, but a hollow space – a *tafoni* – in one of the detached rocks, the gigantic broken eggshells that give an other-planetary ambience to parts of the Corsican south. The opening is blocked with masonry; the interior is generally used, today, for storing hay. Possibly the word *oriu* derives from the Latin *horreum*, granary. But it

179

is certain that the *orii* – as the bard indicated – were once also used as dwellings. Probably they served the two purposes simultaneously, or interchangeably. Some have even been arranged with windows and doors, like the *oriu* I saw at Saparelli, near Chera, which with its crazily high-pitched roof made by the natural slant of the granite resembles nothing so much as a gnome's house in a Walt Disney cartoon.[13]

This *oriu* has long been empty; but quite recently I came upon two that were inhabited within living memory. Both are in the desolate megalith country of the south-west, a country peopled only by a few scattered families of shepherds. The *oriu* of Piaggiola-Pastina stands on a rock eminence amid colossal boulders. It is one of those granite formations such as only Corsica produces, so daring and improbable that one may fancy its substance to be light and pliable, like sculptor's clay. The rock is an oval, hollow shell, some thirty feet long and fifteen high, joined only at one end to the ground, which it overhangs, for all its length, by no more than a foot or two. This narrow space has been carefully filled with masonry. One enters, stooping, by a natural aperture at the end free from the ground; the interior, where one can stand more or less upright, has been divided into three little rooms by waist-high stone partitions. Here lived a certain Vinceguerra Pietri, owner of the surrounding land, until he died in the 1880s at a great old age.[14]

At that period the *bergerie* had not yet been built, a mile or so away, where I stayed with a friendly shepherd and his wife. The *oriu*, fit lodging for Salvador Dali, had been the home of all who occupied the land, generation to generation, perhaps since prehistoric times. And in fact conditions are still only a few steps removed from the Neolithic level. Not that the country has been left in its primordial untamed splendour; on the contrary, though crowded with extravagant rock formations it is none the less permeated by the human presence. But man's relationship to his environment, here, is modest, undemonstrative. Working obscurely, without any pretensions to dominating nature, he is less often seen than his domestic animals: wandering donkeys, cattle resting in the shade of rocks, goats leaping about the mock mountains of piled boulders, or posed like statues on ledges and pinnacles. There are tiny gardens, too, isolated but well-tended by rivulets, and a few olives; paths, unpaved but worn, wind mysteriously, as in Africa, through rocks and trees to unguessed destinations.

One leads to a dolmen, about half a mile from the *oriu*, composed of immense slabs of granite, roughly but perceptibly shaped and smoothed. *Oriu* and dolmen are in harmony: the cave that was a dwelling, and the tomb that was made in the likeness of a cave. And as always in Corsica more care was given to the home of the dead than to that of the living: the dolmen is a clumsy but ambitious essay in architecture; the *oriu* is simply a cave, slightly improved, but perhaps only by its latter occupants.[15]

Another *oriu*, which I came upon by accident at Zilega, near Grossa (when walking through the flowering May maquis with Jean Cesari in search of megaliths and legends), was inhabited by shepherds until about a hundred years ago, and later served both as granary and occasional dwelling, as we learned from two old men living in a stone cabin a few yards away. Some twenty feet high, shaped like an upturned egg, the *oriu* is surrounded by great tilted rock slabs and concave boulders making a labyrinth of shelters and covered passages, where flocks are still folded, as of old. The *oriu* is still used for storing fodder.

Both these *orii* are in a poor, pastoral country where no villages were formed. But in more fertile areas the *orii* sometimes became the nuclei of communities. Not one but several cabins or houses were built near the *oriu* which, abandoned by its inhabitants, came to be used exclusively as the communal granary. But as the first home of the founder-members of the village the *oriu* may be the object of a respect verging on veneration. This, at least, is what has happened at Chera, where the '*oriu* of the Culioli' is honoured both by priest and bard.[16] The old people of Chera believe, however, that the *oriu* resents the hand of the Church; it is haunted, they say, by a phantom goat with iron hooves that can be heard trotting over the rock by night; and it was the goat that bent and twisted the iron cross on its summit.

The performance of the bard of Chera was unsurpassed by any I later heard in this genre. There are poet-singers, less inventive in their style of verse and music, who better represent the indigenous tradition; Jean-André Culioli is outstanding because his personal talent gives new life to an ancient art. His voice, too, is exceptional. The Corsican musical tradition is disintegrating very rapidly under the onslaughts of radio and television. Young Corsicans with good voices become TV singers, and sing trash, or worse still, horribly denature their ancestral music to suit the sentimental tastes of today; the laments of bandits and bereaved women become holiday lovers' whines. As a result the traditional airs are most often heard in the hoarse frail voices of tired old men, who by the strained intensity of their expressions, postures and vocal efforts seem intent on capturing some winged creature inexorably receding into the shadows of the past. Culioli is an exception, his voice unimpaired by his seventy-odd years, rich and true and lusty in all its notes.

Some months after my first visit I returned to Chera with Jean Leblanc and his wife to record his singing. We reached the village early one summer morning; the bard, though unprepared for us, was in form; indeed his voice was so powerful that we had to move the recording apparatus out of the room, too small for the resonant volume of sound. He sang hour after hour, almost without interruption, laughing, miming, lamenting; although he is not really a very big man he seemed, that day, a giant, at once hero, satyr and sage.

People came to join us while he sang. First the women of his family arrived with their children and sat quietly in the background; then friends and neighbours began to drop in. Later a party of young men returned from a boar hunt, carrying two boars they had killed tied by their legs to poles. The boars were hung on a tree and skinned and divided; the meat was cooked on the embers of the open fire. By midday the room was crowded; news of our visit had mysteriously reached the surrounding hamlets; men came on foot, on donkeys, and a grinning cripple in a wooden box with wheels in which he punted himself very fast along the ground with his hands. We sat down to the meal with the bard, still singing, and all the men of his family, packed elbow to elbow round the circular dining-table; the women made an outer ring on chairs, eating from their laps; the children and dogs were on the floor with the cripple in his box; other visitors, who kept arriving, stood propped against the walls, drinking wine.

The boar was too fresh; but so was the meat of the Homeric banquets, the oxen and sheep and deer cooked as soon as slaughtered and washed down with 'mellow wine'. These Corsican feasts with singing and wine-drinking are a survival from the ancient world; they compensated for its horrible hardships; and they are still a compensation, today. They may last all night, until all the meat has been eaten and the wine bottles are empty and the men have sung themselves hoarse and the children have fallen asleep. I have attended many and I know that the pleasure they give is unqualified; for after all what more can a human being reasonably want than to eat and drink and sing in good understanding with his family and friends?

The memory of that heart-warming day was fresh in my mind when I accepted an invitation to spend Christmas in a little village to the north of Chera. My hostess was a middle-aged woman I had met in Nice.

Christmas is not a colourful event in Corsica: the elaborate religious ceremonies with processions are reserved for Easter and the summer feast-days of the Virgin; the winter occasion for rejoicing is profane New Year's Day. All the same every family sits down after Midnight Mass to a Christmas supper which often lasts till dawn, and there is a charming custom in the north of the island of lighting a bonfire outside the church: one stops to warm oneself at its flames going to and from Midnight Mass and its glow gives a cheerfulness to the whole village.

In the south, always more austere, there are no bonfires; the rich kill a sheep for the after-midnight meal and the poor a goat or a wild boar, and that is the limit of the festivities. The slaughtered animals blazed our route as I travelled by bus with my friend south-east from Ajaccio over the mountains thinly crusted with snow; everywhere their bloody carcasses were hanging outside the houses on dead or leafless trees.

The last lap of our journey was by taxi, up a road that soon petered into a trail. The village was a few stone houses and ruins standing just below the snowline on a plateau littered with loose stones. A dense vegetation of maquis, cork trees and olives, growing to its lower edge, sprawled, unalleviated, over the rolling hills that fell to the gulf of Porto-Vecchio, an empty, glass-calm, inland sea reflecting only its own shores. When my hostess took me out to buy bread then I knew that this village was a miserable place; the baker was a widow living in a hut where her seven children, all coughing, sat on the bread chest, dangling skinny bare legs over the side. 'The whole family is tubercular,' my hostess explained.

The widow took the loaves from the chest. 'It's good bread,' she said, 'it's baked in the stone oven; it's better than the bread of the towns.' She smiled; though by no means old she had very few teeth, and her face was terrible, for one of her eyes was sunk back in her head and closed. I was so upset by this family that I gave the children most of the money I had on me, which they received unsmilingly. 'It's because of the lack of vitamins,' said my friend, 'most people here over thirty have lost the use of an eye.'

Such poverty is supposed not to exist in Corsica: everyone has a bit of land and enough to eat, one hears, and social insurance looks after accidents like T.B. But social insurance does not necessarily cover a self-employed widow, and there may not be much to eat for peasants on a stony mountain shelf with a bad water supply. The water in this village, I was told, was insufficient for growing vegetables in summer; in fact the people grew no vegetables at all, only vines. They sold most of their wine and lived on the produce of their goats and olive trees, together with what they could buy in the single shop, a wooden shack stocked mainly with spaghetti and sardines. No doubt they could have done better for themselves; but for generations the race had been worn down by malaria and Malta fever, so my hostess told me.

We were to spend Christmas Eve with her uncle and aunt. Their house had two rooms, one above the other; a goat's carcass was hanging on a dead tree outside. In spite of their obvious extreme poverty they were a dignified couple; they were old and small and their bodies looked dry as the withered tree; they had lost most of their teeth and one of the uncle's eyes was sunken and closed; yet their movements were lively and they carried themselves well. The ground-floor room was half-filled by a huge wine barrel reaching nearly to the ceiling; there was also a bread chest, a table, and some wooden chairs. Small black olives, lying on sacks, almost covered the beaten earth floor. The mud-brown walls were unpainted, but some sheets of newspaper had been pasted round the fireplace. I had seen this kind of wallpaper in Corsica before, and I was still so far from realising quite how little money such people handle that I thought it corresponded with an instinctive taste in decoration; rather good taste, for the result resembles the *collages* of the painters of the 'twenties and 'thirties. Only later I came to understand that newspaper is actually the only thing they can afford to put on their walls; much cheaper than paint, and a dual-purpose luxury: Corsicans may be undernourished, toothless and one-eyed, but they do like to know the news.

I had hardly sat down before the uncle began talking to me, intelligently, about Russia, America, the Cold War, international treaties and obligations. 'I listen to the neighbours,' he said, 'since my children have gone abroad there's no one to read the papers at home. I'm an illiterate; I learnt my grammar from the goats. But all my six children can read. I was determined to give them instruction. You remember what Marshal Pétain said? "I would make the gift of my body if I could save France." I don't know if he was sincere, but I know I'm speaking the truth when I say that I made the gift of my body to educate my six children. And now they have all succeeded. They are all

183

abroad; my three sons are government officials and my three daughters are schoolteachers.'

'Our son in Africa invited us to spend Christmas with him,' the woman said, 'he wanted to send us the tickets for the plane.' 'But my wife wouldn't hear of it,' said the man, 'because the olives have begun to fall.' 'One can't leave the olives to rot,' she said gently, 'the oil is holy.' 'You see how she is,' the old man said. 'Yes, the oil is holy,' she repeated, 'like the bread and wine.'

Then I knew that I had to do with privileged people. They had not been broken by their poverty, for the little they had, their bread and wine and oil, was to them holy. The idea of the sanctity of those three substances is of course inherent in Roman Catholicism, and indeed reaches far back behind Christianity;[17] but I had to come to a village as wretched as this, which knew hunger, to find these beliefs intact and alive. Though most country Corsicans will make the sign of the cross with a knife on the underside of a loaf before cutting it, they are generally only too willing to let the olives rot on the ground.

The man was stacking logs by the hearth. 'You see, it's the custom here to burn a log on Christmas Eve for every son who is abroad, and the grandsons too,' my friend explained. 'My uncle has three sons abroad, and they all have sons of their own, so the fire tonight will be very large.' 'Everyone in the village will have a big fire tonight,' said the aunt, 'almost all the sons have gone away.' 'And the daughters and granddaughters?' I asked, 'does no one burn a log for them too?' 'It's not the custom,' said my friend, 'I'm sure no one ever burned a log for me. But we shall be warm enough without the girls.'

Yet the women, I discovered, were not without prerogatives, for it was the aunt who accompanied us to Midnight Mass in a neighbouring village while the uncle stayed at home to prepare the meal. This too was customary; on this one night of the year the men cook and mind the children while the women go out to pray. The aunt had put on her best black clothes for the occasion; her smile, youthful and expectant, transformed her deep peasant's wrinkles. 'It's really important to her,' said my friend, 'she believes, you see.'

The night was bitter. Far below, an orange half-moon was rising out of the sea. The gulf of Porto-Vecchio which all day long had lain a shining ice blue mirror to the winter sky, was now stained red by the moon's rays, as though it had cleansed Macbeth's murderous hands. But before we reached the village, stumbling downhill over the freezing mud, the moon had purified itself and the waters in its passage to the zenith, where it hung like a flamboyant festive decoration. There was no other. The village streets were dark, and soundless save for the footsteps of women leaving their homes, neat and dedicated in their ankle-length skirts and black shawls. The air, utterly still, seemed about to solidify, to congeal. So intense was the silence that I started when I heard a rhythmic bumping inside one of the houses, a noise hardly louder than the ticking of a clock.

'We'll see what it is,' said my hostess, 'I know the people who live there.' We opened a door to find a bare room, cruelly lit by an unshaded overhead electric bulb. A young man was sitting by a very small fire; with one hand he was cooking a lump of meat stuck on a skewer; with the other he rocked a baby in an old-fashioned wooden cradle that made the bumping sound as it rolled back and forth on the naked boards. 'The Christmas supper,' said my friend. 'I'm doing my best,' he answered, 'this is not a night like others.'

When we returned to the street it was full of women marching five and six abreast towards the church. Their white faces, framed by their shawls, were intimidating, for each was set in an expression of extreme resolution as though in a moment of crisis it had been turned to stone. The church, like the rest of the village, was modern, and ugly, although someone had hung a garland of green maquis branches across the altar; the cold was even more oppressive than outside. The women hardly greeted each other when after the service we stepped out into the blackness of Christmas Day.

But at the end of our trudge up the mountain track, now frozen hard as granite, the air was fragrant with the smoke of fires. My friend's uncle had made a great blaze in the hearth, and he had stewed the goat. In the manner of an accomplished host he filled our glasses, handling the wine bottle tenderly, a large, circular bottle encased in leaf-shaped strips of cork held together by wire. Later, by way of entertaining us, he sang.

His song was a ballad relating the deeds of the bandit Tomasino; he chanted its fifty-two verses in a high, tremulous voice to a wailing air that seemed unconnected with himself, so that one could fancy he were transmitting a music carried on the wind. Tomasino lived some sixty years ago. When two of his cousins were found murdered, his brother was arrested, convicted of the double crime on the evidence of supposedly false witnesses, and condemned to life imprisonment on Devil's Island. On hearing the news Tomasino immediately deserted from the regiment in which he was serving, returned to Corsica, took to the maquis, and killed the men who had witnessed against his brother. After which he managed to escape to America with his sister and engineer his brother's escape from Cayenne. The three of them ended their lives in the United States, prosperous and respected. The story – more intricate than can be related here – was sometimes hard to follow, the music was monotonous; yet the performance had a hypnotic fascination. This was the kind of song that enchanted Boswell when he heard Paoli's followers celebrating the deeds of their heroes, the kind of song that must have stirred the pride of generations of Corsicans ever since Filitosa's barbarous heroic age.

'Tomasino was a good man,' said the aunt, 'he defended justice. Like the bandit Santa-Lucia. He was even more celebrated. Everyone respected Santa-Lucia. He never robbed, and he protected the poor. You know what he did? There was another bandit in the district who used to take money from poor people by menaces. To make himself more feared he used the name of Santa-Lucia. When Santa-Lucia heard of this he searched for the bandit and found him; he pointed his gun at his stomach and said: "Hand back the money you've collected in my name or you're dead." The bandit gave him the money and Santa-Lucia returned it to all the poor people who had been robbed. Ah,

185

yes, he was a very good man.' 'And he saved his brother who had been wrong-fully accused,' said the uncle, 'I will tell you how.' And so I came to hear the story of the most admired of all the Corsican bandits, Antoine Santa-Lucia.

His name was derived from Sainte-Lucie-de-Tallano, where he was born. Like almost every village of the south in the 1830s it was divided by a ven-detta. Antoine and his brother Jean, a priest, were accused of the murder of two men on the evidence of witnesses who, they insisted, were lying. Antoine took to the maquis; Jean, the priest, allowed himself to be arrested and sentenced to ten years' imprisonment. Antoine was condemned to death by default.

Thereafter he lived for a single purpose: to revenge himself and his brother on their accusers and anyone who supported them. From the shelter of the maquis he watched their movements closely, to appear, from time to time, to murder, in cold blood, and with incredible audacity. Having tracked one of his enemies, an elderly doctor, to Ajaccio, he shot him dead in the main square and then calmly walked out of town. On the road leading from Pro-priano to Sartène (later the scene of one of Muzarettu's murders), he inter-cepted a man known as Mezza-Notte, a witness who had testified at his brother's trial. Mezza-Notte was old, and guilty, and at the sight of the bandit he became stupid with fear. 'You do not seem to recognise me,' said Santa-Lucia. 'No, I do not recognise you,' muttered Mezza-Notte. 'Look me in the face and search your memory,' ordered the bandit. 'No, no,' Mezza-Notte mumbled, 'I do not recall ever having seen you before.' 'Yet at the Court of Assizes,' said Santa-Lucia, 'you swore that with your own eyes you saw me, and my brother, commit double murder. Now you will never see me again.'

No doubt the wretched old man expected to be killed on the spot. But worse was in store for him. Seizing him by the throat, Santa-Lucia gouged out his eyes with his stiletto. Mezza-Notte took eight months to die. The revenge, undeniably, was appropriate; but was it not also influenced by unconscious recollections of the patron saint of the bandit's village, the beautiful Lucia of Syracuse who tore out her own eyes rather than allow them to be a tempta-tion to her numerous suitors?

The bandit's deed became notorious; as Jean Cesari told me, it so marked the spot where it was perpetrated that passers-by, ever since, have been liable to see spirits there. Yet it in no way shocked the population; Santa-Lucia is remembered as a hero. And by Corsican standards, he was. His vengeance drew official attention to his brother's trial, and with five murders to his credit Santa-Lucia was received by the Préfet in Ajaccio and given assurance that his brother's case would be reviewed. The peace-loving Bishop Casanelli d'Istria threw in his influence, with the result that Jean Santa-Lucia was released and rehabilitated. A magistrate at the Court of Assizes in Bastia, addressing some witnesses whose evidence seemed unreliable, went so far as to say that he wished there were more men in Corsica like Antoine Santa-Lucia. By then the bandit had left the island and enlisted under Garibaldi; later he emigrated to Brazil where he transformed himself into a respectable, well-to-do citizen.[18] 'That was only to be expected. He was a good man, a very good man,' the gentle old woman commented, as her husband concluded the tale.

'Tomorrow you'll meet a living bandit,' my friend said to me, when we made our way back to her house in the early hours. 'I've arranged for us to lunch in Porto-Vecchio with Bornea.'

I had been long enough in Corsica to know that François Bornea was not a 'good man' among bandits, that he was not cast in the heroic mould of those uncorrupted outlaws who had lived by the total conviction that they killed in the sacred names of justice and honour. Bornea had not taken to the maquis to right an injustice, nor even to avenge an injury; he became a bandit simply for the sake of adventure. He had not found it, or not enough of it, as a member of the French police, from which he was dismissed on account of his connections with the underworld of Toulon. At the age of twenty-two he returned to Corsica, disgraced and dissatisfied; a couple of years later – early in 1930 – he attached himself to Bartoli, a reigning bandit of the new 'tax-collecting' category, already famous for his robberies, his murders, and the rape of a Dutch tourist. In his company Bornea got the life he wanted; for a while.

Their base was Zicavo, from which they controlled all the central, mountainous part of the south. Together they held up the bus from Ajaccio and exacted tribute from its owner. They sent out their emissaries to the operators of transport services, merchants, exploiters of the forests – to whoever, in fact, had a little money – to demand sums of three to eight hundred pounds on behalf of 'Bartoli, Bornea and Co.' Few dared resist them. Chieftains of a bodyguard that soon swelled to a private army, at the height of their reign of terror they were able to peal the bells of the *gendarmerie* of a mountain village while the *gendarmes* prudently cowered out of sight, inside. They lived luxuriously, by maquis standards: supplies of champagne and ammunition were sent to them on order from Ajaccio; their firearms – of the best quality – were imported from the mainland. For Bornea only one thing was lacking: full acceptance in the society he had chosen. He had come by his success easily; too easily, without killing; and to rank as a qualified bandit he had to kill.

His chance came in May 1930, in an argument with a road-mender. What happened is obscure: the road-mender was drunk, it was said; Bornea was drunk; the road-mender threatened him; at any rate he failed to hurry off the road when Bornea drove up in his car. That alone was sufficient pretext for murder: Bornea shot him dead. The road-mender was in fact armed; his revolver was found in his coat pocket, but the coat was lying on the ground some two hundred yards from the scene of the crime.[19] 'Bornea killed from snobbery,' Martin Baretti, the hotel proprietor in Ajaccio, told me.

It was Martin Baretti who later persuaded Bornea to surrender to the law. His glory had been brief. He had taken part in a big coup – his biggest – a few days after the murder, when he and Bartoli exacted a handsome bribe from

187

Paul Lederlin, candidate in a senatorial election, in return for their protection; the bargain was sealed at a champagne banquet in a tavern near Ajaccio. A month later they had racketed a timber merchant for a smaller but still sizeable sum. Then they had quarrelled and parted. Thereafter Bornea's exploits were less spectacular. In November 1931 Bartoli was killed, and the *gardes mobiles* launched their anti-bandit campaign. Bornea joined forces with a minor bandit, Morazzini; when Martin Baretti went to see them they had been on the run in the maquis for more than two years. 'I found them in Carbini, where they were being sheltered by an old woman,' he told me. 'I reached the village after dark; it was a stormy night. I can't describe to you the atmosphere in that cellar where the three of them were living. The monotony of their lives, their constant suspicion of each other, their fear of being captured, denounced or betrayed, had created a terrible tension. I shall never forget the smile of relief on that old woman's face when I arrived. After some blustering talk they agreed to give themselves up. I was in a position to tell them that they wouldn't get more than five years. Actually I think they were glad to go to prison. They were both ill; Morazzini, at any rate, was spitting blood.'

Bornea served a prison sentence of five years; then he settled in Porto-Vecchio, where he had married, fathered a family, and found a job in a small cork-processing factory. He earned a little extra repairing clocks and watches, his unlikely hobby which he had managed to pursue even in the maquis, so my hostess told me.

It was raining when we reached his home on Christmas Day. Porto-Vecchio is surrounded by scenery of a rare exotic beauty; but its streets are depressing at the best of times. An unstable town, heavily stricken with malaria until the Second World War, always subject to setbacks and false starts, it is full of houses abandoned or in construction, so that almost every one appears to be a ruin. The half-finished are the dreariest: built of unmellowed stone in the gaunt local style, with overlarge windows, black gaping holes that glare like dead eyes. Few people were about that Christmas Day except some young men with dark knife-blade faces loitering in the doorways of the cafés.

The house where Bornea lived was no exception to the general rule; there was a gap in an outer wall of the staircase through which blew wind and rain. We found him in a high cold upper room, squatting on the floor filling water pistols for two little sons; the only pistols, presumably, that he handled now. His wife was crouching by the smoking fire, a serene, large-eyed girl, much younger than he, together with her father – a bearded peasant – and some old woman relative draped in black cotton.

'Why this is wonderful!' Bornea exclaimed, springing to his feet, stepping towards us with an engaging smile. He was better looking than I had expected, and in a different way: tall, slender, with greying fair hair and bright blue, sunken eyes. His movements were graceful, his manner worldly; he suggested not so much a lord of the maquis as another type of delinquent: the cocktail party parasite, the Mayfair man.

'We must drink!' he cried, 'unfortunately I can only offer you wine.' He filled glasses, rinsing the one that served for the water pistols with wine which he then dashed onto the tiled floor; a gesture no doubt left over from his tavern-drinking maquis days. He had forgotten that the wine was holy; perhaps he had never known.

The old crone took the pot off the fire and we sat down to stewed goat with spaghetti. A very small child appeared in a doorway, blue with cold. 'Yes, he can come to table,' Bornea said. 'We had to punish him,' his wife explained, 'he laughed this morning at Mass.' 'He's so young,' I suggested, 'perhaps he didn't understand.' 'There are things one must learn to understand when one is young,' said the reformed bandit, 'otherwise one may not come to understand them until it's too late.'

Although we made an oddly assorted party, the conversation went well enough until my friend foolishly mentioned that I was a writer. At this Bornea stiffened visibly, slammed down his knife and fork. 'Then we're not friends!' he flared at me. 'I don't like your profession! I've been pestered by romantic-minded female journalists for years. I've nothing to tell you, nothing at all.' But I too was angry. 'I don't want to write about you,' I told him. 'I've come here to write about the cork factory. That at least has a future.' It was a cruel remark, for I knew that the cork factory was a ramshackle, tottering concern. Bornea glowered with those hypnotic pale blue eyes that must have terrorised in the past. No one spoke; I had insulted the bandit; he had killed for not much more. But Bornea was a reformed character, and he knew how to charm. His face relaxed into a devastating smile: 'You're probably right,' he said, 'I'll take you to see the factory one of these days.'

My blunder had broken constraint, and now he talked freely. 'Don't believe what you hear about Corsica,' he said. 'Corsica isn't neglected. Everyone blames the French government, but the government isn't to blame. The French pour money into the island; they're always giving us millions of francs, for roads and bridges and so on. And what happens? Everyone takes his cut, from the mayor and contractor of public works down to the last labourer, and then only half the job gets done. Haven't you noticed? You drive along a fine tarred road and then it turns into a dirt track?' I had: the road to the village I was staying in was an example. In fact I had noticed many half-finished undertakings such as bridges and roads, but no one had offered me any explanation until I met this retired gangster who knew just what rackets could be pulled off in Corsica and had lived by bullying the rich out of their often ill-gotten gains.

'But why do I tell you about Corsica?' said Bornea. 'There are plenty of people in high positions who can tell you more than I.' 'I've met some of those people,' I said, 'and very often they don't know very much, or if they do they prefer not to talk.' Bornea's face lit with the smile that must have been one of his major assets. 'I know what you mean,' he said, 'my life was more real than theirs.' He spoke tensely, as though of a heresy he had wholeheartedly believed in and unwillingly abjured. Then he lapsed into self-pity. 'When I was young and handsome,' he said, 'people used me in the wrong way. Now I'm old, no one has any use for me at all.'

Bornea, I thought, had always seen himself as persecuted by forces outside his control; the tool of unscrupulous friends, the victim of the law, of Corsica, of life itself. 'But one mustn't despair at fifty,' he added. 'Despair of what?' I asked. 'Of comfortable circumstances,' he replied, suddenly eager, sincere. 'Why, I haven't even got a radio or a car! Tell me truthfully, d'you think it's possible for me to achieve a comfortable standard of living now?' 'Of course,' I said, but without much conviction; for I did not really see how Bornea, that permanently displaced person, would be able to integrate himself into middle-class society. And that was what he wanted; he would never be content, as his wife and her father were, with the bare room, the stewed goat, the smoking fire; he was not at home in this peasant household.

I left feeling sorry for him. But sorry, too, for almost everyone I had met during that bleak Christmas: for the widow with the bakery, of course, and her ill children, and also for the old couple, my hosts, who had made the gift of their bodies to send their six children away. Their educated sons and daughters would not, of course, find the Utopia their parents imagined. They would be rather better fed, perhaps, but probably even worse housed in cramped flats opening on to streets and courtyards. They would be harassed by rents and bills, humiliated by their superiors as their parents never were. They would forget that the bread and wine and oil are holy, or indeed that anything is; they, or their children, might come to doubt that life has any purpose or meaning.

Yet they could never have borne to stay at home. They would not have starved – Corsica provides the necessities – but the old way of life would have been for them insupportable. Poverty can only be accepted when it seems inescapable, the lot of one's fellow men, and they would have seen factory workers from Paris, in the summer camps near Porto-Vecchio, spending more money in three weeks' holiday with pay than they themselves handled in a year. And that would have appeared a monstrous injustice, and against injustice even the traditional faith and fortitude are of no avail. In the past a Corsican who suffered an injustice killed; but one cannot kill the social system; there is no choice, one must leave home and join in. The ancient order, so little changed since the Neolithic Age, is finished, superseded; it will no longer serve. But these peasants' children, who abandon it, exchange a system that was complete in itself, framed in a valid philosophy evolved through the millennia, for one that is experimental, uneven, raw. The modern world pampers some human needs at the expense of others.

I tried to explain these thoughts to my friend as we drove away from Porto-Vecchio in the damp twilight of Christmas Day. The forested maquis stretched out of sight, dark and despairing. 'What would you?' she said, 'this is the land of the disinherited.'

12 FALLEN CAPITALS

The green desert – Roman ruins – night-pleasures of Bastia – a singing duel – ruins of time and war – Genoese agricultural campaign – the Governor's palace – the Corsican flag – the British Viceroy

I REACHED Bastia in late afternoon, an afternoon of the dog days, feeling shrivelled and desiccated by my journey up the east coast plain. At that time it was still a forlorn, neglected area; the mosquitoes had certainly been done away with (not even a common housefly remained), but no one had yet thought of going to settle there. The scientific agriculture, the military air base and the archaeological researches that have combined to recreate this region belonged to the future; the expanses of vines and citrus fruit plantations one now sees, the brash new houses, restaurants and hotels, the splendid museum at Aléria were then all equally unimaginable.[1]

Porto-Vecchio, where I spent a night in a widow's home, was still a stagnant, ramshackle place that seemed overwhelmed by its subtropical environment. Everything in the town was seedy, but the surrounding country was luxurious. I bathed alone from a sandbar at the head of the great empty lagoon; picnicked in a pine grove where the air was dusky and perfumed as in a pasha's tent; wandered through salt pans in an inner lagoon enclosed by wooded round-topped mountains that recalled the landscapes in Chinese paintings.

The opulent oriental scenery withered the following day as I travelled by bus along a road that cut dead straight through the maquis under a martyrising sun. The mountains receded to become a hazy blue boundary wall for the plain that stretched unbroken to the sea; the vegetation was uniform, dense and implacable as the African bush. This was the country that Lear described as a 'green desert', where the inhabitants were all yellow-faced with fever, shaking in their rags;[2] and indeed the sluggish rivers and darkly glinting marshes still looked able to breed death. It was hard to believe that this coast had once been a valued acquisition for the most civilised peoples of antiquity, the site of Greek and Roman cities, of the dozen ports listed by Ptolemy.

At Ghisonaccia, a broken-down one-street village of drab houses built in a rough-cast of river pebbles, I found what must once have been the coaching inn, its interior courtyard now given over to pigs. The ground-floor room was full of bearded old men sitting solemn and silent at café tables; I felt I was intruding on some assembly of elders that had been in session, and at a standstill, for months and years, a kind of Long Parliament of the forgotten plains.

An exhausted woman provided me with some small brown fish to eat and a car to take me on to Aléria, a few miles to the north. My driver was bored by the excursion; but some workmen dozing on a pile of rusted agricultural machinery by the roadside directed me to the Roman town. It had been built on a platform of low hills overlooking the steaming coastline; the confused remains of a small amphitheatre appeared rising above small trees. A broken arch and some unidentifiable lumps of masonry were stranded in a sea of thistles; these, when later excavated, proved to be relics of the *praetorium*, the seat of the governor in the days when Aléria was the capital of a Roman province. But I could make little, then, of these shapeless ruins, unusually lacking in romantic appeal. The litter of shivered bricks and tiles and mosaics lying underfoot among the thistles spoke more directly to the imagination, by evoking the catastrophes that had reduced a thriving capital to fragments small enough to hold in one's hand.

It would be several years before Jean and Laurence Jehasse revealed the ground plan of the city, the foundations of forum, temple and baths, and longer still before their discovery of the pre-Roman necropolis brought to light a marvellous collection of Greek ceramics dating from the sixth century B.C.[3] Baffled by the site and dazed by the sun, I picked up some blue and white mosaic cubes, looked at the stark Genoese fort dominating the existing miserable hamlet, and from a hill-top viewed the inland sea, the vast Etang de Diane that once harboured the Roman fleet and now appeared entirely imprisoned in vegetation, like a lake in Central Africa, secret and unpossessed. Beyond, a humped phantom form floated on the horizon: the Italian island of Monte Cristo; but Italy seemed as remote as ancient Rome.

No bus was due to pass through Aléria; I was spending too much hiring cars; eventually I hitched a lift with a couple of men in a truck bound for Bastia. We crashed ahead through a sick, savage landscape that was almost uninhabited until we neared the town. I asked them to suggest a cheap hotel; they sent me to one that turned out to be a flat in an old mansion. My room gave on to an alley; but no matter, I cared nothing for the sun. Almost at once I fell asleep, with the notion that I was being pressed down the shaft of a well.

When I woke up, in the twilight, I found myself looking at a vaulted and painted ceiling. There was a delicate pattern of scrolls and mermen and caryatids and stylised foliage – faded, restored, flaking, damp-stained – something left over from the Genoese occupation, and bordering the cornice a set of fresher, cruder medallions with sentimental little views of Italian castles and lakes. I remembered, then, that I had reached Bastia, the Genoese capital, the Italianate town of Corsica that flourished, in an obscure provincial way, for some four centuries until Napoleon degraded it in favour of his birthplace.[4] As I opened the shutters its life was carried in to me on the warm air; the life of a Mediterranean backwater town where there is little traffic and the sounds are human: voices in conversation, feet tapping and shuffling on paving-stones, the notes of a guitar. With the sounds came the prevailing smells: the stale odour of drains, the insidious water-scent of the harbour, the pungent scent of Gauloise cigarettes, for on that stifling summer evening most of the inhabitants were walking and smoking out of doors.

Evening is the best time for exploring a strange town. One sees it, then, relaxed, given over to pleasure; the nightly human holiday has begun. These first impressions are indelible, and significant; for people differ more vividly in their pleasures than in their work. That first evening in Bastia compares in my mind with my first in Budapest, when long ago, travelling to Romania filthy and aching after twenty-four hours in a third-class carriage, I saw its lights, left the train on an impulse and spent a summer night wandering about its riverside boulevards, full of the wailing of gypsy violins. Bastia is of course not Budapest; but I had been living in remote rough country places and I entered its streets with the same acute sense of anticipation.

Within a few steps I came to the main square: a vast square designed for the pride and pleasure of the citizens, and as so often happens in Corsican towns and villages, out of scale with everything surrounding it. Cafés line all its length, facing an avenue of planes, a shady promenade, barred to traffic, fanned by a constant breeze blowing in from the sea on the empty side of the square. The lights that give this strolling place a nightly theatrical bravura were already corroding the soft dusk: neon café lights shedding a spectral glare; electric bulbs, hanging in garlands from tree to tree and adding a necromantic intensity to the green of the leaves. Waiters were folding up café parasols made of segments of contrasting canvas, yellow with scarlet, emerald with turquoise blue. The street vendors were packing away their wares, mirrors and scissors and morocco leather notecases and flashily printed ties; an old man was piling into a donkey cart the melons he had displayed all day in a golden pyramid at the foot of a plane. But the night merchants were going into action, advertising pleasures for sale; innocent fairground pleasures: a shooting range; a wheel of chance whirring against tiers of gaudy prizes, peacock-blue satin cushions embroidered with camels, Negro dolls, toy ships with magenta cellophane sails. Outside a café an orchestra was playing a Viennese waltz that gave a lilt to the steps of the passers-by.

Swarms of people were passing by; all the younger members of the population, it seemed, were walking under the trees. Three or four girls abreast, three or four boys, they paced, languid and solemn; but not so tense, I thought, as the youth of Ajaccio and Sartène. The girls were less sleek and sly-looking, the young men less poker-faced, and words and laughter were exchanged now and then between the sexes. Although traditions have been only slightly relaxed in Bastia there is an absence of constraint about the town that recalls northern provincial Italy. To me it seemed voluptuous in comparison with the austere villages I had been visiting. The proprietress of the café I had chosen came to talk to me, recommended a restaurant; it was near the old port, which was picturesque, she said, and the food was the best in town.

Following her directions I made my way along a dark road immediately

193

above the sea, lying motionless under a moonless sky and visible only for brief moments when intermittent red and green lighthouse beams swept its black surface. But the old harbour, recessed between tall Genoese houses, sparkled with a galaxy of lights reflected from their superimposed windows. Stacked up a hillside, they stand six and seven storeys high; but now their outlines were indistinct, so that their windows appeared as lamps hanging in mid-air. Hundreds of families are crowded in these great tenements; but the port itself was deserted. Only a shack on the far side of the harbour pool showed sign of life by its blazing windows. As I approached I could see fishermen sitting inside; with their rutted, unshaven faces, they made me think of a gang of pirates, feasting, after looting the town.

In fact they were mild-mannered, friendly people. 'Yes, it's a good restaurant. You go up those steps, then turn right,' one of them told me. 'You'll get *langouste*,' his drinking companion said, 'we brought in plenty this morning.' The restaurant overlooked the harbour pool which, seen from above, seemed to derive its glitter from gold massed in its depths, so that one could fancy it had sucked into itself, through the centuries, the treasure of the wrecked merchant ships that plied the Mediterranean shores from Syria to Spain. But now it has become a place of phantoms and memories; for business has moved to a new port at the opposite end of the town, leaving the old city and its harbour to decay, the haunt of fishermen and the poor.

The girl who served me *langouste*, followed by wild wood strawberries brought down from the mountains by a friend, had no suggestions as to how I could spend the rest of the evening. There were a couple of cinemas, but she thought their programmes had already begun; there was a night club, but she doubted it was a place a woman could go to alone. It was not. Later I was taken there and found it full of husky brown shepherds from the interior hungrily courting pathetically plain dance hostesses, all dressed in black, as though in mourning for themselves. So after dinner I wandered back to the empty quay (where even the fishermen's shack had closed), and into the alleys of the Genoese town. They too were empty, except for cats picking the rubbish heaps at the base of the canyon walls. Voices came from lighted windows, and seductive tangos; but all this sociable life belonged to other levels, far up towards the sky.

A solitary lamp like a seaman's star finally guided me out of the maze of passage-streets to a church in a little square. Its haughty classical façade fronted a flight of steps, grandly conceived, but dilapidated, for each had dropped a sprinkling of rubble onto the one below. And here indeed were people enjoying the night life of Bastia, sitting about in family groups, reclining on the steps as gracefully as Fragonard's languid revellers. Trees and palms appeared in sombre foliate masses above a creeper-covered wall; a fountain stood in a vaulted loggia on which the scrawled words, '*Eau dangereuse à boire*', reminded one that this arcadia was after all downtrodden and decayed.

I squatted on a step; no one took any notice except a neighbour who silently offered me a cigarette and went on playing with his baby daughter as before. And then the air, or rather the murmuring that pervaded it, was sliced by a high-pitched, long-drawn wailing, a phrase of music wandering through unfamiliar quarter tones. Another voice, deeper and more assured, answered with a similar, slow, meandering call. The first replied, the second rejoined: somewhere, not far away, a couple of men were conversing in song.

I followed the sound, tracking it up and down streets, built almost entirely in steps and spanned by many arches, which so much resembled stairways that I could fancy myself in a huge old rambling mansion, hesitating, between each phrase, in panicked fear that its closing notes might be the last. But the continuing music led me to its source, a closed café from which the voices issued full and vehement. It was a small bare brightly lit room where four men, one in jeans, one bearded, the other two middle-aged, wearing country corduroys, sat drinking at a table. The one in jeans and the bearded one were chanting, alternately, in three-lined rhyming stanzas. The sound was remote and blood-kindling; this was the ancient indigenous music which until then I had only heard faintly echoed in the Bonifacien fishermen's songs. I had gone out in search of urban amusement, and I had come upon a much rarer type of entertainment such as one would normally have to look for in a mountain cabin.

'Come in and listen,' the proprietor said, 'you're welcome, and we're serious here.' The two men continued singing without interruption, ejecting their responses with a mordant conviction. They were engaged in a contest, the proprietor explained; each had to improvise, in rhyming verse, a suitable reply to his opponent. He who first failed to answer was the loser. Known as *chiama e rispondi* – question and answer – this poetic duelling in song is an immemorial Corsican diversion. Its conventions are rigid: the stanzas are made up of three sixteen-syllable rhyming lines, each broken by a caesura. The airs used are traditional, and closer to Arab music than those of some Corsican poets, like the bard of Chera, who so often recall the chants of the mediaeval Church. The style of singing, too, is fixed by tradition: the voice is thrown out with violence, like a jet of water, at the opening of each line, falls through a sequence of involutions until it breaks off short with the caesura, then enters another, swelling phrase, to close the line with a full-throated long-drawn climax which is characterised by a change from minor to major key. The competitors, who take as much pride in their musical accomplishment as in their talent for verse improvisation, often vary or embroider the airs according to the inspiration of the moment.

The difficulty of this double art gives a particular intensity to their performance, irrespective of the subject under discussion. Usually it is some everyday matter: the pair I was listening to in Bastia, for all their wild wailing, were simply comparing notes on how they had spent the day. Another duel I heard, sung to a particularly tragic air – in a cabin in a pine forest, at the end of a boar hunt – concerned the merits of gas stoves as opposed to open fires. *Chiama e rispondi* has little to do with poetry; yet those who can appreciate the subtler nuances of the dialect maintain that words are skilfully, sometimes brilliantly handled, and delight in the sharpness of the repartee between star performers, the innuendos, double meanings and puns. Verbal aggression fuels the competition; singers and audience have been goaded to murder within memory; but today the Corsicans take their pleasures less seriously and the loser of the duel is usually knocked out by mere exhaustion.

This was in fact what happened in the Bastia café, when after an hour or so the bearded singer, whose voice had been grating and creaking like an unoiled hinge, stumbled over his opening words, gave in and admitted defeat. The two men ceremoniously shook hands, after which the loser ordered a round of drinks. I congratulated them. 'It's a gift, one has it here,' the winner told me, tapping his forehead. 'Practice helps, of course,' said the bearded loser, 'when I was young I sang more often; I was invincible then.' 'And wine helps, and sympathetic company,' said one of the listeners. 'No, it's a gift,' the winner insisted, 'either one is born a poet or one is not. One has it inside.' 'All these men are poets,' the proprietor said in prudently conciliating tones. Three of them, I learned, were shepherds who had come down from the Niolo on business; the fourth, the winner, was a dockworker who had originated in the same part of the country. 'You're lucky to hear them,' the proprietor continued, 'there are not many poets left today. The young have lost the gift.' 'They have education instead,' said the man with a beard. 'I've done without education,' said the dockworker, 'all I know comes from here,' he tapped his forehead again. 'He's very intelligent,' said the proprietor, 'even though he can't write his name.' 'Yes, I'm intelligent, I know it,' the dockworker said, 'if I'd had education I'd have gone a long way.'

Perhaps; yet amid the universal applause of education may one not say a word for these inheritors of an ancient cultural tradition, these men with 'a gift', who use it, spontaneously, for their own pleasure? And when subjected to the dreary procession of feeble crooners and pop singers on television, may one not regret the passing of this exacting, spirited art, this music that rakes and tears at the roots of sensibility, known to Corsican dockhands and shepherds?

My craving for entertainment was satisfied, and luckily, for when I walked back to my hotel I found the main square deserted and all the cafés closed. In spite of a certain grandeur of design, Bastia is a torpid little provincial town that offers almost nothing in the way of entertainment to visitors or to its own more prosperous citizens. Later I came to know them: solidly established bourgeois families with businesses, and descendants of the local country gentry who have gone into trade. I visited their houses, where they meet to chat over coffee and cakes, and delighted in their Napoleonic and Louis-Philippe couches and consoles, their Second Empire armchairs covered in beadwork and needlework, the leafy wallpapers accompanied by loose covers repeating their pattern, so that the whole room looks like a midsummer forest;

an extravagant range of nineteenth-century interior decoration such as one must go far to find today. Yet these well-behaved householders, doggedly recreating a way of life that once held sway in Lyons and Bordeaux, have always seemed to me displaced persons. The impressions of my first night proved valid: Bastia is a town that belongs to its poor.

By daylight I discovered its dilapidation. The plaster of the tall houses was pitted and flaking; there were holes in the streets and holes in walls; piles of rubble were swollen by the accumulated rubbish that drifted about the pavements with every gust of the hot breeze. Bastia is the only place in Corsica that was seriously damaged in the Second World War. In September 1943 eighty thousand Italian occupying troops laid down their arms; but some eight thousand Germans remained to be dealt with, increased by the remains of the ninetieth Panzer armoured division passing through Corsica in retreat from Sardinia. Harried by the local Resistance, the Germans made a hurried getaway from Bastia; during the first days of October the town became a battlefield and there were grisly sights in the cemetery where bombs sent the bones of the long-dead flying. But the cruellest incident occurred on 4 October, after the last German had left, when the U.S. Air Force, by one of the horrible misunderstandings of war, bombed the town from a great height, demolishing many buildings and killing a number of the inhabitants who had crept out of their cellars to celebrate their liberation.[5]

This battering brought down the city's tottering pretensions. The old quarter of the town, where Genoese governors and prelates had lived in state, had been decaying for some two centuries; the so-called new quarter, mostly built under Napoleon III, was already shabby; the war reduced both to an east of Suez condition. The damage took years and years to repair (some of it is still apparent); when I first saw Bastia the ruins of time and neglect and war were indistinguishable.

The opera house had received a direct hit. Built in the 1870s in imitation of the Scala of Milan, it was regularly visited by Italian provincial opera companies; to the delight of the local bourgeoisie, which still had cultural affinities with Italy. The Genoese were an essentially mercantile people, and those who went to Corsica were not among the élite. All the same, the wealthier colonial merchants had a taste for painted interiors that gave Bastia a semblance of elegance unknown to the rest of the island. With the French conquest only the Genoese troops and administrators were repatriated, while numerous more or less distinguished families stayed on to form the nucleus of the city's growing population.

More, however, was probably contributed to the culture of the town, before the French conquest and after, by the Corsican lawyers, doctors and clerics who had studied abroad, sometimes in Genoa, but more often in Rome, Padua, Bologna, or at the university of Pisa which ever since the Pisan occupation had held a high reputation for learning in Corsican eyes. Bastia became the meeting-place for these educated, travelled Corsicans; a literary society founded there during the Genoese regime was named the *Accademia dei Vagabondi* because its members, who specialised in the composition of Italian sonnets, had wandered in search of learning far and wide.[6] Respect for Italian scholarship endured long after the Genoese domination had come to an end; well into the nineteenth century gentlemen's sons were still sent to complete their education in Pisa, and what little learning existed in Corsica was concentrated in Bastia, with Italian as its language. The last remnants of this decaying tradition were obliterated only in the Second World War, when Mussolini's troops made themselves even more detested than the Germans and Bastia crumbled under gunfire and bombs. Since then the town has reverted to robust, rustic Corsican ways; improvisers from the mountain have taken over from the Italian tenors, inheritors of an immemorial indigenous culture that has outlived successive foreign influences.

I found my way into the opera house by a back stage door. Though the roof had fallen the walls were still standing almost to their full height. On the stage a young man was sitting in a chaos of burnt beams and twisted iron, placidly repairing a wheelbarrow. Some faded backdrops which he had draped overhead as a shelter against the sun suggested the canopy of an impoverished oriental potentate. This was his workshop, he proudly told me. But it paled in comparison with the auditorium, open to the sky, a spectacle grander, surely, and more extravagant than any that was ever seen upon that stage. In the semicircular wall three tiers of gutted boxes, painted crimson, gashed with dead white naked plaster, all ablaze in the hard sunlight, might have been the cliff homes of anchorites, recalled those sights which eighteenth-century travellers to the East described on their return with awe.

The collapsing buildings of the old port, too, were beautiful, arrayed in shrubs and creepers and wild flowers. I had returned there prepared for disappointment. But no. The harbour pool, balancing sailing yachts and fishing boats on its buoyant surface, shone in a luminous air that bathed all the scene in a golden radiance. Ancient skyscraper walls, rising from the ruins, had assumed the earthy tints of rock precipices; superimposed balconies, hanging over the void, were so crowded with pot plants and creepers that each resembled a tropical mountain ledge. The palace of the Genoese governors, flanked by a stout round tower, rode high above the harbour on a cliff smothered in dusky foliage. Everywhere vegetation flourished; shrubs and grass sprouted from ledges and doortops and the grey-green schist-tiled roofs; fig trees, springing, incredibly, from cracks in crumbling masonry, were spreadeagled high up on walls like monstrous squashed insects. Only the two-towered classical upper storey of the church of St Jean-Baptiste, serene above the crazy rooftops, was unblemished, symmetrical, intact.

Yet Bastia must have been a place of pomp and pageantry in the heyday of the Genoese ascendancy. The Governor had an escort of sixty or seventy horsemen, and received a special allowance from Genoa for trumpets, banners and clothes. The Bishop of Mariana resided there, while those of Aléria and Nebbio contrived to spend a large part of their time in the town. Services were celebrated with a solemn magnificence of chanting and resplendent vestments in the cathedral up near the Governor's palace on the citadel, a poor substitute for the Pisan Canonica of Mariana as a work of architecture, but suitably furnished with carved wood and marble polychrome marquetry.[7]

Genoese piety favoured elaborate, showy decorations and an appearance of costliness. The sight of plenty of sculptured and inlaid marble, of gilded wood and stucco, with *trompe-l'œil* painting simulating lordlier perspectives of architecture than actually existed, perhaps reassured the expatriate soldiers, merchants and administrators as much as the promises of their religion. An ideal of sumptuousness is achieved at St Roch and La Conception, neighbouring chapels in the old town of Bastia built in the sixteenth century by rival fraternities. Lined from top to bottom, like jewel boxes, with crimson damask, illuminated by crystal chandeliers hanging from vaulted and painted ceilings, they would seem the audience rooms of princes but for the processional crosses tipped with silver and the gilded and painted saints and angels swooning and leaping and flying in the glitter of clustered tapers. No private residence in Corsica can have rivalled this display of mundane luxury. La Conception was in fact recognised as the finest room in the island and was accordingly used for sessions of the Corsican Estates all through the French monarchical regime, and again for the inaugural meeting of the parliament of the Anglo-Corsican Kingdom.

I found my way to the citadel after a dragging walk the length of the town's main thoroughfare; seen close to, from the landward side, the fortifications appeared absurdly unimposing. Bastia, built on a flat promontory overlooked by hills, was never a stronghold comparable with Bonifacio or Calvi.[8] In the Corsican wars it several times changed hands, and in the eighteenth century it was twice seized by Britain, even though in the second siege, led by Admiral Hood and Nelson, the attackers were outnumbered two to one.

The site, one might think, was singularly ill-chosen for the capital of a colony where rebellion was always likely. Yet Bastia prospered, between wars, because of the commercial advantages of its position. Well placed to trade with Genoa, Leghorn, Rome and Marseilles, it could drain off the exportable surplus of the hinterland, which was always the most productive part of the island. Not that it was more fertile than the south – if one excepts the hardly habitable east coast plain – but its people, progressively civilised by the Romans, the early Christian missionaries, the Pisans and the Franciscans, were considerably less arrogant and fatalistic. They actively cooperated with the agricultural policy of the Genoese; and whatever may be said against the Genoese as colonists it is undeniable that from the mid-sixteenth century they made strenuous efforts to improve Corsican agriculture.

Their motives were of course not entirely disinterested; they had their own chronic cereal shortage in mind; Corsican prosperity was a secondary aim. They exercised a monopoly on the purchase of cereals at low prices that they fixed themselves; Corsican exporters had to buy licences and pay customs dues on all produce leaving the island. Yet in spite of crippling colonial restrictions some Corsicans could and did benefit by the facilities offered. The government provided loans for the cultivation of cereals at reasonable rates of interest, as opposed to the 100 per cent sometimes extorted by the usurers in the towns. An ingenious system of rewards and punishments was put into operation to stimulate the planting of vines and olives, fruit trees and chestnuts, chestnuts being encouraged because their flour could serve as an alternative to cereals for home consumption. A necessary corollary to this campaign were countless severe edicts to restrict the movements of herds and reduce the number of goats, those worst enemies of trees. Penalties ranged from fines to the confiscation or slaughter of livestock and the corporal punishment of the negligent shepherd.[9]

In trying to make peasants out of the Corsicans the Genoese ran full tilt against a formidable opposition of temperament and tradition. In the south their failure was almost total: the people either went abroad in search of a better life or stubbornly stuck to their immemorial, land-squandering pastoral ways. But in the *Diqua dai Monti*, where agriculture was already better developed, the population responded: areas of the west and centre became wheat-and-barley growing regions; the Balagne specialised in the production of olive oil, Cap Corse of wines, which the people exported with profit in their own ships. The continuous olive groves of the Balagne (where barley was sown under the trees), and the great chestnut forests of the Castagniccia, are permanent picturesque evidence of the civilising work of the Genoese. But this success bounced back on them. It was the prosperous productive north that manned the eighteenth-century rebellion. Pasquale Paoli was born of a family of rural notables of the Castagniccia.

The Governor's palace, scene of so many desperate, drastic or niggling decisions, often attacked and several times seized, is appropriately forbidding. This official residence was above all a fortress, and served, also, as a prison for Corsican rebels; compared with the Doge's palace in Genoa it is a barn. Yet the interior, with its rib-vaulted portico and open courtyard overlooked by vaulted, colonnaded galleries, must once have had a certain haughty magnificence. Much of the building is in ruins, for it was partly blown up by the Germans in 1943; after which what remained was turned into an ethnographic museum. Fragments of frescoes came to light during the restorations, life-size allegorical figures that must have given a welcome warmth and colour to the echoing stone-paved halls.

The agricultural implements on show in the museum are so archaic that one can scarcely believe that most of them were in use almost till the present day. Some hardly distort natural forms: a sack made from a whole goatskin, including the skin of the thighs, which served for carrying it; hollow gourds for water or wine. Human creativity here appears in a very rudimentary form: there is little attempt to improve on nature; plant and beast are simply taken and killed and used. The loose-jointed wooden swing-plough, its parts held together with thongs made of plaited reeds, without metal except on the share, is designed in deference to a tyrannical environment, being the type least likely to break on the Corsican rocks and stones. A huge, cumbersome contraption for manufacturing wax candles for churches, and some pretty baroque pavilions made, in Cap Corse, of interlaced palm leaves ('tabernacles' carried on poles in religious processions), alone speak of man's obstinate aspiration to transcend the soil.

Rooms have now been arranged to include souvenirs of the Graeco-Roman, Pisan and Genoese occupations; but these alien cultures that temporarily alighted in Corsica are less convincingly illustrated than the stalwart, impermeable underlying culture of the Corsicans themselves. Its triumph is symbolised in the eighteenth-century rebel flag, bearing the national arms: a Negro's head, in profile, bound by a white bandeau, enclosed in a crowned escutcheon upheld by a pair of winged giants with shaggy satyrs' legs and cloven hooves.

This enigmatic emblem was inherited from the kings of Aragon who, in the Middle Ages, when the Pope invested them with the sovereignty of Corsica, had temporarily adopted, as their coat of arms, four Moors' heads, each with a white bandeau (perhaps a deformation of the turban), in commemoration of their victory over the Saracens. The four Moors' heads became the arms of Sardinia after Aragon conquered the island, and though Aragon never succeeded in conquering Corsica, the kings continued to regard it as their rightful possession and represented it on their pennants with the head of a single Moor. The Moor's head was shown alongside maps of Corsica published from the seventeenth century in different parts of Europe, the Moor being usually somewhat Negroid. One such map, appearing in Augsburg in 1731, caught the attention of a high-flying German adventurer, Theodor von Neuhof, who was planning to make himself king of the Corsicans, then in rebellion against Genoa. Five years later Theodor was in fact crowned king; the Moor's head figured in his engraved portrait and on the single silver coin issued by the Corsican mint during his brief, precarious reign.

Paoli, developing his idea, proclaimed the Moor's head as the official emblem of independent Corsica. It appeared on the flags and banners of the national army, on the white flags of the Corsican rebel fleet, on the national money, and engraved on all official documents, the escutcheon usually upheld by a pair of Herculean giants, mermen or satyrs. Under the French monarchy the Corsican arms included both the Moor's head and the fleur-de-lis; but after Paoli broke with the revolutionary government the national flag again floated from Corsican ships. Sir Gilbert Elliot, as Viceroy, took steps to replace it by the British flag, pending George III's approval of one proposed for the Anglo-Corsican kingdom, in which the Moor and the royal arms were combined. Later, when he was created Baron Minto in recognition of his services in Corsica (already lost to Britain), he elected to have the Moor's head included in his coat of arms.[10]

Sir Gilbert never occupied the grim old Genoese fortress; he chose as vice-regal palace a patrician house in the lower town, something much more like a British gentleman's home. It is a huge house between the old harbour and the main square, which though now hemmed in by cinemas and a garage then opened on to a garden sloping to the sea. Here Lady Elliot gave receptions that for sheer enchantment can never have been equalled in Corsica, before or since. At the 'really splendid ball' with which she celebrated her arrival in December 1794, the rooms were decorated with myrtle, orange and arbutus trees, and there was a long passage 'enclosed by a myrtle hedge' making 'a perfect garden'. Regimental bands played at her assemblies in the real garden outside; her guests danced on a terrace overlooking it; the moon, rising from the sea, shed its beams through the trench window leading from terrace to ballroom; the scene, she wrote, 'was quite like a fairy tale'. Between parties she explored the surrounding country with her six children, riding and on foot. Just above the town she discovered a monastery surrounded by oranges and lemons, bergamot and vines, lying 'in a sort of bosom of the hills'. 'If I felt it likely I should spend another winter here,' she wrote to her sister, Lady Malmesbury, 'I should certainly make it my palace.'[11]

Sir Gilbert also planned a palace for himself, in the uplands near Corte, which he described as like his native Scotland, 'but with a fine climate'. The freshness and vitality of the Corsican landscape enchanted him; particularly he was struck by the limpidity of the mountain streams, 'rapid, craggy and crystal'. 'The brightness and splendour of the Restonica make it what one may call precious water, as one talks of the precious stones. I had heard of the water of a diamond before, and now I see it, for it is really diamonds in solution,' he wrote to his wife. 'I purpose to pass the hottest months still higher up in the hills amongst the chestnut groves. I thought of building a summer palace in some such situation, and my first idea was to build it of jasper and porphyry, but fearing that as you are not acquainted with the quarries of this country you might think me extravagant, I believe I shall go cheaply to work, and run it up of common marble.'

The Elliots are a likeable couple. Well endowed with that gift for enjoying life characteristic of the British aristocracy, they were cultured and sociable, lovers of outdoor life, poetry and flowers. Sir Gilbert was also a conscientious and humane administrator; indeed he was almost the best sort of man Britain produces for such jobs, being sincerely anxious to reconcile the interests of the people he governed with those of his country and king. 'I am very fond of Corsica,' he wrote to Lady Elliot, 'I mean of its cause and interests; and I have a real ambition to be the founder of what I consider likely to prove its future happiness.' Sir Gilbert spoke fluent French and Italian, the result of an education supervised by David Hume in Paris, where he had been befriended by Mirabeau and Madame du Deffand. Elected to Parliament as an independent Whig, he was appointed Civil Commissioner in Toulon after the British occupied the town in 1793. His role, while Napoleon's artillery battered the outposts, consisted in evacuating thousands of French Royalists, whom he treated with considerable kindness. 'His character is very gentle . . . His natural inclination is to do good . . .' so commented the Corsican soldier and politician Matteo Buttafoco in his memoirs; his great-niece and biographer, the Countess of Minto, recalls his 'natural moderation, candour and liberality of mind, joined to a temper of unfailing sweetness'.[12] Such were his qualifications for governing Corsica. They were insufficient.

Corsica fell into the hands of Britain, a gift of great value, at a critical juncture in the nation's history. At the opening of the Napoleonic Wars Britain had no naval base east of Gibraltar. Toulon for a time supplied the need, so that when Paoli appealed for British protection in the summer of 1793 the British government hesitated to commit itself. But after the fall of Toulon in December Paoli's offer assumed the character of a godsend. In the following January Sir Gilbert Elliot, accompanied by two military advisers, was sent to ratify Britain's possession of the island, the strategic value of which was becoming every day more apparent in the light of the reverses of war.

They landed at Ile-Rousse; Calvi, Bastia and Saint Florent being occupied by the French Republicans.[13] Their arrival was wonderful. Crowds of Corsicans, armed to the teeth and looking like brigands, accompanied them on their long walk over the mountains to Paoli's headquarters at Murato; in every village they were greeted with volleys of gunfire and cries of 'Viva Paoli e la nazione Inglese'. 'I was very much struck', wrote Sir Gilbert, 'by this first specimen I had seen of a real national militia; the inhabitants of a country carrying arms of their own, for their own defence and their own purposes.'

He found Paoli (whom he had already met in London), living in a 'ruinous monastery', without 'papers, books, or any of the conveniences of life'. It was thereupon decided, evidently on Sir Gilbert's suggestion, that Corsica should be governed by a Viceroy, appointed by the King of England, who would be vested with control of the armed forces and the executive and have a negative veto on all legislation. Paoli expressed his satisfaction. What else could he do? He was then in a desperate position. A torrent of unforeseen events had swept him, in the space of three and a half years, from a great personal comeback to the very edge of disaster. Returning to Corsica triumphant in 1790 after twenty years exile in England, he had been welcomed as a national hero; but his temperate political views, combined with a less moderate liking for personal authority, had soon alienated him from the French government and a faction of his own compatriots. The Bonaparte, with the Corsican Jacobins, had turned on him; arraigned by the Convention he had set up an independent government at Corte; in July 1793 he had been outlawed.

Thanks to his boundless popularity with the mass of the Corsicans he had succeeded in confining the French troops to three coastal towns; but now he was at the end of his resources. He had confidently led his country into rebellion against France; and if at one time France had seemed on the verge of anarchy and defeat the revolutionary armies were now holding their own against the combined forces of the rest of Europe.

Paoli knew what to expect if the French invaded Corsica: a hopeless resistance, civil war, and for himself flight or the guillotine. This was no time for bargaining; he accepted whatever Sir Gilbert suggested and asked only for emergency supplies for his army: money, ammunition, biscuits and cheese.

203

He also declared his intention of retiring from public life as soon as the new regime was established, or as Sir Gilbert put it: 'as soon as he has brought his country safe into a British haven'. Sir Gilbert was much relieved, for he was of opinion that no British government could operate in Corsica if Paoli 'more powerful than a veritable monarch' had any hand in it.

In believing Paoli's protestations Sir Gilbert gives proof of a calamitous simplicity of mind. The projected constitution, though liberal enough in British eyes, was certainly not what Paoli hoped for; he might have abandoned the dream of Corsican independence, but he still, it seems, envisaged a protectorate status in which all but military affairs would be left to the Corsicans. If he appeared to accept the constitution it was no doubt because he assumed that he himself would be appointed Viceroy. His talk of retiring was surely no more than a courtesy gesture, calculated to provoke an invitation to remain at the head of the government. Sir Gilbert made the typically British mistake of attributing to words their literal meaning, whereas for the Corsicans words are instruments, to be used for obtaining specific results. The Anglo-Corsican Kingdom began with a misunderstanding.

Both men expected to be called to the post of Viceroy;[14] but they had to wait nine months before the British government made any pronouncement on the subject. In the meantime the French-held ports had to be captured. Saint-Florent fell in February; but the siege of Bastia was delayed more than six weeks by the refusal of two successive British generals to attack the town. It was finally taken by the navy and marines, on the courageous advice of Nelson (captain of the *Agamemnon*), while the army looked on, unemployed. The siege of Calvi (in which Nelson lost an eye) began only in June; but Paoli, regarding the outcome as certain, had already summoned a *consulta*, a national assembly, at Corte to ratify the union of Corsica and Great Britain.

This was another of the stirring occasions that compensated Sir Gilbert for his many frustrations and made him confident – overconfident – of the success of his mission. Riding to the upland capital through chestnut woods 'with glens and burns in abundance, and peeps of the Mediterranean at every opening', he was escorted by the usual crowds of exuberant armed Corsicans, and the 12th Regiment of Light Dragoons whose uniforms created a sensation. Hospitality was offered at every village, with bonfires and the firing of muskets; no wonder Sir Gilbert wrote to his wife: 'There was never an act of the sort better sealed by the hearts of the people.' The Corsican delegates he met on his route appealed to him in the same kind of way as the citizens' militia; as a cultured gentleman of his time Sir Gilbert was not insensible to the ideas of Jean-Jacques Rousseau: 'We were joined on our way by deputies ... coming to this famous Assembly, in all the simplicity of primitive legislators, on their little mules, with their muskets always slung over their backs and their little portmanteau strapped behind them.'

The primitive legislators approved the union of their country with Great Britain. In fact the matter was already settled, and Paoli had published a proclamation to this effect on 1 May.[15] The deputies, all loyal Paolists, merely endorsed his decision. Thirty-six of them, presided by Paoli's brilliant young protégé, Charles-André Pozzo di Borgo, were entrusted with the framing of the new constitution. This, too, was little more than a formality: the constitution, produced within two days, adhered to the model already fixed by Sir Gilbert in his conversations with Paoli and his correspondence with the British government. Sir Gilbert was delighted. 'I was crowned last Thursday, June 19th, and I send you my Majesty's speech . . . it produced on my subjects a kingly effect', he reported to his wife, with understandable vanity. It was then that he imagined his summer palace of jasper and porphyry.

Paoli's approval of the constitution was enough to ensure its acceptance by his devoted partisans. Yet some of them must have realised that it fell short of the democratic principles that had inspired Paoli's own constitution in 1755, when Corsican autonomy was a reality. The Viceroy, head of the executive and commander in chief of the armed forces, had a negative veto on all legislation, thus depriving the so-called Parliament of any real authority. This Parliament was to be elected by universal male suffrage; but its members, two per *pieve*, had to own property worth 6,000 *lire*. The Viceroy could dissolve Parliament, though he had to summon another within forty days. He was assisted by a Council of State, which he nominated; he appointed all functionaries except the administrators of the towns and villages (who were elected according to tradition). In fact his power was almost unchallenged.

Yet in theory Corsica was not a colony, but an independent kingdom that voluntarily acknowledged the same sovereign. Certain clauses in the constitution bear out this idea. All government employees (except a Secretary of State attached to the Council) had to be Corsicans. Parliament could petition the King for the Viceroy's recall. And as in Britain, citizens were protected against arbitrary arrest and the seizure of property; liberty of conscience and the freedom of the press were guaranteed. Viewed in relation to the period the constitution was liberal; remarkably so when one considers that Sir Gilbert was an aristocrat who dreaded nothing more than what he describes in his correspondence as 'democratic anarchy'.

The success of such a constitution would obviously depend on the personality of the Viceroy. Sir Gilbert never doubted that he would be appointed. But he had to wait for official notification, and pending its arrival Paoli remained at the head of the provisional government. Paoli, too, was counting on becoming Viceroy; in fact he had applied for the post through the Corsican delegates who had gone to England to carry an address to their new sovereign, George III.

The summer went by without news from London, to the growing exasperation of the two men. 'I have been straining my eyes every day . . . for messengers on the roads and cutters at sea', wrote Sir Gilbert. Meanwhile Paoli, who was no doubt also straining his eyes, and for the same reason, began putting about ugly rumours that Britain was planning to hand over Corsica to some foreign power.

Sir Gilbert's nomination came on 1 October, when he had almost lost patience. The delay had merely been due to the pressure of more urgent affairs; but it had seriously shaken public confidence; in Sir Gilbert's words, the Corsicans felt themselves 'strangely slighted'. But he was far from understanding the reactions aroused by his own appointment. Paoli's supporters were alienated, and Paoli himself was mortally wounded. He can hardly have been appeased by a letter from the Duke of Portland assuring him that the pension of £1200 a year paid to him by the Crown during his exile would be renewed, and that he would shortly receive His Majesty's picture set in brilliants to be worn on a gold chain round his neck as a mark of the King's favour. As an afterthought Portland suggested to Sir Gilbert that Paoli should be officially decorated with this miniature, that its presentation, in fact, should assume the character of an investiture.

The proposed ceremony would have been comic opera; what happened was farcical. When, in November, the messenger arrived who was to have brought the portrait, it was not found in his luggage. Heaven knows what had happened to it; but it had certainly not been deliberately withheld by the British ministers, as Paoli affected to believe. Nor had Sir Gilbert stolen it, as the Corsican deputies in London suggested ('on which', wrote the Duke of Portland, 'I fairly lost my temper . . .'). It is of course unlikely that Paoli and the deputies really believed what they said; they were unbearably offended, and a Corsican, when offended, is liable to make absurd and outrageous accusations against the offender, with the object of enraging him, breaking his self-control, and so driving him to discreditable behaviour. By such tactics he makes a victim of the offender and so enjoys a psychological revenge.

Sir Gilbert, to his credit, ignored the provocation. He was busy and interested at the time, nominating the various functionaries, organising elections to Parliament, and negotiating with the Pope, who had put in a half-hearted claim to the political domination of the island. Meanwhile Lady Elliot had arrived from England with her children and opened her season of assemblies and balls.

When Parliament met in February 1795, in Bastia, in the luxurious chapel of La Conception, its first act was to elect Paoli as its President, even though he had refused the seat offered to him by his constituency. Sir Gilbert intervened in remarkably strong terms for so mild a man. He gave it to be understood in no uncertain language that he would regard Paoli's acceptance as 'a virtual deposition of the King', and that if Paoli did accept he would immediately withdraw British armed forces from the island. In the face of this formidable threat Paoli and Parliament gave way; one can hardly understand how Sir Gilbert could have made it unless he was thoroughly scared.

French historians have unanimously condemned British treatment of Paoli as impolitic and ungrateful. Paoli had invited the British to Corsica, they argue, therefore the British owed him the government of the island; he had the people behind him, therefore he was the only person capable of ruling it. By excluding Paoli the British lost the sympathies of the majority faction, of precisely those Corsicans who could have supported them against the pro-

Bonaparte, pro-French minority, which was to become increasingly powerful and menacing. Such reasoning, sound so far as it goes, leaves out of account two very important aspects of the situation. The Viceroy of the King of England was his delegate in a foreign land; a first qualification for this role was surely that he should be British born. Secondly, it would have been inconceivable for the British government, engaged in a major war, to leave this newly acquired strategic base in the hands of a man who had twice led his countrymen to rebel against their rulers.

There were also serious ideological divergencies between Paoli and the British government which most historians have neglected. They come out clearly in one of Sir Gilbert's dispatches: 'The ideas expressed in the General's [Paoli's] speeches on all political matters are absurd and crude . . . They are, moreover, in direct contradiction to the system of government established here. . . . Paoli seems to me to have strong tendencies to democracy.' 'Democracy' was not at that time a sacred word in Britain. For the nation's rulers it meant government by the ignorant masses, the atrocities of Jacobinism, the end of civilisation. Paoli now appears as an outstandingly creative statesman because he gave the Corsicans a national parliament partly elected by universal suffrage, and a regime in which almost every position of authority was acceded to by election, well before anything of the kind had been attempted elsewhere. Sir Gilbert and his superiors seem not to have been aware of the nature of his constitutional experiment; but had they been so they would have undoubtedly condemned it. The citizens' army and primitive legislators might take Sir Gilbert's fancy; but he was far too set in the principles of his class to want to see a primitive democracy in action. Had he thought otherwise he would never have been appointed Viceroy. The Anglo-Corsican Kingdom was handicapped from the start by the impossibility of ruling the island with Paoli no less than by the impossibility of ruling it without him. Paoli's position, too, was false; only Republican France could give his country the sort of government he believed in. All the same, one can hardly condone the British government's clumsy, unfeeling, treatment of Paoli. If his influence in Corsica was so much feared, why was he not invited to England early on with really substantial advantages? Since he was technically a British subject (as, incidentally, was Napoleon), and seeing that he had no direct heirs, could he not have been given a peerage?

Sir Gilbert never took the measure of Paoli's resentment. There was an unsatisfactory explanation between them and then, in June 1795, Sir Gilbert set out on a tour of the south. This was the last of his happy and encouraging experiences in Corsica. Travelling by bridle paths through wooded, romantic country that reminded him of *As You Like It*, *A Midsummer Night's Dream* and the *Faerie Queene*, he was everywhere accompanied by cavalcades of Corsicans, greeted in every village with gunfire, triumphal arches of myrtle boughs and showers of wheat 'to make me fertile', he commented, 'as they do brides. Then comes a dinner with fifty people in a small room, succeeded by a walk with a hundred people in the party. This is the style everywhere.'

Exhausted but impressed Sir Gilbert made his way over the mountains to Ajaccio, south to Sartène and Bonifacio, and back to Bastia by a slightly different itinerary.

The storm broke on his return journey. The pretext chosen by Paoli and his supporters was grotesque, but it served their purpose. They circulated a rumour that Paoli's bust had been wilfully smashed by Sir Gilbert's aide-de-camp at a ball given in the Viceroy's honour in Ajaccio. The bust was of plaster; it had been removed to make room for the dancing; Sir Gilbert, on examining it, saw no damage 'except about the thickness of a wafer rubbed off the tip of the nose, which appeared like an old sore'. No matter; 'the assassination of the bust', as the supposed incident came to be called, was something concrete and picturesque, fit to rouse popular indignation. Paoli's partisans flocked to his home in the Castagniccia; copies of the acts of Parliament were burnt in the villages, along with effigies of Pozzo di Borgo, Paoli's talented young protégé who now, as President of the Council of State, had transferred his allegiance to the Viceroy. Delegations swarmed on Sir Gilbert to demand Pozzo's dismissal, Paoli's recall to power; to declare the existing government illegal, to refuse payment of taxes, or to ask, quite simply, for money. Sir Gilbert listened to them patiently; he must have been even more worried, at this time, by news that the population of Mezzana (near Ajaccio) had refused passage to a regiment of Anglo-Corsican troops, an act tantamount to rebellion.

Paoli made no show of encouraging these disorders; his tactics were far more astute and more damaging to Sir Gilbert. He came out with a proclamation urging the people to remain faithful to their constitution and King, while at the same time letting it be known that according to his private information Sir Gilbert had fallen into disgrace with the British government and would shortly be replaced. By himself, it was implied.[16]

Perhaps Paoli really believed he had a chance of being called on to succeed Sir Gilbert in the interests of Corsican tranquility. At all events his manœuvres completely unnerved his opponent. The situation, surely, called for a display of authority; but Sir Gilbert contented himself with appointing a commission to enquire into 'the assassination of the bust' and issuing a proclamation to remind the Corsicans of the blessings of British rule. While rioting spread from village to village he cowered in Bastia, complaining of the 'monstrous ingratitude' of the Corsicans and writing stricken dispatches to England begging for the re-exile of Paoli and a confirmation of his own authority.

By the autumn Sir Gilbert had his way: Paoli was invited to retire to England with a large increase in his pension. To his honour, he left almost at once. With his tormenter thus disposed of Sir Gilbert opened a second session of Parliament, this time at Corte. The winter passed by quietly; Sir Gilbert was convinced that the country was quiet and contented.

But he was gravely mistaken. Paoli's supporters, together with the many people who had been disappointed in their hopes of obtaining government jobs and favours, were now joining forces with the French Republicans, who were filtering agents into the island in small boats on orders of Napoleon. For by the spring of 1796 events were moving rapidly in favour of France as a result of Napoleon's lightning advances in northern Italy.

In April a serious revolt exploded when the population of Bocognano, a tough mountain village on the route leading from Ajaccio to Corte, fired on British troops; in May an armed band of eight hundred Corsicans occupied the road between Corte and Bastia. Sir Gilbert, who had courageously accompanied a force marching from Bastia on Bocognano, found himself caught between the two groups of rebels. He behaved prudently, received a delegation, and agreed to all that was asked, including the dismissal of Pozzo di Borgo and a reduction in taxation. The Corsicans had won the day. 'The people . . . has never been in so happy a situation under any regular government', Sir Gilbert wrote, with incorrigible *naïveté*.

But there was little time left to test the advisability of giving in to almost whatever they demanded. In June Sir Gilbert was in daily expectation of an invasion by the French army, massed at Leghorn. In July he gave orders to Nelson, now his firm friend, to capture Porto Ferrajo, in Elba, and in September – after a rupture with Genoa – to seize the little island of Capraja. On these occasions Sir Gilbert gave proof of real capacities as a man of action when his composure was not disturbed by what he describes as 'the baseness and rascality, the absolute absence of sentiments worthy of a gentleman' deployed, in his opinion, by Paoli's and his supporters.

Sir Gilbert's experience of the Corsicans had been little short of appalling; yet when, on 29 September, he received instructions to evacuate the island, he was genuinely distressed. The new French alliance with Spain was responsible for the decision, not the internal broils of Corsica, to which the British Cabinet had probably hardly given a thought. Sir Gilbert kept the news secret to the last moment in the hope of counter-orders. They came, on 14 November, when he had already reached Porto Ferrajo and the last British troops had left the island and a detachment of Napoleon's Army of Italy had already landed in Cap Corse. Britain muddled her way out of Corsica, as she had muddled her way in.

A number of Corsicans elected to leave with Sir Gilbert. Kind as always, he procured pensions for them and arranged for them to live in Italy, except Pozzo di Borgo, whom he took with him to England, then to Vienna, and so set him on the path of a brilliant international career. Pozzo became diplomatic adviser to the Tsar Alexander I and ended as Russian Ambassador to the court of Louis XVIII. Sir Gilbert got his peerage, with the Moor's head in his arms, and later made a satisfactory Governor-General of India. As for Paoli, in spite of all his humiliations he had been well provided for, and he held his own in London society. Sir Gilbert, describing his attendance at court in June 1804, after speaking of the King and Queen and their fashionable company, adds: 'Old Paoli was there.'[17]

13 SAINT AND ADVENTURERS

Journey through no-man's-land – Paoli's town – gentry of the
Balagne-Calvi, a pleasure ground – Nelson's siege – aristocrats
in exile – adventurers in Spain and Peru – Don Juan, rake's
progress to saintliness

I T was a pioneer's train, a single coach with a trailer, running on a single track
into the sunset through empty, arid hills. The passengers were in keeping: a
pair of unshaven brigandish-looking men with guns – hunters? prospectors?
A party of bronze unsmiling youths and girls bent double under their ruck-
sacks might have been recruits to a collective farm. A backwoods peasant
family – father, mother, grandmother, children, baby – made an encampment
at the end of the coach between their baskets and packages; a young Franciscan in patched robe with dusty sandalled feet was reading his breviary, a
missionary to the lawless. I had to remind myself that I was on my way to the
tourist resorts, Ile-Rousse and Calvi.

I had spent the first half of the day driving with some friendly Corsicans
from Bastia across the leafy Castagniccia, through a continuous forest of
ancient chestnut trees that covered hills and valleys like a green foam. This
landscape, that looks so natural and timeless, is in fact mainly the work of
man, and perhaps man's most remarkable achievement in Corsica; the forest
was cultivated between the sixteenth century and the nineteenth, the trees
seeded, transplanted, grafted, watered and pruned. The chestnut crop, more
reliable than cereals, made the district prosperous: a hundred years ago it
was the most populated part of the island. The schist villages, strung out on
spurs, are within calling distance of each other; often one can see a dozen at
a time, like a flock of grey birds alighted on the hills. Though almost empty,
now, and decaying and neglected, they repay visiting, for this was one of the
few regions of Corsica able to support skilled craftsmen. Here fresco painters
were at work from the fifteenth century, if not before; aloof incorporeal
figures in the Byzantine manner cover walls and apses of neglected Romanesque chapels;[1] swirling baroque saints float on the vaulted ceiling of the
former procathedral of Cervione, and many naïve, anecdotic, colourful illus-
trations of Bible stories decorate the walls of the crumbling parish churches.

Here, too, furniture was made from chestnut wood and walnut, tables and
chairs and chests that now fetch high prices, and pottery was moulded by
hand by the women until the interwar years. Crude and heavy, often, as the
least accomplished Corsican prehistoric ware, it contained an admixture of

asbestos, quarried locally, that gave a particular resistance to cooking uten-
sils,[2] much in demand in this region where cooking was unusually elaborate.
Twenty-two different dishes made from chestnut flour were served at marriage banquets, and one can still enjoy some of them, today.

But the most valuable contribution of local craftsmen was without doubt
the firearms, admired by Boswell; the guns that kept the eighteenth-century
rebellion alive. The Castagniccia became a centre of the national independence
movement: here Paoli was elected head of state and King Theodor was
crowned; in the large Franciscan monasteries assemblies were held, vital
decisions adopted and systems of government hammered out by a people with
a tradition of democratic organisation dating back to the time of the Giovannali and Sambocuccio d'Alando.

The Castagniccia harbours many memories of the patriots' struggle, yet its
aspect is reassuring: it is an area where human beings flourished and multiplied and the art of living developed; more than any other part of the island
it evolved an authentic indigenous style. This I could already sense as I drove
through the tunnels of green boughs with my Corsican friends, always in sight
of the little villages, each marked by a campanile lancing the trees. Some of
the churches, built in apparent stone, though classical in design, from a distance had a strangely Gothic air.

Later I became familiar with the district, in autumn, at the time of the
chestnut harvest, here the most beautiful of all seasons, when the myriad
leaves graduate from lemon to gold to burnt sienna, with every leaf on a single
spray different in tone. The people, then, are all out of doors, men and women
and children gathering chestnuts in oval baskets made from interlaced laths
of chestnut wood, and loading them in sacks on donkeys which make long
caravans homing to the villages in the blue dusk.

I came to know these people well; my most intimate friends in Corsica,
apart from the Cesari, live in the Castagniccia. It was due to their generosity
that I was never hungry while writing this book; the bag of chestnut flour, the
smoked sausages, arrived every Christmas and lasted till early summer.
There was never any condescension in the gift, or suggestion that I would do
better to run a shop; the country that bred Pasquale Paoli has a traditional
regard for intellectuals.

His home was at Morosaglia, on the western border of the forest, the house
of modestly prosperous notables, now arranged as a museum. Many souvenirs
of his regime are on show there: proclamations, manifestos, records of the
resolutions of his national parliament, all handsomely printed by the press he
inaugurated in Corsica and bearing a baroque version of the Moor's head, the
national arms. On the walls hang dozens of engravings of the portraits made
all over Europe of this statesman who sat for many distinguished painters of
his day, including Reynolds, Cosway, Lawrence, Drolling and Gérard.[3] The
ground floor is a chapel for his remains, transferred there in 1889 from Old
St Pancras cemetery in London.

How appropriate, I have always thought, that Paoli should have been born

here, in the crutch of the island, on the frontier between the tamable sch.
country and the anarchy of granite. To the south and west of the village the
mountains of the Niolo appear, rising in seven and eight tiers. That afternoon
when I first saw them they were drenched in a glistening sunlit haze that
made them seem two-dimensional, airy as gauze. The spectacular shapes of
the nearest ranges, silhouetted in oblique ascending lines of spiked peaks,
none the less allowed one to glimpse the remote cold summits of the highest,
innermost mountains, those that reach eight thousand feet and more. Paoli,
I reflected, woke up every morning of his boyhood in sight of this exalting
view.

The mountains were closer, and overwhelming, when I took the train at
Ponte-Leccia, then receded into a fiery blaze as I was rushed westwards into
what was apparently a desert. I had supposed that this second lap of my
journey would be through a country as gentle and civilised as that I had seen
in the earlier part of the day; after all the Balagne had been described to me
as 'the garden of Corsica'. But here were only stones and dry grass, abandoned terraces and circular threshing floors and ruined stone huts with dry
grass growing from their flat roof-tops. We passed a station, a single building
gutted by fire; no one lived there, the population had surely been driven
away by fire and drought and hunger.

The little train running on diesel oil, known as the *micheline*, was gathering
speed. It charged into a cutting with mournful two-noted blasts of its horn,
emerged on to hills devoid of any life at all. The resorts, I thought, must be a
hoax; and I hardly cared. All the way round the island I had thought, now
and then, of the days – a couple of weeks perhaps – that I would spend on
holiday with other people on holiday. I would lie under parasols on soft-seated
chairs, I would eat food cooked in the French style; I would walk on soft
carpets and soak in hot baths; I would talk about what I had left behind me.
I had promised myself this interlude; when I arrived in Corsica it had seemed
to me indispensable; and now that I began to doubt its possibility I realised
I no longer wanted it. I had hardly found any comfort of that kind in Corsica,
and I had not missed it after the first few days. And I had no need, now, to
talk to strangers about the paperbacks they were reading, the films they had
seen at home. Since I had been in the island (the span, I felt, of a reincarna-
tion) I had touched life's grain; nothing, after this journey, would seem the
same as before.

The railway was heading towards a hole in a mountainside; beyond that
tunnel, perhaps, by one of the dream-transformations common enough in
Corsica, the garden of the Balagne would appear, a sylvan landscape golden
in the sunset falling to the resorts strung out on a voluptuous shore. The exit
from the tunnel in fact brought a golden sunset view, but of utterly naked
mountains heaving range beyond range to the north and west. Their covering
of tawny earth seemed a skin stretched over living muscles and bones, the
hide of lions, at rest, but menacing. The one village in sight was a pile of earth-
brown cubes, far below us, scorched and decrepit as any village of the Atlas.

Morosaglia, in the Castagniccia, birthplace of the Corsican liberator and legislator, Pasquale Paoli. (*Louis Bianchetti*)

Ruined Franciscan monastery at Piedicroce d'Orezza, in the chestnut
forest of the Castagniccia. Rebel leaders met here during the seventeenth-century rebellion against Genoa. (*Louis Bianchetti*)

A twist in the lions' hide, as though a muscle had been flexed, exposed the flash of far-off breakers beating on desolate dunes.

The train now rode the edges of descending ravines, burrowing into high cuttings, and tunnels where the headlamp revealed only sections of curved wall, engineering feats of the last century. The driver was rounding the bends at a reckless speed as though infected by the wildness of the setting; I was sitting beside him in a glass-walled cabin like a cockpit, with the sensation, as we hurtled towards the blind corners of the mountains, of taking off into the evening sky.

We stopped at a spot where the railway met a road; a wreck of a bus was drawn up beside the train; the peasant family climbed from one to the other; the bus made off with the driver shouting to ours. The monk got out soon afterwards at an apparently derelict station, strode away up a mountain track, breasting the wind, image of the first missionaries of his order. This was Belgodere, one of the gun-carrying brigands told me; Belgodere, in the sixteenth century a village welfare state where men and women, voting on equal terms, had operated an enlightened democratic regime. But all I could see of it were ruins of a fort against a square-headed rock, speaking of war.[4]

The campers were now droning out French marching songs; the brigands talked to me about boar hunting while the train careered through virgin maquis into the setting sun; they were sportsmen on their way to a shoot. The fleeting shapes of tossing olive trees suggested a new type of country; but I could barely take it in before we met the white-crested sea. I saw a scattering of pink islets offshore, with the sun sinking between them, glimpsed pink-plastered, pink-tiled houses in flowering gardens; but we had halted beside the harbour, heaving in the gale. 'Enjoy yourself!' said the driver. Nothing in sight suggested a tourist resort; I could hardly stand up to the wind. I beat my way to a small inn on the waterfront where a managing, motherly peasant woman gave me soup in the kitchen and put me to bed in a plank-panelled, whitewashed room like a ship's cabin. 'You've come from the interior so you won't be hard to please,' she told me. That night all the building rattled and shook while waves lashed its foundations, so that I ever afterwards thought of that inn as '*Le bateau ivre*'.

By the following evening I had decided to move on; Ile-Rousse in a *libeccio* was not what I had been hoping for. Paoli founded the town in the 1760s as a port for the oil-producing Balagne, Calvi being still held by the Genoese. The site offered a tolerable harbour sheltered by a little promontory and the pink islets that gave the town its name, Isola Rossa (although Paolina was also suggested). In the manner of heads of new nations Paoli planned it from scratch, laid it out its first streets, three of them, running parallel. This tidy design is contrary to Corsican ways. Born of the will of one man, Ile-Rousse still seems alien to its setting; two centuries, enough to make a town of the United States a historical monument, are negligible in a country of long traditions. Improvements carried out since then by municipalities anxious to do justice to their founder have merely emphasised the artificiality of the place:

213

the covered marketplace with a peristyle on the lines of a classical temple, added under Louis-Philippe, the overlarge main square planted with planes. In the 1930s the *palazzo* of local notables was turned into Corsica's first and until recently only luxury hotel; pink villas went up beside it; Paoli's town came to imitate a minor resort of the French Riviera of the interwar years. Yet shops and amusements are not up to Riviera standards; hunters and shepherds play cards in the shabby cafés alongside the more appropriate fishermen, the demon scent of the maquis blows through the garden flowers. The first day I spent there the sea was also blowing across the waterfront in spangled sheets of spray, while the leaves of the planes, already brown, eddied about the deserted square.

The wind went on blowing that night; but by the following afternoon, when I took a bus going to Calvi through the foothills, it was no more than a strong bracing breeze spiced with the biting scents of maquis and sea. It swept over a landscape stripped clean of superfluities: pastures and olive groves rising in smooth uncluttered planes to low bare ranges, between which the mighty jagged walls of the Niolo occasionally appeared. As the road climbed inland the coast to the south came in view: bay after bay, semicircular, foaming, unoccupied, ringed with arcs of naked granite and sand. The villages were hill-perched; there were none near the sea except Ile-Rousse (implausible enclave); only scattered huts, flat-topped, earth-brown, such as shepherds use.[5] The myriad olive trees had practically ousted all other vegetation, including the mountain oak (dark companion of the south) and even the maquis, so that I marvelled at the heady perfume until I realised it came from the inconspicuous tufts of golden everlasting, growing everywhere from the dry earth and the cracks of boulders. That afternoon the hard light which goes with the *libeccio* sharpened every silhouette; simple, straightlined silhouettes: the cubistic shepherds' huts, the mountain peaks, the cubistic villages, their houses set one above another on the hillsides, their flat roofs looking like flights of stairs. Corbara, the first we passed, recalled Cézanne with its pale plastered buildings stacked between prickly pears; one might have been in Provence, but also in Morocco or Spain.

A large white building just beyond the village made a landmark on a mountainside; a monastery, I later learned, that came to public notice a century ago as the retreat of Father Didon, an inspired Dominican preacher exiled from Paris for his too liberal views. This man with 'great brown eyes in which dwelt a flame' (to quote Maupassant, who went out of his way to visit him), apostle of fashionable Parisian society, was also at home in Corsica; his letters to Flaubert's niece, Caroline Commanville, seize the essence of the hard pure brilliance of the Balagne. 'Everything here is vigorous,' he observed, 'one knows oneself to be on a granite soil. The sun darts its splendid beams with violence, the wind roughly shakes its wings. The sea has steely lights; its blue grace seems shielded by a metal breastplate.'[6]

I heard his story when I returned to spend a day in Corbara, a week or so later, and called on Tito Franceschini, a collateral descendant of Paoli[7] (the

Corsican liberator never married, he was too completely dedicated to his cause). The large rambling old mansion, hung with fine paintings and handsomely furnished in Second Empire style (a member of the family was private secretary to Napoleon III), is full of personal mementos of the national hero. A travelling case that Paoli is said to have taken with him on all his campaigns is equipped with everything that could ease the discomforts of military life: a stand-up shaving mirror, ivory-handled razors, silver jugs and bowls and canisters, a flowered porcelain cup and saucer, a green leather writing pad with quills, quill sharpeners, a folding ruler and pots for ink and sand. Paoli might contend with Johnson that there was no beauty independent of utility, but his utilitarian possessions were beautiful; a silk scarf my host showed me was woven in lovely soft sea tints of blue and green. Letters addressed to him came tumbling out of a cupboard, including one from Catherine of Russia, in her own hand; an assurance of friendship written 27 April 1770, soon after Paoli had retired to England (at this period the Empress offered him an appointment in Russia, which he refused).

The gentry of the Balagne developed a standard of living unknown to the haughty *sgio* of the Sartenais, or, for that matter, to most other Corsicans until very recent years. At the opposite end of Corbara, in another large mansion, standing amid castle ruins, I met Count Savelli de Guido, who traces his ancestry to a Roman family settled there since the ninth century. Suites of Florentine furniture are arranged below museum paintings, a Philippe de Champagne, a Breughel de Velours, along with a table and sideboard from the *palazzo* of the Genoese Lieutenant-Governor of the Balagne; surely local work, for the table tops are of chestnut wood and the legs are thick columns shaped from the trunks of small olive trees. During the hours I spent there I had the sensation of being plunged into the accumulated Corsican past, as I sat at this regally-rustic table in a carved throne belonging to the sixteenth-century bishop Alessandro Sauli, reading Sir Gilbert Elliot's decree appointing a Savelli President (chief magistrate) of the Balagne, with a polished prehistoric axe-head serving as paperweight to a letter signed by Nelson, and a clutter of delightful Roman terracotta figurines found in the neighbourhood dotted between our coffee cups.

Such family seats are the outcome of very long traditions; the Balagne has been civilised ever since the Romans introduced the olives, known as the *sabinacci*.[8] The oil, stored in huge earthenware vats, was exported abroad, and bartered far and wide over the island until the First World War; barley was grown under the trees. The big landowners, some of them apparently descended from mediaeval crusading noblemen from Italy, were people of wealth and culture; and even today, with the old agricultural economy ruined, their way of life serves as a reminder of what Corsica has been able to achieve. Several, besides Count Savelli, are perceptive antiquarians; Pierre Simonetti de Malaspina of Ville-de-Paraso has made his home a veritable museum of prehistoric finds. And one may see French and Italian eighteenth-century furniture in their houses, and libraries stocked with the French, Italian and

Latin classics; the country gentlemen of the Balagne were brought up in the traditions of European scholarship. They are probably the last of their kind, for their children have joined the exodus that has been gathering volume in the Balagne for the past hundred years. Today the land brings little profit except to the shepherds, those red-faced winter visitors from the Niolo, obvious aliens from a tougher environment.

What I saw on my way to Calvi was a mellow, declining countryside, once well tended and inhabited; the stately declining villages are set close together, looking at each other from hill to hill. In almost every one a baroque church focused my attention with an elaborate arched and domed campanile, a cupola or octagonal-roofed dome, a classical façade higher than the body of the building, statues in niches, a gracefully curving pediment; the parish churches of the Balagne are designed with fantasy and verve. Connoisseurs of the baroque would probably dismiss them lightly; as Sacheverell Sitwell says of those of Guatemalan Antigua, 'they should be looked at scenically'.[9] Nearly always they are sited with a fine sense of drama, on open terraces and platforms facing the sea. Painted, often, dead white, they stamp the brown and silver landscape with their bold volumes; their campanili, pierced by three and four storeys of arches, spear and capture the sky.

The villages were glimpsed kaleidoscopically as the bus meandered to Calvi through the old gnarled olive groves: below the road, as a geometry of Roman tiles, and above as compact cliffs of superimposed façades gashed by dark archways and arcaded galleries. The silver crowns of the olives fluttered over the shelving miles to Algajola, collapsing Genoese fortress jutting into the waves; Sant'Antonino brooded over us, a circular mediaeval village that from afar looks like one great castle, something on the lines of Krak le Chevalier.

We were mounting, now, to a lateral ridge, marked by a small Pisan chapel; beyond the pass the landscape unrolled in authentic Corsican dimensions. The Niolo mountains, until then an occasional backdrop between hills, reared up ahead in a forbidding wall throwing great buttresses across the plains. Monte Grosso, its upper zone all rock, might, I thought, have been the archetypal model for those sculptured temples of Angkor with towers designed in the image of mountain peaks. Its presence lay like a shadow over the bright landscape, annihilating detail. The citadel of Calvi, far off on the extremity of a semicircular bay, was dwarfed, irrelevant; one expected that remote promontory to be desolate, like the one that closed the southern horizon beyond it with the shape of a Mesozoic reptile.

This northern escarpment of the Niolo is one of the most secret areas in all Corsica, practically waterless, shunned even by the shepherds. As we approached it I could see dark valleys disappearing into rocks, pathless and uninhabited. Yet Calenzana, standing so close under the mountains that one could catch the cold aroma of the pines, was a much larger place than any we had passed that day, almost a town, laid out round its imposing baroque church and campanile overlooking the graveyard of five hundred Germans, allies of the Genoese, killed during the national rebellion. The inhabitants, too, looked urban; in fact they are said to rule the gangster hierarchies of Marseilles, emigrating there generation after generation just as young men in the other villages of the Balagne regularly enlist in the army, the merchant marine. At all events they are 'not of the flour that makes the host' – the bread of the Eucharist – to use a local expression; if one enters the cafés one is likely to meet with the hooded stares of expensively dressed men with gold-ringed fingers busy at the card tables; once I blundered, unwelcome, into a curtained alcove where the game was unlegalised baccarat. Others are hunters who alone know the topography of Monte Grosso, where they vanish in contempt of the law to stalk moufflon, the strictly preserved, fast disappearing curly-horned Corsican wild sheep, delicious forbidden eating. Calenzana belongs only geographically to the serene, squirearchical, outdated, Italianate Balagne; almost the last village before the sixty-mile-long no-man's-land of untamed maquis rolling south to Porto, it is linked, in a wary, competitive intimacy with that other outpost, seabound Calvi.

We were speeding there now head on into the flaming sunset, most beautiful, however, for the light it cast on the receding mountains, emphasising their crests and chasms, revealing unsuspected hollows, folded in the rocks, hidden to sight by day. By the time we reached Calvi the sun had dropped behind the citadel, now dominating the little port with its bold high ochre bastions. By a twist of the coastline the port faces due east; I stepped on to the quay to find myself looking back at the panorama of the mountains, which appeared as though falling straight into the sea. Their lower slopes had sunk into a lilac mist; but their heights still glowed with an unearthly pink, impossible fields of roses drifting in mid-sky. The semicircular sweep of the shore, edged by an arc of sand, a band of pines, was so perfect and unbroken that one felt it must be drawn with a compass; the whole scene might have been the work of a romantic landscape painter who had rendered his subject at once more shapely and extravagant than any landscape could be.

The human actors, too, had a finer-than-life appearance. My companions on the bus had been dowdy elderly couples, like most of the scarce tourists I had met in Corsica. But the port of Calvi was crowded with cowboys, Mexican toughs, pirates, Polynesian dancing girls, or people dressed up as such; I had stumbled into a small but very lively cosmopolitan playground. Pleasure-seekers of all ages and – I suspected – many races, packed the quay, the cafés, the yachts moored to the waterfront; the red-kneed pair in lederhosen were wearing national, not fancy dress. I had neglected to book a room (nowhere else had this been necessary); after calling at the few hotels I realised that Calvi was full. Eventually I found a room in a widow's flat; for one night only, she told me. One night, in a place of such rending beauty! I determined to spend as little of it as possible in my stuffy lodging.

The ambience of the port had intensified when I returned there, as though in the catastasis of an ancient drama the scene were prepared for some climax of conflicting human passions. The sun had set; the water gleamed with

217

brilliant reflected lights. Roulette tables had been set up along the quay in scarlet bunting booths with blazing electric bulbs; the traditional accompaniment, I was told, of the festival of the Assumption of the Virgin, which had been celebrated that very day. They were operated by a little dark curlyheaded man whose grin displayed a set of teeth all silver and gold; Bijoutier, 'the jeweller', a well-known character from Calenzana. The Wild West and South Sea island crowd, increased by real and fake sailors from the yachts and women in full floating evening dress, seethed round the tables in a state of compressed excitement not to be accounted for by the low-staked gambling. One was conscious, here, of currents between person and person charged with potential explosive.

I found a seat in a café close to an attractive English woman, drinking alone. She was bitter. 'I read so much about Corsica; Colomba, the bandits of honour. Bandits d'honneur! Call them bandits d'amour! Bandits of love! Look at them! I ask you!' They were easy to distinguish, though they were wearing a costume as outlandish to English eyes as any visitor's: dark slacks, tight jerseys, brightly printed scarves, cloth caps set straight and low over the eyes with the dandyism of Marseilles. Very superb they looked, pacing in twos and threes, ignoring the very pretty women of all ages who hovered in their passage. They were an extreme product of patriarchal society, these Calvi men, so I later came to understand. Not that they are inevitably more dictatorial than a Swedish businessman may be; but the ancient division of labour that long, long ago excluded women from the hunt and relegated them to humble chores has become, here, unchallenged through the ages, a complete cleavage between the sexes, so that these men are less aware of themselves as human beings than as males. A man acts, thinks, feels like this or that, they often explained to me, as though I belonged to another zoological species. 'A real man must kill and go to prison', I several times heard. And many have had occasion to live up to this code in a perfectly praiseworthy way, having fought in the Second World War in the Resistance, which was very active in Calvi where it was known how to smuggle in arms.

A party of them filed, poker-faced, into the back room of the café; my companion brightened (she had been looking desperate) and led me inside. The men had taken possession of the bar counter. 'Drinks all round!' one of them called, as though commanding a military manœuvre; glasses of *pastis* were thrust into our hands. Drinks all round again; they had begun to sing. The song was the flashy, martial Ajaccienne, composed in 1848 by a Corsican poet to welcome Napoleon, son of Jérôme Bonaparte, the first member of the family to set foot in Corsica after the repeal of the law that had exiled the Bonaparte from the soil of France. The men ordered us to their table: 'You don't like sitting by yourselves, it's not natural,' one of them informed me. Another was paying attention to my companion; she was happy and in love. Now they were chanting the dirge of the bandit Spada, said to have been composed by a fellow prisoner to whom Spada, awaiting execution, told his tale: an interminable ballad relating in flat, tragic detail how he took to the maquis, robbed and loved and killed, hid and was captured and condemned to the guillotine.

We were released very late for dinner, haphazardly served in an overfull quayside restaurant, but redeemed by a great red moon rising above the mountain ranges. An orchestra was playing tangos on a café terrace; but my companion was unwilling to join the dancing there; she was looking unhappy again. 'I'd rather take you to Tao's,' she told me. Tao Kerefoff was a White Russian, she explained; he had been in Calvi for years; he ran a night club in the citadel.

We left the glittering port by a stepped arched alley, came abruptly to the neck of the promontory, an unlit wasteland overlooking the open spaces of the western sea. The citadel sprang sheer from the ground at our feet, its bastions and glacis rising to a great height in smooth, inclined planes. They chilled me as we walked in their indeterminate shadow, up a cobbled ramp and over the drawbridge into a tunnel of masonry, our steps echoing from the invisible roof.

These defences were sufficient to keep Calvi secure and isolated through the warring centuries, though the city took a fearful battering in the sixteenth century when the Turkish fleet, allied with Sampiero Corso and the French, hurled eleven thousand cannon-balls inside its walls, and the inhabitants in their extremity paraded their ebony crucifix on the ramparts, ever since regarded as miraculous. It was to suffer even worse when the British attacked in 1794. The siege began in June after the town had been blockaded by Paoli's partisans for the best part of a year; the defenders numbered about eight hundred soldiers and a corps of volunteers, the enemy some two thousand. The British did what was least expected of them: landing well to the south by the reptilian peninsular of Revellata, Nelson and General Stuart, with a sure sense of strategy, dragged their artillery to the undefended hilltops behind the town. They began by bombarding a secondary stronghold, Mozella, which still stands, bleak as an Arab fort, on an inland plateau facing the citadel. By mid-July it had fallen and Nelson, manning a battery on a ridge near the shore, had been wounded in the right eye by an explosion of stones. The bombardment of Calvi then started in earnest; over eleven thousand shot and nearly three thousand shells were fired into the town during the four weeks before the garrison surrendered with more than half its number out of action. 'The place is a heap of ruins,' wrote Nelson. In fact some of this destruction is still apparent, on the western edge of the citadel, above the cliffs raked by the winds from Spain.[10]

We climbed into the stronghold by a winding cobbled way; the streets circle the site, coil within coil. A gap in the walls revealed the moon, risen clear above the peaks and pouring its light into the bay, transforming it into a deep silver bowl. Mountains and sea were of the same phantasmal consistency, less material, far, than the darker, more familiar sky, pricked by many stars. This was surely a mirage of the imagination's eye, glimpsed inwardly in dread of its wonder and likely any minute to dissolve. I stayed leaning against the parapet in spite of my companion's impatience; after all I had only one night to spend in Calvi and I might never come here again.

Stumbling in the shadows of walls and archways and towers, we passed below the cathedral, its domed lantern swelling into the constellations, made our way between high houses, ragged ruins, down steps, over rubbish where old tins glittered like diamonds, through rubble and loose stones. Tao's music poured through an open door. The room was orange and vaulted, once the chapel, I later learned, of a bishop's palace; a champagne bottle was cooling in the holy-water stoup. An unaged man with cat-like movements and large compassionate brown eyes welcomed us, and I knew him at once as a friend. We often wondered if we had met years before in the Russian *boîtes* of Paris, where the tzigane music wailed the whole night through; but I hardly think so, for before I began going to such places Tao had already settled in Calvi.

'Ah, you have had a good idea, you make me much pleasure,' he said, with a particular note of approval in his pidgin English, as though congratulating us on some very difficult and worthy action. Entering Tao's night club with my distraught companion I was made to feel like a prodigal daughter being received back into respectable society; and that was the feeling he was to give me every time I went there.

Tao arrived in Calvi by accident, young, but with a life of adventure behind him. A Muslim of the Caucasus, one of the legendary Tcherkess, famed for their looks, their matchless horsemanship and valour, he had got away from the Crimea after the defeat of the White cavalry regiment in which he served, reached Constantinople with his comrades in arms. 'We all wandered about the streets,' he told me, 'no one knew what to do.' Tao only knew how to do one thing apart from ride a horse: dance Caucasian dances. He danced before the last of the Turkish sultans, and before the Sultan's harem; the Tcherkess concubines, victims of their beauty, wept for the Russia they had been exiled from for many years. This was the start to a career in which Tao danced his way westwards, to Paris, to New York, in night clubs, cinemas, at charity balls, on dance floors, on stages and the tops of tables, while the women wept again and again.

In New York he ran into that supremely handsome nobleman, Felix Youssoupoff, murderer of Rasputin and benefactor of innumerable exiled compatriots. Together they returned to Paris; in 1928 they went to Calvi where Youssoupoff had already bought a couple of houses. They landed with a party of Russian friends, a guitarist and a flute player and a mechanical nightingale picked up in the old town of Marseilles. In Calvi Tao danced, the musicians played, the mechanical nightingale sang; the Russians waltzed on the port, sailor style, with the fishermen (no women were allowed out dancing then). The fishermen descended on Youssoupoff's farm one night with *langoustes*, kid, fruit, wine and champagne and coloured lanterns to hang on the trees. 'Don't worry,' they said, 'we won't be sending you in a bill.'[11] This was a period of reckless high living that has never been forgotten; the glamour of it clung to Calvi after Youssoupoff had left and the Russians dispersed, grown

The citadel of Calvi. (*Louis Bianchetti*)

old, taken to drink or died. But Tao, always resilient, acquired the bishop's palace and married a Corsican girl whose Slav looks – high cheekbones, slit eyes – give her a ballerina's allure.

There has been scope for Tao's skills in a Calvi night club; his dancing; his personality, which projects a particular sense of well being; his aristocratic way of treating all his guests as equals and bringing out their best; and their worst would have defeated a less accomplished host. I have seen bands of shepherds arrive fresh from the Niolo with their guns and dogs, after driving across half Corsica shooting on the way, to spend two or three days and nights in uninterrupted eating, drinking and dancing: 'Take a room? What for? Beds are for invalids!' one of them protested. Leaders of parallel international hierarchies have elbowed the bar: a Rochefoucauld and a Bourbon Parme alongside Tiberius, Corsican king of the Tunis gambling saloons, his face scarred with vitriol. Scottish schoolteachers and London ex-debutantes dance with merchant seamen and foreign legionaries, models with peasants; straggle-haired young Parisian Bohemians are more reassuring than the well-dressed, unnaturally quiet men from Calenzana and Marseilles. And always Tao is imperturbable, working, sometimes, from sunset to sunset to the following sunrise (the record marathon was eleven hundred tango records played in uninterrupted succession), imposing himself by the gentle answer, by his mere presence.

The night club was crowded the first time I went there, with visitors from various nations, Corsicans from the interior in heavy corduroys, and the suave Calvi men who sat in tight, conspirational groups, pounced on their partners, swayed them solemnly round the room and left them at the end of the dance without a word; their approach to pleasure was ritualistic. We were seized, danced with, left, seized again, constantly on the floor, where one caught sight of the stars, the moon, the spectral mountains through the tall windows above the dancers' heads. We would be danced to extinction, for the women were far outnumbered by the men. The women of Calvi, until very recently, have been kept in the background, perhaps more heartlessly than those of the Sartenais. I saw them occasionally at that period, carrying buckets between pumps and houses with set, fatalistic expressions, or sitting in rows on benches, like black crows. I think that most of them had rather wretched lives. But now their daughters are taking a revenge, for no one can stop them slipping out after dark to jerk at Tao's till dawn.

The night was gathering impetus; it carried us with the rising moon into dark, unexplored, fathomless places. The music was hypnotic; no one resisted it; the dancers moved with a taut, controlled violence, the men crouching over their partners as though intent on kindling a fire. And this, after all, is what most women, if they are honest with themselves, enjoy; in the words of Colette: 'to feel the certitude, from head to feet, of being the prey of one living man, and to obey, in his arms, a rhythm as intimate as that of sleep.'[12]

They were all enjoying themselves, except my companion; she was in tears.

221

'I'm not like this normally,' she sobbed. It would be safe to say that no one at Tao's that night was behaving normally (except Tao himself, at ease in the realm he had created); not the party of dark-faced peasant boys fresh from some village where talking to girls may still have incurred the dire alternatives of death or marriage, now glowering hotly at their foreign dancing partners; certainly not the beautiful red-haired woman in a dress I recognised as a Balmain model of the year before, absorbed in concentrated conversation with a Corsican bronzed-skinned and arrogant as a picture-book Red Indian.

At Tao's masks and attitudes slip away, as though the superstructure of the personality were decomposed by a powerful acid. People go there to lose their individual and social identities, to rediscover in themselves an area of instinct, common to all. Corsica gives few opportunities for this kind of satisfaction; in the villages it has always been stamped on with relentless penalties. Visitors, on the other hand, have been starved of it, while their hunger for it has grown abnormally as they travel to and from work, work long hours, shop and cook and accumulate things they hardly need or enjoy. In Calvi Corsicans and foreigners meet on terms more intimate than elsewhere; not as hosts and guests, travellers and guides, but as anonymous human beings driven by their compulsions. They come together on the ground of shared pleasure; a perilous ground, undermined by misunderstandings from the start.

For the visitors, these Corsicans of Calvi are magnificent simple primitives. But few Corsicans are simple, and those of Calvi are not so at all. There is nothing truly primitive about Calvi except some of the surrounding scenery; it is an anciently civilised town that has gone downhill. The inhabitants are aware of its historic past, and they are haunted by the idea that more is due to them than a hand-to-mouth living as fishermen, labourers, and operators of a short tourist season. The haughty citadel, the *Commissario*'s *palazzo* with its colossal towers, the cathedral, where the light from the domed lantern picks out the gilding of the resplendent Genoese altarpiece,[13] the inscription over the drawbridge, *Civitas Calvi semper fidelis*, in memory of Calvi's loyalty to Genoa during the Turkish siege: such sights constantly serve to remind them that their predecessors were not poor backward islanders, but wealthy, valorous Genoese patricians.

One knows what they looked like. Augustin Canava, a stone mason apparently descended from a Genoese family (the name is un-Corsican), showed me half a dozen marble busts in the cemetery, funeral monuments dating from the late sixteenth and early seventeenth centuries. The faces of these High Renaissance notables are autocratic, their clothes soberly sumptuous. Viola Silvestri, buried on Palm Sunday of 1616, daughter of the *castellano* – the commander of the fortress – wears a double starched ruff and a heartshaped jewel on a ribbon necklace; her hair is drawn up on a frame above her long nose and aggressively salient chin. The costume is rather old-fashioned for the date; this was provincial dressing, conservative, overcharged, but obviously expensive. One can imagine her among the ladies who attended Mass in the cathedral, seated in the little balconies, like opera boxes or Muslim moucharabies, placed high up in the walls and screened by wooden lattices to shield their occupants from vulgar eyes.[14]

Where did the money come from? Not from the land. At first the citizens of Calvi cultivated vineyards; but production had so fallen off by the seventeenth century that they were short of wine for themselves. Unlike the Bonifaciens they were uninterested in agriculture; much less numerous – little more than a thousand until recent years – they lived on their windswept rock in disdainful isolation. They were sea-going traders who profited by tax concessions from the Republic; or so it was assumed until a modern historian brought evidence to show that their most lucrative occupation was usury. Like the Indian moneylenders they 'sucked the blood' of the peasants.[15]

The more enterprising, it is true, made fortunes abroad, such as the illustrious Baglioni, supposedly surnamed Liberta in recognition of the courage of Bayon Baglioni, who assassinated a pair of citizens who were plotting to deliver Calvi to the Aragonese. In the sixteenth century the Baglioni Liberta had moved to Marseilles where they distinguished themselves by a deed of patriotic valour curiously similar to that which had earned them their name: in 1598, during the disturbances following the Wars of Religion, Pierre Baglioni Liberta, with his two brothers, murdered the quisling who was about to surrender the town to a besieging Spanish fleet and established the authority of Henri IV, who largely rewarded them. Two and a half centuries later the family reappears, it has been asserted, as the Libertys of Regent Street.[16]

By the sixteenth century an enduring relationship was established between Calvi and Marseilles. But Spain and the Indies were the greater lure; Spain in the aureole of the New World, and the New World itself, adventurers' Eldorado. The chronicler Filippini gives a list of the Calvais who had piled up wealth in those lands. Surpassing them all was his kinsman (also related to the dispossessed Cinarchesi), Giovann'Antonio Vincentello, 'one of the richest men in Christendom' who, it is said, followed the Emperor Charles V to North Africa as a soldier of fortune, made his way to Peru, scooped up Inca gold, lived luxuriously in Lima, and afterwards, ascertainably, built himself a palace in Seville and married his daughter to a prince of the royal house of Portugal. He 'opened the road and lent a hand' – in the words of Filippini – to numerous Corsican relatives and friends, who came to form a thriving, powerful colony in Seville.[17]

These success stories are well known in Calvi; the deeds of Giovann'Antonio are in fact recorded in Gothic lettering on Tao's walls, where one can learn that he founded a charitable institution in Calvi and lent five thousand *livres* to Philip II of Spain. Past glories weigh as heavily on Calvi as violence does on the Sartenais. With the example of these magnates behind them, and no agricultural tradition, the Calvais are convinced that money is something to be got by daring initiative and clever manipulation. Less oppressed by Destiny than most other Corsicans, they have a strong belief in another mythical figure, *La Chance* (the French feminine gender accords with the concept): one waits for her, seizes her and profits by her; she favours or abandons one.

La Chance was rather ungenerous after the French conquest. The Genoese families lingered on in Calvi – the Pittalunga, Cataneo, Lecalupi, the Canava – and grew poor. Some sought and found *La Chance* in the French colonies, as their predecessors had done more brilliantly in the Spanish. The army, the merchant navy, provided endurable alternatives to fishing. There was Marseilles, of course, ever an abode of *La Chance*, where young men still occasionally disappear, to return in new clothes, driving large cars. But since the time of Youssoupoff foreigners have brought *La Chance* to Calvi. Not only with the money they spend; the inhabitants, who see no reason why they should be deprived of the good things of life, join in their pursuit of pleasure with a biting zest and a facility for living in the present that are in themselves wonderfully exhilarating. Their philosophy is a rudimentary existentialism: 'There's no such thing as happiness or unhappiness,' one of them told me, 'those are your illusions. All that counts is to feel oneself alive.' A point of view irresistible to many visitors, who may not have felt truly alive for years and years.

They, on the other hand, offer the Calvais the novelty of their carefree ways, their disregard for convention. In Corsica prostitute and Englishwoman are not designated by the same word, as happens in Sicily; on the contrary the Corsicans are shrewd enough to realise that the women who arrive unguarded by husbands, fathers or brothers are well-placed in their own societies. But this merely confirms their suspicion that there is no morality abroad. The foreigners' world is one of unbounded wealth and freedom, to be enjoyed for the moment, as a gift of *La Chance*, but not to be taken too seriously. Which no doubt explains why foreign women are not always treated with much consideration. My companion was kept waiting at Tao's till two in the morning before her man came to join her. He knew how to counter her resentment. 'Corsica's not the country of love and flowers!' he exclaimed. 'It's the country of hate and harm!' She looked radiant.

What begins at Tao's in the night-soarings of love can lead to satisfactory marriages – I know of several – but may also end in smashed homes, hopes, lives. My companion seemed to be heading that way. The men of Calvi are known as Don Juans. And for this they have a precedent: Miguel Manara, the historical Don Juan, was born of parents who emigrated from Calvi to Seville.

It is a pity that over-optimistic attempts to prove that Christopher Columbus was a native of Calvi have obscured, or discredited, the historical facts of Don Juan's parentage. The arguments for Columbus's Calvi origins are unscientific and rejected by all serious historians, Corsicans and others; the most one can say is that he may conceivably have been a Genoese of Calvi but that there is no proof whatever that he was.[18] None the less a ruined house on the citadel overlooking the western sea is shown as his birthplace, while the Manara home has been forgotten. Yet the evidence seems irrefutable: Miguel de Leca y Colonna y Manara y Vicentello, born in Seville in 1627, was the child of Corsican parents: Tomaso Manara of Calvi, and Jeronima Anfriani of

224

Montemaggiore, in the Balagne, both of them descended from branches of the Cinarchesi.

We know this because when Miguel was eight years old his father took steps to secure his membership of the Order of the Knights of Calatrava. To be eligible to this extremely exclusive religious and military association it was necessary to produce proof of noble ancestry. Tomaso Manara applied to the Genoese senate, which authorised an official investigation in which fifty-four Corsican witnesses certified that Tomaso Manara was the great-grandson of Francesco da Leca, 'of the counts of Cinarca', and that his father-in-law, Antonio Anfriani of Montemaggiore, was likewise descended from the Leca in direct line. In a parallel enquiry four descendants of the Leca confirmed that the Manara and Anfriani were legitimate branches of their family.

The facts, first published by Colonna de Cesari Rocca, one of the best Corsican historians, were used in a recent biography of Miguel Manara by Esther van Loo. Her book has never received the attention it deserves: it relates one of the most extraordinary life stories ever told. Essential material comes from the very detailed evidence collected by the Vatican with a view to Don Juan's canonisation; for Miguel Manara, known as the worst man of his day, repented, reformed, and died in odour of sanctity. The Vatican has accorded him the title of Venerable, the first step towards recognition of sainthood.[19]

Popular ideas of Don Juan have been muddled by the confusion of two distinct figures: Miguel Manara, a real man, nicknamed Don Juan by his contemporaries, and the fictional Don Juan Tenorio, hero, or rather anti-hero, of a play by the Spanish monk Tirso de Molino: *El Burlador de Sevilla*. The well-known plot, which was followed by Molière, Byron, and nearly all the writers inspired by the Don Juan theme, tells how the nobleman Juan Tenorio, an unscrupulous seducer of women, murders the Commander Gonzalo de Ulloa, father of an intended victim of love, mocks the dead man's statue and invites it to dinner. The man of stone comes to the supper table, lays hands on Don Juan at the end of the meal, and thereby removes him, too late repentant, to the flames of hell.[20]

The play, moral in intention, was a smash-hit; produced around 1620, it ran for years. Miguel Manara first saw it in 1641, when he was fourteen; at the end of the performance he announced (so it is said): 'I will become Don Juan.' The anecdote is credible, and very interesting as an early indication of his peculiarly Corsican cast of character. Like the young Corsicans of respectable families who enrol, eyes open, in the underworld of Marseilles, Miguel Manara chose his career of crime deliberately. For crime it was, and he knew it as such. Who could be more thoroughly versed in the code of feminine honour than this son of devout Corsican parents living in seventeenth-century Spain? Better than most of the writers who have handled the Don Juan theme, he knew that to seduce and betray a wife or virgin and then publicise her seduction meant her irretrievable disgrace, the loss of social and private consideration, of her self-respect; in short the destruction of her personality.

I am unable to envisage Miguel Manara as the tormented romantic in anguished quest of an unattainable satisfaction, as imagined by some writers (but with the legendary, not the historical, Don Juan in mind). The facts of his life point to a hard Corsican realism and overbearing pride. The Corsican writer Lorenzo di Bradi seems to me nearer the mark in likening him to a Corsican bandit at loose in a foreign land, bent on asserting his worth. I would go further: Miguel Manara, I think, was consciously rebelling against a puritanical code, doing wrong for the joy of wrong-doing, as a puritan will. He was out to defy society, but also the morality society upholds: in fact to defy God. And there are parallels among the Corsicans, in a less elegant sphere. The Corsican doctor in law, Madeleine-Rose Marin-Muracciole, marvels at the 'strange social phenomenon' presented by 'the sons of peasants and shepherds, of a healthy mentality, respectful of their mothers and fiercely sensitive to the honour of their sisters and cousins' who earn their living 'by the abasement of women'. Strange indeed; and only to be understood as an aspect of Corsican pride; pride that makes poverty insupportable, wealth a necessity; pride, too, that glories in the breaking of laws and the sacred precepts – moral, religious, maternal – imbibed since childhood.

Miguel Manara was not looking for money; his father was immensely rich. His victims were ladies of the high society of Seville. At first his exploits were no worse than scandalous: 'duels, amorous follies and other vanities of the world', the 'terrible furies' of passion, to quote his contemporaries. For preference he chose the most inaccessible married women and young girls; those with a reputation for blameless virtue. He was irresistible. Not that he was very good-looking: his portraits show the long Corsican nose and irregular features; but he must have been well endowed with the Corsican fusion of primitive vitality and physical refinement, and this, joined to the education of a Sevillian gentleman, made him the most fascinating of men.

His love affairs were often discovered; he intended them to be. He relished risks, went so far as to make a rendezvous with a young girl in a shooting lodge, having sent word to her brother that he would seduce her there at the appointed hour. The brother arrived, incredulous, challenged Miguel Manara – already in his sister's arms – and was promptly killed. For almost every broken heart and home there was a corpse; the women were left to mourn their virtue, their reputations, their husbands and brothers and fiancés; and also Don Juan, for he was a seducer of the most deadly kind: more than physically attractive, one who could engage his victim's total capacity for devotion.

Then came an adventure which found its way into the records of the time and crowned his ambition of incarnating the Don Juan of the play. The name of the woman is remembered: Dona Teresita Sanchez de Linden y Olmedo. Like Clarissa Harlowe she was known for the perfection of her purity; Don Miguel had to serenade her for several weeks before she consented to open her window to him. This affair lasted longer than most; Teresita's love was sincere, idealistic, worth bringing to full flower before destruction. One night as she lay with her lover her father entered her room. Miguel Manara killed him on the spot and fled.

This was a serious matter that could hardly be passed off as a duel. Don Juan had to take to the maquis like a Corsican bandit; that is to say he went to the Netherlands war. There he made himself known by his heroism in the field, as a result of which judicial proceedings against him were dropped and he was able to return to Seville.

His rake's reputation was now at its height; only a very unusual feat of seduction could add to it; one that exceeded, in infamy, the last. He decided on incest. He knew that his father, years ago before leaving Corsica, had seduced a cousin, one of the Anfriani, and that the child of this liaison was a daughter by the name of Vannina who was being brought up in the family home at Montemaggiore. Miguel Manara travelled to Corsica, presented himself to the Anfriani under an assumed name, posing as a close friend of the person he in fact was. He was welcomed with the hospitality due to the bearer of a letter of introduction from a distinguished cousin abroad. He courted Vannina, succeeded in entering her room; she, no doubt, intended to anticipate and so hasten their marriage in accordance with the customary guile of Corsican girls. Then, at the very moment when she was about to yield to him, Don Miguel revealed his identity; the conquest, to be total, demanded that she should share his guilt. But in Corsica the taboo on incest is absolute: no act is regarded with such horror. Vannina repulsed him, woke the family with her screams; Don Miguel had to fight his way out of the house by a back staircase (which was shown to me by Charles Colonna d'Anfriani, the present owner).

Failure acted on him as a spur. On his return to Seville Miguel Manara conceived a project even more abominable, by the standards of his day: he would seduce a nun. This, in itself, might not be very difficult; the immorality of certain Spanish convents was notorious. But Don Miguel had the refinement to choose a former victim, that Dona Teresita whose father he had killed, and who had since taken the veil. He found her in her convent, contrived to speak to her, declared his love and convinced her of it, persuaded her to elope with him, fixed a day for the abduction; and planned to abandon her afterwards.

He was dissuaded by a sequence of experiences that run true to Corsican tradition. Walking through the streets of Seville with his equerry, one night shortly before the day fixed for the abduction, he heard a strange humming; like the sound Jean Cesari described to me as heralding the spirits of the dead. It was followed by funeral chants mingled with lamentations issuing from the church of Santa Cruz. Through the open door he could see lighted tapers. He entered; the singing ceased, the lights were extinguished; the church was empty. Much shaken, he continued on his way. At the sinister cross-roads of the Calle del Ataud and the Calle de la Muerte (the Street of the Coffin and the Street of Death), Miguel Manara felt a violent blow on the back of his neck; a blow such as the *mazzeri* deal. It knocked him senseless; when he came to he heard a voice saying: 'Bring the coffin, he is dead.'

Had he been told of such psychic experiences by his Corsican mother? Or

227

did they arise, spontaneously, from the collective racial unconscious? At all events he heeded them; they changed his life. His equerry, Don Alonso Perez de Velasco, who related the incidents of that decisive night to the court of the Vatican, describes how he thanked God afterwards for these warnings; for Miguel Manara, killer of hearts and lives, still believed in God. The next day he learned that three private enemies had been waiting for him in the house he had intended to visit.

He had been warned; but he had still not given up his villain's scheme. Then, on the very night before he was to remove Dona Teresita from her convent, he had another vision, less Corsican in its imagery. A beautiful woman called to him from a window, invited him to her house, threw down a rope ladder from her balcony. He climbed it, entered the room; and found only a skeleton lying on the floor.

The following morning he counter-ordered the coach in which he was to fetch Teresita and sent her a letter. It told her the whole, the unbearable, the unnecessary truth: he had planned to elope with her only to abandon her; he had never loved her, never, at any time. Alas for the victims of the newly converted! Did Teresita rejoice in her deliverance, his conversion, thank God for saving her from perdition, and her lover from yet further crime? She collapsed and died that same night, always repeating: 'He never loved me.'

Soon afterwards, on 31 August 1648, Miguel Manara married Jeronima Carillo de Mendoza, a girl barely fifteen years old of an extraordinary sweetness and strength of character. He was then twenty-one. He became a loving and faithful husband, a conscientious landlord, a magistrate and municipal councillor of Seville. They lived together in flawless harmony until after thirteen years she suddenly died. There were no children.

His despair marked the next step in his metamorphosis. In the monastery of the Carmelites, known as the Desert of the Snows, up on a wild *serra*, he prayed day and night over his wife's tomb until the monks began to fear for his reason, his life. Back in Seville six months later, aged and unrecognisable, he had visions, intimations, which even more precisely than those that had preceded his marriage conform to Corsican tradition. One night he met a funeral cortège and stopped the coffin-bearers to ask who was being buried at that unusual hour. 'Don Miguel,' they replied. A few nights later he met another procession, this time of hooded penitents passing by with soundless steps and carrying lighted tapers that remained strangely steady in the breeze. 'We are burying Don Miguel Manara,' they told him. He followed them into the church of San Isodore, heard the Mass of the Dead from beginning to end, tore the velvet covering from the coffin; and saw himself lying inside. When he was picked up the next morning on the church steps he was thought to be dead.

But this was the time of his rebirth, of entry into the religious life. Although he was attracted to the contemplative orders he never became a monk; the tasks he imposed on himself were in the realm of action; his saintliness was of a practical, Corsican kind. He joined the lay fraternity of Santa Caridad (the

Blessed Charity); its members were men of wealth and position who rather negligently devoted some of their spare time and money to good works. Miguel Manara reformed the organisation, was elected prior, and thereafter gave all his energy, mind and vast fortune to fighting illness and poverty; and in seventeenth-century Seville their proportions were appalling. He built a hospital; nursed the sick through a plague; distributed relief during a famine, a flood; carried food and clothing to the destitute families of the slums. The sick, the poor, the down and outs, were not to be treated as outcasts, but honoured and loved, for they were the image of Jesus Christ, so he insisted, in the Franciscan tradition, as the Corsican monks might have done. 'The poor are born free, like us, they are our brothers,' he wrote. And he performed funeral rites for executed criminals, rites of great splendour with a Corsican sense of what is due to the dead.

So he lived, in absolute dedication, until his death in 1679: seventeen years. His tombstone was inscribed according to his own wish with the words: 'Here lie the bones and ashes of the worst man who was in the world.' The first investigation for his canonisation was opened the following year.

Miguel Manara's life story follows a recognisable Corsican pattern, but exceeds it, as a masterpiece exceeds rough sketches. In his enormous pride, his wilful choice of wrong, his abrupt changes of direction, his absolutism, his realism, no less than in the nature of his visions he was a Corsican. The drastic conversion in middle life is one of the Corsican possibilities. True, I have not heard of any Don Juan turned saint; reformed gangsters and adventurers, murderers and wreckers of women normally stop short at an early stage on that road; they marry respectable girls (like Bornea) or return to long-neglected wives, become conscientious husbands and fathers, worthy citizens, municipal councillors and mayors. But their rehabilitation is most often accompanied by an austerity unusual among regenerated rakes: it involves a total, conscious rejection of their past.

The type may become less familiar from now on. Traditional values are dissolving in Corsica, as elsewhere. There are fewer Don Juans in Calvi today because there are fewer women who can really be ruined. The companion of my first night at Tao's believed in unique love, irreplaceable and lifelong; the present visitors are more likely to subscribe to the slogan: 'Make love not war.' The myth of Tristan and Iseult is losing ground, like the complementary myth of Don Juan. At the same time pleasure is becoming accessible, approved by local society, now that Calvi is on the way to prosperity with a score of hotels open nearly half the year and campers crowded in the surrounding woods and maquis. Almost anyone can find work, earn money and spend it on what he enjoys: skiing holidays are the latest wholesome craze of the Calvais. Pleasure is part of the accepted scheme of things, a commodity to be bought, a right; no longer that forbidden game to be tracked and trapped with craft and treachery, caught on the wing, pinioned and devoured in the anguishing euphoria of guilt and destruction.

14 THE CORE OF THE ISLAND

Journey to the centre – the lugubrious Scala – the peaks – a
sombre fair – *voceru* and *paghiella* – nomad shepherds –
paradise in decay – primitive living – archaic *bergerie* – pastoral
decline

I HAD my holiday after all; one less restful than I had planned but more
interesting. When I called on Tao to say good-bye, the day after my arrival in
Calvi, he offered me a room. It was a very large room at the top of the fifty-
two steps of a regally vaulted staircase; the windows gave on to the bay. One
looked across it straight into the mountains; the sunrise and the moonrise
would be mine. I saw both in recurring succession during my stay there, came
to know the two heavenly bodies as never before. Night after night the moon
flooded in under my ceiling, drenching me in the same vaporous essence as the
ranges and the sea. It held me at the windows until the music floating up
from the bishop's chapel became too insistent: seldom jazz, but the corrupt
haunting airs of the Mediterranean, paso doble, tango, java, the spinning-top
waltz of Marseilles, last dross of that millennial civilisation which in its vigour
of youth gave birth to the dances sacred to Dionysus. It stayed with me, the
moon, all through the night, sailing into Rimbaud's sidereal archipelagoes
over the dancers' heads; it had usually disappeared by the time I got back to
my room to see the rising sun recreating sea and mountains, giving them colour
and consistency, lighting the peaks as it would again, at the day's end,
before it made way for the moon's return.

My holiday ran from the feast day to feast day; from the Assumption to
the Nativity of the Virgin. I wanted to stay in Calvi for that occasion when
almost the whole population climbs to the chapel of Notre Dame de la Serra,
set like a fortress amid huge granite boulders on a rock far above the sea, and
the pilgrims picnic after Mass among the rocks while Bijoutier operates the
roulette tables. But I had to remind myself that Count Peraldi had arranged
for me to see this festival in the Niolo, where it is accompanied by a three day
fair, and that my time in Corsica was running low.

The *micheline* left before six in the morning; Tao helped me carry my
luggage to the station. We had neither of us slept; as often happened we had
made ourselves breakfast in the kitchen after the last dancers had left, the
last tune had been played, and the only sounds were the cocks crowing and
the fishing boats chugging out to sea, and the sea itself, washing all round the
citadel so that one could fancy one were living on a ship. We picked our way

230

down the crumbling steps and along the ramparts, surprising a donkey rummaging among old tins and bones, and a pair of lovers, too absorbed in each other to know that day had come.

Passing under the great arch of the drawbridge we crossed the wasteland below the bastions, where one could see the rugged coast winding to Revellata, and the rock coves where I had bathed each morning in a sea so sparkling and revitalising that I could never believe it was just salt water. The rocks continue beyond Revellata, fifty miles south to Porto, in almost uninterrupted high cliffs, rose and violet and orange, the colours of sunset and sunrise, the hours when they outflame the sky. As though in a mescaline dream I saw that coast, after a long night's dancing at Tao's, from a fishing boat sailing to landlocked Girolata, where a dozen or so Corsicans, without a road, exist in a weird fusion of biblical and Bohemian simplicity, gardening, hunting, and selling food and drink to passing fishermen, off-beat tourists and artists, and gangsters cheating the law.

Nothing could efface the memories of those weeks, I thought, as we walked through the waking village filled with the scent of wood smoke and coffee coming from the houses of the early risers, greeting some who would rise much later, now straying home with the disjointed steps of people who have danced all night. At the station close to the beach – the lunar crescent edging the vacant bay – we said good-bye; not, I felt, for ever. The *micheline* sounded the two sad notes of its horn, rattled into the pinewoods past the sleeping campers in their little tents; as the train gathered speed the citadel, my home, became a vignette of a fortress surmounted by a cupola; the bay that had been the ornamental pool of my private mythical domain receded into the shining spaces of the morning. At Ile-Rousse only a few people boarded the train; I fell asleep during the dragging climb into the mountains, was jerked awake barely in time to change at Ponte-Leccia.

The second train took me south up the valley of the Golo, through maquis and rock and holm oak and young pines, the rough parkland scenery of Corsica. At Francardo I changed to a bus, already packed with travellers to the fair. It headed westwards slap into the saw-toothed ranges, nosing between the enormous mountain masses like an icebreaker. I had been sleeping again when I realised we had entered a gorge. The road was a shelf on a vertical wall of blackish rock; beside it rose another bare rock wall slashed with a multitude of crevasses and chasms. We were passing through the Scala di Santa Regina, grim corridor to the Niolo; the rock walls actually rise more than a thousand feet sheer from the river bed. It was a place much dreaded by travellers before the building of the road, a grave for men and beasts; its name, Scala – ladder – described the terrible mule track cut into continuous steps along the cliffs. 'Imagine houses a hundred or two hundred storeys high, which one must successively climb and descend,' exclaimed the Abbé Gaudin, describing his journey into the Niolo in 1787, and concludes with the splendid words: 'It seems that one has reached the limits of nature.'[1] The road, a triumph of its kind, was not opened till the end of the last century. It is the lifeline of the Niolo; for the only other access is by the Col de Vergio, to the west, snowbound from November till April.

Many people had spoken to me of the Niolo; the Corsicans regard it as a national curiosity of which they are proud. It is the most isolated inhabited part of the island, and the highest: the plateau lies at around 2600 feet, the topmost village at 3000; the shepherds' cabins up to 5500, some two or three thousand feet below the peaks. These Alpine herdsmen, I was told, were tall and fair; they were the descendants of the original population of the island, pushed up into this mountain stronghold by early invasions.[2] They were the most hospitable Corsicans, the best singers and improvisers, and also the most violent and vindictive; they were the last to be converted to Christianity and held to their ancient practices in divination until very recent times. They were intransigent patriots; this, I knew, was borne out by their history: they were staunch supporters of nearly all the anti-Genoese rebellions and they resisted the French conquest to the end; they even raised a suicidal revolt in 1774, as a result of which their leaders were broken alive on the wheel and their bodies hung on trees outside their homes. Niolo, I had heard, is a deformation of *niello*, meaning sombre, or afflicted; the whole area had formerly been covered by one dark forest; the Forêt de Valdoniello, on the western slopes, was its residual survival.

The bus rumbled through the gorge at walking pace behind a truck piled high with planks and people sitting on top of them among stacked pots and pans and kitchen chairs. They were on their way to the fairground, where they would set up camp for the duration of the festival. Young men travelling on the roof of the bus hailed them, climbed from bus to truck; the voices echoed and re-echoed in the gorge where only the changing colours of the cliff-face convinced me that we were moving; colours of ashes, rust and sand. We negotiated one sharp corner after another below anarchic rock formations, until at long last, and as suddenly as release comes from a nightmare, the walls went down, sunlight flooded over us, blue space engulfed us: we had entered the Niolo.

Nothing I had been told had prepared me for this landscape. I found an oval plateau entirely ringed by mountains, crenellated as castle walls. The prodigious peaks I had so often glimpsed between, above and behind lesser ranges, snow-streaked at the beginning of my journey, sun-drenched when seen from Morosaglia, always mysterious, inaccessible and phantasmal, were now exposed close at hand in naked materiality. Square topped Monte Cinto, often cloud-veiled, reaches nearly 9000 feet; the Paglia Orba, though considerably lower, appears as high, and far surpasses the Cinto in the majesty of its silhouette: a swelling curve to the west, to the east a precipitous escarpment. Its hooked shape is visible from all over northern Corsica, like a scythe for ever hanging above the horizon. Paglia Orba: the words are numinous to English ears, suggest the opening, or refrain of an incantation, an orison to a divinity which is the peak itself, but in fact – in accordance with the realistic Corsican mind – merely mean 'curved straw'. Giant among giants it outsoars

232

minor peaks, in line as bold: the Cinque Frati – the Five Monks – an ascending file of ragged spires like a procession of hoary beings climbing into the heavens; Monte Tafonato, on the western boundary, pierced by a hole or window through which the sky is seen.

All these summits are so sharply cut that one would think them to be of some light material, like paper, and less substantial than the sky; the mountains, however high-flying, and the plateau itself, are ruled, possessed, by that shining vault joining range to range. Its blueness seems to flow down the mountains like a liquid, filling the rock clefts and gullies, seeping through the bands and patches of pine forest on the upper slopes, pouring on to the plateau and coagulating in the shadows of the small chestnut trees dotted on its rolling surface. The Niolo, whatever its name may mean, makes no impression whatever of darkness, but rather of a sphere filled with a luminous blue substance in which one floats, as in a celestial realm. Yet it is harsh, mineral, puritanical heaven: the trees are dwarfish, the maquis shrivelled; the unveiled sun reverberates from naked sheets of granite and the scattered stones, the millions and millions of stones all burning under the sky.

The bus drew up in a street of unashamedly plain stone houses with glaring red-tiled roofs. The Niolo has prospered over the last half century, and during this time its villages, so often ruined and abandoned after rebellions, have been largely rebuilt or restored. Yet their lack of patina is not alone, I think, responsible for their harsh uninviting air: life here is for the most part lonely and loveless. According to custom wives and children and old people are often left in the villages, while the able-bodied men, the hearty, heroic nomads, travel with their flocks two to three thousand feet higher up the mountains in summer, and down to the coasts in winter, fifty miles away and more. For the shepherds the villages are halfway halts, where they spend only a week or two in the year; the permanent inhabitants are transhumance widows, fatherless children, grandparents and the ailing, people who go about their affairs with the muted doggedness of those who wear out their lives waiting.[3] Coming straight from erotic Calvi I was particularly struck by the triste aspect of Calacuccia, the head village of the Niolo, where the bus dropped me. I saw no sign of the fair.

The hotel where Comte Peraldi had reserved me a room is a base for visiting mountaineers with photographs of rock and snow and a moufflon's curling horns decorating the walls. The heavy-booted red-faced crowd in the diningroom was forbidding, and I was reconciled to my arrival only when I spotted Jean Leblanc and his wife, that friendly couple who long ago, in Ajaccio, had showed me the Fesch museum. They were lunching with members of an expedition from the *Musée des Arts et Traditions Populaires* that had come to Corsica to record local singing; at once I found myself engaged in an excited exchange of ideas about statue-menhirs, Pisan churches, *voceri*, Roman ruins. The fair, they told me, was a rendezvous for the best singers; it took place at Casamaccioli, a neighbouring village; they were going there at once; they would give me a lift.

We drove in a jam of trucks and cars along a dust road winding through fields divided by little stone walls, as in the Cotswolds. The village, set at the foot of a range loaded with chestnuts and pines, was rather less raw-looking than Calacuccia, though I saw nothing from the past until I was shown an enormous free-standing boulder in which were hewn a pair of inter-connecting basins, once used for washing wool; a dateless monument, no doubt historic, but which by its nature belongs to the stone age.[4]

We dined that evening in a café sitting on benches at a trestle table; the meal consisted mainly of *boudin*, a type of sausage made from the blood of sheep or goat or pig, much favoured by the Corsicans and rather like black-pudding. An uneven tapping on the cobbled street, as of a disastrously lamed horse, announced the arrival of the proprietor. He was a crippled dwarf who moved himself about sitting astride a short-legged chair, holding the uprights of its back and propelling himself on its legs by an action of his extremely muscular arms. His lean old wrinkled red face peered cheerfully over the crossbar from under a wide-brimmed black felt hat, and he kept us laughing all through the meal. Afterwards he gave me eau-de-vie by the open fire, where I crouched beside him huddled in my jersey, abruptly robbed of the voluptuous subtropic nights of Calvi.

I was up at dawn, pricked awake by the mountain chill. The morning had a nostalgic northern freshness; dew glittered on the grass and the air held the tang of wood smoke. The smoke was rising in countless fine trails from the fairground, a tree-shaded meadow where many cabins had been set up the day before, roughly put together with planks brought on trucks for the purpose. A few women were about, carrying fuel and water; but it was a curiously secretive, subdued encampment, as though of a tribe, scared, on the run, flying some terrorising foreign invasion. Hushed voices came from the huts where I could see, through the chinks of blankets hung across the entrances, faces crowded round little fires, red in the flamelight. There was nothing to suggest a fair, as fairs are generally understood; no merry-go-rounds or side-shows. A few booths had been set up; but only one seemed to be functioning; it belonged to a barber who was already trimming a patriarch's beard. The scent of coffee mingling with the wood smoke reminded me that I was ravenous; what with sea and mountain air, nights spent dancing, days walking and swimming, my appetite had become habitually colossal.

The barber sent me to a shed that served breakfast out of doors; I was given coffee and eau-de-vie, raw ham, bread, and the soft dark burning goat's cheese of the Niolo; not to me the best of the Corsican cheeses but one much prized by the Corsicans. Afterwards I wandered into the livestock market, where horses, donkeys and mules were standing tethered to the trees, with a few very small bulls, tied by their horns. The horses, too, were small, but fine limbed, with shining bay and chestnut coats, last specimens of the highly valued, incredibly resistant Corsican breed that must have Arab blood. The dealers were villainous-looking men, like horse-copers anywhere, rakishly dressed in check shirts, cloth caps and mufflers; some were still asleep on bales of hay.

234

The sun, now, was slanting through the branches; when I returned to the main fairground I found it full of people and the stalls displaying their wares. The objects for sale were unfrivolous, the sort of things shepherds need: horse and donkey shoes, bells for animals, aluminium milk buckets and bales and bales of the near-black corduroy that nearly all the men were wearing. It was a dark crowd, elderly and preoccupied. Old men and women moved silently from stall to stall, staring, fingering, seldom buying, while the stallholders, similar black-kerchiefed old women, old men in corduroys, waited, seated on kitchen chairs, without a word of welcome or encouragement.

But there were young men, too, at the fair, and they were already enjoying themselves in their own hard way. I found them packed together at the roulette tables set up in scarlet tents and blazing with electric light laid on from the village. Their ruddy, long-nosed faces were taut with a ravenous excitement as they pressed round the whirling wheels. They were shepherds who had walked or ridden two to four hours from the *bergeries* for this, their supreme pleasure. Most, I noticed, were taller than the average Corsican, and some had fair or reddish hair. Though not exactly handsome they had the well-balanced bodies of people who live actively out of doors, and they wore their black hats, their corduroys and checked shirts and mufflers with a jaunty rustic elegance. They would gamble day and night till the end of the fair, one of the stallholders told me; and not only at roulette: the house-holders of Casamaccioli organised illegal baccarat in their homes and often cleared the equivalent of £1000 in a night.

The Niolins are not poor. While the Corsican landowning peasants have been sinking into depressed circumstances during the past fifty years, failing to sell their surpluses, going out of business, going abroad, the shepherds have flourished as never before. Sheep-breeders can now sell their entire winter milk production to the Roquefort Company at an assured price; and if this hardly makes them rich by other than Corsican standards at least they have what is rare among the peasants: reliable cash incomes.[5] Paradoxically, the Corsicans have been encouraged in their most archaic vocation and one of the most backward areas of the island has become prosperous. Yet the influx of ready money has done little to change it. There is no obvious way of improving *bergeries* isolated in the rugged mountains half a day's walk from the nearest road. Shepherds continue to spend the summers there in almost pre-historic conditions while their new cars wait for them at the end of the mule tracks. A few rent houses near the coasts where their families can join them in winter; others still spend winter, as summer, in bachelor quarters of a hardly believable primitiveness.[6] These people bear the stamp of an austerity that was once the condition of survival. Women still wear the traditional black in the Niolo villages (though they may copy the fashion magazines when they go to the coasts); gambling is still the men's one amusement; the women, apparently, have none.

Though few of the gamblers left the tables to join in the religious ceremony the congregation was far too large for the church. Mass was celebrated at an improvised altar under an elm tree, beside the venerated statue of the Niolo, *Santa Maria della Stella*, the Virgin of the Star. Crude repainting and a smothering of tinselly jewels have degraded the little baroque figures of Virgin and child, though they have kept their original crowns, daring, delicate constructions of gilded metal with glittering star points. The statue is said to have come from the monastery of Selva, an ancient Franciscan foundation in the desolate valley of the Fango, an immemorial winter grazing ground for the goatherds of the Niolo. But the traditional story is confused; perhaps one has to do with yet another legend of a Virgin, heiress of star-goddess Astarte, miraculously issued from the sea.

After Mass she was carried into the fairground, followed by the congregation chanting the *Dio vi Salvi Regina* in a chorus of strong voices. The black hats came off at the roulette tables as the *Santa* went by; the players lifted their heads for a moment from the wheels; the Virgin was carried into an open space under the trees. There the people fell into double file behind the statue for the *granitola*, a traditional labyrinthine procession that must surely be of distant, pre-Christian origin. With measured, solemn steps they wound round and round until they made a tight dark knot at the foot of the gorgeous figures, then mysteriously unwound, were blessed and dispersed, and the joyless fair continued.[7]

The Leblancs and their companions spent a hard day looking for singers in the thick crowd, which was increased, hour by hour, by truckloads of visitors arriving from beyond the Niolo. Recording began only towards sundown, after the priest had lent a hand in finding performers. The apparatus was set up in the school, a single room furnished with an antiquated stove and massive tables inscribed with the initials of generations of pupils; remarkably bright pupils, so the priest assured me; many heads of civil service departments had started their climb in the social scale walking to such rudimentary schools through the Niolo snow.

The priest had found two elderly men who were prepared to improvise in *chiama e rispondi*; one a Niolo shepherd, the other from the Castagniccia. Their dialogue, ejected in the long, broken, sixteen-syllable lines of Corsican tradition, seemed to me particularly aggressive, the gestures unusually emphatic; they were becoming abusive, the priest explained. At the height of the argument the man from Orezza took a goat's bell from the pocket of his corduroy jacket, jangled it in his opponent's face and thrust it into his hand. 'Now we can weigh [judge] you as an animal,' he chanted. The retort was unhesitating: 'The man who can weigh me does not exist and will never be born because only God weighs men.' No reply was possible; the priest pronounced the Niolo shepherd the winner.

He then introduced a very old woman; her long black dress hung loosely over her bony, upright figure; her hair was scraped into a knot above her paper-white brow. She was to sing a *voceru* she had once improvised on the death of a favourite niece. In a frail thin voice with piercing tones, which she must have used to terrible effect in wailing lamentations at the time of the
236

death, she sang some verses in shortlined rhyming sextets. The melody was pitched very high – it made me think of ice – and composed of few notes, a statement of anguish so naked as to seem impersonal. I had the feeling, which I have experienced since when listening to *voceratrici*, of hearing something unconnected with the singer. It was as though these words, this music, were always drifting on the air, a cry from afflicted humanity, but inaudible to common beings, and the singer, possessed of a finer receptivity, had the grave privilege of apprehending and transmitting them. She rose serenely when her song was ended, ignoring compliments, moved round the room with a regal step (she filled it) to shake hands with her audience. 'May I wish you good health,' said the head of the mission, at a loss how to thank her. 'Wish me rather long life!' she said in a downright manner, and strode out of the room.

This was the first *voceratrice* I heard, and the last for several years; though some of the mourning songs are reproduced by folklore groups in the towns, authentic, improvising, practising *voceratrici* are becoming extremely rare. I was engaged in a very different kind of quest when I eventually met one: I was travelling by bus to a seaside village, in the blinding rain of a winter evening, to interview for a British daily paper some men who had been sent there in temporary forced residence as being potentially dangerous to Khrushchev during his state visit to de Gaulle. At one of the bus stops, a passenger, an elderly woman, caught her finger in the door; while the wound was being dressed in a café as well as might be I was struck by her serene aloofness to blood and pain.

I spoke to her; she told me her life story while we travelled on through the storm. She came from a small village, she told me; she had married very young on the understanding that her husband would take her to live in mainland France; she had been a modern woman of her period. She had spent forty years in Paris; her husband had been employed in the Préfecture de la Seine; she herself had worked in the Ministry of War. Now, widowed, she had retired to her village; but she had an occupation: she improvised *voceri*. 'I speak for the dead,' she explained.

Even though I was impressed by a certain authority in her speech and bearing, a calm consciousness of exceptional status, I could hardly believe her. How could this urbanised woman who had spent her life in a government office make a convincing *voceratrice*? How could she, who had turned her back on tradition, assume the immemorial accents of the Corsican mourners? Why should she even wish to do so? Her explanation was carefully worded: 'It was death herself who unleashed the gift.' Her husband, she told me, and then her two sons, had all three died at close intervals during the first years of the Second World War; when the third, untimely, unbearable death took place, of her younger son, she had improvised a *voceru*. 'It came to me, I don't know where from,' she said. 'Yes, I must have heard *voceri* when I was a girl; but not since then, and of course I'd never even dreamed of improvising one myself. I don't know how it happened; I heard myself singing for my son.' From this moment she recognised her vocation. After the war she had returned to her village, and since then she had regularly 'spoken for the dead' of the neighbourhood; only a fortnight before, she told me, she had performed a *voceru* on the death of an eighty-four-year-old man. 'The priest disapproves,' she added, 'he says it's a pagan custom. But I don't pay much attention; it gives great comfort to the relatives.'

The personality of this strange woman lingered in my mind through the night that followed, as I listened to the reminiscences of the Russian, Polish and Central European victims, misfits, adventurers and counterrevolutionaries who crowded the little hotel. Their tales – of prison, torture, escape, exile, destitution, the massacre of family and partisans – were more eventful than hers, and also less shapely and meaningful. Or rather they had been unable to perceive any shape or meaning in their misfortunes; each ghastly incident stuck out of their memories with an excoriating edge, like the iron hook that served as forearm for a mutilated young Russian who used it to waylay reluctant listeners by digging it into their clothes. Their lives, I thought, would not end like hers, in quiet, close converse with death, but in frustrated resentment, drink or suicide.

Later I visited this woman in her home. All one sultry afternoon, behind closed shutters, she sang to me: her *voceri* for the deaths of friends and neighbours, and even that first, revelatory improvisation when her grief for the loss of her son had wrenched away the mask of urban behaviour and left her, a Corsican country woman, stricken but at one with her kind. The searing, repetitive music came from the Corsican past: each *voceratrice*, she explained to me, 'found' a certain air which she used for every performance, with little variation. Her verses were cast in the rhyming sextets habitual to the *voceri*; the images, forthright and artless, vibrated with the immediacy of pain. 'That miscreant, death/Is never satisfied/She roams round the houses/And enters without knocking/She blocks her ears/And leaves us to cry aloud.'

It had been after all quite a good day for the mission, better than its members expected; yet they had not heard the full variety of songs current in the Niolo. Always it has been the home of Corsican singing and improvising. These ancient arts were what made life endurable; they were the one entertainment in Spartan homes and remote *bergeries*, and a mould into which might be poured, and so transformed, feelings otherwise too painful to be borne. The Niolo has been a country of separations; heartbreaking, inexorable separations such as are hardly known in the modern world. The young shepherd set off for the coast in the autumn, leaving his fiancée or bride; the young woman bore his child in his absence; the child died without setting eyes on its father (the infantile mortality rate in the Niolo has always been high); the girl sickened; the young man hastened back to her too early in the year, was caught in a blizzard, died or almost died of exhaustion and exposure, struggled home to his village just in time to hear the funeral bell tolling for the death of his loved one: such tragic situations are the inspiration of the Niolo songs.

I had to wait till the last night of the fair to hear one of these laments, and it branded my memory. The mission had left; during the past two days I had

238

haunted the fairground alone, walking there and back through the fields from the hotel at Calacuccia. I discovered short cuts by mule tracks sunk like trenches between the little stone walls, or across the turf under the chestnut trees; I made detours to follow the Golo, here splashing through rocks like a Scottish burn. The going was good for the air was effervescent with the first stirrings of autumn; I walked without effort or thought; at times I felt slightly lightheaded. I was suffering, of course, from a lack of sleep during the past weeks, and also from the shock of the sudden transfer from Calvi, hothouse of human intimacies, to the severity and solitude of the Niolo (after the mission left I knew no one). But the Niolo is always likely to induce a sense of alienation, for it is unrelated to the remembered world. All Corsica has a quality of remoteness; it has often been called the nearest of distant countries. Yet the sight of the dark blue Mediterranean curling round headlands, or glimpsed in dazzling triangles at the mouths of valleys from deep in the interior, is enough to remind one that the island lies within the antique sphere of Odysseus and the Roman legions. Only the Niolo is completely barred from the sea, the civilising sea, familiar to eye and mind and imagination; this high blue shining plateau circled by towered ranges evokes no associations. except, perhaps, travellers' tales of Tibet.

The fair had become livelier each time I reached it. Carloads of young people kept arriving from outer Corsica, and caravans of shepherds from the mountains on their jingling donkeys and mules, and they were all less interested in buying pastoral equipment than in gambling, and drinking in the improvised cafés. Even the old men who had gone about their business so seriously on the opening day were now hovering at the roulette tables, or smoking their pipes with a glass of *pastis*, clutching some warily chosen object – a sheep's bell – an enamel coffee pot – and spending or gambling away far more money than they could ever have wasted in less careful shopping. The same people I had watched checking prices from stall to stall were now losing piles of notes at the roulette tables and standing rounds to fifteen and twenty acquaintances.

I had decided, late in the afternoon, to go back to the hotel, when I was drawn to a plank café by a sound of strange singing. I found a trio of youngish, husky men standing together by the bar, and their song held the noisy drinkers spellbound. The sound was like none I had ever heard before; yet I recognised it as one I had always longed to hear. The three strong voices – tenor, baritone and bass – rose and fell in a sequence of deliberate discords; this rich harsh clashing music was more poignant, far, than any of the wailing solos I had heard, even the *voceru*, so remote and rending that it seemed to issue from the birthpangs of the world.

What was the subject of the song? Probably some tragic separation; for such is the recurrent theme of this mode of part singing, known as the *paghiella*. But to me, that evening in the fairground café, unable to grasp the words, it seemed rather a primitive, warlike incantation, like the *barritus* of the ancient Germans described by Tacitus, a chanting that served to kindle their courage and help them to forecast the issue of the coming battle. And

239

perhaps, originally, the *paghiella* had some such function, for it is of an immemorial antiquity, and the same airs, used by generations of poet-singers, no longer have an organic relation to the words.[8] The cries of loneliness and thwarted love, however moving, seem insufficient for this music, which by its violence and mystery exceeds the range of even the more extreme personal emotions. I was in a way fortunate, when I first heard the *paghiella*, in that the words were incomprehensible to me, so that I was free to imagine the subject as what it seemed to be, and may once have been: an invocation to the hidden, demonic forces in the universe and in man.

The three singers were standing close together, side by side, in the traditional posture for the *paghiella*, each with his elbow resting on his neighbour's shoulder. They were singing in a state of self-absorbed euphoria; their voices, drowned at the end of each stanza by the applause of the drinkers, took up the theme again and again, gathered force, collided, faded, swelled. Their bodies, slightly swaying, were pressing ever closer together; they had become one instrument, a single three-headed monster. The song was interminable; perhaps – as often happens in *paghiella* singing – they were running one song into another. Corsicans will sing in this way for hours on end, all night sometimes, as though hypnotised by their own voices. They never, I think, feel so united in their apartness, their insularity, as when performing this indigenous music inherited from their unremembered past. Fathers and sons and brothers and cousins stand or crouch in close formation, body to body, ear to ear, linked in the communion of singing with each other, with their race and with the hosts of their ancestors.

The villages remained full of people after the fair ended. This is the holiday period in the Niolo when the ewes, no longer in milk, are left to wander alone in the high pastures, while their owners join their neglected wives and children, sleep on sprung beds instead of stone or wooden platforms, loose their mules in the meadows and drive from café to café in their cars. It is a brief respite; for in a few weeks' time they must return to the highlands, collect their flocks and set off for the coasts, two to three days' journey on foot or by mule.

Even in a country so little modernised as Corsica the transhumance seems an anachronism. Two or three men guide a herd, walking beside the animals with long, swinging, dogged strides, heading them off traffic with the help of a mixed lot of alert, highly intelligent hairy mongrels. The mules follow, laden with blankets and milk pails and cauldrons that mingle their clatter with the jangling of the bells. Often cattle are taken along with the sheep and goats; during the first weeks of October the roads are covered with slow-moving livestock. The halts on each route are fixed by custom; as late as the 1930s the shepherds slept by the wayside on the ground, and though today it is more usual to spend the nights at inns or the houses of friends, very few have thought of transporting their flocks in trucks. The goatherds still follow a roadless route to the Fango over the shoulder of the holed mountain, Monte Tafonato, by difficult paths known only to a few mountaineers besides them-

240

selves; the journey is broken at an accepted stopping-place where they gather to pass the night round an enormous fire; its flames, visible from far off in the valley, serve to herald their arrival.

These men live as their remote ancestors did, in the time of Diodorus, and long before: the traditional routes of the transhumance are dotted from over 6000 feet to sea level with the rock shelters and tools and weapons used by the Neolithic Corsicans.[9] The transhumance is a fact of nature; no one invented it: the animals, left to themselves, now as always, will move spontaneously uphill *en masse* in early summer in search of fresh grass and back towards the coasts with the first autumn chill. Each herd is led by a female animal that will guide it successfully over ranges, down escarpments, through forests, across rivers in flood; one may imagine that the first Corsican stockbreeders simply followed their half-wild herds.

Stockbreeders also, by necessity, cultivated cereals, each family producing just enough for its essential needs, in accordance with the subsistence economy that prevailed over most of Corsica until the First World War. By then the shepherds of the Niolo had evolved an elaborate and painstaking system, designed for making full use of the land they occupied at different altitudes. In winter they grew wheat near the coasts which they harvested before the summer transhumance; they also sowed barley and rye in the Niolo in early autumn, before leaving, not only on the plateau near the villages, but in the high mountains: I have seen abandoned threshing floors at over 5000 feet in rock-strewn areas that one would hardly think could yield anything useful to man. These crops, maturing late, were reaped when the shepherds returned, and the land ploughed and sown again with the first autumn rains. Meanwhile the women and old men were fully occupied on the plateau, growing flax and vegetables, spinning and weaving, and breeding chickens and pigs. There were chestnuts, too, to be gathered and dried in autumn and winter; everyone, men and women, old and young, was kept continuously at work in a labour chain reaching from snowline to sea.

'We all had enough to eat, but the work was unending,' an elderly man told me, recalling his youth. 'One sowed and reaped three and four crops in the year. If the first rains came early there was sometimes not a single day's interval between harvesting one piece of land and ploughing another.' The Niolins might be models of industry, but they never got over the Corsicans' innate aversion to tilling the soil. Thanks to the Roquefort Company, and the ready money circulating since the First World War, the shepherds, over the last fifty years, have been able to sell their milk and cheeses, buy food and clothes. Today they have practically discarded agriculture, their unloved secondary occupation, and thankfully reverted to the primitive pastoral life of their early ancestors.

Can it last, one wonders, this prehistoric method of production for a twentieth-century industry? Civilisation is closing down on the shepherds. The tourist resorts and the new agricultural developments on the coasts are rapidly eating into the areas they once occupied. True to nomadic tradition the shepherds have always resisted the landowning system; many possess only small strips and patches near their villages. For grazing they have always relied on the vast common lands in the high mountains, and on the desolate coasts, and have paid rent for pasture only under compulsion. And now winter grazing space is being drastically reduced, and rents are rising for what remains, on the east coast, and in the Balagne where the fields, every year, are critically overcrowded.

And at the same time the free mountain pastures are failing; the shepherds' immemorial Alpine kingdom is pitifully denuded, degraded. To make matters worse the shepherds' sons are rebelling against a life deficient – one cannot say in modern but – in mediaeval pleasures and conveniences. A major complaint is that girls are unwilling to marry these land navigators and spend months on end waiting for their short visits. In the face of this crisis the agricultural authorities are advising the shepherds to buy land at low altitudes, fence it, grow forage with irrigation; in short change their way of life completely. But so far few have responded, in spite of the financial help offered. Their primordial conviction that all the land in Corsica belongs to all Corsicans, their contempt for the earthbound, sedentary farmer, are as ingrained as the dogma of a creed.

I never got above the plateau during my first visit to the Niolo; the shepherds had left their *bergeries*; the weather – though radiant – was declared unreliable; it was too late in the year. I came to know the high mountains much later, and with difficulty: guides are hard to come by and to wander uphill alone is a folly that has killed quite a number of foreigners. The tracks are intermittent, paved only on risky stretches where mules might otherwise slip and crash into ravines; it is easy enough to do the same, or lose one's way in rock-deserts where no one will pass by in days. For above and out of sight of the villages one is unlikely to meet a single being: only rocks and torrents and pines, and cliffs and peaks that grow in stature as one mounts towards them. And even more awe-inspiring are the voids below and between: a bird is a dust-mote in the gulfs that cleave range from range; the pebbles one dislodges with one's feet rattle down the vertiginous abysses in an interminable echoing decrescendo.

Many people have died here, stifled and frozen in snow drifts, knocked senseless by falls. Others have been shot down by private enemies: until well into the interwar years the Niolo shepherds, constantly engaged in vendettas, hunted their human prey with the tenacity of Red Indians.[10] Wooden or iron crosses mark the spots where these people fell; yet they do not bring death to mind, but rather the comforting assurance that others have been there before one. In these areas one rates the human race high. A length of paved track, an abandoned threshing floor, even stepping-stones laid across a brook are heartwarming; and how much more so that black forked insect on the skyline which one recognises as man! One never asks oneself whether he has murdered anyone or is likely to do so, whether he is a good father and husband and pays his debts: he is made in one's own shape; he has the same needs for food and drink and shelter; he belongs to the same species.

242

It is the hereditary empire of the shepherds, this upper, concealed, un-violated Corsica, which in fact amounts to about a quarter of the total area of the island. Not all of it is hostile to human survival. After the first hideous climb above the villages up some two thousand nearly vertical feet, one comes to rolling tablelands, high valleys and level ridges lying under the rock peaks, a secret world on the cornice of the island with its own way of life, its own culture, thinly spread and several thousand years distant in time.

Here the shepherds have ruled undisturbed since the prehistoric era, true lords of all they survey. Army, police and functionaries, builders of roads and villages, have never followed them with the cramping paraphernalia of civilisation; at the altitude of Briançon, French town of some seven thousand inhabitants, one finds, in Corsica, only a few scattered cabins. There are *bergeries* grouped within hailing distance of each other, and isolated cabins separated by three and four walking hours from the next settlement; distances are measured, here, by a man's walking speed. Physical stamina, resourcefulness in danger are his most valued assets; violence is less often a fault than a necessity; loyalty and hospitality are his virtues: the Homeric values still prevail among these last free men of western Europe.

Eventually I reached their kingdom. First the Lac de Nino, at over 5800 feet, which appears, after a journey of four to six hours according to the route chosen, as something unreal, a lost mountaineer's mirage. I went by the long trail from Casamaccioli along the upper reaches of the Tavignano, the river a torrent pouring between overpowering rock ranges, the mule track an often-broken thread through a primal chaos of boulders. Colossal pines are the landmarks: old trees stricken by lightning, battered by snow and storm, withered by age, dying, with spectral white boughs piercing their greenness, or dead, standing bleached corpses, monuments to all tragedy, or crucified on precipice and cataract. They must be the last, mutilated veteran relics of a former forest, destroyed by erosion and climatic changes and the merciless greed of pigs and goats which have consumed young shoots, torn up the vegetation, so that now the soil bears only cushions of spiky dwarf juniper and broom.

The epic grandeur of the scene accumulates as one follows the river upstream, cudgels and crushes the senses, until abruptly, when one nears the valley's head, the fury of the landscape fades, dissolves, as when in an orchestral symphony a climax of sound makes way for a tender theme. Green pastures then appear between boulders, where sheep are feeding; the earth bubbles with springs and rivulets; the mighty pines are superseded by beeches casting an idyllic shade. But this forest, too, is a relic; the trees are dying, their upper branches are leafless; I felt I had struggled back to the earthly paradise only to find it withered and in decay.

Yet the lake itself is joyous, large and diamond shaped, lying just above the last beeches on a plateau flat as a billiards table and as green. Hundreds of sheep and horses and cattle are grazing on the spongy grass, between countless channels and pools. The tired mules break into a trot, a canter, at the touch of the springing turf; the lake glitters and beckons like a jewel; it is full of a pinkish weed which under the blue sky gives it the tint of amethyst. The surrounding slopes, for all their granite nakedness, are unoppressive; one mistakes them for independent ranges of moderate height. Only the view to the south of the massif of Monte Rotondo, a vision of unguessed stupefying rock castles and pyramids piled one above the other, reminds one that this happy grazing ground clings to the island's roof.

It is an oasis at a junction of thoroughfares now almost forgotten: the tracks down the Tavignano leading to Corte in six to seven hours' walking, through the pines to the Col de Vergio in three or four, to the south-west, in less than a morning, to the dark, bewitched pine-circled Lac de Creno, only a couple of hours from the nearest western villages. Carlo Bonaparte and Letizia, six months pregnant with Napoleon, retreating from the victorious French army, probably rode their mules from Corte up the Tavignano and over the mountains to the west coast;[11] shepherds used this route in both directions until the interwar years, sometimes pushing on beyond Corte down the lower valley of the Tavignano to Aléria and the Roman plains.

The *bergeries* near the lake are specks in the landscape, arrangements of stones among stones distinguishable to the untrained eye only at close quarters. One or two small rectangular cabins are enclosed in a courtyard by a stone wall, a yard or so high, without an opening, to be climbed by stone steps built into its thickness. Three shepherds were encamped in the *bergerie* where my guides to the lake led me, besides no less than seven visitors, men of all ages who had ridden up to join the shepherds in their particular style of gay, abstemious, sociable living. They crowded to the walls of the courtyard as we arrived, eager to shake hands, to unload our mules; the unaffected warmth and gusto of their greeting was something that normally requires generations of aristocratic training. The evening milking had just been completed in the adjoining stone-walled pens; the oldest shepherd, who was also the cook, had made a soup of onions and tomatoes in a black cauldron; a boy was frying sardine-sized trout caught in a near-by stream. 'He went to Paris to play the caïd, but he came home quick enough; he was starving,' said one of the men. 'Yes, I got a job but I didn't get enough to eat,' said the boy.

Now was the moment for building up the fire that would soon be the only light; for these men, owners of good cars and houses, lived in the *bergerie* without so much as an electric torch or a candle. It is not quite true to say that nothing has changed in the *bergeries* since prehistoric times: there are such innovations as metal milk pails, copper cauldrons for making *brocciu*, knives and guns and invaluable matches. But the general feeling and aspect of life, I thought, must surely be that known to our Stone Age ancestors, as we squatted on rocks in the courtyard with our bowls of soup and mugs of spring water, while the dogs waited for the leftovers, and the mules and donkeys and sheep and goats wandered in the enormous spaces outside the walls and the light withdrew from the unconquered mountains.

We slept that night in lines of seven in the two cabins, each furnished with a

244

wooden platform raised a hand's width from the ground. The platform filled the whole cabin except for a space at our feet a few inches wide where the fire was burning; the smoke crept out through chinks in the unmortared wall and through the open door. Belongings were lodged on a stone shelf under the pitched roof; clothes were hung on sticks protruding from crevices between the stones. 'We live like the men of antiquity,' one of the shepherds explained, laughing, but proudly.

Though I was tired after the day's riding on the wood and metal side-saddle (such as the shepherds use), I lay awake as long as I could for the deep satisfaction of seeing the fire flicker against the rough-surfaced granite, the huge deformed shadows of the men when they rose to feed it, the white ghost shapes of the rocks through the open door, under a small moon, and a sheet of snow on the opposite mountainside. As I dozed off I had an almost physical sensation of being drawn down and back to the roots of humanity, to my lost origins, in a dream more comforting than any I have known in sleep.

The *bergeries* are built by the shepherds with whatever comes to hand. There is enough wood near the Lac de Nino to make beams, and wooden planks for roofs, which are held down by loose stones. But on the treeless slopes of Monte Cinto, on the northern side of the Niolo, the *bergeries* are entirely stone-built, roofed with corbel vaults in the technique of the *torri*. A report by an Englishwoman who travelled there in the 1930s spurred me to visit them; the circular *bergerie* of Urcula, she writes, suggested a stronghold of 'primordial warriors'.[12]

The departure, on foot from Corscia with a friend, was delayed while we vainly asked for directions; the villagers had apparently forgotten Urcula. The summer sun was rising in a blazing red ball over the Scala di Santa Regina as we plodded up the first escarpment. A path that seemed to head in the right direction took us round an elbow of the mountain, marked by a wooden upright, a cross that had lost its arms. And here a new landscape unfolded; the one we would live with all day. The deep gorge of the Rudda cut windingly into the massif; the torrent was audible miles – it seemed – below, but invisible beneath the feathery crowns of the laricio pines. They were perhaps giants of their kind, but dwarfed by the vertical rock formations that sprang from the riverbed almost to the full height of the range, cones of violet granite streaming into the early light like the images of a waking dream. They stayed with us, a hardly changing panorama, as we crept along a path halfway up the opposite escarpment, a path sometimes no wider than a footprint, but continuously paved. Stepped like a ladder up and down the ravines, bordered with upstanding stones above chasms, it twisted into the heart of the mountains, mile after empty mile, no less a symbol of human creativity, I thought, than the Parthenon.

We followed it until the floor of the valley rose to meet us; a *bergerie* no larger-seeming than a matchbox stood by the stream. It was a single, corbel-vaulted cabin, and empty, planted on the bare grey granite. But there was shade under a bridge, a rudimentary bridge consisting of a corbelled half-vault joined to an overhanging rock. We plunged to our necks in the icy water, gulping it like desert survivors.

Higher up the mountain, but still far below the stripped white summits, we found two similar, deserted *bergeries*; then a man, the first we had seen. He was trying to fill a bucket from a nearly exhausted spring. He lived alone in his cabin, where we rested awhile. It was corbel-vaulted, like the others, but so low that one entered crawling and could only sit up inside; a home, I thought, very like a grave. I asked if I could photograph it. 'As you will,' said the shepherd, 'but give me a moment if you want me in the picture.' He burrowed into the cabin, reappeared with a shining new metal suitcase, took his pose holding it well in evidence in front of his home. It was the symbol of his deliverance. He was leaving, he said, in a week's time, and for ever; no one could stay in a *bergerie* alone, and the springs were running dry.

The air grew ever lighter as we toiled on up the valley, and more sharply scented with the small blue-flowered mint that smelt also of pepper, the main vegetation apart from the dwarf alders by the stream. The sun was nearly overhead when we caught sight of Urcula on a mountain crest; the fortress of primordial warriors, as it in fact seemed to be. A man was lying atop a high wall that entirely enclosed it, reclining on his side in the pose of the figures on the Etruscan tombs. He remained quite motionless as we dragged ourselves towards him, until our feet were actually looking for the stones that made a staircase jutting from the ten-foot high fortress wall. He reached out a large hand, heaved me over the parapet: 'Go lie in the cool,' he said, pointing to the cabin.

The cabin was not a free-standing hut; one of its walls joined that which enclosed the courtyard. The courtyard was large and shaped curiously: it ended, opposite the cabin, in three semicircular apses of unequal size, divided by high walls. Low stone benches and hearths were built against the inner walls of the apses, and square niches were made in their depth at various heights. The cabin itself was oblong, and rounded at one end like the old Corsican bread ovens. The roof was a very perfect and accomplished corbelled dome. The whole elaborate and ingenious complex of stone structures called to mind the Neolithic community of Skara Brae.

The archaic appearance of the Corsican *bergeries* can be extremely misleading. One very ancient-looking corbel-vaulted cabin I visited in another region was built, so its owner remembers, in 1914. It would be hazardous to suggest any date, or even period, for Urcula. Certainly the walls are higher than would seem necessary for keeping out livestock, and suggest that more dangerous intruders had to be reckoned with. Bears, that roamed the mountains till the sixteenth century? Hostile neighbours? The Moors? The tri-part courtyard obviously provides convenient working spaces for preparing cheese and *brocciu*, and might correspond with the needs of three shepherds, sharing the same cabin but, as often happens, owning separate flocks. Yet the curved walls and the apses (unique, so far as I know, in the *bergeries*) have a primitive style that evokes the *torri*. Every feature of Urcula is explicable; but the place

246

as a whole, remains mysterious. Its single, silent occupant was unable to enlighten us; in fact at first he was so withdrawn that I could fancy him as the ghost of its first owner.

'Shall I make the coffee?' he said, after he had watched me sketching and photographing his weird home without apparent reaction. Coffee is the shepherds' ritual offering of hospitality, and also their one luxury, their indispensable standby, as tea is to the English worker. They smoke little, drink wine seldom, eat sparingly: milk and cheese are, of course, unrationed; but bread is limited; fresh meat and fruit are luxuries. No one complains; austerity is a small price to pay for the shepherds' heritage: the majestic spaces they rule and wander over, their freedom of men in the youth of the world. Only solitude makes the *bergeries* intolerable; our host at Urcula, unbending with the mug of black coffee drunk sitting on the stone platform bed, confided that since his two companions had gone out of business he could hardly face spending another summer at Urcula, even though the habit of the mountains would be hard to break, for himself and for his goats.

As I later learned, he owns a comfortable house in a village, and a herd of cattle. But though well-off, and handsome enough for his fifty-odd years, no one will marry him. Sooner or later he will sell his flock, like many others in the Niolo who have no sons to succeed them, or sons who are bent on becoming civil servants. This may be a cruel necessity for men who are attached to their flocks as to a part of their being. 'We found the old man crying under a chestnut tree after his goats were taken away,' a shepherd told me, recalling one of these occasions.

But even if brides and sons were less averse to the pastoral life it could hardly continue in its present form much longer. The human defection has synchronised with a deterioration of nature. Sheep and goats are driven immense distances to areas almost without grass, without soil. On the arid slopes of the Cinto I found none of the zest for living of the *bergeries* near the Lac de Nino; only ruined and empty cabins, discouraged, solitary shepherds, failing springs. And even the miraculous pastures round the lake are overcrowded, and the green parklands at the head of the Tavignano are shrinking under the dying beeches. The mountains have been ruined by millennia of overgrazing; too many animals have fed there, too long; too many trees have been cut, or have burned; there is too little vegetation to retain the water; erosion has set in. The immemorial wasteful use of the land has brought the inevitable penalties; the island is withering at its core.

At the same time, the coasts are being civilised, cultivated, subtracted from the shepherds' domain; conditions conspire to oblige them to change their ways. Yet most would rather change their occupation. Rather than transform the free challenging nomad's life into tame sedentary stock-breeding, they will throw up their vocation, cut loose from their origins and push themselves into modern urban society. The shepherd cries under the chestnut tree and then contentedly ends his days with his family running a grocery store in a town.

Whatever the shepherds decide for their future the economy of the Niolo is on the way out, with its poetry and its privations.[13] The parting laments will soon become meaningless, the *bergeries* empty; at the time of writing I am endeavouring to have Urcula preserved as a historic monument. It is the same story everywhere: the civilisation born in the Neolithic era has run its course; the earth can no longer stand it, nor can women or men.

15 LIBERATION: TRADITION AND THE ENLIGHTENMENT

Military Corte – struggle for freedom – Paoli's constitution –
Rousseau's ideal – Boswell's visit – death of a nation

THE journey to Corte began, like so many of the past weeks, just before dawn. I had come to value those early starts; that silent dew-scented hour preceding sunrise when I gulped down coffee in sight of huge ghostly landscapes and pale seas had become a precious private luxury. The hour was always kindled with excitement, as I tried to conjure the scenes that lay ahead; scenes – so I had learned by experience – that invariably exceeded my expectations. This departure from the Niolo had also the added painful poignancy of pleasures not to be repeated; for Corte was my last stopping-place before Ajaccio and my remaining days in the island were down to three. My feelings went beyond regret for leaving. The summer's journey had effectively severed me from my life, or rather from what I already thought of as my past life. In Corsica I had seen a basic expression of the human predicament and the roots of history laid bare; and as I packed in the sleeping hotel of Calacuccia – the worn-out clothes of my past life, the note books and sketches that were all I had to show for the new – I was dismayed that the vision was about to close before I had fully grasped it.

The sky glowed red above the Scala di Santa Regina when I joined the little group waiting for the bus by the road. Then golden streaks appeared simultaneously on the topmost eastern and western peaks. The light slid down the western slopes swiftly, giving a coral glow to the rocks; but it remained a gleaming streak on the eastern heights until, when the bus was almost loaded, the sun at last rose over the rim of the ranges and flung its beams across the plateau to meet the blaze on the western side. Its brilliance was pouring down from the sky as we drove away, flooding the single street of Calacuccia; but we had almost reached the Scala before it flowed into the deeper hollows of the land.

Entering the gorge was a return to the pre-dawn twilight; the sun touched only the upper strata of its walls; the mineral tints of the raddled rocks were dull in the stale night air. Daytime came much later, when the defile fanned out into parklands and maquis, all bathed in a luminous mist that promised extreme heat. At Francardo we turned south for Corte into a glaring bare upland valley. Forests have been cut and burned in this district that formerly

249

specialised in the cultivation of corn. One can still see the abandoned terraces carved from top to bottom of the ranges, like grass steps in an English garden, but scaled to the stride of giants. There, until a generation ago, wheat was cultivated by methods little improved since Neolithic times. Many of the ledges were too narrow to allow a team of plough oxen to turn, so that the soil had to be broken by hand. On the way to Corte I saw only two small, high-perched villages; whoever worked these lands began and ended the day with a cross-mountain excursion that would intimidate most people who do such things for pleasure.

Corte stands in a well or hollow of this country, close against the bastions of the Niolo at a point where the Tavignano and the Restonica, issuing from rugged gorges, join. Since we were approaching the town from higher ground one saw, at first, only its topmost edge, the walled citadel on a rock pinnacle that springs sheer from the base of the well. The fortress was a little white silhouette apparently suspended, like a picture on a wall, against the sombre mountains behind.

The town itself came into sight as we dipped downhill. The fortified pinnacle, with a spawn of dark old houses clamped to its lower slopes, now looked like the uptilted hull of a sinking liner. But this amazing rock formation, ejected some 360 feet high from an almost level plain, was dwarfed by the majestic massif in the immediate background. On either side of it the river valleys that climb back to the high lakes appeared receding through a succession of lateral ranges, all serrated by the spearhead shapes of rocks and pines.

Corte is an extraordinary place, and not least because it is ugly, viewed as a whole. One feels that this incomparably romantic site deserved better, that a great opportunity in city planning has been thrown away. The fortress makes an unsatisfactory acropolis, for the ancient defence walls enclose nothing more than a group of homely little pitched-roofed houses instead of the mighty mediaeval towers the eye demands. They must have been run up after the French conquest, when the original castle built by Vincentello d'Istria was reconstructed. Since when Corte has remained a garrison town, subject to periodical large-scale, disastrous building, so that huge yellow-stuccoed barracks now blight its lower zone alongside huge yellow-stuccoed blocks of flats.

Yet as a symbol Corte has power. Only Corsica, one feels, could have produced it; Corte epitomises essential characteristics of the people: intransigence, valour, a flair for the grand gesture that is so often crippled – as here – by disdain for the graces of living. The unique strategic position of the fortress gave it importance all through the island's history. It was a natural centre for the nation, for it controls the passage from north to south, from the Diqua to the *Dila dai Monti*, and is linked by river valleys and mountain passes with the east and west. The eighteenth-century rebels recognised its appropriateness as a rallying point and increasingly held the national assemblies there; Paoli made it the official capital. The site was geographically ideal; yet one must admire his courage in planting a university at Corte rather than in one

250

The citadel of Corte, focus of the Corsican struggle for independence.
(*Louis Bianchetti*)

Statue of Pasquale Paoli in Corte, capital of his independent government. (*Louis Bianchetti*)

of the more civilised but peripheral communities, such as Corbara. Corte is the Corsican Ankara, indigenous and dour. Paoli's experiment, at any rate, was too brief to change the essentially military character of the place. Corte's outstanding men have been soldiers: Gian'Pietro Gaffori, who came to the fore of the rebel movement just before Paoli; Jean-Thomas Arrighi de Casanova, a kinsman of Napoleon who created him Duke of Padua in recognition of his bravery on many battlefields.

The bus dropped me close to the square named after him, dominated by his outsize figure in bronze. There I found a hotel with an astringent, varnished interior where I was given trout for lunch, fished in those waters of the Restonica that Sir Gilbert Elliot likened to 'diamonds in solution'. The weather warnings I had heard in the Niolo were taking shape before the meal was done. When I wandered into the town I saw black clouds swelling over the mountains, like boils that must soon be lanced by the peaks. The air was spitefully scorching, yet shot through from time to time by steely warning draughts discharged from the apocalyptic gatherings above.

Black against black, the roofs of the old houses rose one behind another against the darkening mountains and sky, all tiled in the local slate that also makes their walls and the paving-stones of the stepped streets. The old town of Corte, like the newer quarters, is built with more regard for status than appearances. The arcaded galleries, arches, pilasters and broken pediments of some of the larger houses suggest no more than that their owners felt some such display was due to their personal distinction. They must have been strangers to the idea of elegance or even comfort, just as their equivalents today, retired army men with high records in the world and colonial wars, are content with flats in the brash yellow blocks hardly distinguishable from the neighbouring barracks, or those – most likely – in which they spent the greater part of their lives.

In a little square at the end of the main street a lugubrious bronze statue of Paoli stares at forbidding housefronts. Further up in the town I found a similar sort of statue of Gaffori, standing outside his own large plain house and pointing an accusing hand at the parish church. Bas-reliefs on the pedestal recall that his wife Faustina, besieged by Genoese troops in her husband's absence, her retainers muttering of surrender, brandished a lighted torch over a barrel of gunpowder and threatened to blow up the house with the lot of them unless they continued resistance. Doubly menaced, they held out until Gaffori arrived to deliver them at the eleventh hour. This is an extreme example of the desperate happenings recurrent at Corte. The fortress was fiercely fought for in nearly all the Corsican wars and changed hands several times in the course of the eighteenth-century rebellion prior to the ascendancy of Paoli.

The rebellion had been going on for over a quarter of a century when Paoli was elected head of state in 1755.[1] Its record had been one of inconclusive fighting, expedients, setbacks and confusion, but redeemed by the Corsicans' unbreakable underlying resolution to free themselves from Genoese colonial rule. It had broken out, accidentally and dangerously as a maquis

251

fire, in December 1729, when a village near Corte refused to pay taxes heart-lessly demanded by the Genoese Governor after two bad harvests in suc-cession. Troops sent to quell the riot returned to Corte empty-handed and cowed; the news spread over the island, village to village, within twenty-four hours; patriots and bandits armed, assembled, threatened Bastia; Genoese control of the interior was at an end.

Why did a full-scale rebellion erupt at this time, after the Corsicans had accepted Genoese rule during a hundred and sixty peaceful years?[2] And why was it more successful than all those that in earlier centuries had been waged with reckless bloodshed and bravery, high hopes and horrible atrocities, to their tragic conclusions? Successful enough, in spite of all errors and dis-sensions, to paralyse the Genoese government during forty years and to give the Corsicans, under Paoli, a virtual autonomy with an enlightened govern-ment that could be overthrown only by the armed might of France?

The answer seems to be that while Genoa had become an impoverished, declining power, the Corsicans, in spite and because of oppression and condi-tions that were sometimes desperate, had developed a new awareness of national aims and of the means of achieving them. This rebellion differed from all previous ones in that it was not the personal adventure of any noble or warlord, but a spontaneous uprising that mobilised almost the whole population. The people might be starving after bad harvests, divided by vendettas that caused some nine hundred deaths a year; but they had ac-quired a long experience of democratic organisation in the self-administrating rural communes and a technique of collective action. They had moreover men of education and ability to lead them; not nobles (the nobility had by then fallen into decadence), but members of a rural bourgeoisie that had evolved under Genoese rule. These were the people who, taking advantage of the Genoese encouragement of agriculture, had benefited by the colonial regime, and also, paradoxically, most resented it. Genoese trade monopolies restricted their profits; the colonial hierarchy blocked the road to advance-ment and power. Many of them knew enough of the world to realise how far such a system was exceptional. Sons of notables habitually went to the Italian universities, to study medicine, theology, law. This travelled, learned élite provided the patriot leaders; the Corsican national rebellion, like the French Revolution, was propelled by an ambitious, frustrated bourgeoisie.[3]

No conflict of interests however divided notables and peasants: the rebel-lion drew its strength from the union of classes (though not always of indi-viduals) in the face of the common enemy. The clergy, too, sided with the rebellion, long outraged because the five Corsican bishoprics were reserved for Genoese nationals. Ecclesiastics served the patriots' cause as polemists, publicists and politicians, ambassadors and guerrilla leaders; the Franciscan monasteries sheltered the innumerable rebel assemblies.

There was precedent for such gatherings. Popular assemblies on a national or regional scale had been a recurrent phenomenon in Corsican history at least ever since Sinucello della Rocca had endeavoured to establish an insular government in 1264. In every political crisis they had been summoned: by the population of the *Diqua dai Monti* which in the fourteenth century had launched the anti-seigneurial revolution; by the many Cinarchesi rebels; by Sampiero Corso, waging a hopeless war on the Genoese after the French abandoned Corsica with the Treaty of Cateau-Cambrésis. Sanctioned by patriotic tradition, the assemblies – known as *consulte* – were resumed, naturally enough, in the eighteenth-century rebellion. They took place, usually, two or three times a year; they became a symbol of national unity, the mainspring of patriotic propaganda; they shaped the policy and structure of the rebel state.

From the beginning the Corsicans knew what they wanted: nothing short of national independence with a system of government designed according to Corsican ideas. At a *consulta* at Corte in January 1735, attended by delegates from all the villages, national independence was declared and a constitution adopted. Andrea Ceccaldi, Luigi Giafferi and Giacinto Paoli (a doctor, and the father of Pasquale), all three notables from the *Diqua dai Monti* who had already been elected Generals of the rebellion, were appointed 'Primates'. They were to govern through a Junta of six members and a Diet consisting of a delegate from every village. A numerous subordinate executive was divided into specialised departments: an office of war, an office of supplies, a committee of four fathers of the commune charged with the upkeep of the roads (those terrible paved mule tracks still used by the shepherds today).

Created in the stress of revolution and war, and conceived, most likely, by the ruling Generals, this first national constitution was hardly democratic; the Primates and their Lieutenants had power to nominate some if not all the members of the Junta and the Diet; the executive officials were apparently nominated by the Junta.[4] All the same the system had features remarkably modern for the period: the separation of powers, concessions to the principle of national representation. It marked the first step in the political evolution that led the Corsicans, in 1755, to adopt a constitution more liberal than any that existed in its day.

At this same *consulta* of 1735 the newborn nation was placed under the protection of the Immaculate Conception. The solemn magnificent *Dio vi salvi Regina* became the national anthem and the image of the Virgin was portrayed on the national banners (I have seen one in Paoli's village, Morosaglia, with a touchingly awkward embroidered figure, the work, perhaps, of some patriot's wife). Soon after the *consulta* eighteen Corsican theologians met in the Castagniccia to declare Corsica free of allegiance to Genoa.

Confident in their constitution and in divine favour, the patriots went to war; at first with startling success. Saint-Florent and Algajola, the two weakest Genoese fortress towns, were captured, the rest blockaded by land. But the struggle became unequal when Genoa obtained the assistance of six battalions from the Emperor Charles VI: Algajola and Saint-Florent were recaptured; in May 1732 the rebels submitted; a settlement was guaranteed by the Emperor according to which Genoa made certain concessions to

Corsican grievances. Like subsequent settlements proposed by foreign intervention it satisfied neither of the belligerents; the rebellion broke out again after the Emperor's troops left. Meanwhile *consulta* followed *consulta*, in the monasteries of the Castagniccia, the Casinca and Corte.

The patriots were however more successful in holding *consulte* and proclaiming constitutions than in winning battles: the achievements of the national rebellion, viewed as a whole, were political rather than military. The Corsicans were poorly armed and short of footwear; supplies could only reach them by ships running the Genoese naval blockade. Democratic traditions proved a handicap in war: every military action had to be preceded by interminable discussions; the unpaid citizens' army dwindled with the harvests or according to mood. Battles, too, were lost without necessity, by the Corsicans' custom of leaving the field to carry away their dead, sometimes back to their distant homes.

When, in March 1736, a gorgeously dressed foreigner landed at Aléria in a ship freighted with money, guns, ammunition and Turkish leather boots, promising more to come, the patriots readily agreed to his request to be crowned king. This fanciful adventurer was Theodor von Neuhof, son of a Westphalian baron, who had been brought up at the court of France, had served in the Bavarian army, and learnt the craft of political intrigue from Alberoni and Ripperda, successive scheming, parvenu ministers of Spain. He had also speculated in the wake of John Law, dabbled in alchemy and done spells in debtors' prisons before the Corsican gamble occurred to him after meeting some exiled patriots in Tuscany. The expedition had been financed by Greek and Jewish merchants of Tunis whom he had somehow inspired with confidence in its success.[5]

Whether the Corsicans were really hoaxed by this professional charlatan is beside the point; after six years' indecisive struggle they were desperate; almost anyone who brought them boots and money and munitions would have been well received. Theodor was welcomed by the Generals and their followers with salvoes of gunfire and the singing of songs, conducted into the interior through festive villages, and crowned with a laurel wreath at the monastery of Alesani (in the Castagniccia) in the presence of a crowd 'drunk with joy' while all the church bells pealed.[6] Not that the Corsicans were prepared to accept an absolute monarch. Theodor was made to swear fidelity to a constitution devised for the circumstances by a certain Sebastiano Costa, a Corsican lawyer who had recently returned from Genoa to support the rebel cause. A Diet of twenty-four members was to be instituted; three of them were to be constantly in attendance on the King who could take no decision relative to war or taxation without their consent. True to their political inventiveness, the Corsicans had given themselves a constitutional monarchy. The only clause contributed by Theodor was a guarantee of liberty of conscience, designed to allow Greek and Jewish merchants to settle in the island in accordance with the undertakings he had given to his backers in Tunis.

254

The constitution, it seems, was never put into practice; at all events the merchants never arrived, nor did the promised money and supplies. Theodor's eight months'reign was spent in futile military manœuvres, much handicapped by internal dissensions. Trained in the classic methods of eighteenth-century warfare, he naturally conceived a campaign as a succession of sieges, a type of fighting alien to the Corsicans, who lacked patience and discipline but excelled in the lightning surprise attack (a technique later perfected by Napoleon). While the royal army camped ineffectively in front of the Genoese fortresses, the Corsicans deserted and betrayed their king and quarrelled between themselves; while the national mint entrusted to a notorious counterfeiter of Genoese coins remained unproductive, Theodor was running out of funds. By midsummer he had sections of the patriots against him and had to put down a rebellion within the rebellion at Corte; by September he was heading south, accompanied only by Costa and a handful of retainers. In November he thankfully escaped from the island after a harrowing trek to the east coast over the mountains from Sartène.

Yet the patriots, disorganised and divided, cheated and disabused, none the less kept the rebellion alive: muddle and endurance, according to a pattern now familiar, characterised this first decolonisation movement of modern times. By 1738 the Genoese were again in need of foreign aid. Their former ally, the Emperor, being then at war with the Turks, they turned to France. The French agreed the more readily to lend troops because they themselves had their eye on Corsica. Already, in 1735, the foreign minister, Chauvelin, had laid down the policy that France was to follow with a refined cunning until the invasion of 1768. There could be no question, he stated, of forcibly annexing the island; it was necessary to gain the sympathies of the Corsicans and lead them to beg spontaneously for the blessings of French rule. At the same time Genoa must be persuaded that French troops were in Corsica to defend her interests, unless, added Chauvelin, Genoa judged it expedient to accept a 'treaty of sale'.[7] Thirty-three years went by before the Genoese resigned themselves to this solution, during which the Corsicans struggled through many disappointments and false hopes until they had set up an operative autonomous government. But all this time their fate had been predetermined by the most powerful nation in Europe.

The aim of the French in 1738 was to disarm the rebels and restore Genoese rule. When this became apparent the rebels issued a long, hurt, manifesto ending with an appeal to the God of Battles, fell on a French detachment at Borgo, to the south of Bastia, massacred a good number of troops and sent the rest flying. The commander, the Comte de Boisseux, died soon afterwards, afflicted with dysentery and disgrace. He was replaced by a firmer man, the Marquis de Maillebois who, killing and burning, mastered the rebels within a matter of weeks.

This was a second decisive defeat for the patriots. A thousand or so went into exile. Some chose Naples, among them that staunch pair who had headed the rebellion from the start, Luigi Giafferi, and Giacinto Paoli, taking with him his fourteen-year-old son Pasquale. Others joined the Royal Corse, a regiment formed by Louis XV with a view to drawing Corsican fighting men into the service of France. With the island so pacified Maillebois was able to impose an efficient administration until he was recalled with the outbreak of the War of the Austrian Succession.

Corsica now became a prize, or prey, for powers waging a war in total contempt for the self-determination of peoples, France, Spain and the Two Sicilies, allied with Genoa, being lined up against England, Austria and Sardinia-Piedmont. England was alive to the advantages of securing at least a port or two in the island; the King of Sardinia was prepared to annex the rest. Bastia was besieged and actually captured in 1745 by British warships and a Corsican force armed by Sardinia, only to revert to Genoa after fighting between the citizens and rival factions of Corsican patriots.[8]

The Treaty of Aix-la-Chapelle put an end to British ambitions and schemes for a Corsican partition. French troops, already occupying Bastia, commanded by the skilful Marquis de Cursay, kept peace in the island during the next four years. Their departure was the signal for the rebellion to revive under Gian'Pietro Gaffori, a doctor of Corte who had come to the head of the movement since 1745. At a *consulta* in October 1752 a new national constitution was proclaimed with the assurance of a people that had been experimenting in systems of government during the past twenty years.

For the determination of the patriots to establish a valid national government had persisted in spite of the defection of Theodor, defeat by France, foreign interventions and civil strife. *Consulte* had taken place all through this confused period; provisional governments had been formed and reformed in close succession. The ruling power in the nation was however not so much these precarious governments, lacking in representative institutions, as the *consulte* that created them and elected their members. These huge popular gatherings had increasingly assumed the functions of a national parliament. They appointed Generals – usually several at a time – as leaders of the rebellion, designated magistrates, negotiated Corsica's relations with foreign states, enemy and allied, raised taxes and enacted legislation. Their membership, in theory dependent on the invitations issued by the war leaders who summoned them, had in fact become fixed by custom: podestas and fathers of the commune attended as though by right, together with varying numbers of outstanding patriots; a deputy was elected by each parish. The *consulte* were really representative of the nation, if in an irregular, rough and ready way; the majority of their members – who might number a thousand or more – had been elected by universal suffrage either to administer or represent the communities to which they belonged.

The constitution of 1752, like those that preceded it, was based on the rule of military commanders and magistrates.[9] No Diet was provided for; the *consulte* had come to fulfil the role of a national assembly. Gaffori was head of state with wide but apparently undefined powers. It seems he abused them. At all events the Genoese had no difficulty in finding personal enemies to

256

assassinate him the following year. A Regency of four was promptly appointed, one of whom was Clemente Paoli, Pasquale's elder brother. A natural soldier and a dedicated patriot, this weird sombre man with leanings to the monastic life was however not the leader the nation was then in search of. In 1754 Pasquale was invited to return to Corsica to save the rebellion.

He was then a twenty-nine-year-old sub-lieutenant in a Neapolitan regiment stationed in Elba. He had apparently received a superior education in Naples, where he may have studied under the distinguished physiocrat Antonio Genovesi. The books he asked his father to send him before leaving for Corsica were however classics of the French Enlightenment: Montesquieu's *Grandeur des Romains* and *Esprit des Lois*, together with Rollin's ancient history and a manual on engineering. To the old man's gloomy forebodings he replied: 'I regard my departure as an invitation to a feast day.'[10] Paoli's courage was equal to his opportunities.

He had accepted his mission with the fixed determination to make Corsica an independent state; there was no question for him, at this period of his career, of bartering away any part of the nation's sovereignty. His conviction was that the Corsicans could drive out the Genoese by force of arms, institute a regular, autonomous government, and impose its recognition on the world at large. Yet during the fourteen years of his generalship the military part of his programme, the key to the rest, was in fact never achieved. Courage and confidence were insufficient for leading the patriots to victory, and Paoli became General of the Nation without any experience in active warfare. Though he progressively evicted the Genoese from the last towers and villages they held in Cap Corse and elsewhere on the coasts, they remained in possession of the six fortress towns, periodically aided by France, until the French conquest.

Paoli's military schemes were certainly handicapped: by a desperate lack of munitions, artillery, warships; by small-scale but potentially dangerous internal rebellions in the early years of his regime backed by Genoa or France (which he put down); above all by the almost constant presence of French troops in the principal Genoese towns. All the same, his operations seem to have lacked dash and vigour. Attacks on Ajaccio and Saint-Florent in periods when French garrisons were absent failed, as did a later attempt on Bonifacio; in fact his only outstanding feat of arms before the French invasion was the conquest, in 1767, of the little Genoese island, Capraja, in which he himself took no part. His resistance to the French invasion, when his citizens' militia successfully opposed the troops of Louis XV for the best part of a year, astonished Europe; but it probably owed less to his generalship than to the fanaticism of Clemente and his ferocious guerrilla bands. Paoli's record invites the conclusion that unlike most Corsican leaders he was an indifferent soldier.

Where he excelled was in the art of government: in creating a national constitution and making it work. As a political philosopher he was indeed more original and enlightened than Napoleon. In action he employed a comparable calculating realism; while consistently proclaiming the sovereignty of

257

the people Paoli often assumed the role of enlightened despot in the interests of getting things done. What he achieved must be measured against the enormous obstacles that confronted him.[11] After over a quarter of a century of rebellion the Corsicans were discouraged; and as always they were divided. The Genoese naval blockade caused a chronic shortage of boots, salt, paper, arms and ammunition; most of the patriots' cannon had been captured in battle or salvaged from wrecked ships. The country was dismembered of its best ports; it was without roads or industries and almost without money. Paoli tackled each overwhelming problem with audacious countermeasures, never wholly successful, but always more effective than anyone could have hoped. He formed a small navy and sent it to patrol the coasts flying the Moor's head; trading vessels from Tuscany and Naples began to reach the rebel ports. He founded a mint, made it function, and induced the people to accept its currency. He successfully encouraged the manufacture of guns in the Castagniccia. The rebel state was unrecognised by any of the foreign powers: Paoli solicited, and obtained, an apostolic visitor from the Holy See, who remained with him four years and in so doing gave an *ipso facto* acknowledgement of Corsican autonomy.[12] When French troops arrived in force to occupy five of the coastal towns in 1764, Paoli must have realised that the rebel state could exist thenceforth only on sufferance. Yet he calmly went ahead with plans for inaugurating a university and for developing Ile-Rousse as a substitute port for Calvi. In his subsequent negotiations with the French minister, the Duc de Choiseul, he defended the nation's independence, with firmness and dignity, writing as the spokesman of one sovereign state to another, until the eve of the invasion.[13]

The poet Gray, after reading Boswell's *Account of Corsica*, observed that Paoli was a man born two thousand years after his time,[14] so difficult it was, at that period, to conceive of a revolutionary statesman outside the context of antiquity. But Paoli's tragedy was in living two centuries before Fidel Castro and Makarios, in an age when governments were monarchical or aristocratic and small nations were habitually bought and sold and exchanged and divided without regard for their inhabitants. Such was the climate of his time, that while certain progressive minds applauded his struggle for national liberation, his political innovations were never properly understood, nor esteemed at their worth. Less explicably, this incomprehension has persisted. Paoli's pioneer experiment in representative government went almost unnoticed, and has remained neglected to this day.[15]

He landed, secretly, in Corsica in the spring of 1755, was elected 'General of the Nation' in July at a *consulta* composed of deputies from the parishes assembled in a monastery of the Castagniccia. His constitution was proclaimed at another *consulta* in November of that same year. The original record of its proceedings has survived, forming a constitutional document; the earliest, to my knowledge, of its kind. The preamble is a clear, bold, noble statement of the sovereignty of the people, of the people's right to create a constitution for its own well-being: 'The General Diet of the People of Corsica, legitimately

258

master of itself, convoked according to the form [established by] the General in the city of Corte, the 16, 17, 18 November 1755. Having reconquered its liberty, wishing to give durable and constant form to its government, reducing it to a constitution from which the felicity of the Nation will derive. [The Diet] has decreed and decrees. . . .'[16] Such principles were of course lurking in the advanced political philosophy of the age; but historians have hitherto supposed that they were not fully formulated, nor acted upon, before the Constitutional Convention of the United States, thirty-two years later.[17]

Was the constitution really as democratic as these splendid words might lead one to expect? It would be unreasonable to suppose that it conformed to the criteria by which democracy is defined today; neither Paoli nor the Corsicans could have had any such criteria in mind. Undeniably systems more democratic than Paoli's can be imagined; but undeniably, too, his was exceptionally liberal in the context of his age.

Paoli had been appointed head of state at the July *consulta* with limited authority: he was to be 'economic and political chief' but – so it was stipulated – could take no action in 'matters of state' without the consent of the representatives of the people. By this was meant the consent of the members of the *consulte*; Paoli was made responsible to the traditional national assembly. In November of that year he summoned the *consulta* that proclaimed the constitution, and gave it the title of General Diet. This simple semantic device was in fact a master-stroke by which he transformed the whole shape and character of the rebel government. The customary *consulta*, which until then had been an irregular, unofficial body, always outside the structure of the governments it created, now became a properly instituted national parliament. According to the constitution Paoli, as head of the executive, had to summon it once a year; he was to render account of his government at the opening of each session and await the verdict of the assembly 'with submission'. In giving the national assembly a status that allowed it to balance the executive Paoli may well have been indebted to Montesquieu; yet he effected this vital change without any break with Corsican custom. His constitution issued from a convergence of the Enlightenment, as represented by Montesquieu, and Corsican political tradition as it had developed since the outbreak of the rebellion.

His election was for life, though in theory he could be deposed by the Diet. In 1764 provision was made for electing a new General in case the post fell vacant by his death or for other reasons. He was permanent president of the executive council (though he did not appoint its members), and had a double vote in its deliberations. In military matters his voice was decisive. He was also solely and personally responsible for Corsica's relations with foreign states. In reserving for himself these very important spheres of power Paoli again may well have been inspired by Montesquieu: had not Montesquieu said, in his chapter on the English constitution, that the executive power belonged to the monarch, and that military and foreign affairs should be controlled by the executive? Paoli probably saw himself as a constitutional regent. Perhaps he thought he had produced something similar to the English constitution; this, at any rate, was believed by the Corsicans: they were pleased with their constitution, a chronicler observes, because they thought it had resemblances to those of republican Rome, Sparta and England.[18]

The executive council, the Supreme Council of State, was elected by the Diet. At first, following the lines of Gaffori's regime, its members were exceedingly numerous: a hundred and forty-four in all. The full Council met only twice a year; during the rest of the time its members held office, turn by turn, for periods of a month or ten days. According to the constitution of 1755 they were elected for life; an arrangement no doubt designed to give a much needed stability to the Corsican government but which, if continued, would have created a ruling caste. The form of the Council was, however, soon recognised as unsatisfactory and was modified by the Diet; by 1764 the Council was reduced to nine members, elected only for a year.

Paoli's constitution was very exactly suited to the Corsican temperament. Almost every position of authority was to be won by election: membership of the Diet, of the Council of State, of the provincial magistratures (which the Diet elected), besides minor posts that none the less gave spectacular prestige, such as those of the captains and lieutenants in arms, who combined the functions of police officers and local military commanders. Meanwhile the yearly parish elections of podestas and fathers of the commune continued as always. Elections provided a constantly recurring opportunity for acquiring status and power, and dull indeed must have been the citizen who could not hope to advance himself thereby.

The Diet, in the early years of the regime, was composed in much the same way as the customary *consulte*. Deputies – *procuratori* – were elected in every parish for each separate session; Paoli insisted that voting should be secret. It was no doubt this feature of the constitution, unique in its period, that caused Boswell to describe the Corsican constitution as 'the best model that hath ever existed in the democratical form'.

Not all the members of the Diet were however elected; a fact that Boswell overlooked. Paoli made full use of the customary prerogative of the Corsican Generals to invite other categories of people to the national assembly. He had no hesitation in summoning ex-councillors of state, provincial magistrates, and even commanders of the *pievi* (who had been appointed by the executive, that is by himself), besides – on occasion – podestas and fathers of the commune, not to mention the sons and brothers of patriots killed or wounded in battle. From 1762 the clergy and monastic orders, on his invitation, sent their own deputies according to a system that gave them a much higher representation per head than was allowed to ordinary citizens: about 137 members as compared to some 325 elected by universal suffrage. The reason for this favoured treatment is not hard to find. The relative wealth of the clergy was invaluable to the rebel state. The Church was persuaded to melt down ecclesiastical ornaments to provide metals for the mint, to finance the university by a voluntary gift, and supply money to the treasury in moments of

260

crisis in exceptional levies. Paoli (who had inaugurated his regime by confiscating the revenues of the Genoese absentee bishops) was not himself a very orthodox Catholic; at heart he seems to have been a Deist.[19]

Though he had no seat in the Diet, he could influence its legislation. After his opening speech, in which he gave account of his conduct (which was in fact never questioned), he proposed subjects for discussion. The evidence suggests that he took advantage of the occasion to impose his will. Paoli had promoted the traditional *consulta* to parliamentary status, confirmed its powers and used them to secure his own; having done so he exerted himself to curb and subjugate this influential assembly. In 1763 the Diet, apparently acting on his instructions, passed legislation to limit the elected non-ecclesiastical deputies to one per *pieve*, to be chosen by indirect election. Had this law been respected the members elected by universal suffrage would have been reduced to a minority in the Diet. But the records show, unambiguously, that it was not respected; the parishes stoutly defended their customary right by which each sent its directly elected member to the national assembly.[20] The following year Paoli openly attacked the authority of the Diet by asking it to give the Council of State a negative veto on its legislation; the Diet resisted, and Paoli had to content himself with a suspensive veto by which the passing of a law could be delayed for a year. Further legislation was enacted to control village elections in 1766, again, it seems, on Paoli's prompting: candidates had to be proposed by the podestas and fathers of the commune; only heads of families had the right to vote. The records do not suggest that these regulations were much better observed than that of 1763.

A close reading of contemporary documents suggests that Paoli was already master of the political guile which so distressed Sir Gilbert Elliot, and that he employed it to ensure, and if possible increase, his personal power. Some of his contemporaries were not unaware of this; yet the majority of the Corsicans remained proud of their leader and constitution. It is easy enough, now, to fault Paoli's regime, to show that his position was irreconcilable with present-day ideas of a liberal government, and that the Diet that excited Boswell's enthusiasm was never entirely elected by universal suffrage, and after 1766 in theory not at all. But these objections would not have carried the same weight for Paoli's contemporaries. Nowhere was there a national assembly elected by universal suffrage; moreover no political philosopher had ever advocated such a system. The councils of the old Italian city states, Venice and Genoa, were exclusively patrician; the British parliament was returned by a limited electorate and dominated by the aristocracy. Certain Swiss cantons, it is true, adhered to the practice of direct, or pure democracy; but by the mid-eighteenth century Swiss democratic institutions were in decay. Everywhere in Europe aristocracies and oligarchies were in the ascendant; absolute monarchs ruled by divine right; despots now termed enlightened wielded powers far beyond those possessed by Paoli.

If Paoli owed part of his success to a well-developed political astuteness, he was also aided by a charismatic personality that must have faded by the time he had to do with Sir Gilbert Elliot, after his long exile in England. By all contemporary accounts he was a very handsome man: tall, fair, well-built and imposing. Both Boswell and the Jesuit man of letters Bettinelli (who met him in Tuscany in 1769) remark on his eloquence, his charming and easy manners; both were struck by his classical scholarship and wide range of learning. His conversation, always stimulating, was sometimes shot with brilliance: 'I regret that the fire with which he spoke so dazzled me that I could not recollect his sayings', wrote Boswell, who was after all a connoisseur of conversation.[21]

But the quality that most impressed Boswell and Bettinelli was of another order, and both regarded it as a mark of greatness. It can be described as buoyancy, aloofness, serenity, the ability to rise superior to circumstances. It showed itself in all aspects of his life, from the smallest: he ate and drank sparingly; he was impervious to climatic changes. Though courteous and chivalrous to women – as Bettinelli had occasion to observe in Italian society – he lived in voluntary celibacy; on this both writers insist. He was constantly composed, cheerful and resolute, in his time of defeat, when Bettinelli saw him, as when Boswell visited him, head of a newly formed state menaced from without and within. For Boswell, tormented by his own instability, melancholia and excesses, Paoli's example was nothing less than an inspiration: 'The contemplation of such a character really existing, was of more service to me than all I had been able to draw from books, from conversations or from the exertions of my own mind. . . . I saw my highest idea realised in Paoli. It was impossible for me, speculate as I pleased, to have a little opinion of human nature in him.' The portrait was of course idealised; Boswell saw only one facet of Paoli's complex character.

All the same, his account of Paoli and his regime is of the greatest historical interest; and one can only regret – and regret is too mild a word – that his visit did not coincide with a session of the Diet and that he never witnessed this large, vehement, primitive assembly in action. It met either in a monastery at Corte (now demolished) or in the former *palazzo* of the Genoese Lieutenant-Governor. I found the historic building with difficulty the first time I went there, for though still known as the *Palais National* it had been neglected and forgotten. The plain old mournful house, which has nothing of a palace about it, stands in the heart of the old town, up against the outer bastions of the citadel. An enormous schist boulder incorporated into the foundations protrudes from the mouldering stucco; the lower windows, haphazardly placed, are protected by iron bars that look like weapons of war. I could see nothing but darkness through them and I was unable to go inside.

Here representative democracy was tried out, decades before the French and American revolutions, in conditions that denied all the princely heritage of Europe. The deputies rode to the assembly on their mules, two and three days' journey across landscapes fit to illustrate explorers' tales, over the forested mountains and through the maquis burning with wild flowers, for the sessions usually took place in May. In the large beamed rooms (that now house

262

a historical museum), they debated and passed resolutions concerning the constitution, taxation, trade, agriculture, criminal law. And here, too, resided professors and students of the university inaugurated in January 1765. Poorer students, with minimal scholarships, were lodged in the Franciscan monastery; it was an example of high thinking and low living in a period when few honours went to the poor. One of the scholars, at least, has been heard of since: Napoleon's father, Carlo Bonaparte, who studied law at Corte while also acting as private secretary to Paoli.[22]

The professors, nearly all, were Franciscan monks; there were just enough intellectuals in the Corsican monasteries to man a small university. Only the rector, Father Mariani of Corbara, had to be summoned from abroad. A very disinterested as well as distinguished scholar, he gave up his chair at the university of Alcala, in Spain, to give the students of Corte courses in ethics and civil and canon law. The other subjects taught were dogma and ecclesiastical history, and – in line with contemporary trends – natural science, mathematics and philosophy. The latter did not imply only – if at all – the philosophy of antiquity, but 'philosophy according to the most plausible systems of the modern philosophers',[23] by which was meant the political and social thinkers of the age. The contemporary French writer Pommereul saw volumes by Locke, Montesquieu, Helvetius, Hume, Voltaire and Jean-Jacques Rousseau in the libraries of the professor-monks. One needs no further proof of the liberalism of the Corsican Franciscans than that they gave instruction in these works widely condemned as dangerous, subversive or atheistical. Paoli's regime performed the unusual feat of reconciling Catholicism with revolutionary institutions and ideas.

The Corsicans must have gained great self-assurance from learning that many of the principles they held to by instinct and custom, and had now integrated in a national constitution, had been promoted by the leading thinkers of their age. But in fact the *philosophes* had more to learn from the Corsicans than had the Corsicans from them. They could have seen a living society acting on the ideas they had conceived in studies, argued in drawing-rooms. The sovereignty of the people, the subordination of Church to State, absence of privilege, hereditary functions, arbitrary authority: all these principles of the Enlightenment were illustrated in the Corsican regime. That this should be so in a country notoriously backward would not have struck most of them as a paradox, but rather as an exhilarating proof of their faith in the sane reasoning of natural man. Rousseau, in particular, might have seen in the Corsican experiment the concrete expression of a passionately held creed.

In fact he knew nothing of the Corsicans' political system; but their struggle for national liberation was sufficient to recommend them in his eyes. In the *Contrat Social*, published in 1762, he singled them out as the one people in Europe fit to produce just laws: 'There is still in Europe one country capable of legislation, and that is the island of Corsica. The valour and constancy with which this brave people has known how to recover and defend its liberty well merits that some wise man teaches them how to preserve it. I have some presentiment that one day this little island will astonish Europe.'[24] Hardly could he have thought that two years later he would himself be offered an opportunity to become that wise man.

The proposal came to him in August 1764 from a certain Matteo Buttafoco, a young officer in the Royal Corse. He had read the *Contrat Social*, so he wrote to Rousseau, appreciated the gratifying mention of Corsica; would Rousseau deign to become the legislator of the nation? Rousseau sent an enthusiastic reply, but hesitated to commit himself, given the precarious position of the rebel state. Buttafoco was at pains to reassure him, sent him some works on Corsica; Rousseau procured others; the idea of a Corsican constitution began to take shape in his mind. But before he could settle to the task he became the victim of Voltaire's venomous attack following the publication of his *Lettres écrites de la Montagne*. Unnerved by persecution, in March 1765 he appealed to Buttafoco for a refuge in Corsica. He had abandoned the projected constitution; he refused any involvement in Corsican politics; but he would repay his hosts by writing a history of the Corsican people.

It is uncertain what part, if any, Paoli played in the early stages of these negotiations; but one knows that he invited Rousseau to Corsica in the spring of 1765; in the *Confessions* Rousseau speaks of receiving several letters from him (which have never come to light). Whether Paoli ever wanted Rousseau to produce a rival constitution to his own is debatable; but he undoubtedly understood the enormous prestige value of Rousseau's interest in the patriots and any work he might write about their country. Buttafoco prepared for his arrival. But at the last moment Rousseau, in understandable dread of moving to a semibarbarous island, dropped the whole scheme.[25]

After this Buttafoco and Paoli lost interest in him; they were increasingly preoccupied at this period by the insurmountable difficulties of coming to terms with France, then controlling the coastal towns. But Rousseau had not forgotten the Corsicans. In spite of his personal troubles, in spite of all he had told Buttafoco, he was secretly working on a Corsican constitution in 1765; the rough draft was probably sketched out before he left Switzerland in October. No doubt he intended to complete it and offer it to the Corsicans, had they remained independent. The French invasion cut him to the quick; no Corsican could have resented it more. 'It will be known', he wrote to Saint-Germain, 'that I was the first to see a free people, capable of discipline, where all Europe still saw only a horde of bandits.'[26] But in fact his views on Corsica were not fully known until nearly a century later; his *Projet de Constitution pour la Corse* had to wait for publication till 1861. Neither Paoli nor Buttafoco nor any contemporary Corsican ever read it, and it has attracted little attention in Corsica to this day.

Incomplete, disjointed, and moreover as excessive and irrational as Rousseau's political writings can be, it is none the less a fascinating document. Rousseau has little to say about political institutions; those he proposes for Corsica more or less corresponded with those already existing, under different names. It is the economy and way of life he advocates that makes such enthralling reading. When counselling the Corsicans Rousseau was speaking to a people after his own heart, a people still 'almost in the natural and healthy state'. For him their factions and feuds were the direct consequence of their 'servitude' to the Genoese. They had only to revert to their primal condition, barely out of sight, to recover 'concord, peace and liberty'. This, he was convinced, they could do with the help of good laws.

So he proceeds, with his incomparable force and fervour, to portray his idea of a legislated Utopia. It is based on the 'simplicity, the equality of the rustic life'. 'The rustic system', by which he meant elementary subsistence farming, was the source of all blessings and virtues. Not that it made for the wealth of individuals; but so much the better: 'It is necessary that all should live and none grow rich.' Money should be discredited, and if possible abolished altogether; trade, internal and foreign, should be reduced to a minimum. The different districts, he suggests, could exhange their surplus products by a system of barter supervised by the public administration. But barter, Rousseau reflects, is always awkward; money is liable to creep into any transaction; preferably each peasant should provide for all his needs even if this meant growing certain crops on unsuitable soil. As for foreign trade, it was practically unnecessary: Corsica could be self-supporting, as the experience of the rebellion had shown.

Nothing at all should be spent on the 'idle arts'. Rousseau's austerity programme recalls the early phases of Russian communism: 'We need neither sculptors nor jewellers, but carpenters and blacksmiths.' Coaches were to be forbidden except for the clergy, women and the sick; the rest should walk or ride.

Urban life should be discouraged. When Rousseau speaks of towns his voice becomes sombre and moving. In his references to the soft pretentious burghers, the wasters and idlers and swarming vagabonds, the peasant corrupted and his children depraved, one glimpses the squalour of the magnificent eighteenth-century cities as seen through the eyes of an inspired reformer. A capital was 'an abyss where almost the whole nation loses its morals, its laws, its courage and its liberty'. But since an administrative centre was indispensable to the Corsican nation, let it by all means be Corte, which owing to its remote mountain site seemed unlikely to acquire 'that fatal splendour which brings about the lustre and fall of nations'. Let the brave Corsicans be content with the life of the fields, and a modest prosperity; in this way their island would never be coveted by the foreign powers. Rousseau forgot that it might be coveted for its strategic value alone.

His arguments are still compelling, despite their extravagance. As one reads this passionate summons to the simple life a picture forms itself in one's mind; the picture of free, equal sturdy men living from the soil, exchanging their produce, walking and riding across country on their sober business, operating their administration from a rural mountain capital. It is a picture of Corsica. Rousseau, scrappily informed about the island, and with his own ideal always in view, unknowingly painted a portrait of Corsica as it then was and as it still appears to have been. Had he gone to Corsica he would have come face to face with his Utopia, his life's vision. He would have found a people equal in status and without great differences in fortune, who lived by the land and had bartered their surpluses since time immemorial (and without supervision). He could hardly have met a people less given to luxury and 'the idle arts'; he would have been satisfied, surely, to see that there were no coaches, because no roads,[27] and that Corte showed no signs whatsoever of 'fatal splendour'.

Rousseau would have found all this, and more, in the image of his ideal society; but also the vendetta. True, it was somewhat decreasing under Paoli's severe and impartial justice, and Rousseau would no doubt have rejoiced to see that the Corsicans were singularly innocent of the faults of city dwellers, sober in their habits and in sexual morals puritanical. No doubt he would have regarded their vindictive violence as a legacy of Genoese rule, soon to disappear. Yet more than a century after the Genoese had left the island the Corsicans were still killing each other, though still living according to the 'rustic system', and favoured with an administration of justice that could have been uncorrupt if they had wished it so.

Had Rousseau been able to foresee Corsica's future, he would surely have been led to revise some of his basic ideas. One cannot observe men close to the state of nature without being drawn to the unhappy conclusion that man is not naturally good and mild. Indeed the 'rustic system' may actually encourage feuds, by giving men a great sense of independence and self-assurance but few outlets for their pride. Rousseau would certainly have been shocked to know that the ending of the vendetta in Corsica coincided with the large-scale introduction of motor cars. Men cannot satisfy all their instincts living under the lid of a subsistence economy; only some. There is a whole critique of Rousseau's doctrine to be made in the light of the Corsican record. Diodorus's description gives it monumental support, Corsican history less; its limitations, surely, are traced by the nineteenth-century vendetta.

In the absence of the book Rousseau might have given us about the Corsican people we have Boswell's, certainly less profound, but brilliant of its kind, and though uncritical, remarkably well informed. He set sail for the island on 11 October 1765, armed with a passport from the commander of the British Mediterranean fleet designed to impress Barbary pirates, and a letter of introduction to Paoli from Rousseau himself (whom he had visited the previous year).[28] He had chosen a trading vessel bound for Centuri in Cap Corse, not Bastia; for Bastia was then in the hands of the French and Boswell feared (though in fact mistakenly) that they would try to prevent him travelling into the rebel zone. The journey had an aspect of adventure less common then than today. Boswell was experiencing the same kind of thrill a young writer might now feel when setting out to interview a hero of the decolonisation of some newly born African or Asiatic state.

He approached the shores of Corsica in high spirits mingled with trepidation. He had been warned that he ran the risk of his life in 'going among those barbarians'; the Corsican sailors, who movingly sung the Ave Maria at sunset, told him, more sensibly, that if he 'attempted to debauch any of their women' he could expect 'instant death'. The warning sank in: Boswell behaved himself all through his stay in Corsica, the most virtuous and probably the happiest period of his life.

The note is struck in the opening pages of the well-known journal, in his delight at the 'extremely agreeable prospect' of mountains all covered with vines and olives, and the 'very refreshing odour' of the 'myrtle and other aromatick shrubs and flowers'. By landing in prosperous Cap Corse he was able to ease himself into Corsican conditions gently. At Morsiglia and Pino he stayed in the houses of well-off notables; at Canari, reached on foot with 'a couple of stout women' carrying his luggage, he lodged in the beautifully sited Franciscan monastery (now the home of the parish priest) and reflected on the serenity and peace of mind to be found in such places. As he had confided to Rousseau, he had become a Catholic some years before; and though he had since lapsed he always felt at home with the tolerant, hospitable Corsican Franciscans.

His route continued through the Nebbio to Murato, where Signor Barbaggi, a kinsman of Paoli's, entertained him to dinner with 'twelve well-drest dishes, served on Dresden china' and different Corsican wines and liqueurs. It must have been the overwhelming sort of banquet distinguished visitors are still treated to; the chestnuts and eggs he got in the south where what people more normally ate. Barbaggi was in charge of the national mint, and Boswell was able to take away specimens of the silver and copper coins.[29]

A rough day's journey through 'a wild mountainous rocky country' brought him to Corte of which, unfortunately, he tells us rather little. He lodged in the Franciscan monastery, which had become a guest house for university students and government functionaries, and for Paoli himself, whose rooms Boswell occupied. Paoli, he learnt, was away in the south presiding over the *sindicato*, a travelling court of appeal; he had to prepare himself for another long journey. The delivery of a passport from the Great Chancellor is recorded with an anecdote that surely conveys the style of Paoli's regime: 'The Chancellor desired a little boy who was playing in the room by us, to run to his mother, and bring the great seal of the kingdom. I thought myself sitting in the house of a Cincinnatus.'

Heading for distant Sollacaro, Boswell passed some 'immense ridges and vast woods': the bastions of Monte d'Oro, the great forests of chestnut and beech and pine on the flanks of the pass of Vizzavona. From now on, till he reached Paoli, he was living right down to the basic Corsican level. Yet Boswell, the man about town who had recently made a delighted tour of the German courts, never utters a complaint; on the contrary he rejoices in his primitive surroundings. Though he shared the eighteenth-century insensitivity to romantic scenery he was captivated by the way of life that here went with it. Like many other highly civilised visitors to Corsica he experienced a wonderful revival of spirits, that feeling of a return to origins, as though to scenes of childhood which by stirring long dormant memories are as much familiar as strange. So we have his memorable description of walking through the forests with his guides: 'When we grew hungry, we threw stones among the thick branches of the chestnut trees which overshadowed us, and in that way we brought down a shower of chestnuts with which we filled our pockets, and went on eating them with great relish; and when this made us thirsty, we lay down by the side of the first brook, put our mouths to the stream, and drank sufficiently. It was just being, for a little while, one of the *prisca gens mortalium*, the primitive race of men, who ran about in the woods eating acorns and drinking water.' Boswell lived, that day, what Rousseau had constantly imagined.

The country he crossed has changed little, so that one can easily visualise his journey: over the haggard pass of Vizzavona and down to Bocognano in the chestnut woods; over another high ridge to Bastelica, a large shepherds' village, birthplace of Sampiero Corso, where he harangued the inhabitants on the dangers of luxury and the blessings of liberty. From there he proceeded to Ornano (now Sainte-Marie-Sicché), a day's walk by a very steep mountain path with the sight, at the end, of Sampiero's ruined castle, which still stands, a gaunt granite pile beside ancient elms.

The next lap of the journey brought him to Paoli, at Sollacaro, in a state of acute anxiety. There follows the famous account of their meeting, of Paoli's fine looks and his terrible scrutinising gaze. 'I had stood in the presence of many a prince', writes Boswell, 'but I never had such a trial as in the presence of Paoli. . . . For ten minutes we walked backwards and forwards through the room, hardly saying a word, while he looked at me, with a stedfast, keen and penetrating eye, as if he searched my very soul.' As Paoli later admitted to Fanny Burney, he at first took Boswell for a spy;[30] but he soon changed his mind, disarmed, perhaps, by Boswell's genial conversational opening: 'Sir, I am upon my travels, and have lately visited Rome. I am come from seeing the ruins of one brave and free people: I now see the rise of another.'

Then began that enchanted period, the marvellous days Boswell spent with Paoli,[31] eating at his table, attending his audiences, constantly enjoying his company. He was visited by all the men in Paoli's entourage, accompanied by a party of armed guards whenever he 'chose to make a little tour'; he rode Paoli's own horse, caparisoned 'with rich furniture of crimson velvet, with broad gold lace'. The lesser known account of his visit by the Corsican chronicler Rossi confirms these marks of attention; Boswell was not boasting. The common people, writes Rossi, were convinced that Boswell was an envoy from the British Crown.[32]

Oddly enough the misapprehension has persisted in Corsica, and is even shared by some otherwise perspicacious modern French historians. But it is unlikely that Paoli was so deluded even though Boswell, with incorrigible forwardness, spoke to him of 'an alliance between Great Britain and Corsica'. Paoli, in Boswell's words, 'with politeness and dignity waived the subject'; he was not naïve enough to suppose that this enthusiastic young traveller really had it in his power to reverse the policy of Britain, then at peace with

268

France after the Seven Years War. Yet he none the less appreciated, while somewhat overrating Boswell's social position, that he could give valuable publicity to his cause. When Boswell asked him what return he could make for his kindness Paoli replied: 'Only undeceive your court. Tell them what you have seen here. They will be curious to ask you. A man come from Corsica will be like a man come from the Antipodes.' Both men, at the time of this first meeting, were motivated by self-interest: Boswell the writer and lion-hunter in pursuit of his quarry; Paoli the revolutionary statesman building up goodwill abroad. But their relationship ripened into a genuine friendship: Boswell worked very hard for Paoli after his return to England, and over the next twenty years Paoli had a good influence on Boswell unequalled by any of his friends, Johnson not excepted.

It began here, at Sollacaro. Every day Boswell felt happier, experienced a 'luxury of noble sentiment' in the company of his host. One knows what they talked about: the being and attributes of God (always Boswell's favourite subject); Epicureans and Stoics (Paoli preferred the latter); the history of Britain; the infidel writings of the King of Prussia (who once sent Paoli a sword inscribed *Pugna'pro Patria*); marriage, a condition Paoli approved in theory but refused for himself; the nature and intelligence of beasts; virtuous habits and sentiments (which for Paoli were 'beyond philosophical reasonings'); wits, who bored him; Sir Thomas More's 'calm resolution on the scaffold', and whether it were true that the Romans placed towers full of armed men on the backs of elephants. There were discourses, too, from Paoli that reduced Boswell to the role of admiring listener: on Corsica and the Corsicans, full of shrewd, vigorous sayings; on the 'revolutions of ancient states' and 'the most distinguished men of antiquity' (the occasion when Boswell was 'dazzled by his fire'). And there were confidences, as when Boswell learnt that Paoli was gifted with second sight; like many Corsicans he had prophetic dreams.

Boswell's departure was made the more depressing by what he took to be a chill caught in the old Istria mansion, where he had been lodged in the absence of its owners; the house where Alexandre Dumas later stayed. It was much decayed, Boswell complained, 'like the family of its master', and the October wind and rain blew into his room. The malady soon declared itself as 'tertian ague', in other words malaria. The journey back to Corte in appalling weather was a test of endurance; yet Boswell managed to enjoy a 'truly savage' war dance performed for him at Cauro, perhaps a choreographic episode of the *Moresca*, a traditional pageant celebrating the Corsicans' early mediaeval victory over the Moors.[33] At Corte he had another good welcome from Chancellor and monks, besides a meeting with the erudite Rector of the university, Father Mariani, before making his way to Paoli's home in the Castagniccia, where he just missed his strange brother, Clemente. Reaching Bastia, really ill, he called on the Comte de Marbeuf, the French commander, collapsed and was put to bed in his host's sumptuous lodging, pampered with delicacies and treated by a doctor free of charge, and was so able to record a glimpse of the incomparable warm gay elegant manners of an accomplished nobleman of the Ancien Régime.

Boswell kept faith with the Corsicans and Paoli. On his return to England he bearded the elder Pitt, calling on him at the Duke of Grafton's house in Bond Street at nine in the morning and resolutely waiting until he was admitted at eleven; as often in his dealings with the great he had no fear of making himself ridiculous. But there was nothing ridiculous about the interview, as he reports it. 'Pitt: "How are their harbours?" Boswell: "One or two excellent, with some expense." Pitt: "Sir, that is of great consequence to a fleet on some grand enterprise. We have no such place in Italy."' And Boswell must have for ever treasured Pitt's thundering parting phrase: '"Sir, I should be sorry that in any corner of the world, however distant or however small, it should be suspected that I could ever be indifferent to the cause of liberty."'[34]

But he had obtained nothing for his hero. Undeterred, he went back to the attack, badgered Pitt, now Earl of Chatham, by letter, to do what amounted to declaring war on France for the sake of Corsica. The wonder is that Chatham replied with so courteous a refusal, and that Boswell nevertheless persisted, sending him extracts from Paoli's letters and an announcement of the publication of his book. The correspondence ran on for over a year. After which Boswell acted on his own initiative. In August 1768 he raised £700 in Scotland by private subscription and used it to send a shipload of cannon to Corsica, then fighting the French invasion. It was a courageous as well as a difficult enterprise, for by a proclamation following the peace with France in 1763 which Boswell had pestered Chatham to repeal, British subjects were forbidden to aid the Corsican rebels. The government was however hardly in a position to enforce this ruling, for according to the *Cambridge Modern History* it had also 'privily furnished Paoli with arms' that summer. Perhaps Boswell's clamouring had been more effective than he knew.[35]

Meanwhile his book had appeared, in February 1768, and been instantly acclaimed. Men of letters, including his enemies, agreed in recognising the quality of one of the most enjoyable travel journals in the English language. Nor was the *Journal* all. It was preceded by the *Account of Corsica*: a general description and history of the island. The history, like all those so far attempted, makes rather a hash of the early periods; but the contemporary section, written with the bite of firsthand experience, is vividly informative.

With a generous absence of the writer's craving to monopolise his subject Boswell also collected and edited twenty anonymous *British Essays in Favour of the Brave Corsicans* (himself contributing seven, unsigned). The volume was published at the end of the year. In December, he launched another appeal for funds for the Corsicans, openly this time in the *London Chronicle*, where he had been placing snippets about Corsica ever since his return. In September 1769 we hear of him at the junketings at the Shakespeare Jubilee at Stratford, disguised as an armed Corsican chief and endeavouring to interest the rowdy revellers in his poem on Corsica's resistance to the French invasion. 'From the rude banks of Golo's rapid flood, Alas! too deeply tinged with patriots' blood'

270

it begins. This dreadful composition was probably as good a means of stirring the public as any other.[36]

But it was too late to help Corsica. The patriots had been defeated and Paoli was already on his way to England. The span of Corsican independence had been, after all, only a reprieve while France waited for the appropriate moment to execute a sentence decreed years before. On 15 May 1768 the Traité de Versailles was signed, whereby Genoa abandoned her rights to Corsica with the proviso that she could reassert her sovereignty if she were ever able to repay France the cost of annexing the island. By a secret clause France undertook to pay Genoa an annuity of 2000 *livres tournois* for ten years. Corsica had been sold.[37]

In these negotiations Louis XV treated Genoa with the probity and courtesy due from one sovereign to another; he admitted no such obligations towards Paoli. The Corsicans were never consulted about the transaction that disposed of their persons, nor even informed when it was concluded. The invasion of June 1768 was undeclared; French troops had already occupied Cap Corse in the face of a determined resistance before the Marquis de Chauvelin saw fit to issue a manifesto. One knows what Paoli thought. One can hardly remain unmoved when he compares the Corsicans to a 'flock of sheep led to the market', when he writes: 'Men are not inanimate things; one cannot transfer the possession of them to another by act of cession or conveyance. Their obligations are founded on their freely expressed will.' Yet his appeals to the nation are marked by a dignified restraint. It was the university student Carlo Bonaparte, speaking on behalf of the youth of Corsica, who uttered the solemn suicidal call to arms: 'If it be written in the book of destiny that the greatest monarch in the world shall measure himself with the smallest people on earth, then we can only be proud, and in these circumstances we shall be certain to live with honour and die with glory.'[38] Historians seldom fail to observe that he was one of the first to collaborate with the conquerors.

All the same a great many Corsicans died as he had predicted, and during the best part of a year. Paoli had only six hundred regular paid troops; disliking professional soldiers, he had always relied on levies of the militia, to which all men from sixteen to sixty could be called. The Corsicans responded loyally to the mass levy to meet the invasion; tough bands of shepherds came down from the mountains, often recruited by the clergy. According to his own statement Paoli could count on about four thousand fighting men; others came and went, as in all the Corsican wars.[39] The French invasion force numbered about nine thousand, not including the garrisons of the towns, plus some hundreds of Corsican volunteers won over by propaganda or promises of advancement.

But though the patriots were lamentably inferior in numbers and in arms, though they had been betrayed by some of the best-trained Corsican soldiers, the young French courtiers who arrived in expectation of marching over a rabble of peasants were in for a disappointment. The shock came in September 1768, after Cap Corse, the Nebbio and the Casinca had apparently submitted. Following their age-old tactics the Corsicans retreated before the enemy only to spring back on it in rapid, unpredictable attacks in which all the rocks and maquis came alive with hostile men. In the Casinca they drove the French from their positions, led by Clemente Paoli, a matchless marksman who prayed for his enemies' souls as he shot them down. At Borgo, always unlucky for the French, they forced a garrison to surrender. There was no question for the Corsicans, now, of interrupting battles to carry home the dead; Voltaire, of all people, describes how when defending a bridge they fought behind a rampart built with the corpses of their fellow-fighters while the wounded voluntarily added their own bodies to the pile.[40]

In November Chauvelin was actually reduced to sending envoys to Paoli who, supported by a couple of Englishmen who had brought him funds from London, coldly refused to treat. The French crept into winter quarters while the Corsicans, back in possession of most of the Nebbio, sniped at them continually so that no soldier dared stir abroad. In January, with Chauvelin recalled, Marbeuf obtained an armistice, which was broken when Paoli reopened hostilities the following month.

April saw the landing of fifteen fresh battalions under the Comte de Vaux, 'a hard severe man' and a master of strategy;[41] the French Army now numbered more than thirty thousand men. Even so the Corsicans resisted, in the Nebbio and the neighbouring mountains. On 8 May a group of some two thousand risked a counter-attack a little to the north of Ponte-Leccia. This was probably the first time the Corsicans had challenged a foreign army in open combat since Roman times, and the consequences were just as disastrous. Fighting fanatically, suicidally, they were driven back from rock to rock to Ponte-Nuovo, a bridge over the Golo. It is unnecessary to enter into the discussions of whether there were misinterpretations of orders, or whether Paoli failed in his duty by not being present on the field of battle: the Corsicans were hopelessly outnumbered and outarmed. They had no bayonets, and the French made good use of theirs, plunging down on to the bridge where about a quarter of the Corsicans were trapped and killed. Bodies were found months later in the surrounding rocks and maquis, of the wounded, who had crawled into hiding to die. The war ended with Ponte-Nuovo; what the Corsicans had achieved was to give the French a lasting respect for Corsican valour.

16

THE END OF AN EPOCH

Paoli in exile – Paoli and America – Napoleon and Corsica –
Corsicans abroad – legendary victory – death of a tradition -
pageant of the seasons

PAOLI was not the man to rally his disheartened supporters after the massacre of Ponte-Nuovo, to lead a hungry, heroic resistance in the mountains in
the style of the warlords of the past. His retreat to the south resembled a
flight; he evacuated his headquarters at Morosaglia with the French at his
heels, abandoned Corte the night before they entered the town, unopposed, to
ransack the meagre national treasure: two pieces of crimson damask embroidered with the Moor's head, ten gilt armchairs, a stuffed tiger – a present
from the Bey of Tunis – and Paoli's library, which according to an officer who
looted a hundred volumes was admirably chosen and worthy of 'a man of
genius and a great statesman'.[1]

But Paoli the intellectual, the liberal political philosopher, had no use for
guerrilla tactics; he headed towards the south-east coast without ever making
a stand. Futile bravery and needless bloodshed were alien to his concept of
leadership. Moreover he must have known that not only had Corsica too few
men for challenging the French army but that too many of those few were
now fighting on the wrong side. The victims of Ponte-Nuovo were outraged
by the sight of their fellow-countrymen in the enemy ranks; and after the
battle the defections multiplied. Paoli's judgement was correct: Clemente, the
true Corsican warrior, who after Ponte-Nuovo fell back on the Niolo and
crossed to the western watershed, failed in a last-hour counterattack with two
thousand hastily assembled partisans and had to join his brother's retreat.
Together they got away from Porto-Vecchio, on 13 June 1769, with two or
three hundred supporters, in a British ship that carried them to Leghorn.

Clemente thereupon retired from public life; Pasquale was fêted by the
sovereigns who had sympathised with his cause but done little or nothing to
help it. Lord Pembroke (who had paid him a flying visit in Corsica earlier in
the year) was at Leghorn to meet him, to bear him company to Pisa;[2] in
Florence he was entertained by Leopold, the enlightened Austrian Grand
Duke of Tuscany. The Emperor Joseph II, touring northern Italy, went out
of his way to meet him with the young Archduchess Marie Antoinette: 'Let
us go to see the Themistocles of our century,' the Emperor is reported to have
said.[3] In Holland he banqueted with the Prince Stadholder; in London he was

273

received by the Prime Minister, the Duke of Grafton, given an audience by George III, welcomed by numerous members of the peerage, and of course by Boswell, who introduced him to Johnson (the occasion when he felt like 'an isthmus which joins two great continents').⁴ He was granted a Civil List pension of £1200 a year, painted by his new friend, Sir Joshua Reynolds, and many others, lionised in aristocratic and intellectual circles; compared with every other Corsican rebel leader Paoli had got off lightly.

But the meaningful period of his life had ended with Ponte-Nuovo; the rest was a postscript. Europe had no further use for him. His system of government had been crushed before it was really understood by the world at large; when the same principles triumphed in France twenty years later they were propelled by a younger generation that owed nothing to his precedent. Corsica's role has been to prophesy, not to lead; to innovate but not to influence. The sculptors of Filitosa had no successors; Paoli's experiment in representative government played no part in freeing Europe from monarchical and aristocratic rule.

Only in America, where another colonial people was struggling for its independence, his example became a stimulus to revolutionary action. Benjamin Franklin, one of the first to greet him in London, had already written letters to the press comparing the position of the Americans with that of the Corsicans, those 'last brave assertors' of Civil Liberty 'within the bounds of the old Roman Commonwealth'. Thanks to Boswell's book Paoli became the hero of the American patriots; the Sons of Liberty and other radical groups toasted him at their banquets, along with Boswell and a heterogeneous collection of statesmen and princes thought to favour the sacred cause of freedom: Chatham, Shelburne, Burke, Wilkes, the King of Sardinia, the King of Prussia. Sympathy with the Corsicans in their last stand against the French found expression in such resolutions as: 'May the attempts of France upon Corsica meet with the same fate as those of Persia upon Greece', and 'May Paoli meet with equal renown, but a happier fate than the younger Brutus.' The cult of the 'uncorrupted Patriot General' and 'the brave Corsicans' ran highest in Boston, New York, and above all Pennsylvania. Patriots met at an inn near Philadelphia called the General Paoli Tavern; the name was given to the town that eventually grew up on the site, and three other towns were later named for him, in Indiana, Oklahoma and Colorado.⁵

As for Paoli, dining out, visiting, touring the mild British countryside as far afield as Scotland, he was none the less harbouring his ambitions with true Corsican tenacity. He refused a pardon offered to him in 1776; he was not disposed to return to Corsica as a private citizen, subject of an absolute monarch, to see the island ruled as a conquered province by a military governor.⁶ Paoli still believed in his mission as Corsican liberator; he continued believing in it while year after year he watched the political scene, waiting his chance. That chance seemed to be offered – at last – on 30 November 1789, when the Constituent Assembly of revolutionary France lifted the ban on Corsican political exiles. His landing in Bastia on 17 July 1790, amid salvoes of gunfire and chiming of bells, was a great personal comeback. It was also a great blunder. For by then Paoli was an elderly man softened by twenty years of English social life, and the time for Corsican independence had gone by.

In fact authentic independence, permanent and recognised, had never been possible. Paoli's dream, inherited from the Cinarchesi, the recurring Corsican dream since the fall of Rome, had always been condemned; the European powers were at no time prepared to allow such an important strategic naval base to escape their control. The Corsican nation had been able to rise to a temporary existence during the delay entailed in transferring the island from one foreign ruler to another, as a plant thrusts out of the earth during the mending of a road, when an old, cracked paving-stone is lifted, before the stone to replace it has been laid. The interval had sufficed – just – for Paoli to transform the rebel territory into an organised, autonomous state. In this he satisfied at once his personal aspirations and the age-old hopes of the Corsicans. The consciousness of human worth and dignity that appears, rude and uncompromising, in the statues at Filitosa, that was kept alive through centuries of colonial rule, achieved its final expression in Paoli's regime. In his hands the two histories of Corsica, hitherto at odds, the spectacular turbulent political history, and the slow, covert social evolution, fused, and the insular culture came to maturity.

Paoli never understood – or perhaps was unable to admit – that he had been favoured by a unique opportunity. All through his years of exile he nursed the hope that he might yet be instrumental in giving Corsica, if not complete independence, then at least a protectorate status. The amnesty that allowed him to return to his country was for him paradoxically tainted with disappointment; for on the very day it was granted the Assembly had also decreed, swayed by a petition of the Corsican deputies, that Corsica was an integral part of France and would thenceforth be governed by the same laws. The Corsicans had spontaneously voted themselves into the French revolutionary state as first-class citizens.

At first Paoli, it seems, loyally accepted their decision. He approved the principles of the French Revolution; he expelled the members of the small aristocratic party from Corsica; he actively enforced the Civil Constitution of the Clergy.[7] Yet he remained first and foremost a Corsican, and as head of the insular administration had small patience with interference from Paris. As the violence and disorders of the Revolution increased he must have been haunted by the idea of Corsican autonomy; when the Convention indicted him as a traitor, the old dream suddenly presented itself as the only practical course of action.

But it ran counter, then, to the currents of European history, and also to the best interests of the Corsicans. Neither France nor Britain, locked in war, was prepared to leave the Corsicans to their own devices, and the Corsicans stood their best chance of enjoying democratic liberties as subjects of France. This was not the moment to revive the chimera of Corsican independence, nor to experiment with a British regime that turned out to be hardly more liberal, and a good deal less efficient, than that of the French monarchy.

Thanks to the Terror and to his enormous popularity Paoli was able to drag the majority of the population in the wake of his ill-judged adventure. But he had few men of ability beside him; too many of the younger, educated Corsicans had joined the French Republicans and left the island; the Corsican élite was fighting in the French army. Whatever the monarchy had failed to do in Corsica, however inept the official schemes for planting mulberries, starting silk and soap factories, France had at least offered the Corsicans military careers. The generation born after Ponte-Nuovo had responded with enthusiasm; young men engaged at sixteen and seventeen in the Royal Corse and its offshoot regiments; scholarships in the French military academies were competed for with the asperity given to electoral campaigns. Among the successful candidates was Napoleon Bonaparte. He had already done with insular politics and local ambitions when Paoli appealed to the British, had driven the British out of Toulon while Paoli was still awaiting their protection; he was earning his reputation as General Vendemaire in Paris while Paoli fought the last, losing round in his duel with Sir Gilbert Elliot. Paoli was dining out in London again, finished, while Napoleon advanced from victory to victory across Italy with eighteen Corsican generals or future generals in his ranks. Seen against this record Paoli's aims appear outdated and provincial.

The number of soldiers Napoleon levied in Corsica has been estimated at some ten thousand. The names of his Corsican generals have been listed: forty-three in all.[8] They came from all over the island: Abbatucci from Zicavo, in the central south, Cervoni from Soveria, a hill top village near Corte; the astonishing Casabianca of the Castagniccia and the Casinca produced three generals and several high-ranking army officers besides the famous naval commander who perished on his burning ship, with his twelve-year-old son, at the battle of Aboukir. These men were often promoted young (General Abbatucci was twenty-six when he died at the battle of Huninguen); some rose to very high positions. Felix Baciocchi became prince by his marriage to Napoleon's sister Elisa, Arrighi de Casanova Duke of Padua, Horace Sebastiani count of the Empire, marshall of France and later foreign minister to Louis-Philippe. They followed their hero to Egypt, to Moscow, fought across Europe from the Atlantic to the steppes; they made and unmade rulers, rode in Roman triumph through legendary cities; they knew the extremes of experience – luxury, plague, carnage, famine, the Russian winter – they changed Europe. They, with thousands of fellow-Corsicans left the violent, claustrophobic, unrewarding struggles of insular guerrilla sniping to create an empire. Paoli brought about the fulfilment of Corsican democratic traditions, Napoleon the apogee of Corsican valour.

His birth, just three months after Ponte-Nuovo, at a time of national defeat and mortification, can be considered as an act of providence, a manifestation of compensatory synchronicity, or simply and undeniably as a very fortunate historical coincidence. Everything, perhaps, has been said about him; though with rather little emphasis, I think, on the essentially Corsican quality of his genius. He was a ruler and warrior in the authentic Corsican style. His grasp of essentials, that X-ray vision that showed him the core of every problem, every opposition; his over-indulgent loyalty to his kindred; his love of display – less for itself, he cared little for luxury – than for its status value: these are characteristic Corsican traits. So was his stoicism, that went beyond Paoli's dignified composure in misfortune; one is amazed by the sheer gaiety of some of Napoleon's recorded sayings during his retreat from Moscow, his exile at St Helena. And typically Corsican was his fatal failing: like Paoli, like the Cinarchesi warlords, like Sampiero and all the Corsican leaders, he attempted too much, for too long.

What he did for Corsica was of permanent, incalculable value; but it was not apparent during his lifetime. Given his possibilities, he neglected the island. His ascendancy was an uneasy period in Corsican history; he never commanded the unanimous, unconditional respect of his countrymen, as commander of the Army of Italy, as First Consul or as Emperor (although, faithful to lost causes, they rallied to his support during the Hundred Days). Republican severity to the clergy, after Fructidor, excited a holy war in the Castagniccia which was relentlessly put down;[9] in the mid-winter of 1799 a more serious uprising was instigated by anti-Republican Corsican exiles in Tuscany with the fanciful aim of giving the island to Russia.[10] Miot de Melito arrived with orders from Napoleon to suspend the constitution, execute rebels out of hand and burn their homes; he was succeeded in this role by General Morand, the worst dictator the island had ever known, who was said to ensure the happiness of the Corsicans by executing a man a day.[11] Berthier, sent to replace him in 1811, was hardly better liked; British troops landed in Bastia in 1814 on the appeal of the town, to be recalled after Napoleon abdicated in April of that year; the population of Ajaccio, it is said, greeted this news by hurling his bust into the sea.

Yet Napoleon had done more for Corsica than anyone then realised; or rather more for the Corsicans: he had sowed the seeds of ideas which, germinating slowly, changed their attitude to the world and their very image of themselves. Armed rebellions and dreams of independence came to an end after his reign: Napoleon had given his countrymen a nationality and so solved a problem that had bedevilled their history for the past fifteen hundred years. His career brought home to them as nothing else could have done that they were citizens of France and as such might win the highest honours. It weighed powerfully against the instinctive feelings of victimisation, frustration and underprivileged apartness that had dogged them for centuries. Never again could it be said that they were a base, benighted, insignificant people. The Cinarchesi heroes might be dismissed as irresponsible warlords, Sampiero Corso as a brutal soldier of fortune, Paoli as an ineffectual idealist; but no one could deny Napoleon's stature. Little by little the Corsicans came to realise that they need no longer squander their talents in civil wars and rebellions and schemes for self-government predestined to failure; they could go to France, as he had done and his soldiers and generals, and play their part in the history of a wealthy, powerful nation, which was theirs.

Emigration was of course nothing new to the Corsicans; but until then it had been either a privilege or a risky adventure. In the nineteenth century it became the normal procedure for young men of promise. Need was a spur to ambition; as the population began to outgrow the island's static resources more and more Corsicans chose to make careers abroad.[12] The élite became generals, ministers, ambassadors, crack lawyers; the rest found their level in the army and navy, the civil service, the professions, and the world outside the law (none joined the wretched industrial proletariat). Some remarkable men emerged from rather humble homes: Xavier Coppolani, born in a small mountain village, became a scholar of Arabic and the tribal dialects of the Sahara, where he promoted the peaceful penetration of the French until he was murdered by fanatics in 1905.[13] By then the Corsicans had made their mark all over the French empire, as explorers, soldiers, governors and administrators, doctors and missionaries, adventurers, traders and pioneers. Whole villages were built and peopled by Corsican families. 'We pitched our tent, my brother and I, at a spot where the Foreign Legion had the habit of halting,' one of the empire builders from Algeria told me. 'We slept with our guns in our hands. We put up a bar and sold drinks to the Legion. Then we sent for our younger brothers from the village at home and put up a general store. Our cousins came out to join us with their wives and children, and we built a hotel and another store and in the end we had a real village.'

Until the Europeans' retreat of recent years Corsicans were to be found thriving, multiplying, and often commanding in Morocco, Algeria, Tunisia and all the French African colonies, in Madagascar and in Indo-China. Others settled in the French Antilles and Pacific isles; the writer Francis Carco was born of Corsican parents in Noumea. They made colonies, too, in whichever foreign countries allowed them a foothold. The *sgio* of Sartène associated with the building of the Suez Canal paved the way in Egypt for their relatives and friends; Raoul Léonie, former President of Venezuela, was of Corsican origin, as are some six thousand or more citizens of that country, mostly descended from merchant adventurers of Cap Corse.

For all these people Napoleon has been an inspiration, a model ever in view. Coppolani was noted for the Napoleonic caste of his features, though his nature seems to have been very different; the innumerable Corsican colonial army and police officers were certainly closer in temperament to their hero. And so Napoleon's image continued to grow in the Corsican mind, became a national cult and legend, while Paoli was relegated to the history books. He is remembered with affection as a sincere but misguided patriot, architect of an independence that hardly anyone thereafter seriously envisaged, with irritation as a poor soldier and the dupe of Britain, with respect – by the well-educated – as an enlightened political philosopher; but more often, realistically, as a man whose ideas were too great for his field of action. His remains were reverently brought back from London and reinterred in his home at Moro-saglia; but the old house was a rather pitiable place before the Leblancs restored the museum there, and the *Palais National* at Corte, when I first saw it, had become a dilapidated dump for military stores.

The summer was ending with my journey. Climbing, towards evening, past the *Palais National* to the upper edge of the old citadel of Corte, I watched the sun sinking through a tumult of red-stained clouds. Helmeted with baroque cupolas, each monstrous form encased in a fiery aureole, they crowded above the summits of the Niolo, greater and more menacing than the mountains themselves. Shafts of unnaturally gilded light, slanting through the gashes in their ranks, illuminated small patches of rock and forest, suggest-ing not so much the eye of God as death rays that had singled out these innocent spots for total destruction. The rest of the huge spiked tumbled landscape was shrouded in shadow. A feeling of approaching cataclysm was accentuated by the only sound: the steady rushing of the rivers over their stony beds.

By morning the clouds had worked all round the horizon. Massed, en-throned, on the ranges, they smothered the peaks, poured their dark fumes into the gorges. Ragged outriders were flying ahead down the river valleys, heralds of the hosts of wrath. Though the sun still blazed from an inviolate sector of the eastern sky, the storm was very near. The parish priest, young, handsome and athletic (the modern type of militant Christian that has super-seded, here and there, the traditional, patient old leisurely priests of the Corsican villages), showed me a little square in the heart of the old town which he had cleared of rubble and ruins, by voluntary labour, to lay bare the site of the birthplace of Blaise Signori, the Franciscan Saint Theophile. This one latterday Corsican saint was a man of extreme austerity who travelled about the island during the early phase of the national rebellion in an uphill en-deavour to convert the insular Franciscans to the strict rule of the Ritiri, based on penitence and prayer.[14] 'He only succeeded in one monastery, at Zuani,' the priest told me. 'Our Franciscans were poor enough, but they were patriots rather than ascetics, passionately involved in politics, as most Corsi-cans are. All the same, their religion is something very real to them; but felt, seldom thought, and insufficiently lived, sometimes not lived at all.' He went on, more cheerfully, to tell me about the ruined mediaeval churches in the region, which had apparently been a centre of militant Christianity after the defeat of the Saracens.

Later in the day I found my way to them, walking through the scorched maquis under a heavy sky: pre-Pisan Santa Mariona on a bare hillside, reduced to little more than its two juxtaposed apses; San Giovanni, a mile or so along the railroad track, a much larger ruin with a handsome arcaded apse rising above tangled briars. Close by stood an unbeautiful, intact, trefoil-shaped building, used as a barn, which Geneviève Moracchini-Mazel has since identified as a baptistry. Both are pre-Pisan, dated to the first half of the ninth century. This was precisely the period, according to a Corsican chronicler, when a heroic national leader besieged and defeated the Saracens, entrenched at Corte.[15] It is conceivable that church and baptistry were built to commemorate this victory, and convert the enemy survivors; Paoli, perhaps, chose for his capital the scene of a great insular Christian triumph of Corsica's legendary chivalrous age.

Fat drops were falling, singly, into the dust as I hurried back to the station to catch the *micheline* to Ajaccio; gusts of sharp mountain air rattled the maquis. Whirlwinds were swirling leaves and waste-paper about the platform, where travellers huddled with bellowing babies. The storm and the *micheline* arrived together; in a majestic rolling of thunder, as of celestial drums, the rain crashed down, a battering, blinding enemy; it had drenched me before I boarded the train. There was nowhere to sit, barely space to stand; for the single coach was packed with young Corsican parents and their children besides the familiar elderly peasants with their baskets and guns. The time had come when for a week or two public transport would be even more crowded than usual. Schoolteachers, university professors, pharmacists, doctors and civil servants were ending their holidays, taking their children back to school on the mainland; all those Corsicans who will never forgo their yearly visit to their home villages, where the population, in summer, may be multiplied by ten, and beds are put up in every room and the old peasant women think nothing of cooking for parties of fifteen and twenty for the joy of being with their grandchildren and daughters and sons. Carefully dressed in town clothes oddly out of keeping with their environment, these bourgeois Corsicans far outnumbered the tourists, also on their way home: some tousled campers, a contingent of boy scouts.

Standing pressed against the door I watched Corte sway out of sight in the rain. The citadel, topped with its unsuitable houses, lashed by the storm, appeared a mere knob of rock against the dark masses of the mountains, confounded, now, with the greater masses of the clouds. As we crept up the barely visible valley the storm poured over the ranges in continuous opaque squalls, so that one could hardly judge their dimensions: a rift in the cloud rack would reveal unsuspected heights of gnarled and fissured rock, forest and scree, unfathomable ravines and cataracts just created. I should have a jumbled view of this country which travellers have described with wonder, where Boswell rediscovered the youth of mankind, and the vagabond poet, Albert Glatigny, was moved to exclaim, overwhelmed by its beauty: 'Here there is only one thing to do; stop and weep.'[16] I should see this landscape confusedly; yet in its most characteristic mood; for the watershed of Vizzavona bears the brunt of the elements, is constantly visited, summer as winter, by mists and gales and storms. 'It's marvellous to see nature suffer so,' a taxi-driver said to me who regularly covers this route.

Few people live here; some chestnut gatherers in the forest hamlets; some shepherds and goatherds; a few lumberjacks, mostly Italians (the Corsicans refuse such hard labour) who camp for months on end in wooden shacks. The blows of their axes, the faint jangle of goats' bells, are the only sounds besides

280

Village in the central mountains. (*Louis Bianchetti*)

High Peaks of the central mountains. (*Louis Bianchetti*)

Mountain landscape. (*Jean Bianchetti*)

the rushing of waters, and the wind, like the ceaseless washing of an ocean, in the upper branches of the trees. One can walk for hours and hear nothing else, and see only pines and rocks and water, and the cloud-burdened sky, which as one advances up the gorges sometimes seems almost within hand's reach, a substance barely divided from the earth, so that the ancient myths of creation come to mind and the cosmic battles of the gods, as when Marduk the merciless, driving the chariot of the storm, severed Tiamat, mother of monsters, and set up half her body to make the heavens.[17]

The train jerked slowly uphill, burrowing into tunnels through shoulders of mountains, flying mist-veiled ravines on high viaducts. This stretch of the railway is a man's triumph; when one caught sight of the line running obliquely across precipices, miles above or below, one marvelled that the shaking little *micheline* could hold to it. The stations were sheds in the wilds, yet all crowded with well-dressed parents and children who pressed patiently into the train. Squatting, now, on a suitcase at the feet of all these Corsicans, observing their lined, dramatic, masterful faces, mostly a little sad, I found myself speculating on the future of their race. Would it produce any more great prophetic figures like Paoli and Napoleon; Paoli who anticipated representative democracy, Napoleon the unification of Europe (though one hopes it may be achieved by other means)? Or was he the last of those astonishing leaders periodically produced by this obscure, technologically backward island?

The question was less easy to answer then than it is now; for now one knows that the indigenous culture of Corsica has run its span. The way of life, the concepts that prevailed there since the Neolithic era in an unbroken, slowly evolving tradition, are being annihilated day by day, and the Corsicans will soon become like other people, like those of continental France and of Europe as a whole, and eventually of the world, all forced into the same mould that is shaping our work, our homes, food, thoughts, and perhaps our very dreams. If Corsica gives birth to any outstanding individuals they will no longer be marked by the peculiar insular genius, for the characteristics of the people – as of most others – will have disappeared.

But on my first visit to Corsica these changes were not foreseeable; the Corsicans were still a people apart. Though Ponte-Nuovo had killed their belief in themselves as a nation, their culture lingered on, an anachronism in modern France, until a few years ago. It survived, because neither the continental French nor the Corsicans had done anything much to disturb it. Count Peraldi was perhaps unjust in complaining that France had given Corsica nothing except roads and school; but certainly the roads and schools were then the most obvious signs of nearly two hundred years of French rule.

In fact the nineteenth-century governments launched a number of optimistic development schemes; but either they failed, or else their results were so completely absorbed into the country as to become unnoticeable. Potato growing was successfully encouraged; but no one now marvels at the potatoes in every village garden. Bonuses given for grafting and planting olive trees during the Restoration made for the prosperity of the Balagne; until, that is, Corsican oil was pushed off the market and the new mansions of the gentry fell into decay beside the neglected groves. The fruit trees distributed gratis under Louis-Philippe give a Japanese splendour of blossom to the spring landscape; the eucalypts planted in the early antimalarial campaigns could be taken for native trees, so perfectly their drooping foliate forms harmonise with the Claudian vistas. Industries were started, flourished and collapsed: mining proved uneconomic; iron foundries on the east coast boomed in the mid-century until they were bankrupted by larger enterprises overseas.

All this time, it is true, the island had been growing less poor; emigration, gathering volume through the nineteenth century, brought money to Corsica with those who returned to retire. But not very much: enough to build larger houses, to buy the endearing Louis-Philippe and Second Empire furniture one sees jumbled up with garish Moorish and oriental souvenirs. These home-coming Corsicans had not been radically changed by twenty to forty years abroad. They were still Corsicans, with Corsican values: careless of money but avid for prestige; stubborn, solemn and unindulgent; potential political chieftains one and all, competing for local eminence.

Meanwhile those who stayed in the island continued in the immemorial routine, cultivating their terraces with wooden swing-plough and *zappone*,[18] bartering their surpluses, driving their flocks up and down the mountains as their ancestors had done. Agricultural advisers, model farms and training centres had small effect on their methods; the Corsicans were disinclined to tamper with a relationship with nature which they had fashioned, through the centuries, into a delicately balanced partnership, demanding neither too much of her nor of themselves. In the long, quiescent twilight of Corsican tradition every act, almost every gesture, was fixed and hallowed by im-memorial usage: the beating of chestnuts, the yoking and unyoking of oxen no less than the ritual kiss of customary marriage. Some Corsicans who grew up in this archaic world now seem like people walking in their sleep. A goatherd had always driven his goats to the coast by a certain route; he continued doing so, a few years ago, while a house was being built across his path, even though a detour would have been easy. The goats swarmed over the walls, encouraged by their owner, knocking down bricks, scattering plaster, cement and tools.

In conversations with people who remember the old Corsica two contrasting pictures emerge. One is of a deep contentment, something approaching Rousseau's ideal. 'You can't begin to imagine what it was like when the harvests were in and we knew we had enough food to get through the winter. The chests stuffed full of chestnut flour and corn, the apples and walnuts gathered and stored, the figs picked and dried, the wine in the barrel, the pig killed and the sausages and hams hanging from the beams, below the cheeses. Nothing I've achieved has ever given me a comparable satisfaction.' This man is now a successful architect; others, who have remained peasants and shepherds, like the Cesari and their friends, have spoken to me in almost the same words.

But there are also those who remember mainly hunger, flies, fleas, bugs, fever and sudden death. Both pictures are true; which was uppermost depended on whether one owned just enough land to feed the family or just too little, whether one lived in a peaceful or a feuding village, in the bracing mountains or the malarial plains. The people were no doubt physically stronger then than now, but suffered atrociously in the absence of doctors from malaria, epidemics, and appendicitis that killed off many before they could get to a surgeon. Talking to those granite-faced survivors of a tougher age one has the impression of extraordinary mental and physical robustness. Sure of their principles and their beliefs, confident in themselves, the Corsicans of the older generation were more generous and hospitable as well as more abstemious than their presentday descendants; very much more hard working, yet less materialistic; warmer in affection but implacable enemies; capable of the extremes of violence and devotion. Life was harder and shorter than it has since become, but lived with far greater zest and passion.

The darker aspect of passion was the vendetta. If the record number of killings in a year during the nineteenth century was only a hundred and sixty-one[19] (as against nearly a thousand under the Genoese regime), the rate was still extravagant for the size of the population. The vendetta made the French despair of Corsica, and certainly deterred governments from financing the very improvements that could have brought it to an end. Unfortunately it was officially regarded as a form of crime, to be repressed, rather than as an archaic institution that might be expected to disappear with archaic conditions. Clemenceau was the first French statesman to grasp the connection between the vendetta and living standards. 'A man who has a home, who possesses a certain well being, does not willingly take to the maquis', the 'Rapport Clemenceau' pertinently observes.[20]

Following the findings of his commission of enquiry, Clemenceau, in 1909, proposed a long-term programme of public works, to include the draining of the east coast plain. The First World War prevented its full execution, but brought other advantages, along with mourning and death. The gradual modernisation of the island has been less due to anything done by governments or the Corsicans than to exterior, world events, backwashing on its shores. The soldiers who returned in 1918 (less than half the number who left) brought money in the form of disability pensions; acres and acres of land were abandoned but shepherds and peasants were able to count on selling their produce for the first time.

The Second World War seemed a time of regression, with a reversion to subsistence farming under a galling occupation and fighting in the maquis as of old. But the American Army killed the malarial mosquitoes and so prepared the way for tourist resorts and commercial agriculture. Even so, developments hung fire. At the time of this, my first journey to Corsica, the east coast was still a green desert; roads were rough, cars rare, hotels scarce and dowdy, plumbing was unknown outside the towns; public transport was crowded, battered and inconveniently timed; only two per cent of the land was cultivated, the prewar winter tourist season had not revived and summer visitors held off. The social code was correspondingly archaic; in fact I constantly had to defy it in order to get my work done at all. And so I had the incomparable good fortune of knowing the traditional Corsican culture in the final years of its existence, threatened and decadent, but still vibrating with spasms of elemental vitality; to glimpse the primaeval world of the bards and the *mazzeri*, and to experience the satisfactions (as well as the defects) of an archaic rural society.

Within the last decade that society has been disrupted, and its hereditary culture is going under; the fate, of course, of all small-scale archaic cultures in the present age. And now, surely, is the time for describing it, before it is completely forgotten. Its achievements, though unrecognised, were prophetic and nobly inspired: Corsica has been a sibyl, but speaking unheard. The statues of Filitosa, the village welfare states, Paoli's regime, are different expressions of a faith in man's dignity and freedom that has become the creed of the western world. One can hardly withhold one's interest from the people who lived by it and practised it, however imperfectly, throughout their history; one is too often asked to die for these ideals. The Corsicans were, after all, privileged: technological backwardness and a high murder rate were the price they paid for their immunity to feudal and capitalist oppression. Almost alone among Europeans they never lost sight of their original status as free men.

Whatever remains of the Corsican democratic spirit will now be absorbed in the political struggles of France and Europe; for contrary to all expectations the Corsicans are energetically joining the ranks of the modern bourgeoisie. Once again exterior influences have been decisive. Nearly all the land cleared and equipped on the east coast by government intervention has been taken up by refugees from North Africa. Some seventeen thousand (many of Corsican origin) found homes in the island, with mass arrivals after the liberation of Algeria in 1962. They came equipped with the capital and know-how for exploiting the opportunities Corsica offers: for vine and fruit growing, running restaurants and hotels.

The latter have multiplied; Corsica can hardly remain a preserve of primitive customs while Abyssinia advertises a tourist season. French and foreign capitalists have bought, built, transformed; the old Corsican idea that to sell land is dishonouring has collapsed before the fancy prices offered. During the past few years twentieth-century civilisation has been reaching the island's shores – one cannot say in waves – for its action has nothing in common with the rhythmic motions of water: it barges and grinds its way into a country by fits and starts with the bulldozer, the excavator and the electric drill. The immemorial jungle of the maquis goes down in a matter of days; hotels, villas, bungalows jump out of the ravaged earth; unbeautiful, but bringing welcome creature comforts and bewildering glimpses of an affluent society. True, the rate of development is still slow, much slower than on the devastated Costa Brava or Majorca; miles of coastline and nearly all the interior are still unimpaired. The yearly intake of tourists is estimated at around 420,000; small numbers by the standards of today. All the same this pleasure invasion has done more to change Corsica than all the conquering armies of the past.

Not that the Corsicans have taken to the new jobs offered with any alacrity: the hotel staffs are mainly continental, the building workers and agricultural labourers Italian, Spanish, Arab, Portuguese; as always there is little work in the island its people are prepared to do.[21] It is the spectacle of all this easy living that has brought down the traditional Corsican culture, already far gone in decay. Young Corsicans see no reason why they should toil in biblical conditions while their contemporaries from overseas revel on their doorsteps. They too want spending money, cars, comfort, new houses, new clothes; and they get what they want by making full use of what the French welfare state offers. They crowd the secondary schools, grind for exams, make careers on the mainland; most often in the teaching profession since the army has reduced its numbers, the girls as well as the boys. Especially the girls, now in full revolt against the traditional role of Corsican women: the submerged half of the population is surfacing. Meanwhile their parents sell their flocks, their land, and set up businesses in the towns.

Hardly anyone, so far, is rich by standards other than Corsican; payments for flats and cars weigh heavy; small businesses are threatened; ex-peasants find themselves in debt for the first time in their lives and some are on the edge of ruin. But for all these people a choice has been made, a way of life adopted, regardless of its disadvantages; and this means that the ancestral code has been rejected wholesale. Those who blamed the government for Corsica's troubles made an accurate diagnosis; a rise in living standards, slight in absolute terms but dramatic for Corsica, has eliminated the proverbial faults of the Corsicans, together with some of their proverbial virtues. The new bourgeoisie looks back on the vendetta as a benighted barbarity; murder today usually has less to do with honour than *pastis* which everyone can now afford in plenty, a drink that sends men mad. Wives rejoice in television as a means of keeping their husbands out of the bars; but its introduction has coincided with other innovations from overseas: theft, burglary with violence, teenage gangs in the towns. Accepting the new culture often seems like exchanging one set of afflictions for another.

Yet few people under sixty regret the passing of the old order. If some elderly peasants lament the falling off of the traditional heroic virtues – stoicism, abstemiousness, disinterested generosity – the rest are proud that the Corsicans have adapted themselves so readily to the modern world. Families, they point out, that grew up sleeping three in a bed, eight in a room, are now spread over smartly furnished houses; girls who carried water barefoot as children are holding their own in the professions. And here, really, there is room for congratulation. The Corsican career girls have acceded to their status without any of the neuroses that beset Englishwomen of the 'twenties; they are nearly all married, the mothers of several well-behaved children, accomplished flat-keepers and impeccably groomed. If Corsica once again prefigures the future it is surely in these amazingly serene and efficient young women doctors, lawyers and university professors. As for juvenile delinquency, this, the Corsicans reasonably contend, is the problem of every modern country, something to be solved; modern civilisation is bound to have snags; it is only just starting, it will improve. More than any people I know the Corsicans are acutely aware that one epoch has ended, another begun.

The process is almost unanimously felt as a liberation: from manual labour, physical hardship, isolation, old houses, from old servitudes and fears. Tales of the spirits and the *mazzeri* are dismissed, of course, as benighted superstition. Catholicism is still the framework of existence for the great majority, but one may wonder for how long; in the churches one sees mainly old people. The religious festivals are celebrated with more decorum, but less conviction: public gambling has been prohibited; the processions, now swollen by crowds of agnostic tourists, journalists and television reporters, shuffle between parked cars. Family solidarity is the traditional trait that has best resisted this clean sweep of the past, with the result that the aged are still tenderly cared for and elections still fought with unscrupulous acrimony; no less than thirty-six local elections were invalidated in 1966 for flagrant irregularities. The country that set the world an unheeded example in representative democracy has become one where democratic procedure is notoriously corrupt.

Feminine morals are now aligned on those of continental France, to the satisfaction, most often, of girls, and the horror, sometimes, of their parents; the liberties of the pill era cause more nervous breakdowns among outraged fathers than their intrepid daughters. Hospitality is waning: one cannot keep open house in a two-roomed flat in a town. And that is where more and more Corsicans choose to live (if they happen to stay in the island); the population is gathering on the coasts, stacked in the apartment blocks that ring the towns in expanding zones. Bastia and Ajaccio have now sucked in about half the island's inhabitants.

The interior contains mainly old people; those who cannot and will not leave, whose survival is bound to their crumbling villages, their awkward stone houses, their hams and chestnut flour, their tiny, prized gardens, their domestic animals, the evenings by the smoking fires. They include types of human beings now superseded: thundering old soldiers, the First World War veterans; patriarchs of dispersed families; the guides and friends of the bandits; bards, poets, *signadori* and *mazzeri*; hermits, the transhumant shepherds, eccentric addicted sportsmen; the black-robed women who improvised the *voceri*; people who have fulfilled their now obsolete functions with so total a conviction as to be disqualified for the modern world. While they live the interior will remain much as I first saw it, and as it still appears.

But one can imagine Corsica twenty years from now: on the coasts the spreading resorts and residential towns, joining up where the lie of the land allows; civilisation eating inland, up the slopes, the river valleys, where

286

properties are already changing hands at inflated prices. The mountains, then, may be almost empty; for mountains are what resist civilisation best. But not, perhaps, for very long. 'Just wait,' an enthusiastic young agricultural official said to me. 'The great cities are exploding; people can't stand the life there, the anonymity, the overcrowding, the inhuman rush and noise. The refugees from the towns will come streaming back to the land; just wait and see! One can cultivate even the terraces today without too much labour with the new small modern machines.' When the world's population has doubled, he assured me, all Corsica will be inhabited, farmed, exploited, right up to the lost prairies of the Lac de Nino.

No vision could have been further from my mind as I sat in the *micheline* swaying and jerking through the mountains still clothed in their primal forests, so little changed since they had come into being and seeming unlikely to change ever. The landscape was phantasmal behind the rain curtains; only the boughs of the laricio pines could be clearly distinguished, tossing within arm's length of the train's windows. I had thought of spending the night at Vizzavona, where a hotel dating back to the 'nineties once welcomed leisured English winter visitors with log fires and ballroom dancing and a skating rink in a forest clearing. But the raging storm, which almost obscured the old gabled buildings, was enough to deter me. Much later I came to know the forest in its frozen splendour of winter, when the snow, encrusted on the pine needles, turns every tree into a panache of spangled white ostrich plumes, and in midsummer too, when one walks through beech glades carpeted with pink cyclamen to bathe in icy green rock pools under the cascades.

Now we plunged into a tunnel under the pass, a couple of miles long, and emerged to see only the faintest sunset glow beneath the stacked clouds at the mouth of the valley of the Gravona. The valley seemed uninhabited, with stupendous dark mountain heights materialising here and there between drifting cathedrals of mist; but at Bocognano, the village of the Bellacoscia bandits, several urban-looking families were waiting for the train. Stations were rare as we jolted seawards; nothing at all was to be seen during the last lap of the journey except a girl with Nefertiti's profile standing at the door of a hut with a hurricane lamp in her hand. The lights of Ajaccio were blurred by the unremitting rain.

But the next morning, when I woke up in Martin Baretti's hotel, brilliant sunlight was streaking through the shutters on to the ochre ceiling, and the garden flowers were already shining dry. The outlines of the mountains across the bay were sharper than I had ever seen them; the whole scene might have been carved in sapphire, the mountains being only a little greyer, the sea a little darker, than the sky. This, Comte Peraldi told me, was the beginning of the luminous autumn weather, the season of blue light and hard silhouettes, that would last, between storms, with luck, till Christmas. Some of the storms would bring snow, and then the mountains would be crowned and streaked with white, glittering by sunlight and by moonlight, glowing pink at sunrise and sunset. 'Get away from here before you're completely bewitched and enslaved,' he said to me, 'but I hope and trust that you already are.' We were sitting in the fishermen's café at the hushed midday hour; the town, then little more than a village, was flooded with the scent of reviving vegetation blown in from across the bay.

'You've seen nothing,' Martin Baretti told me, as I ate my last meal in the hotel. And he spoke to me of the autumn maquis, when the arbutus bushes bear flowers at the same time as their fruit, turning as they ripen from lemon to deep crimson, and of the red and gold tints of the beeches, the chestnuts, the vines, and of the blue myrtle berries, and the holly of Vizzavona: 'You've never seen berries so red and clustered outside a Christmas card.' Soon, he told me, it would be the season to go mushroom picking, and then would come the time for gathering the chestnuts and making the chestnut flour, and killing the pigs, and making the sausages and hams. 'You've eaten nothing either,' he said, 'all our best food belongs to winter.'

Yet the winter was short, he told me, and so mild that one often thought oneself to be in spring. With the autumn rains the flowers would bloom again, the roses and geraniums in the gardens, and in the new year the mimosa would splash the villages with gold and the oranges hang so heavy on the trees that one had to prop their boughs with forked staves. And in February came the 'white spring', sung by the Corsican nature poet, Diane de Cuttoli,[20] when the almond blossom and the white heath simultaneously appear, and after that the blossom of the cherry, the peach, the plum, while asphodels and golden broom light the maquis, mile on mile, and then, finally, the climax of May, when all the cistus plants, all over the island, break into white and yellow and lilac flowers until they fade under the steady blaze of June.

I did not sorrow, as I listened to him talking, that I should leave without tasting the first fruits of winter, or seeing the pageant of the seasons. When I went aboad the ship that night under the bright stars I felt confident and serene; for I already knew, by one of those decisions taken below consciousness, so as to seem like a judgement passed, an order received, that Corsica would be my lot.

HISTORICAL SUMMARY

CORSICAN records are written in Italian until the French annexation in 1769, and afterwards, increasingly, in French. Throughout this work I have given the names of people who became adult after 1769 in the French forms, and those of people who were adult before the annexation in the Italian. Since the spelling of the latter is variable in contemporary documents, I have used the forms that appear most frequently. The history of Corsica, especially in the Middle Ages, is still imperfectly known. I have taken as my guides the outstanding scholars Xavier Poli, Colonna de Cesari Rocca and Abbé Letteron when speaking of periods that have not been the subject of specialised, more recent studies.

While Italian was the official and written language until the French annexation, the people also spoke the Corsican dialect, which is still used by the majority, alongside French. Supposedly evolved from Latin during the Middle Ages, the dialect presents various deviations from Italian; the substitution of u for o is very frequent, and will be observed in the words quoted from the dialect here and there in this book. Since the end of the last century literary works have been published in the dialect, and its structure is at present a subject of serious study.

GRAECO-ROMAN PERIOD *c.* 560 B.C.–*c.* A.D. 430

Greeks and Carthaginians

c. 560 B.C. Greeks from Phocaea (Asia Minor) founded a colony at Alalia (Aléria). In the naval battle of Alalia, *c.* 535, they held their own against a combined Carthaginian–Etruscan fleet. Carthaginians occupied the city 278–259.

Romans

259 B.C., the Romans conquered Aléria and Corsica, but the interior was not pacified till 162 B.C. 93 B.C., Marius built Mariana; 81 B.C., Sulla rebuilt Aléria. Christianity took root in Aléria from *c.* 200; from the 4 c. the Church was very active at Mariana. The two cities were the seats of bishoprics; the bishoprics of Nebbio, Sagone and Ajaccio were founded either in late Roman times or soon afterwards.

EARLY MIDDLE AGES *c.* 430–1077

Vandals attacked the coasts from *c.* 430, mastered Corsica by 460, were defeated by Belisarius, 533.

Byzantine Domination

From 533 Corsica was incorporated in the Byzantine Empire. This domination was interrupted, 549–53, by an Ostrogothic invasion. Pope Gregory the Great, 590–604, endeavoured to check Byzantine exploitation, encouraged the evangelisation of the interior and supposedly created the bishopric of Accia in the north-central mountains.

Lombards attacked from *c.* 581. By 725 Corsica was annexed to the Lombard kingdom of Italy.

The Papacy

756, Pippin the Short promised to donate Corsica, when liberated, to the Papacy. The donation was confirmed 774 by Charlemagne, during whose reign Corsica was freed. The Pope was thenceforth titular sovereign of the island.

Saracens raided the coasts from 712 and occupied parts of the island from 810. A temporary reconquest was achieved after 825 when Count Bonifacio II of Lucca was appointed 'defender of Corsica' by Louis the Debonair and Lothair. But the Saracens returned and were not expelled till the early 11 c. The Saracen king of Valencia controlled ports, probably in the south, as late as 1150.

Seigneurs and Popular Regime

With the retreat of the Saracens a unified government was apparently established, *c.* 1000, under a Count of Corsica. It collapsed in the 11 c. when power fell into the hands of local nobles. Certain communities administered themselves according to a 'popular regime' with elected chieftains, who often succeeded in making their authority hereditary.

Pisan Protectorate 1077–c. 1284

1076, Pope Gregory VII sent Landolfe, Bishop of Pisa, to reassert his authority over the bishops and nobles of Corsica. 1091, Pope Urban V gave Corsica in fief to Daibertus, Bishop (later Archbishop) of Pisa. The Pisans rebuilt the cathedrals on or near the sites of the Roman coastal cities and hundreds of churches in the interior. The units of ecclesiastical administration were the *pievi* (the word derives from the Latin *plebs*); each had a church, *plebania*, built on a site roughly equidistant from the various communities in the *pieve*.

Pisa Versus Genoa

Genoa disputed Pisa's possession of Corsica. 1133, the Pope divided the control of the bishoprics between the rival republics, three to each. Fighting between them continued: the Genoese took Bonifacio, 1187, Calvi, 1278, and decisively defeated Pisa, 1284, in the naval battle of Meloria.

Sinucello della Rocca, profiting by the discord between the rival republics, made himself master of Corsica, promulgated a primitive constitution at a national assembly at Mariana, 1264, was captured by the Genoese after the defeat of Pisa and died in prison *c.* 1306.

The Franciscans founded monasteries from 1236.

GENOA AND ARAGON 1297–1453

1297, Pope Bonifacio VIII, to replace the domination of Pisa, invested the kings of Aragon with the sovereignty of Corsica. Aragonese attacks, 1330, 1335, were repulsed by Genoa. An attempted Genoese military occupation of Corsica, 1347, was prevented by the Black Death. Meanwhile Corsica was controlled by warring seigneurs.

Anti-Seigneurial Revolution 1358–9

Sambocuccio d'Alando, elected leader of the people, led a revolt against the seigneurs. At this same period the *Giovannali*, members of a heresy in the Franciscan Third Order, gained many converts to their doctrines of 'absolute poverty' and community of possessions. They were liquidated in a crusade organised by Pope Urban V, *c.* 1362. Meanwhile Sambocuccio defeated the seigneurs in the north and east and solicited Genoese protection. The Commune of Corsica was incorporated in the Commune of Genoa; the first Genoese Governor arrived 1359. Genoese rule was however only operative in parts of the north and east, known as the *terra del comune*: the Cinarchesi seigneurs remained in control of the south and west, supporting Aragonese claims.

Pro-Aragonese Rebellions

Arrigo della Rocca, supported by Aragon, made war on Genoa 1372–1401, at times controlling the island.

Bastia was founded by the Genoese, 1380, after Arrigo had defeated them at Aléria.

Vincentello d'Istria, Arrigo's nephew, appointed Lieutenant in Corsica by King Pedro of Aragon, 1404, opposed Genoa with success. King Alfonso V of Aragon landed in Corsica, 1420.

Bonifacio, the last stronghold faithful to Genoa, successfully resisted the Aragonese in a historic siege, August 1420 to January 1421. Alfonso then abandoned Corsica; Vincentello continued to control most of the island until he was captured and executed by the Genoese, 1434.

THE OFFICE OF ST GEORGE

After a period of anarchy and confusion Genoa assigned Corsica, 1453, to the Office or Bank of St George, a powerful corporation with its own army. The Office ruled Corsica with military rigour, built watchtowers on the coasts, rebuilt the fortresses and founded the existing town of Ajaccio, 1492. From 1453, by an undertaking given to the Office by Pope Nicholas V, the bishops of Corsican dioceses were Genoese citizens.

Rebellions of the Cinarchesi

The rule of the Office was opposed in a succession of rebellions led by the Cinarchesi seigneurs, who thereby ruined themselves. Rinuccio della Rocca, the last Cinarchesi warlord, fought the Office from 1502 till his assassination, 1511.

FRENCH INTERVENTION AND THE REBELLION OF SAMPIERO CORSO 1553–69

1553, Henri II of France, at war with the Emperor Charles V, invaded Corsica with the aid of a Turkish fleet and Sampiero Corso, a celebrated Corsican mercenary then colonel in the French Army. The whole island was conquered except Calvi and Bastia and was successfully administered by France from 1557 until 1559, when it was returned to Genoa by the Treaty of Cateau-Cambrésis.

Sampiero Corso, secretly assisted by Catherine de' Medici, raised a rebellion against Genoa, 1564. In the ensuing savage war he controlled most of the island until he was assassinated, 1567. His son, Alfonso, continued resistance till 1569.

This period of war was followed by plagues, famines and increasingly frequent attacks by Barbary pirates.

RULE OF THE GENOESE REPUBLIC 1562–1729

From 1562 Corsica was directly ruled by the Genoese Republic. The system was despotic and excluded Corsicans from the central government, but left them in control of local administration. The Genoese encouraged agriculture, and so favoured the evolution of a new class of rural notables. But their colonial trade monopolies and the cupidity and corruption of their officials gave rise to bitter grievances. The vendetta increased and the population declined.

NATIONAL REBELLION AND AUTONOMY 1729–69

1729, rebellion broke out near Corte and rapidly spread over the island. The Genoese were confined to their coastal towns.

First National Constitution
January 1735, national independence was declared at a national assembly at Corte
and a constitution adopted. Andrea Ceccaldi, Luigi Giafferi and Giacinto Paoli
were elected Primates of the Nation.

Imperial Intervention
Genoa appealed to the Emperor Charles VI, who sent troops to the island. The
rebels submitted, 1732, and a settlement was negotiated between Genoese and
Corsicans. But the rebellion was renewed soon afterwards.

Theodor Von Neuhof
March 1736, Theodor von Neuhof, an international adventurer, landed at Aléria
with money and supplies. Crowned constitutional monarch in April, he left the
island in November.

French Interventions
In response to Genoese appeals the French, who already planned to annex Corsica,
sent troops, 1738, under the Comte de Boisseux. His attempt to impose a settlement roused the hostility of the Corsicans who defeated a detachment of his troops.
He was replaced by the Marquis de Maillebois who decisively defeated the rebels,
1739. About 1000 went into exile, including Giacinto Paoli, who retired to Naples
taking with him his younger son, Pasquale. The Royal Corse, a regiment for
Corsicans, was created in France. French troops withdrew from the island, 1741.

British and Sardinian Interventions
Britain and Sardinia intervened on behalf of the Corsicans during the War of the
Austrian Succession with a view to partitioning the island. 1743, Theodor von
Neuhof appeared off Ile-Rousse on a British warship but was ignored by the
patriots. 1745, British warships bombarded Bastia, supported on land by the
troops of Count Domenico Rivarola, appointed Corsican liberator by the King of
Sardinia. Bastia surrendered; but Gaffori and Matra, recently elected leaders of
the patriots, came to blows with Rivarola's troops and both armies evacuated
the town. 1748, Bastia was again bombarded by the British navy, supported by
Austro-Sardinian troops and Corsican patriots. The arrival of French forces in May
under the Marquis de Cursay ended the siege; allied forces withdrew after the
Treaty of Aix-la-Chapelle in October. De Cursay administered Corsica with
success until he was removed in disgrace, 1752, a victim of Genoese intrigue.
French troops evacuated the island towards the end of the year.

Government of the Rebel Territory
Constitutional experiments were resumed in the rebel territory after the French
withdrawal in 1741. One or several Generals were chosen to govern with the aid of
magistratures and councils. The ruling power in Corsica was however not these
shortlived systems of government but the national assemblies that created them
and increasingly assumed the role of a national parliament.

Constitution of Gian'Pietro Gaffori
October 1752, a constitution was adopted designed to take effect when French
troops evacuated the island. General Gaffori, head of state, was assassinated 1753.
He was succeeded by a regency of four members who were unable to agree on
policy. 1754, Pasquale Paoli was invited to return to lead the rebellion.

Generalship of Pasquale Paoli
15 July 1755, Paoli was elected General of the Nation. His enlightened constitution was adopted at a national assembly 16–18 November 1755 and modified at
intervals during the ensuing years. Corte became the capital of the rebel state, and
the seat of a university from 1765. Paoli crushed revolts led by rivals: the Matra

(backed by Genoa), 1755–63; Colonna da Bozzi, 1757. He formed a small navy that sufficed to break the Genoese blockade and ensure the conquest of Capraja, 1767, drove the Genoese from Cap Corse but failed in attempts to take the coastal towns. He founded the first Corsican printing presses, 1758; the first operative mint, 1761; a gazette, 1764, opened mines, started an arms factory and promoted the cultivation of potatoes. In 1760 he persuaded Pope Clement XIII to send him an Apostolic Visitor who stayed in the rebel territory till 1764. Thanks to his severe and impartial administration of justice the vendetta declined.

Struggle with France. By the first Traité de Compiègne, August 1756, France, solicited by Genoa, sent troops to garrison Calvi, Ajaccio, Saint-Florent; they were withdrawn 1759. By the second Traité de Compiègne, August 1764, France guaranteed to occupy the same towns, with Bastia and Algajola, for four years. By the Traité de Versailles, 15 May 1768, Genoa ceded the sovereignty of Corsica to France. French troops were landed in large numbers in August; the Corsicans opposed the French army till their defeat at Ponte-Nuovo, 8 May 1769. Paoli retired to England.

FRENCH MONARCHY 1769–89

Resistance continued in the mountains for several years after the annexation in spite of rigorous repression. 1774, the shepherds of the Niolo rebelled and were severely punished. The year 1776 marked the beginning of a series of amnesties. Paoli, in exile in England, refused the pardon offered to him.

Corsica was made a *pays d'Etats*, that is to say it had an assembly of Estates composed of three orders: clergy, nobility and commoners. Each order was represented by twenty-three deputies, chosen according to a system of indirect election which in certain regions could be dominated by the nobility. The order of the nobility had to be created. At least seventy-seven families were recognised as noble, including the Bonaparte. The Estates met from 1770 to 1781 about every two years, and once again, for the last time, in 1785. The assembly had only advisory powers; every decision depended on the Governor (the military Commander-in-Chief) and the Intendant. Local administration was left in Corsican hands.

Taxation was low and equitable; no exemptions were accorded to the nobility or clergy. Well-intentioned schemes for promoting agriculture, fishing, industries, mining and hygiene were largely ineffective; but roads were built from Bastia to Saint-Florent and Corte and wheeled traffic appeared in Corsica for the first time. From 1775 a small number of scholarships were offered in French mainland schools. The six in military academies were reserved to the sons of nobles; Napoleon Bonaparte was a successful candidate.

FRENCH REVOLUTION 1789–94

The majority of Corsicans welcomed the Revolution, which for them represented liberation from an oppressive regime, not a class struggle (the Corsican nobility was insufficiently privileged to excite hostility). From August 1789 riots occurred all over the island. In November the Governor was forced to accept the formation of a National Guard in Bastia.

30 November 1789, a petition from the National Guard of Bastia, supported by the Corsican deputies to the Constituent Assembly, prompted the Assembly to vote that Corsica should be fully and permanently integrated into the French nation. The ban on political exiles was repealed.

17 July 1790, Paoli landed in triumph at Bastia. At the Congress of Orezza, September 1790, he was elected Commander-in-Chief of the Corsican National Guards.

He was later chosen President of the *Conseil Général* of the *département*. His neglect of the Bonaparte brothers sowed the seeds of a dangerous opposition.

Bastia had become the seat of the sole Corsican bishopric, in accordance with
the legislation of the Constituent Assembly, which reduced the French bishoprics,
to one per *département*. After the deposition of the reigning bishop, who refused to
take the oath of the Civil Constitution of the Clergy, a religious riot broke out in
Bastia, June 1791. It was firmly crushed by Paoli, who marched 6000 National
Guards into the town. The seat of the bishopric was moved to Ajaccio, an arrangement confirmed in 1801 after the Concordat.

February 1793, an expedition for the conquest of Sardinia, ordered by the Convention, in which Corsican Volunteers took part, with Napoleon as one of their
officers, failed. Paoli, suspected of pro-British sympathies, became the scapegoat.
Three commissioners, members of the Convention, were sent to Corsica to investi-
gate his conduct, arriving 5 April.

2 April, Paoli, with Pozzo di Borgo, was indicted by the Convention following an
irresponsible denunciation by Lucien Bonaparte in Toulon. The commissioners,
following instructions, ordered their arrest, 17 April. The order was ignored; the
population of the interior rallied to Paoli at Corte.

27–9 May, a national assembly at Corte condemned the French government and
proclaimed Paoli Father of the Nation. His partisans entered Ajaccio and looted
the Bonaparte home. Napoleon, having failed to capture Ajaccio by sea with the
commissioners, rescued his family, and sailed with them to Toulon, 11 June.

17 July, Paoli and Pozzo di Borgo were outlawed by the French Government. In
the course of the summer they appealed, secretly, for British protection. The
Paolist militia confined French forces to Calvi, Bastia and Saint-Florent.

ANGLO-CORSICAN KINGDOM 1794–6

January 1794, Sir Gilbert Elliot landed in Corsica with two military advisors, met
Paoli and discussed a constitution. British forces besieged and captured Saint-
Florent (February), Bastia (April–May), Calvi (June–August). Nelson, who
distinguished himself in the two latter operations, lost an eye at the siege of Calvi.

1 May, Paoli proclaimed the impending union with Britain.

10–22 June, the Anglo-Corsican kingdom was proclaimed at a national assembly
at Corte and a constitution adopted.

Paoli remained at the head of a provisional government till 1 October 1794, when
Sir Gilbert, to Paoli's mortification, was appointed Viceroy. In February 1795 Sir
Gilbert obliged the first Parliament to cancel its election of Paoli as President of
the chamber (to which he had refused election). Riots broke out during the
summer of 1795 that led to Paoli's re-exile to England in October. In April 1796
riots provoked by French Republican agents occurred in the interior.

29 September 1796, Sir Gilbert received orders to evacuate Corsica. A detachment
of the Army of Italy landed unopposed, 15 October.

ASCENDANCY OF NAPOLEON 1796–1815

December 1796, on Napoleon's advice Corsica was divided into two *départements*
with a view to weakening possible rebellion. Three commissioners, among them
Miot de Melito, were sent to reorganise the administration. After the *coup d'état* of
Fructidor, September 1797, the Civil Constitution of the Clergy was enforced with
renewed severity.

294

1798, the *Révolte de la Crocetta*, inspired by the clergy, broke out in the north of the island and was repressed severely.

1–7 October 1799, Napoleon stayed in Ajaccio on his way back from Egypt and was welcomed by his supporters.

December 1799, a coalition of Royalist, Paolist and pro-British Corsican exiles in Tuscany organised a pro-Russian rebellion in the Fiumorbo which spread to the Sartenais and the north before it was crushed.

1801–2, Miot de Melito, on a second mission to Corsica, suspended the constitution by order of Napoleon, executed rebels and implemented tax concessions known as the *Arrêtés Miot*.

1801–11, General Morand, military Governor, exercised a rule of terror. He was replaced by Berthier, who was almost as unpopular.

1811, the *Décret Imperial* granted Corsica further tax concessions. The island was united in a single *département* with Ajaccio as administrative capital.

1814, Bastia appealed for British protection. British troops were landed, then withdrawn after Napoleon's abdication in April.

4 March 1815, agents of Napoleon landed secretly, raised an army and won the support of the population. The Royalist garrisons submitted; Arrighi de Casanova, Duke of Padua, governed Corsica from April 1815 till Waterloo.

RESTORATION TO THE PRESENT DAY

From 1815 the Corsicans remained loyal subjects of France and increasingly benefited by French citizenship. But conditions improved very gradually. Development schemes were handicapped by changes of regime and the rival claims of the French colonies. Emigration increased through the century, particularly from 1850. The population none the less continued to rise till 1891, after which it rapidly declined. Roads were progressively built, and schools, following the compulsory education act of 1882. The railway was begun in 1887. On the other hand encouragement of agriculture was insufficient to alter traditional methods. Attempts to exploit mines, from 1840, all failed; foundries for working iron imported from Elba were established 1830–60, prospered for a few years but had all closed by 1885. Malaria was endemic on the coasts.

The vendetta declined, but slowly. It gave inspiration to Prosper Mérimée and other visiting writers. From *c.* 1860 British tourists discovered the island.

1908–9, Clemenceau, Minister of the Interior, proposed a long-term programme of public works. Its full execution was prevented by the First World War.

In the First World War Corsica is reported to have lost 20,000 men or more. Bandits terrorised the island after the war until they were liquidated in a police operation from November 1931.

In the Second World War an enemy occupation of *c.* 80,000 Italians and 8000 Germans (for *c.* 180,000 inhabitants) was opposed by a local Resistance aided, from 1942, by Allied arms. The Italians surrendered, 8 September 1943. Fighting between Germans and patriots (reinforced by regular troops from 20 September) ended with the liberation of Bastia, 4 October 1943, and of Corsica as a whole, the first French *département* to be freed.

U.S. troops stationed in Corsica from 1943 cleared the east coast of malarial mosquitoes; the continued use of insecticides has eliminated malaria everywhere in the island.

295

Since 1957 economic development has been accelerated by the Government-sponsored organisations *SOMIVAC* (*Société pour la mise en valeur agricole de la Corse*) and *SETCO* (*Société pour l'équipement touristique de la Corse*). Some 17,000 French refugees from North Africa who have settled in the island (the majority since 1962) have given an added stimulus to insular economy. Agriculture is now flourishing on the east coast and in some other regions. Hotels and holiday villages are being built continuously to accommodate increasing numbers of tourists. Corsica now has 300 hotels, six in the four star and thirty in the three star categories, with accommodation for about 14,000 visitors, besides numerous holiday villages and camping sites offering accommodation for about 21,000 more. The insular standard of living is barely below that of mainland France; cars are actually more numerous in Corsica, in proportion to the population, than in France as a whole.

To preserve Corsica's natural beauty and wild-life a *Parc Naturel Régional* has been created, covering 150,000 *hectares* of almost unspoilt scenery, including nearly all the central mountainous area and some fifty miles of coastline.

NOTE ON POPULATION

The results of recent censuses being regarded as misleading, population statistics have become a subject of specialised research. At present the population is estimated at *c.* 200,000, with more than 40,000 in each of the main towns, Ajaccio and Bastia. This total is above the average estimated population before the 19 c. Giustiniani, writing *c.* 1531, reported *c.* 150,000; a census made by Maillebois, 1741, gave the figure 120,000. The population rose during Paoli's regime, though the clergy's estimate of an increase of 30,000 between 1753 and 1763 was certainly exaggerated. The Plan Terrier (1770–94) records a total of 150,000. During the 19 c. official statistics show a steady rise to 278,000 in 1886, the last census considered to be accurate. The peak was reached in 1891 with *c.* 280,000, after which the population declined; the lowest figure estimated since then is *c.* 150,000 for 1954.

NOTES

References to sources of which details are provided in the Selected Bibliography (p. 320) are given as SB, followed by section and subsection numbers. Other abbreviations are listed at the beginning of SB.

CHAPTER I: *The Imperial City*

1. The Genoese city was founded *c.* 1492 to replace an older city nearer the head of the bay which occupied a site inhabited at least since Roman times.
2. Napoleon Bonaparte, 'Lettres sur la Corse . . .' (see Masson and Biagi, SB IV, 3).
3. The Bonaparte, always short of ready money, supplied their table almost entirely from the produce of their country properties (see works cited SB IV, 3).
4. Concessions were made by the Arrêtés Miot, 1802, and the Décret Impérial, 1811 (see A. Gaudin; Neuwirth, SB IV, 5).

CHAPTER II: *The First Heroes*

1. See Leblanc; Carrington (SB IV, 8, D).
2. Statue-menhir known as Apricciani, see Mérimée, *Notes . . .* (SB IV, 8, A).
3. Although the Saracens are known to have occupied Crete 832–960, no vestige of a mosque of that period has been found. The invaders were 'tough adventurers merely intent on plunder', see R. W. Hutchinson, *Prehistoric Crete* (London, Penguin Books, 1962).
4. Pinello (SB III).

CHAPTER III: *Birth of a Myth*

1. Commandant Octobon, 'Statues-menhirs, stèles gravées. Dalles sculptées' (*Revue d'Anthropologie*, fasc. 10–12, 1931).
2. Described with bibliography by R. Grosjean in *EC*, no. 7/8, 1955 (see SB IV, 8, B).
3. Noted by L. Giraux in 1903; see Grosjean *op. cit.* A fine unsculptured menhir, *c.* 8 ft high, stands near by (see *ibid.*; Mortillet; Grosjean, *La Corse avant l'Histoire*, SB IV, 8, B).
4. Known as Santa-Maria; noted by Mortillet and others; see Grosjean, *EC*, no. 7/8, 1955.
5. See Mérimée, *Notes . . .* (SB IV, 8, A); Grosjean, *EC*, no. 7/8, 1955.
6. Known as Luzzipeo, from the name of the place where it was discovered by Comte Savelli de Guido and Chanoine Alberti. See Grosjean, *ibid.*
7. Filitosa IV, following numbering in Grosjean, *EC*, no. 7/8. See also Grosjean, *La Corse avant l'Histoire* and *Filitosa et son contexte archéologique* (SB IV, 8, B).
8. A large statue-menhir known as Le Paladin (commune Serra-di-Ferro) was described by Maestrati in *Le Petit Bastiais*, 1937. Mérimée (*op. cit.*) and Mortillet (*op. cit.*) reported a dolmen on the left bank of the Taravo, and near it a dozen menhirs of which several appeared to be anthropomorphic. Grosjean found the dolmen destroyed and only two menhirs left on the site, one of which is classed as a statue-menhir; see Grosjean, *EC*, no. 7/8; *Filitosa et son contexte. . .*; *La Corse avant l'Histoire.*
9. Filitosa V. See Grosjean, *EC*, no. 7/8, and *Filitosa et son contexte . . .* According to

Grosjean's recent hypothesis the engravings on the backs of the statue-menhirs may represent corselets worn in battle (see n. 46).

10. Filitosa IX, following numbering in Grosjean, *EC*, no. 12, 1956.

11. See Grosjean, *EC*, no. 7/8, 1955; no. 12, 1956; *La Corse avant l'Histoire*.

12. Filitosa VI; see Grosjean, *EC*, no. 12.

13. Tappa I, discovered in the neighbourhood. Two upper fragments of statue-menhirs were also moved to Filitosa from the sites where they were found; see Grosjean, *EC*, nos. 7/8, 12.

14. See S. von Cles-Reden, *The Realm of the Great Goddess* (SB IV, 8, B); V. Gordon Childe, *The Dawn of European Civilisation* (London, Routledge & Kegan Paul, 1957); Glyn Daniel, *The Megalith Builders of Western Europe* (London, Hutchinson, 1958).

15. Examination of human remains in megalithic tombs has however shown that Mediterranean peoples migrated to north-west Europe, particularly to Britain and Ireland; see Daniel, *op. cit.* and *The Idea of Prehistory* (London, Watts, 1962).

16. The beginning of megalithic building in western Europe has had to be backdated since 1959, when carbon-14 tests on material from megalithic tombs in Brittany gave surprisingly early dates *c.* 3000 B.C. (see Cles-Reden).

17. The word 'megalith' means large stone (from the Greek *megas*, great, and *lithos*, stone). The term 'megalithic' as applied to architecture describes the card-house technique of the tombs known as dolmens. But the megalith builders produced other types of sepulchres: rock-cut tombs, and dry-walled monuments, usually under cairns, roofed with corbel vaults and sometimes built of very large 'cyclopean' stones (see Daniel, *The Megalith Builders . . .*).

18. Even in western Europe the megalithic monuments may not invariably have derived from the same cultural source; Daniel (*ibid.*) concludes that the *doss/dyss* tombs of Denmark, megalithic in construction, which were used for individual burials, originated there independently, before the arrival of the megalithic seafarers.

19. The megalithic faith however penetrated deep into France; from the coast of Languedoc into the mountains and plateaux of Herault, Aveyron and Gard, and up the Seine to the Paris basin. It was also carried up the Bristol Channel to Wiltshire and the Cotswolds, and spread over the interior of Ireland (see Daniel, *ibid.*; Cles-Reden; Childe).

20. Spain has been described as the El Dorado of the eastern Mediterranean Bronze Age peoples; their discovery of silver, lead and copper near the south-east coast is marked by the prehistoric mining town, Los Millares, and its necropolis containing seventy-five chamber tombs under tumuli, some of the *tholos* type (see Cles-Reden). Dr J. Arnal believes that the megalith builders of Herault were searching for the copper and lead of Aveyron, Herault and Gard (Daniel, *op. cit.*). Tin may have been found in Cornwall, where megaliths are quite numerous. But though the tombs of Los Millares are full of copper implements, metal is rare or absent in the grave goods of many megalithic areas, including metal-producing Herault and Britain.

21. See Childe, *The Prehistory of European Society* (London, Penguin Books, 1958).

22. Cles-Reden traces the origin of megalithic concepts to the Natufian culture of Palestine, which dates from *c.* 10,000 to *c.* 6000 B.C., a view put forward by Childe in *The Dawn of European Civilisation*. The Natufians, who may have initiated agriculture, practised collective burial, a fertility cult and a cult of the dead; anthropological evidence suggests that they were 'the predecessors of the ancient Mediterranean race which later played a vital role in the civilisation of the Near East and the Aegean' (Cles-Reden, *op. cit.*). Menhirs and dolmens and other types of tombs found in European megalithic areas were erected in great numbers in Palestine from *c.* 3500 B.C., mostly in pastoral regions. Cles-Reden postulates a relation between the pastoral life and the cult of the dead which is applicable to Corsica: 'A nomadic or semi-nomadic pastoral people is in many ways predestined to an ancestor cult and veneration of the dead. This is the result of its social structure. To protect its flocks and herds and keep them together, it generally lives in big family groups; the consequence is a strong clan or family feeling, which can easily extend into the hereafter.' There are indications that the Palestinian menhirs represented deities or dead people; a carefully trimmed

7 ft high stone known as the Hagar el-Mansub, near the necropolis of El Mreirat, has a round top suggesting a human head. It has been interpreted as a phallic symbol, but according to Cles-Reden 'the impression it creates is much more that of a rudimentary human figure. Particular interest attaches to it in the light of recent discoveries of statue-menhirs in Corsica.' But she considers that the megalithic phenomenon had 'far too many roots for it to be possible to speak of a country of origin in the narrower sense of the word'. Egyptian influences are however excluded, for the practice of collective burial was foreign to Egypt, as it was to Sumer and the Anatolian plateau (Childe, *The Dawn of European Civilisation*; Cles-Reden; Daniel, *The Megalith Builders . . .*).

23. Worship of an archetypal goddess in western Asia dates back to Sumer. She was associated with the bull, symbolising the male fertilising force, and the snake, the animal that creeps out of the earth and also had a phallic significance; see Gertrude Rachel Levy, *The Gate of Horn* (London, Faber, 1948), and for the sacred serpent, Erich Neumann, *Origins and History of Consciousness* (London, Routledge & Kegan Paul, 1954). In Minoan art the goddess is shown with snakes and wild animals; stylised bulls' horns ('horns of consecration') and representations of bulls are numerous; the legends of the Minotaur seem to echo a bull cult; see Hutchinson, *Prehistoric Crete*, and J. R. Conrad, *The Horn and the Sword* (London, MacGibbon & Kee, 1959). The cult of the goddess, coming to the Mediterranean peoples from the Neolithic East, was superimposed on a very ancient veneration of a life-giving female principle, expressed, from Palaeolithic times, in small idols of fat women, and artistic tradition that in certain areas, such as Malta, was carried over into megalithic art. Representations of the goddess in megalithic France and Iberia, on the other hand, are highly stylised and emphasise the divinity's terrifying aspect. The snake motif appears in megalithic contexts in Malta and Brittany. Bulls' horns and bulls' heads are carved in rock-cut tombs in Sardinia, where the sacred bull seems to have been venerated along with the Mother Goddess, represented by stylised idols with protruding breasts and by breasts sculptured on conical stones (see Cles-Reden; Margaret Guido, *Sardinia*, London, Thames & Hudson, 1963).

24. Childe, *The Prehistory . . .*

25. Cles-Reden.

26. The role played by Aegean (Minoan and Mycenaean) navigators in introducing megalithic rites and building styles to western Europe has still to be determined, but they evidently had frequent contacts with megalithic areas of the Mediterranean in the second millennium B.C. Stuart Piggott, in 'The Tholos tomb in Iberia' (*Antiquity*, vol. xxvii, 1953) postulates that the magnificent chisel-cut Aegean *tholoi* were copied from the *tholoi* of southern Spain, and not vice versa. Spain seems to have operated as a centre of secondary cultural diffusion in the megalithic world. By *c.* 1500 B.C. western Mediterranean and Atlantic Europe were linked by trade relations, the migrations of populations and a common religious outlook expressed in similar styles of monuments (see Daniel; Cles-Reden).

27. Peretti (SB IV, 8, B). At Palaggiu (or Pagliaiu); the tomb is situated at the southern end of a group of some 100 aligned menhirs; it contained also a fragment of a copper dagger (see n. 44).

28. The most striking groups are south-west of Sartène, at Caouria and Palaggiu; but since numbers of cist tombs have been found in the south-east (see n. 32) it would be hazardous to assert that the megalith builders first settled on the west coast.

29. See Lanfranchi, 'La grotte sépulchrale . . .' (SB IV, 8, B).

30. See Grosjean, *La Corse avant l'Histoire*.

31. See Grosjean, *CH*, no. 9/10, 1963.

32. The dolmens are the best-known Corsican megalithic tombs; but many stone cists have also been discovered (a cist is a simple type of tomb exactly described by the word from which its name is derived, the Welsh *cistvaen*, meaning large stone box). They have been found singly or in groups, wholly or partly sunk into the ground, in the south-east (near Porto-Vecchio) and the south (near Figari) as well as in the south-western and north-western Corsican megalithic areas. A small pillar is often

placed close to a tomb. Grosjean postulates an upward and expanding evolution of Corsican megalithic building, by which the cists emerged above ground and were superseded by dolmens, and the small pillars were superseded by alignments of larger menhirs set at some distance from the dolmens (see *La Corse avant l'Histoire*). About 100 dolmens are known in Corsica. None measures much over *c.* 6 ft by 8 ft and 6 ft high (dolmen of Fontenaccia, Caouria, see Mortillet). They are almost all single rectangular chambers (chamber tombs).

33. The Corsican menhirs can be counted in hundreds, and these must represent only a fraction of the number that once existed. They appear singly, in pairs and in alignments; the largest groups are at Caouria and Palaggiu. The prevailing north–south direction of the alignments does not suggest a sun cult. But sun disc symbols (common in megalithic art) have been found here and there in prehistoric contexts (see Grosjean, *La Corse avant l'Histoire*; *EC*, no. 6, 1955).

34. See Grosjean, *La Corse avant l'Histoire*. In local legends the menhirs are always described as having originally been human beings (see Cles-Reden).

35. Another characteristic, though less prevalent type, is trapezoidal, wider at the top than at the base. The steles near the cist tombs measure only 3–6 ft high; the menhirs vary from *c.* 8–13 ft high and 1 ft 6 in. to 3 ft wide; they are seldom more than 16 in. thick (Grosjean, *Filitosa et son contexte . . .*; *La Corse avant l'Histoire*).

36. See Mérimée; Mortillet.

37. Cauria II and IV, according to Grosjean's numbering in *La Corse avant l'Histoire*. For their clothes see n. 46. A similar juxtaposition of menhirs and statue-menhirs is known in the Taravo valley (see n. 8). Three statue-menhirs on which the human features are less evident than the engraved weapons have been recognised in the alignment of menhirs at Palaggiu (see *ibid.*).

38. Grosjean, 'Classification descriptive du Mégalithique Corse' (SB IV, 8, в).

39. At Filitosa the statue-menhirs appear outside the traditional megalithic context. Their disposition does not suggest that they were ever set up in alignments and there is no trace of a megalithic tomb. The same is true of the statue-menhirs known in the north, which are considered to be the most recent (see Grosjean, *La Corse avant l'Histoire*).

40. Archaeologists have agreed, since the discovery of the site, that the statue-menhirs are cult figures and represent individual human beings (see Grosjean, *Filitosa et son contexte . . .*; Cles-Reden).

41. See Octobon; Cles-Reden; J. Arnal and C. Hugues, 'Sur les statues-menhirs du Languedoc–Rouergue' (*Archivo de Prehistoria Levantina*, Valencia, Fedsa, 1963).

42. The Corsican sculptors (in contrast to those of mainland France) emphasised the head at the expense of the rest of the body. Heads are well over life-size: that of Filitosa IX is 18 in. long, that of Filitosa VI no less than 24 in. This was surely not accidental, but rather an expression of primitive humanistic concepts. Recognition of the head as the ruling member of the body is reflected in mythology (see Neumann, *Origins and History of Consciousness*), in traditional marriage customs (see E. O. James, *Marriage and Society*, London, Watts, 1951), and in ritual (see J. Pitt-Rivers, 'Honour and social status', in *Honour and Shame, the Values of Mediterranean Society*, ed. J. G. Peristiany, London, Weidenfeld & Nicolson, 1965). The head was regarded as sacred, the source of creative energy; the skull cult (for which archaeology gives evidence from very early times) is an expression of this idea. Belief in the supernatural powers of skulls survived in Corsica into the present century: in times of drought the members of a village would walk in procession with one or several skulls carried aloft on poles; the skulls were laid in a river bed and were thought to bring rain. The custom is well remembered at Cauro (*c.* fifteen miles from Ajaccio). According to Cles-Reden, the same custom is reported from Sardinia. The aggressive Corsican custom known as the *attacar* may derive from an ancient belief in the sacredness of the head of woman (see chap. V). The concept of the creative power in the head of man may be emphasised in the Corsican statue-menhirs by the rounded form on the backs of many of the heads, which has been variously interpreted as a page-boy hair-style, a helmet (see n. 46) or a phallic symbol. Phallic representations were not alien to megalithic

iconography: phallic idols appear in Malta and Sardinia (see Cles-Reden), a group of unambiguously phallic menhirs exists in the Sudan (see Octobon), and tapering menhirs in themselves are held to have phallic connotations.

43. See Grosjean, *EC*, no. 18, 1958; *REC*, no. 1, 1961; *CH*, no. 13/14, 1964; *Filitosa et son contexte* . . .; *La Corse avant l'Histoire*.

44. A fragment of a copper dagger different in type from the daggers shown on the statue-menhirs was excavated at Palaggiu in the same tomb as the bell beakers (Peretti, SB IV, 8, B).

45. See Grosjean, 'Les armes portées par les statues-menhirs de Corse' (SB IV, 8, B).

46. Aristotle (*Politics*,VII, ii, 6) may well be repeating an ancient tradition. Similar practices existed among the Turucks of southern Siberia and the Chinese (see Grosjean, *La Corse avant l'Histoire*; Cles-Reden). Examination of the armed statue-menhirs (which according to this theory were portraits of Torréen warriors) has led Grosjean to believe that these people were the Shardana, one of the 'people of the sea' who raided Egypt, in coalition, between *c.* 1190 and 1186 B.C. The Shardana have hitherto been identified with the Sardinians (see Geoffrey Bibby, *Four Thousand Years Ago*, London, Collins, 1962). A bas-relief in the Egyptian temple at Medinet-Habu, illustrating a naval attack *c.* 1190 B.C. by the allied Shardana and Philistines, shows the Shardana armed with weapons resembling those seen on certain Corsican statue-menhirs, and wearing spherical helmets adorned with curved horns and corselets with five grooves slanting obliquely downwards on either side of the centre of the body. Grosjean thinks that the rounded forms of the backs of the heads of certain statue-menhirs (formerly interpreted as phallic) represented the Shardana's helmets, that hitherto unexplained hollows, or cupmarks, on either side of the heads of several statue-menhirs were sockets for holding horns, and that the engravings on the backs of certain statue-menhirs, formerly regarded as stylised indications of spine and ribs, represented the Shardana's corselets. The shapes shown on the lower bodies of the statue-menhirs of Caouria are, in his opinion, Shardanese tunics (see *La Corse avant l'histoire*; F. de Lanfranchi opposes this theory in his forthcoming thesis, SB IV, 8, B).

47. Grosjean believes that the site was not previously fortified; see *Filitosa et son contexte* . . .; *La Corse avant l'Histoire*.

48. For an account of the excavation of this complex monument see Grosjean, *Filitosa et son contexte* . . .

49. See Atzeni (SB IV, 8, B).

50. Tests applied to the top layer of ash in the complex Torréen monument (see Grosjean, *Filitosa et son contexte* . . .; *La Corse avant l'histoire*).

51. The supposition seems to be borne out by an ancient tradition according to which northern Sardinia was populated by Corsicans who emigrated there after a war.

52. See Grosjean, *La Corse avant l'Histoire*.

53. One is a statue in granite, discovered by P. Lamotte near Tavera (in the valley of the Gravona, north-west of Ajaccio). It has the prominent ears characteristic of the northern statue-menhirs (including Apricciani), and a ridge below the neck which may represent collar bones or a necklace (see Lamotte, 'Une nouvelle statue-menhir . . .', SB IV, 8, B). Stone arrowheads and tools have been found near it, but no trace of a tomb. The other known as Nativu, was found in 1964 near Barbaggio (*c.* five miles north-east of Saint-Florent).The naturalistic intentions of the artist were facilitated by the use of local limestone (see Grosjean, *La Corse avant l'histoire*).

54. Known as Capo-Castinco I, following Grosjean's numbering in *EC*, no. 7/8, 1955. See also *La Corse avant l'Histoire*. Possible contacts with the Etruscans from the 8 c. B.C. should be taken into consideration; according to Servius Populonia, an early Etruscan port on the promontory facing Elba, was founded by Corsicans; anthropomorphic steles discovered in the earliest tombs there have a marked resemblance to the Corsican statue-menhirs (see Cles-Reden).

55. F. de Lanfranchi, *Le Peuplement du Bassin de l'Ortolo et du Rizzanese du Néolithique à l'Age du Fer*, to appear shortly.

56. The migrations of the Celts, who originated in east-central Europe, have been adequately traced by archaeological evidence; they reached the Mediterranean

towards 400 B.C. (see H. Hubert, *Les Celtes depuis l'epoque de la Tène et la civilisation Celtique*, 2 vols. Paris, Albin Michel, 1950), after the Phocaean Greeks had already made a settlement in Corsica. There is no evidence to show that they crossed to the island as a people or implanted their culture there, though individuals of Celtic origin may have reached Corsica in Graeco-Roman times. The population at that period was extremely mixed, especially on the coasts. Seneca, exiled in Corsica A.D. 41–9, makes some interesting ethnological observations in *De consolatione ad Helviam*, vii, 8. Corsica, he writes, had been settled by several races before the Romans; first by the Phocaean Greeks, then by the Spaniards, as could be judged by certain resemblances: the Corsican head-dress and footwear were the same as those of the Cantabrians, as were certain words in the Corsican language, which was also much adulterated by Greek and Ligurian. His remarks relative to the Spaniards command respect, seeing that he was himself of Spanish origin; one may postulate that Spanish merchants had settled on the coasts and that possibly the tradition of such voyages had existed since megalithic times. Seneca's references to the Ligurians may be based on fact, but chronologically misplaced. None of the Greek writers who mentions Corsica speaks of a Ligurian invasion, as might be expected if it took place after the foundation of the Greek colony (*c.* 560 B.C.) and not before, as seems more probable. But that Seneca could make such a mistake suggests that Greek and Ligurian implantations might have been made within a fairly short space of time. A Ligurian settlement of Corsica seems to be recalled in a legend, reported by Sallust (*Fragments*, xi, 8) and repeated by Rutilius Namatianus (*De reditu suo*) which relates that Corsica was discovered by a girl named Corsa who, herding cattle on the Ligurian shore, followed a bull, or several oxen, which swam out to sea and so led her to the island. Many place-names mentioned by classical historians in areas inhabited by the people known as Ligurians, including the area known as Liguria today, end in usco, asco, osco or isca (see Hubert). Such terminations appear in place-names in north-central and north-eastern Corsica: Asco, Popolasca, Venzolasco.

57. Gregory the Great writing to Petrus, Bishop of Aléria, 597, speaks of those who had reverted to the cult of idols and worshipped wood and stone (see 'La Corse dans la correspondance de St Grégoire le Grand', *BSSHNC*, 1881, 1882), 1882.

58. See Grosjean, *La Corse avant l'Histoire*.

59. At San Nicolao de Pième, in the Nebbio.

60. At Lozzi, in the Niolo; also at Eccica-Suarella (near Cauro), (information kindly supplied by P. Lamotte). The shepherds of Guincheto, in the Sartenais, until well into the 19 c. practised a yet more primitive method of burial by placing the corpses in rock shelters or caves which they then closed with stone slabs (see Cles-Reden).

61. See P. Lamotte, *EC*, no. 2, 1954; no. 10, 1956.

62. See chap. IV.

63. Diodorus Siculus (V, xiii, 1–14, ii) describes the Corsicans as pastoralists and food-gatherers with an unusual respect for justice. Since his material is considered to be largely derived from Ephorus of Cyme, 4 c. B.C., his description has the great interest of presenting a picture of the Corsicans at the very dawn of their history.

64. See chap. IX.

65. ADC, *Série F*, see chap. XV.

CHAPTER IV: *Night-hunters of Souls*

1. 'Mémoires historiques . . . 1774–1777' (SB III).

2. C. B. Jung, *Modern Man in Search of a Soul* (London, Kegan Paul, Trench, Trubner, 1933).

3. According to a widespread primitive belief reflected in Greek popular custom, a man's shadow represents his soul; midday, when his shadow is smallest, is therefore the hour when he is most vulnerable (see Sir James Frazer, *The Golden Bough*, abridged edn, New York, The Macmillan Co., 1942).

4. Also known as *squadra d'arozza*. *Arozza* has no known meaning in the Corsican dialect; but it seems more likely that Heroda is a corruption of *arozza* than vice versa, for Christian accretions are numerous in connection with Corsican traditional beliefs.

5. My evidence for the custom is from southern and western Corsica. The food and wine are not treated with reverence the following day: reaching a house early in the morning of All Souls' Day I was invited to eat the food that had been left out for the dead, pastry turnovers filled with leaf-beet. G. Faucheux reports purely defensive rites from the south: on the Eve of All Souls' Day (as on the eve of 1 August, see n. 17), fires are lit outside the doors, and metal cutting instruments, and salt, placed on doorsteps, to prevent the entry of the spirits of the dead (see Carrington and Lamotte, 'A propos des Mazzeri', *EC*, no. 17, 1958).

6. For Brittany see Anatole le Braz, *La légende de la Mort chez les Bretons Amoricains* (Paris, Champion, 1922); for Wales, Sir John Rhys, *Celtic Folklore, Welsh and Manx* (London, Frowde, 1901); for Scotland, J. G. Campbell, *Witchcraft and Second Sight in the Highlands and Islands of Scotland* ... (Glasgow, MacLehose, 1902); also W. Y. Evans Wentz, *The Fairy Faith in Celtic Countries* (Oxford University Press, 1911).

7. For these and other survivals of beliefs in connection with megalithic monuments see Gertrude Rachel Levy, *The Gate of Horn* (Rollright), and Cles-Reden (SB IV, 8, B , Brittany).

8. See Carrington and Lamotte, 'Les Mazzeri' (*EC*, no. 15/16, 1957) and supplementary information contributed by the ethnologist Claude Faucheux in Carrington and Lamotte, 'A propos des Mazzeri'.

9. It is believed, in the Sartenais, that one may share the vision of a seer by touching him, for preference by placing one's foot on his. The same belief is reported from Scotland (see J. G. Campbell), the Isle of Man (see Rhys), and Wales (see Rhys; Evans Wentz).

10. See S.-B. Casanova (SB IV, 2), vol. i. *Mazzeri* are not specifically mentioned among the numerous types of magicians condemned by the bishops (many of which are now extinct), but they may have been included among 'those who make a pact with the Devil, explicitly or implicitly' (Costituzione di Mgr Castagnola, 1615, *ibid.*). On the other hand their activities, being performed in a dream-state, without material manifestations, may have remained largely undetected by the bishops.

11. The gestures in these ceremonies are symbolic of contrition, purification and rebirth. I am indebted to Dr John Layard for an interpretation of the ceremony used at Sartène: the axe is symbolic of sacrifice; three is the number associated with transformation; the covering with the vestment illustrates the *mazzere*'s rebirth by entering the womb of Mother Church.

12. Such experiences can be regarded as varieties of the *participation mystique* described by L. Levy-Bruhl as characteristic of primitive societies in *Les Fonctions mentales dans les Sociétés Inférieures* (Paris, Alcan, 1910).

13. I am indebted for this valuable negative information to Dr Marcelle Bouteiller, specialist on European witchcraft.

14. Filippini (SB II) reports the practice in the Castagniccia in the 16 c. An almost identical technique of prophecy is remembered in the Scottish Highlands (J. G. Campbell), and is still employed in Greece, see Patrick Leigh Fermor, *Roumeli* (London, Murray, 1966).

15. As late as the 3 c. B.C. Timaeus wrote (no doubt with some exaggeration) that the Corsicans spent their time hunting wild animals 'without knowledge of any other occupation' (quoted by Polybius, XII, iii, 7).

16. It is I think significant that though ordinary people are thought to assume the shapes of various animals, the *mazzeri* are believed to transform themselves only into dogs: animals that hunt and are not hunted. The *mazzeri* of Chera, on the other hand, kill like dogs while retaining their human form.

17. See Jung, *op. cit.* Some African peoples believe that the only 'natural' deaths are killings in war, or murders; others that even these kinds of death are caused by magical powers in the killers. It is not clear, from the information so far collected, whether the *mazzeri* are considered responsible for homicides. The only practising

mazzere I have met spoke as though death in war were something alien to her function (see end of chapter). The *mazzeri* being themselves mortal, their own deaths had to be explained. In many districts where they practise, on the night of 31 July, the *mazzeri* of each village are thought to go out, armed, in a group, to meet those of a neighbouring village, usually on a mountain pass separating the territories of the two communities. There a dream battle takes place between the two groups; the *mazzeri* who are killed will die within a year. The village represented by the group in which most deaths occur will lose more of its members within the next twelve months than that represented by the victorious group of *mazzeri*. Faucheux reports that 1 August is observed in certain villages as an unofficial feast of the dead; see Carrington and Lamotte, 'A propos des Mazzeri'.

18. Dread of the Evil Eye, or 'the Eyes', apparently deriving from the Eye Goddess aspect of the Terrible Mother, is still alive in Corsica (see chap. V), as in Sardinia (see Cles-Reden who links the Evil Eye with the Eye Goddess) and other Mediterranean countries, including Muslim North Africa.

19. *The Golden Bough*.

20. The term *shaman* more properly applies to a category of people found in Siberian pastoral or fishing tribes who act as seers, healers and exorcisers of evil spirits. They are as often women as men, and like the *mazzeri* they are compelled to exercise their function, which is however wholly beneficial. A *shaman* habitually has an exterior soul, a *yekhuya*, which resides in a living animal; if the animal is killed the *shaman* dies. See W. Howells, *The Heathens* (New York, Doubleday, 1950).

21. W. Lloyd Warner, *A Black Civilisation: a social study of an Australian tribe* (rev. edn, New York, Harper, 1958).

CHAPTER V: *Aristocracy and Honour*

1. In traditional Corsican society shepherds were also in some degree agriculturalists (see chap. XIV) while sedentary peasants often owned livestock and would send one or two members of the family to make the transhumance. The distinction between shepherd and peasant was determined not so much by occupation as by the ownership of land; the shepherds owned little or none.

2. See G. della Grossa (SB II); A. Casanova (SB IV, 5; *EC*, no. 21, 1959).

3. Elliot, *Life and Letters* . . . (SB III).

4. The Cinarchesi apparently originated in the region now known as the Cinarca, to the north of Ajaccio. G. della Grossa (*op. cit.*) however relates that they were the descendants of Ugo della Colonna, a Roman nobleman who in the 9 c. liberated Corsica from the Saracens. Research has shown that Ugo della Colonna was a legendary figure (see Letteron's introduction to della Grossa); Cesari Rocca in *Histoire de la Corse* . . . (SB IV, 1) suggests that the Cinarchesi descended from magistrates, perhaps Corsicans, who established positions of hereditary authority during the Byzantine regime. A. Casanova (*EC*, no. 17, 1958) believes that the story of Ugo della Colonna is a romantic travesty of the historic deeds of Count Bonifacio II of Lucca (founder of Bonifacio), a nobleman of Bavarian origin charged by Louis the Debon air and Lothair, *c.* 825, to rid Corsica of the Saracens. The different branches of the Cinarchesi took their family names from those of the castles or territories they occupied: della Rocca, Istria, Ornano, etc. From the 16 c. they added Colonna to their names. In 1777 Octave Colonna d'Istria was granted the title of count by Louis XVI; his descendant is a doctor now practising in Ajaccio.

5. Quoted by Louis Mumford, *The City in History* (London, Secker & Warburg, 1961).

6. Unrevised version of della Grossa in *Chroniche di Giovanni della Grossa e di Pier'Antonio Montegiani* (SB II).

7. In the megalith country of the south-west until quite recently certain *mazzeri*, known as *lanceri* (who were usually men) were relied on to heal and to control the weather. In the south-east, near Chera, I have heard of men who, some thirty years ago, were credited with powers to raise or quell rain and storms. Apparently the functions of *mazzere*, healer and weather-controller were often interchangeable. The *lanceri*

believed that they had counterparts in northern Sardinia. I was told of a *lanceri* who constantly met a fellow night-hunter unknown to him in real life; years later he recognised this man of his dreams in a Sardinian who came to work in Corsica. The Sardinian likewise recognised the Corsican *lanceri* as a hunting companion of his dreams.

8. 'Black' witches are seldom heard of in southern Corsica; but in some other areas old women known as *strege* were thought to cause illness and death, deliberately, because possessed by the Devil; see Joseph Chiari, *Corsica: . . .* (London, Barrie & Rockliff, 1960).

9. See 'Mémoires historiques . . .' (SB III); Marin-Muracciole (SB IV, 6, в).

10. See Marin-Muracciole; Busquet (SB IV, 6, а).

11. Marin-Muracciole.

12. Vuillier (SB III), writing in 1891, describes a customary marriage which he regards as betrothal followed by cohabitation. The betrothal ceremony was the ritual kiss: *abbracciu*. According to oral sources the *abbracciu*, implying customary marriage, was practised in two villages of the Sartenais until about ten years ago.

13. See Marin-Muracciole.

14. See Pitt-Rivers in 'Honour and social status', in *Honour and Shame . . .*, ed. Peristiany; James, *Marriage and Society*, Frithjof Schuon, *Understanding Islam* (London, Allen & Unwin, 1963).

15. Ample evidence of cousin marriage in the past is provided by the ecclesiastical records. In the Middle Ages the Church prohibited all marriages between blood relations; the Council of Trent restricted the prohibition to marriages between first, second and third cousins. The Corsicans, in spite of the risk of drastic penalties, none the less habitually contracted such unions, which were necessarily 'customary' and are referred to in ecclesiastical reports as 'incestuous concubinage'; see S.-B. Casanova (SB IV, 2); Marin-Muracciole; R. P. Vrydaghs Fidelis, *Notices historiques sur la Rocca* (Ajaccio, Daroux, 1962). Such marriages however could be, and were authorised by special dispensation from Rome, solicited by the bishops. Since 1918 the Church's rulings in this matter have been liberalised. In Corsica today marriages between first and second cousins, at least in the over forty generations, appear more common than elsewhere. The custom seems to have stemmed not so much from a preference for blood relations as marriage partners as a traditional distrust of a family inhabiting another village; the unit of Corsican endogamy is apparently not the kinship group but the village community; see A. Casanova, 'Marriage et communauté rurale, l'exemple Corse' (*Centre d'Etudes et de Recherches Marxistes*, undated).

16. Marin-Muracciole.

17. Until the early 17 c. children were commonly betrothed at the age of seven or eight, or even younger, by notarial contract between their fathers. In theory they were required to ratify the promise made on their behalf on reaching the age of puberty. when, according to custom, they were married. But in fact refusal was hardly possible, leading as it did to scandal, disgrace, and vendettas between the families. Normally the girl's dowry was handed over to her bridegroom's family at the time of the betrothal and was difficult to recuperate if the marriage did not take place. Usually the girl was handed over at the same time and grew up with her future in-laws, sharing the bed of her betrothed. See Marin-Muracciole.

18. Romantic, obsessive love is by tradition regarded as a misfortune or mental illness. Some simple uneducated people believe that a woman can impose this kind of love on a man with a potion consisting of a glass of wine in which she has mixed a few drops of her menstrual blood.

CHAPTER VI: *Law of the Outlaws*

1. See Hubert J. Treston, *Poine, A Study in Ancient Greek Blood-vengeance* (London, Longmans, 1923).

2. Tacitus, 'Germania', in *Tacitus on Britain and Germany*, trans. H. Mattingly (London, Penguin Books, 1948).

3. The *lex lombardica* had a marked influence on Pisan and Genoese law, both of which necessarily affected the administration of Corsica. Pisan law condemned the vendetta but allowed for a remission of penalties if the hostile families made peace; according to the Genoese code of the 16 c. homicide committed in the course of a vendetta incurred no penalty if the opposing families made peace except a fine paid to the state; see Busquet (SB IV, 6, A).

4. See Busquet.

5. See Diodorus Siculus, V, xiii, 1–14, ii; Strabo, V, ii, 6–7; Seneca, *De Consolatione ad Helviam*, vi, 5; vii, 8.

6. See Lucy Mair, *Primitive Government* (London, Penguin Books, 1962); John Beattie, *Other Cultures* (London, Cohen & West, 1964); and for the Murngin, Lloyd Warner, *A Black Civilisation*.

7. See Mair; Beattie.

8. Exogamy tends to break the chain of vengeance between the generations. The Greek Sarakatsan shepherds, for instance, are much given to blood feuds; but these seldom last long because sons and daughters, by custom, marry into families which are not related to their own and are usually unwilling to take up their feuds; see J. K. Campbell, *Honour, Family and Patronage* (Oxford University Press, 1964).

9. Pinello (SB III).

10. The code of the vendetta is described, with small variation, in the 15 c. by Cirneo (SB II), in the 18 c. by Pinello, *op. cit.* and Rossi (SB II). See also Busquet.

11. See Versini (SB IV, 6, A).

12. See *Nice-Matin*, 12 November 1954; 13 September 1958; 19, 20 December 1964.

13. Thorstein Veblen, *The Theory of the Leisure Class* (London, Allen & Unwin, 1899).

14. See Napoleon Bonaparte's short story, 'Nouvelle Corse', in Masson and Biagi (SB IV, 3), in which a Corsican who has failed to execute vengeance explains his misfortunes as follows: 'My ancestors were angered because I had betrayed the vengeance due to their manes'; and F. D. Falcucci, who states that in the Corsican vendetta the blood of the offender is shed 'to appease the manes of him who has been killed', *Vocabolario dei dialetti, geografia e costumi della Corsica* (Cagliari, Bibliotheca della Societá Storica Sarda, 1915).

15. See Busquet.

16. According to the *Statuti civili e criminali di Corsica* promulgated by the Genoese government 1571, and supposedly based on Corsican custom, homicide was punished by various forms of execution; if the murderer evaded capture he was banished for life and all his property confiscated (see Gregorj, SB IV, 4). In fact the undermanned Genoese police seldom made an arrest; murderers were allowed to escape abroad and were even given safe-conducts for the purpose. The Genoese government tried to improve the legal code with a spate of edicts, some brutal, others ingenious, but all ineffective; see Busquet.

17. Montesquieu, *De l'Esprit des Lois* (1748; edn used, Paris, Garnier, 1961), 2e partie, Book X, chap. viii.

18. See Gregorio Salvini, *Giustificazione della Rivoluzione di Corsica* . . . (Corte & Oletta, 1758), who quotes these statistics of murder. They are confirmed by Rostini (who estimates the number of bandits) (SB II), and by Boswell, quoting other contemporary sources (SB III). For population statistics see census of 1741 quoted by S.-B. Casanova (SB IV, 2), vol. ii.

19. Champgrand (SB III).

20. 'Mémoires historiques . . .' (SB III).

21. The history of legislation against the vendetta is treated by Busquet. For 19 c. homicide statistics see Versini; for population see Lefebvre (SB IV, 5).

22. See chap. XIV. All songs improvised for the dead are loosely termed *voceri*, but strictly speaking a *voceru* is for a death by murder and songs improvised for natural deaths are *ballati*.

23. See Ortoli; Marcaggi; Croze (SB IV, 6, c). Most of the *voceri* in these anthologies belong to the periods when they were recorded, but Croze quotes one of 1745.

24. See P. Lamotte, 'Le Caracolu' (*EC*, no. 12, 1956); S.-B. Casanova, vol. iv; Ch. de la Morandière, *Au Cœur de la Corse, le Niolo* (Paris, Desfosses, 1933).
25. The novelist Marguerite Peretti della Rocca.
26. Bourde (SB IV, 6, A).
27. Gustave Flaubert, journal (SB III).
28. For Nicolai and the Bellacoscia see Marcaggi; Versini (SB IV, 6, A).
29. See Emmanuel Arène, 'La Corse familière', in *Voltaire*, avril, mai, juin 1883; for Bellacoscia's acquittal, *Le Drapeau*, 26 juillet 1892. In 1900 an uncle of Martin Baretti took the old bandit to Paris to see the Universal Exhibition. He died at Bocognano, a local celebrity, aged 100.
30. ADC, *Série M*.
31. Marcaggi (SB IV, 6, A).
32. Joseph Carcopino, François Ferrandi, Dominique Santoni, Henry Souyris, commissaires de police, 'Du bandit d'honneur au gangster moderne' (*Revue Bimestrielle de la Direction de la Sureté Nationale*, no. 66, 1967). See also Derick Goodman, *Villainy Unlimited* (London, Pan Books, 1957).
33. Between 1962 and 1966 the average was 6·6 per year, or 0·037 per thousand of the estimated population. This was none the less a higher proportion than for France as a whole (0·016 per thousand) or for Bouches du Rhone, a notoriously lawless *département* that includes Marseilles, where the average for the same years was only 0·029 per thousand. In establishing these statistics I am indebted to the facilities given to me by INSEE, Marseilles.

CHAPTER VII: *Penitents and Bandits*

1. The patricians of Sartène became influential in Egypt in the latter half of the 19 c. Antoine-Marie Pietri and his brother Jourdain were councillors to Khedive Ismail; see Marien Martini, *Les Corses dans l'expansion française* (Ajaccio-Bastia, Editions Les Myrtes, 1953).
2. The Genoese distributed the domains of R. della Rocca to the village communities, but some of the land was apparently appropriated by his collateral descendants and by local notables. Such people continued to usurp vacant land in the 17 c. when large coastal tracts were abandoned after pirate raids. According to the legal code these deserted areas belonged to the Genoese government, but considerable properties were taken by individuals by legal and illegal means (see Janine Pomponi, *La Vie rurale de deux communes Corses: . . .*, Aix-en-Provence, La Pensée Universitaire, 1962). For the ennobled *sgio* see B. de Gaulejac and Pierre Lamotte, *EC*, no. 6, 1955.
3. See Valéry; Gregorovius (SB III); G. Roger, *Prosper Mérimée et la Corse* (Alger, Baconnier, 1945); Busquet. A clause in the peace treaty whereby three members of the Roccaserra group were exiled from the region was designed to give the Abbé Pietri numerical compensation for the death of his three nephews.
4. Born at Grossa, his real name was Marc-Antoine Alfonsi. In piecing together his life story I am indebted to a Franciscan, a shepherd, a fisherman and others who knew him.
5. In theory refugees could only stay three days, but this ruling was often disregarded; see S.-B. Casanova, vol.i.
6. See Gaudin (SB III); similar views are expressed by Pommereul and the author of 'Mémoires historiques . . .' (SB III). For the history of the Franciscan Order in Corsica see Olivesi d'Istria (SB II); S.-B. Casanova, vols. i, iv.

CHAPTER VIII: *Violence and Piety*

1. Jean Monlaü, *Les Etats Barbaresques* (Presses Universitaires de France, 1946). For Hassan Corso see *ibid.*; J. Casenave, 'Hassan Corso: un Corse, roi d'Alger' (*l'Afrique Latine*), reviewed by Louis Villat in *Revue de la Corse*, no. 24, 1923. For the careers of other Corsican renegades see Martini, and chronicles of Ceccaldi and Filippini (SB II).

2. See Roger.
3. Published by Busquet (SB IV, 6, A). For the story of the vendetta see Vrydaghs Fidelis, *Notices historiques sur la Rocca* (Ajaccio, Daroux, 1962); Roger; ADC, *Série M*.
4. These fortified homes were built long before the outbreak of the vendetta, as a protection against pirates. They conform to a type of domestic fortress common in the Corsican villages.
5. See Roger.
6. The statue was commissioned by the population of Fozzano, 1635, from Pompeio Bagnoli of Ajaccio; (Vrydaghs Fidelis). In the light of this information the legend seems more than ever strange.
7. The cathedrals of Mariana and Nebbio were dedicated to the Assumption of the Virgin, as were many Pisan churches; others were dedicated to the Annunciation; see Moracchini-Mazel, *Les Eglises romanes* . . . (SB IV, 8, D). Yet the marble figure of the Virgin on the façade of the cathedral of Nebbio (possibly later than the building) is unique, whereas figures of Eve, in bas-relief, are common. Representations of the Virgin in frescoes (mostly 15 c.) in Pisan churches are later than the buildings they decorate; see G. Moracchini avec la collaboration de D. Carrington (SB IV, 8, A).
8. A hymn composed in the 17 c. by the Neapolitan St Francis of Girolamo.
9. See Fidelis, quoting reports of pastoral visits of the bishops and their delegates.
10. See Moracchini-Mazel.
11. The peacock, for instance, symbolised the immortal soul, because according to mediaeval belief its flesh was imperishable; see George Ferguson, *Signs and Symbols in Christian Art* (London, Zwemmer, 1954).
12. 31 March 1772, at a dinner party given by Boswell; see Boswell, *Life of Samuel Johnson* (London, Dilly, 1791).
13. See Moracchini avec . . . Carrington.
14. See Lamotte, 'Andrea Doria et Rinuccio della Rocca' (*CH*, no. 1, 1953) and Monteggiani (SB II).
15. See Dorothy Carrington, 'Les Tableaux de Sainte-Lucie-de-Tallano' (*EC*, no. 11, 1956); Moracchini avec . . . Carrington.
16. See Moracchini-Mazel.

CHAPTER IX: *Heretics and Revolutionaries*

1. See Moracchini-Mazel, *Les Eglises romanes* . . ., vol. ii (SB IV, 8, D).
2. Della Grossa (SB II). The 'peculiar penances' may have implied flagellation, which was much favoured by the extremist sects of the period and admitted by the Franciscans.
3. The Pisan documents are published by F. Guerri, 'I Giovannali, nella testimonianza di documenti inediti del Trecento' (*Corsica Antica e Moderna*, Jan.–April 1935); Also consulted: Olivesi d'Istria (SB II); S.-B. Casanova (SB IV, 2), vols. i, iv; Bernard Gui, *Manuel de l'Inquisiteur* (Paris, Champion, 1926); Decima L Douie, *The Nature and the Effects of the Heresy of the Fraticelli* (Manchester University Press, 1932).
4. Gioacchino Cambiagi, *Istoria del Regno di Corsica* . . . (4 vols. Leghorn, 1770–2).
5. See Douie.
6. Diodorus Siculus, V, xiii, 1–14; A. Casanova, 'Essai d'étude . . .' (SB IV, 5), no. 18.
7. The interpolation must be by Filippini; see *Chroniche di Giovanni della Grossa* . . . (SB II).
8. Olivesi d'Istria; S.-B. Casanova, vol. i.
9. Della Grossa. For the historical background see Cesari Rocca, *Histoire* . . . (SB IV, 1, A); for social conditions, A. Casanova (SB IV, 5), *EC*, no. 21.
10. See Masson and Biagi (SB IV, 3).
11. S.-B. Casanova, vol. i.
12. See Hans Nobholz, 'Medieval agrarian society in transition' (*The Cambridge Economic History*, vol. i, chap. viii, Cambridge University Press, 1941); Georges Duby,

L'Economie rurale et la Vie des Campagnes dans l'Occident médiéval (2 vols. Paris, Aubier, 1962), vol. II.

13. See Lamotte, studies in *EC*, cited SB IV, 5; Pierre Emmanuelli, *Recherches sur la Terra di Comune* (SB IV, 5).

14. The monastery at Nonza was founded by Giovanni Parenti, companion of St Francis, soon after he retired to Corsica, in 1236, having resigned his position as General of the Order. He founded four other monasteries in Corsica before his death in 1250. For the Fraticelli in Corsica see Olivesi d'Istria; S.-B. Casanova, vols. i, iv.

15. See F. Pomponi (SB IV, 5).

16. See Theophrastus, V, viii, 1–2.

CHAPTER X: *The Outpost*

1. 'Mémoires historiques . . .' (SB III).

2. Words by Pierre Leca, poet in the Corsican dialect active in the 1930s, music by T. Lasciure, recorded in *Evocation de la Corse* with music by Felix Quilici (Vega, F 35 M 3001). The guitar was imported to Corsica, with the violin, in the 19 c.; until then the Corsicans used the cithern, the Jew's-harp, and, most often, wind instruments made from chestnut bark or reeds. See Galletti (SB III); Falcucci, *Vocabolario*.

3. Louis Moulinier, 'L'Episode des Lestrygons dans l'Odyssée' (*EC*, no. 17, 1958).

4. Translation by E. V. Rieu, Penguin Classics, 1946; used in the following quotations unless otherwise indicated.

5. Translation given by Moulinier, *op. cit.*

6. See Moulinier, quoting Ch. Ferton 'Sur l'histoire de Bonifacio à l'époque néolithique' (Actes de la Société Linnéene de Bordeaux, t. LIII, 1898).

7. Reproduced in Georgina Masson, *Italian Gardens* (London, Thames & Hudson, 1961).

8. Bonifacio has been identified with Marianon, mentioned by Ptolemy; see J. Jehasse and J. P. Boucher, *EC*, no. 21, 1959. For Ptolemy's geographical description of Corsica see Ascari; Berthelot and Ceccaldi (SB IV, 7); for Roman finds in Corsica, A. Ambrosi (SB IV, 8, c).

9. Important sources for the history of Bonifacio are: a bound manuscript volume recording municipal statutes and decrees from the 14 c. to 16 c. in ADC; the early statutes published by Abbé Letteron, 'Statuts de Bonifacio . . .' (*BSSHNC*, 1883, 1884); *Le Fonds du Lieutenant de Bonifacio*, ADC; Giovanni Battista Marzolaccio, *Compendiosa descrittione delle cose di Bonifacio* (Bologna, 1625), besides the Corsican chroniclers, particularly Pietro Cirneo (SB II), historian of the Aragonese siege.

10. Bonifacio was by far the largest town in Corsica until its population was reduced by plague to 700 in 1528. The original colonists numbered *c.* 1200; the population is estimated by Marzolaccio, *op. cit.*, at 8000 in 1420, and by Giustiniani (SB II) at 4000–5000 just before the plague, when Bastia had only 3500 and Ajaccio and Calvi considerably less. See also Kolodny (SB IV, 5).

11. The Emperor's stay in Bonifacio, 1–6 October 1541, is mentioned in contemporary works, as has been established by Mlle J. Veillard, of l'Ecole des Hautes Etudes Hispaniques, in her researches kindly communicated to me by the late Maître Emmanuel Musso of Bonifacio.

12. First built, perhaps, by the Pisans, the church was redesigned by the Genoese in the 13 c.; the ornately carved campanile is Aragonese in style, 14–15 c., perhaps the work of craftsmen from Sardinia. See Camille Enlart, *Quelques Monuments du Moyen Age en Corse* (Paris, Clavel, 1925); Moracchini-Mazel, *Les Eglises romanes . . .*, vol. ii (SB IV, 8, D).

13. St Francis is said to have been driven into the harbour in 1215 when sailing between Italy and Spain, and to have founded St Julien *extra muros*, a monastery outside the town; but the story is unconfirmed by documentary evidence and the monastery was more probably founded by Parenti (see chap. IX, n. 14).

14. The only complete Gothic church in Corsica; see Enlart. It was built 1270–1343 by the Dominican Nicolao Fortiguerra, Bishop of Aléria, for an adjoining Dominican

monastery (rebuilt 17 c. and 19 c. and now used by the French army). See S.-B. Casanova (SB IV, 2) vol. iv; Moracchini-Mazel, *Les Eglises romanes* . . ., vol. ii. Two inscriptions on a wall of the monastery record gifts of property to the foundation in 1343; see Jean Serafini, *Bonifacio* . . . (Marseilles, Imprimerie de la Société Petit Marseillais, 1936).

15. The principal works of art described in this church are mentioned in Moracchini avec . . . Carrington (SB IV, 8, A). The altar was transferred to St Dominic from the church of the neighbouring Franciscan monastery during the French Revolution.

16. See Moracchini avec . . . Carrington. The groups of statuary may recall miracle plays once performed in Bonifacio; or perhaps they were made to supersede human equivalents: groups of immobile actors carried in procession on platforms, as is still the custom in Campobasso, in the Appenines, on the feast of Corpus Christi.

17. Built late 13 c. with the adjoining monastery; see S.-B. Casanova, vol. iv; Moracchini-Mazel, vol. ii.

CHAPTER XI: *The Disinherited*

1. C. Levi-Strauss, *Tristes Tropiques* (Paris, Plon, 1955).

2. St Julien *extra muros* (see chap. X, n. 13).

3. ADC, *Série VII*, M 105.

4. 'L'Agonie de la *Sémillante*', in *Lettres de mon Moulin* (SB III).

5. The image of the emperor was also a sanctuary; the urns engraved below and beside the bust are *ollae*, vases for libations; see J. Jehasse and J. P. Boucher, *EC*, no. 26, 1960; D. Carrington, 'The Rediscovery of Roman Corsica', *Geographical Magazine* (London, March 1960); also Grosjean, *EC*, no. 15/16, 1957.

6. See Carcopino; Jean Jehasse (SB IV, 8, c), and Moracchini-Mazel, *Les Monuments paléo-chrétiens de la Corse* (SB IV, 8, D).

7. Philippe Diolé, *The Undersea Adventure*, trans. A. Ross (London, Sedgwick & Jackson, 1953).

8. The Roquefort Company, installed in Corsica since 1893, has kept the traditional pastoral economy alive and fairly prosperous, whereas agriculture declined from the First World War till the 1960s, when the activities of SOMIVAC (a government-sponsored organisation) began to show results on the east coast (see chap. XII). Though herds have decreased since the beginning of the century there are still *c.* 120,000 head of sheep in Corsica, owned by some 1200 shepherds, the average herd being 150–200 head. The Roquefort Company, with half a dozen milk-collecting centres at strategic points on the coasts, buy their entire winter milk yield for cheese-making at an assured price of 1·42F per litre. A shepherd's gross income is likely to reach about 20,000F a year, of which 40–50 per cent may however be deducted for the rent of winter pasture (the shepherds own little or no land). The number of goats is estimated at 40,000; much fewer than in the past. The owners of large herds often do better than the sheep-breeders, for a goat's milk yield is higher than a ewe's, and goats can thrive on the unimproved pasture of common lands; see Renucci, 'L'élevage en Corse . . .' (*Revue de Géographie de Lyon*, vol. XLV, no. 4. 1970)

9. In southern Corsica the shepherds migrate between two fixed points, one near the coasts, the other in the mountains at *c.* 5000 ft where they habitually take their wives and children, unlike the shepherds of the north (see chap. XIV). Both their homes may be at a distance from any village.

10. The pastoral economy dates back to an era when the land was collectively exploited, as described by Diodorus Siculus. In the course of history most of the best lands near the coasts have fallen into private hands; but the high mountain pastures are still owned by the communes and used by the shepherds either free of charge or for low fees. Though given to outward signs of piety, such as nailing wooden crosses on their doors, the shepherds, on account of their isolation, have been little influenced by the clergy. Ecclesiastical records are full of complaints about their godless condition; see S.-B. Casanova (SB IV, 2), 'Missions du Père St Léonard . . .' (SB III); Vrydaghs Fidelis.

11. According to J.-C. Sillamy, musical scholar living in Corsica, many traditional Corsican airs belong to the plagal mode of ancient Greece, which was perpetuated in the liturgical chants of the Middle Ages. On the other hand it seems likely that Corsican music originally derived from a primaeval Mediterranean tradition that was also inherited by the Greeks of antiquity, and later by the Arabs, so that the relationship between Corsican, ancient Greek and Arab music is collateral. For the magico-religious function of music in prehistoric and primitive societies see Walter Wiora, *Les Quatre Ages de la Musique* . . . (Paris, Petit Bibliothèque Payot, 1963; first published Stuttgart, 1961).

12. The tradition was transposed into written verse by the writers of the Corsican *félibrige*, who from the end of the last century endeavoured to elevate the Corsican dialect to the status of a literary language, J. P. Lucciardi (1862–1929) was particularly given to this genre. For the history of the movement see H. Yvia-Croce, *Anthologie des Ecrivains Corses* (2 vols. Ajaccio, Stamparia di U Muvra, 1929–31), vol. ii; Paul Arrighi, 'La vie littéraire et intellectuelle de la Corse' (*Visages de la Corse*, Paris, Editions des Horizons de France, 1951).

13. J. Pomponi, in *La Vie rurale de deux Communes Corses*: . . ., quotes a document of 1589 in which it is stated that the shepherds of Serra-di-Scopamène, in southern Corsica, possessed *case o siano orrii*, 'houses, that is to say *orii*' in their winter grazing grounds, and other documents of that period speaking of the ownership of houses beneath caves. The *orii* may well have served also as granaries. In the Balagne huts known as *pagliaghii* (places for keeping straw) were used for this purpose when the surrounding land was cultivated, and as shepherds' winter dwellings when it lay fallow. The larger *orii* of the south could have been used as granaries and dwellings simultaneously. Several people I spoke to in the south, notably at Pianottoli–Caldarello, believe, by tradition, that the *orii* were used as fortresses during the Saracen invasions.

14. I am indebted for this information to my host M. Jérôme Marchi.

15. Other types of prehistoric habitat certainly must have existed in the neighbourhood; but one may suppose that *orii* were one of the types used all over the south. Their continued occupation through the centuries has destroyed archaeological evidence, particularly because their floors are invariably of rock, not of earth that covers and preserves pottery, etc. No doubt they were chosen for dwellings and granaries precisely because the rock floors protected against damp. At Pianottoli-Caldarello, however, I saw, with R. Grosjean, an *oriu* in a rock-mass near the village that also contained caves where we found fragments of prehistoric pottery. The manmade walls of all the *orii* I have seen appear to be fairly modern, being composed of smallish stones joined by mortar. The masonry of the *oriu* of Piaggiola-Pastina is remembered as the work of its last occupant, Vinceguerra Pietri.

16. The Culioli may well have used the *oriu* when they brought their flocks down from the mountains in winter, before they settled permanently on the site some 200 years ago. One may suppose that after they became sedentary and took to agriculture the family increased on the spot, instead of dispersing with each generation (as tends to happen with shepherds, who require the use of large areas of land). They therefore overflowed the *oriu* and built the village.

17. The olive tree is said to have been cultivated from the second millennium B.C. west of the Nile Valley and in Crete. For the Greeks, this miraculous tree that flourishes on poor soil and provides both light and sustenance was the gift of Pallas Athene; in the Old Testament it is recognised as the first of trees: 'The trees went forth on a time to anoint a king over them; and they said unto the olive tree, Reign thou over us' (Judges 9:8). See Robert Standish, *The First of Trees* (London, Phoenix House, 1960).

18. J.-B. Quilichini's *l'Agonie d'une Vendetta* (Hanoi, Taupin, undated) gives a romantic and probably biased account of the bandit's career; Maupassant's version, 'Un bandit Corse' in *Le Père Milon* (SB III), is superficial; Versini (SB IV, 6, A) regards both brothers as guilty.

19 See *Petit-Bastiais*, 12 juillet 1953.

1. A government-sponsored organisation, SOMIVAC (Société pour la mise en valeur agricole de la Corse), created 1957, has transformed the east coast by clearing and equipping *c.* 3000 *hectares* of land, bought from communes or rented on long leases, which has been allocated in eighty-four lots to individual farmers. SOMIVAC has also built dams in the interior for extensive irrigation, created seventeen farms in the Balagne, and improved 151 private properties in the island. See *Bulletin d'Informa- tion de la SOMIVAC et de la SETCO,* quarterly or bimonthly since May 1960.

2. Lear (SB III).

3. See Carcopino; Jean Jehasse; Jean and Laurence Jehasse (SB IV, 8, c).

4. In 1794 Bastia had 8033 inhabitants as against 4701 in Ajaccio (*Plan Terrier,* SB I). Today both towns have populations of over 40,000, that of Ajaccio being estimated as slightly the larger of the two.

5. For the history of the Corsican Resistance see Raymond Sereau, *La Libération de la Corse (1943)* (Paris, Peyronnet, 1955); Maurice Choury, *Tous Bandits d'Honneur!* (Paris, Editions Sociales, 1956).

6. See Abbé Letteron, 'Les Sociétés savantes de Bastia' (*BSSHNC,* 1915).

7. In 1571 the seat of the diocese of Mariana and Accia was transferred to Bastia, the Pisan cathedral at Mariana (known as the Canonica) having been abandoned on a site recognised as unhealthy and unsafe; see S.-B. Casanova (SB IV, 2), vol. i.

8. Founded on the site of a fishing village, Porto Cardo, Bastia took its name from the tower, *bastiglia,* built by the Genoese *c.* 1380. The fortifications were erected between 1480 and 1575; see *Histoire de la Corse comprenant . . .* (SB II).

9. See Ettori (*EC,* no. 15/16, 1957); F. Pomponi (SB IV, 5).

10. For the Corsican flag see Berthelot and Ceccaldi (SB IV, 7). A representation of the flag of the Anglo-Corsican Kingdom, combining the Moor's head and the royal arms, exists in the storeroom of the Musée d'Ethnographie Corse, Bastia. For the arms of Sir Gilbert Elliot see *Life and Letters . . .* (SB III) and *Debrett's Peerage*; he was created Baron Minto, 1797, and Earl of Minto, 1813.

11. Quotations from letters of Sir Gilbert and Lady Elliot throughout this chapter are from *Life and Letters . . .*, and 'Correspondance de Sir Elliot . . .' (SB III).

12. See 'Extrait des mémoires de M. Buttafoco', in 'Pièces et documents divers . . .' (*BSSHNC,* 1891); *Life and Letters . . .*

13. For the history of the Anglo-Corsican Kingdom see, besides sources already cited, Jollivet; Tomi (SB IV, 1, B); McErlean (SB IV, 3).

14. There was a third candidate: James Boswell, who naïvely wrote to Dundas, Principal Secretary of State, 17 March 1794: 'My knowledge of Corsica, and my having been the first man by whose means authentick information of its importance was obtained, my long and continued intimacy with General Paoli, and the consideration how agreeable it would be to him and to the people in general, that I should be sent thither, seem, I cannot help thinking, to have such weight as almost to preclude competition . . .' (*Private Papers of James Boswell from Malahide Castle,* 18 vols. Privately printed, 1928–37), vol. xviii.

15. 'Il Generale de Paoli ai suoi compatriotti', printed Corte (B.M., B 418 [4]). The people as a whole seem not to have been informed of the impending union with Britain until the publication of this proclamation. It says much for Paoli's popularity that the project encountered no opposition; Britain really owed him a personal debt for the sovereignty of the island. For the *consulta,* 10–22 June 1794, see 'Pièces et docu- ments . . .' *op. cit.*

16. Thrasher (SB IV, 3) interprets the evidence in a light more favourable to Paoli.

17. *Life and Letters . . .* vol. iii.

CHAPTER XIII: *Saint and Adventurers*

1. Notably at Sainte-Christine (Valle-di-Campoloro), a mediaeval chapel rebuilt 15 c., with twin apses at the east end of the nave. These, with the adjoining wall, are

covered with frescoes, suggesting Siennese influence, dated 1473. See Geneviève Moracchini, *La Chapelle Sainte-Christine* . . . (*Bulletin Monumental*, 1954); Moracchini avec . . . Carrington (SB IV, 8, A).

2. See I. Chiva and D. Ojalvo, 'La potérie Corse à l'amiante' (Paris, *Arts et Traditions Populaires*, no. 3/4, 1959).

3. According to the researches of J. Leblanc, Conservator of the Musée de Morosaglia, 137 portraits of Paoli are known. I am indebted to the National Portrait Gallery, London, for a descriptive list of sixteen paintings, five miniatures and two busts, not including Flaxman's memorial bust of Paoli in Westminster Abbey. I have also found mention of a bust of Paoli by Joseph Nollekens which has not, so far as I know, been traced; see J. T. Smith, *Nollekens and his Times* (1828; edn used, London, Turnstile Press, 1949).

4. See Emmanuelli (SB IV, 5) and chap. IX.

5. The *pagliaghii*, used as storehouses, or, in winter, as dwellings for agricultural labourers or shepherds (see chap. XI, n. 13). They are usually roofed with corbel vaults which were covered with earth to make a flat surface.

6. See Guy de Maupassant, 'Le monastère de Corbara', *Au Soleil* (SB III); Comte Savelli de Guido, *Corbara* (Nancy, Bailly & Wettstein, 1938); Maurice Ricord, *Découverte littéraire de la Corse* (Paris, Nouvelles Editions Latines, 1963).

7. The Franceschini Pietri descend from Paoli's only sister, Chiara. J.-B. Franceschini Pietri, Paoli's great-nephew, was secretary to Napoleon III and is buried beside him at Farnborough Hill. He was responsible for exhuming Paoli's remains in London and giving Paoli's home at Morosaglia to the *département* of Corsica.

8. Another type of olive is known as *genovesi*, and yet another as *saraceni*, as though the Genoese and the Saracens were responsible for their implantation; see Gregorovius SB III).

9. S. Sitwell, *Golden Wall and Mirador* (London, Weidenfeld & Nicolson, 1961). The best examples outside Calvi are St Blaise at Calenzana, built early 18 c. by the Milanese Domenico Baino, who was also the author of a remarkable campanile at Porta d'Ampugnani (Castagniccia), see O. F. Tencajoli, *Chiesi di Corsica* (Rome, Desclée, 1936), and l'Annonciation at Corbara, built 1640–1751 with a marble altar and choir balustrade by Pietro Cortese of Carrara (Savelli de Guido, *op. cit.*). See also Moracchini *avec* . . . Carrington.

10. See Horatio Nelson, *The Dispatches and Letters of Vice-Admiral Lord Viscount Nelson* (4 vols. London, Colburn, 1845), vol. i.

11. Prince Felix Youssoupoff, *En Exil* (Paris, Plon, 1954).

12. Colette, *La Fin de Chéri* (Paris, 1926, edn used, Flammarion, 1953).

13. Saint-Jean-Baptiste, said to date from the 13 c., was several times rebuilt and must have assumed its present form soon after it became pro-cathedral of the diocese of Sagone in 1625; see S.-B. Casanova (SB IV, 2) vol. iv. The altarpiece is dated 1498 and signed by the Genoese painter Barbagelata, pupil of Giovanni Mazone; for this and other works of art and curiosities of this church see Moracchini *avec* . . . Carrington.

14. These accomplished, realistic portraits, evidently the work of Italian – probably Genoese – craftsmen, are unique in Corsica and are among the very few portraits of any kind prior to the 18 c., see Carrington, 'Les statues de Calvi' (*Nice-Matin*, 15, 16 juillet 1958). For the moucharabies, see Moracchini *avec* . . . Carrington.

15. For the privileges of Calvi see Abbé Letteron, 'Calvi, franchises et immunités . . .' (*BSSHNC*, 1884); for the decline in wine production, Giovanni Banchero, 'Calvi vers le milieu du XVIIᵉ siècle' (*BSSHNC*, 1885). The Genoese usurers in Corsica are described as 'blood-suckers' by the Genoese themselves in official documents of the 16 c. They seem to have been particularly active in Calvi: in 1454 the citizens requested the Genoese Government to refuse safe-conducts for travel to their debitors (Letteron, 'Calvi: Règlement . . .' *BSSHNC*, 1883); in 1561 they protested against a two-year moratorium on private debts imposed by the government after the Treaty of Cateau-Cambrésis on the plea that income from this source constituted their wealth (see René Emmanuelli, *Gênes et l'Espagne dans la Guerre de Corse, 1559–1569*, Paris, Picard, 1964).

16. See Jean-Baptiste Tristan l'Hermite, seigneur de Soliers, *Les Corses François* ... (Paris, 1667); A. Lazenby Liberty, *De Libertat, a historical and genealogical review* ... (London, Pettit, 1888).

17. See Filipinni (SB II); Colonna de Cesari Rocca, *Don Juan Corse* (SB IV, 3); F. F. Battestini, *Calvi au XVIᵉ siècle* ... (Asnières, Ambrosini, 1968).

18. The main arguments for Columbus's Calvi origin are that a family by the name of Colombo lived there (mentioned in documents only from 1530); that they were apparently weavers (as was Columbus's father); that the sailors on Columbus's voyages had Corsican names; that the few lines written in Columbus's hand are in faulty Italian resembling the Corsican dialect; arguments that are to say the least inconclusive and are dismissed by serious Corsican historians (see Cesari Rocca, *Histoire* ..., SB IV, 1, A).

19. See Cesari Rocca; Van Loo (SB IV, 3), the authors of the historical research on Miguel Manara, also Lorenzo di Bradi's less scholarly *Don Juan, la Légende et l'Histoire* (Paris, Librairie de France, 1930). The texts of the three investigations for Manara's canonization (1680–2, 1749–62, 1770–8) were among the documents looted from the Vatican by Napoleon and are now in the Bibliothèque Nationale, Paris. The testimony of Manara's equerry, Alonso Perez de Velasco, in the first investigation, is particularly revealing. It is corroborated by Manara's friend, the Jesuit Juan de Cardenas, in a biography written 1680 (see Van Loo). Manara's own confession is included in his will, which is preserved in the archives of Santa Caridad, Seville, where his tomb can still be seen.

20. For the sources of the plot see Van Loo. Although the Tenorio were a real Spanish family, several members of which were named Juan, no historical prototype for the Don Juan of the play has been identified.

CHAPTER XIV: *The Core of the Island*

1. Gaudin (SB III).

2. A few families of Albertacce and Calasima are in fact very tall, with flaxen hair and pale blue eyes. At Calasima I recently met a veritable Viking of a man; Vuillier (SB III) visiting the village in 1891, saw two blond giants both, he writes, over 6 ft tall. The people of the Niolo have been given to inbreeding; none of the fair people I have spoken to remember any marriages with foreigners in their families; it therefore seems improbable that the strain was introduced in modern times. But a theory that these fair families descend from the megalith builders who apparently retreated into the Niolo (see chap. III) is unproved. Tall fair people are found in other mountainous regions of the island: at Olmi-Capella (north of the Niolo) and around Zicavo, in the central south (the place of origin of the Cesari, some of whom are fair).

3. The Niolo shepherds, unlike those of the south, seldom take their wives and children with them on their seasonal migrations. Though the longer distances covered in their three-point transhumance may be partly responsible (some winter as far away as Porto-Vecchio, and Tomino, in northern Cap Corse), one reason for the arrangement may have been to leave members of the family to cultivate lands near their permanent home. Until the interwar years shepherds of the Castagniccia practised a similar, but shorter, three-point transhumance, leaving their families in the intermediate villages, where the cultivation of chestnuts had become an activity more important than sheep-breeding. In the Niolo chestnuts were the last crop to be attempted; the small trees are hardly more than a century old.

4. Until the First World War the herds provided wool for clothes and blankets. The women (who also cultivated flax) were the spinners, weavers and tailors of the men's clothes, though they themselves, since the beginning of the century, had taken to wearing black materials imported from France in place of the local homespun.

5. See chap. XI, n. 8.

6. I have found goat-herds wintering on the west coast, three men together, in stone huts as rudimentary as any in the high mountains; in the Balagne, until recently,

shepherds lodged in the *pagliaghii* (chap. XIII, n. 5). On the east coast, where stone is scarce, the shepherds until the interwar years built themselves huts of interlaced branches covered with clay (I am indebted for this information to M. Louis de Casabianca, who has communicated a report on the subject to the Musée des Arts et Traditions Populaires, Paris).

7. The *granitola*, performed at religious festivals in Cap Corse, the Balagne (including Calvi) and other places in the Diqua dai Monti (though not in the Dila), apparently derives from a maze dance widespread in Europe, originating in prehistoric fertility rites (see Violet Alford and Rodney Gallop, *The Traditional Dance* (London, Methuen, 1935).

8. The *paghiella* may be yet another legacy from the Corsican megalithic age; according to the musical scholar Schneider, polyphony originated in megalithic Europe, whence it gradually spread to Asia (see Wiora, *Les Quatre Ages de la Musique*). This view is, however, contested.

9. See chap. III.

10. The last vendetta in the Niolo took place in the interwar years. These feuds involved great physical endurance; men tracked their enemies over immense distances from high mountains to coasts, or waited in ambush for days on end on passes or in the Scala di Santa Regina (see Morandière, *Au Cœur de la Corse ...*). In past centuries practically the whole population was permanently engaged in feuds, as is vividly described in the reports of the preaching missions which visited the region in 1652 (mission sent to Corsica by St Vincent de Paul, see S.-B. Casanova, vol. i), and in 1744 (see 'Missions du Père St Léonard ...', SB III). From 1767 to 1772 a vendetta, started by the wounding of a sheep, raged between two families of Calacuccia, making thirty-six victims, besides a monk who tried to make peace. As a result of this rigorous enforcement of the code of the vendetta theft of livestock in the Niolo has been rare, given the opportunities. Flocks have always been left to wander unguarded, each owner marking his animals by cutting their ears according to a particular sign, a state of affairs that confirms the report of Diodorus Siculus (see chap. VI).

11. The route indicated seems the most probable. According to Nasica (SB IV, 3) the Bonaparte retreated on to the slopes of Monte Rotondo; according to tradition they passed through the Niolo.

12. Edith Southwell-Colucci, 'I laghi di Lancone ...' (*Archivio Storico di Corsica*, July–September 1932).

13. The Niolo is rapidly changing. Tourists are replacing shepherds. A dam on the Golo built by SOMIVAC has created a large artificial lake on the formerly arid plateau.

CHAPTER XV: *Liberation: Tradition and the Enlightenment*

1. For the history of the rebellion see the contemporary chronicler Rostini (SB II) to 1741, and Rossi (SB II), vols. vi–xi, who wrote a few decades after the events and quotes numerous contemporary documents.

2. Corsica had been at peace since 1569, when Alfonso d'Ornano, who had continued the rebellion instigated in 1564 by his father, Sampiero Corso (assassinated 1567) surrendered to the Genoese.

3. See F. Pomponi (SB IV, 5).

4. Rossi, vol. vi. The use of the word 'eleggere' in connection with the executive officials is probably misleading and should be interpreted as 'designate' (as in numerous Corsican documents of the period). A contemporary document recording the reenactment of the constitution in 1735 states that these officials were nominated by the Junta; see Lamotte, 'La déclaration d'indépendance ...' (SB IV, 4).

5. For Theodor's reign see Le Glay, and Bent, who quotes extensively from the journal of Sebastiano Costa, now lost (SB IV, 3). For the monarchical constitution see Rossi, vol. vii.

6. See Bent (SB IV, 3).

7. See Louis Villat, 'La politique française et la Corse au XVIIIe siècle' (*BSSHNC*, 1912).

8. See Le Glay, *Histoire* . . . (SB IV, 1, B).

9. The constitution is published from a contemporary document in Lamotte, 'La formation du premier gouvernement corse autonome' (SB IV, 4).

10. See Pasquale Paoli's letter to his father of November 1754 published in Abbé Letteron, 'Pascal Paoli avant son élévation . . .' (SB IV, 3).

11. Pommereul, a French officer (later director of Napoleon's censorship) who was stationed in Corsica while Paoli's regime was still operating, gives valuable evidence of local conditions, see *Histoire* . . . (SB III), as does Boswell, *An Account* . . . (SB III). All quotations from Boswell in this chapter are from the above work unless otherwise stated.

12. See Rossi, vols. x, xi; S.-B. Casanova (SB IV, 2), vol. ii.

13. See 'Carteggio fra Pasquale Paoli ed il Duca di Choiseul' (*BSSHNC*, 1886).

14. Thomas Gray, *Correspondence* . . . (Oxford University Press, 1935).

15. Fontana (SB IV, 4) uses only printed sources. My introductory study 'The Corsican Constitution of Pasquale Paoli, 1755–1769' to appear shortly (SB IV, 4), is the first attempt to examine the subject in the light of the rich material in the Corsican Archives (*Fonds Paoli* and *Série F*).

16. 'La Dieta Generale del Populo di Corsica, lecitimamente Patrone di se medesimo, secondo la forma dal Generale convocata nella Città di Corti sotto li qui 16. 17. 18. novembre 1755. Volendo, riaquistata la sua libertà, dar forma durevole, e costante al suo governo riducendoli a costituzione tale, che da essa ne derivi la felicita della Nazione./Hà decretato, e decreta . . .' (ADC, *Série F*).

17. See R. R. Palmer, *The Age of Democratic Revolution* (2 vols. Oxford University Press, 1959), vol. i, chap. 8.

18. See Montesquieu, *De l'Esprit des Lois* (1748), Book xi, chap. 6. Paoli counted on his constitution to make a favourable impression on the foreign powers, particularly the English, from whom he continually hoped for support; see his letter to 'Sua Maestà il Re della Gran Bretagna', 10 February 1763 (*BSSHNC*, 1887). For contemporary Corsican opinions of the constitution see Rossi, vol. xi, 28.

19. Rossi, himself a churchman, was under no illusion as to why Paoli gave the clergy a privileged representation in the Diet (see vol. xi, 22). Pommereul (*op. cit.*, vol. ii) writes of Paoli: 'With his friends his ordinary conversation concerned politics, literature and religion, and in connection with this subject he made no mystery of his heterodox opinions, nor of his attachment to those sentiments which the Church has proscribed and which have been so universally diffused and adopted since half a century'.

20. See Boswell and Pommereul (vol. ii) (SB III), confirmed by documents in ADC, *Fonds Paoli I*. Not a single record of an indirect election of a 'procuratore' for a *pieve* has come to light, whereas records of elections of 'procuratori' in the parishes are numerous, including 263 for the Diet of 1768.

21. See Saverio Bettinelli, 'Observations sur M. de Paoli . . .' (*BSSHNC*, 1881); Boswell (SB III).

22. See Chuquet (SB IV, 3), vol. ii.

23. Circular letter from Paoli and the Council of State, published by Tommaseo (SB IV, 3). See also Pommereul.

24. Jean-Jacques Rousseau, *Du Contrat Social* (1762), Book ii, chap. 10.

25. The correspondence between Rousseau and Buttafoco is published by M. G. Streckeisen-Moultou in *Jean-Jacques Rousseau, œuvres et correspondence inédites* (Paris, Levy, 1861), together with Rousseau's 'Projet de Constitution pour la Corse'. According to Ernestine Dedeck-Hery, *Jean-Jacques Rousseau et le Projet de Constitution pour la Corse* (Philadelphia, French Printing and Publishing Co., 1932), Buttafoco first wrote to Rousseau unknown to Paoli. His object, she argues, was to make use of Rousseau to dethrone Paoli and advance his own position. Among the works he sent Rousseau was a manuscript draft of a constitution he himself had written, which gave exceptional privileges to the nobility (to which he claimed to belong). Dedeck-Hery

believes that Buttafoco hoped Rousseau would exert his influence to impose this constitution on Corsica, pending the completion of his own work. A thesis in preparation by Fernand Ettori is expected to present a different view. For Rousseau's version of the negotiations see *Les Confessions*, Book xii.

26. Quoted by Dedeck-Hery.
27. Pommereul, vol. ii, observes that coaches were then unknown in the island. The first roads, from Bastia to Saint-Florent and to Corte, were built under the French monarchy.
28. Boswell was received in December 1764 at Motiers by Rousseau, who later sent him a letter, to serve as introduction to Buttafoco and Paoli. See Boswell, *Private Papers ... from Malahide Castle*, vol. vi, and Frederick A. Pottle, *James Boswell, the earlier years, 1749–1769* (London, Heinemann, 1966).
29. Copper coins were issued worth 1, 2 and 4 *soldi* and silver coins worth 10 and 20 *soldi*. They were engraved on one side with the Moor's head surmounted by a crown, and on the other with the value of the coin and the year of issue, see L. Doazan, *CH*, no. 31/32, 1968.
30. Fanny Burney, letter to Mr Crisp, 15 October 1782, in *Diary and Letters of Madame d'Arblay* (London, Macmillan, 1904).
31. Boswell skilfully worded his book so as to make his journey in Corsica, and particularly his stay with Paoli, appear longer than they in fact were. Examination of his private papers shows that he was in Corsica from 12 October to 20 November, and with Paoli for about a week, ending 29 October (see Pottle).
32. Rossi, vol. xi.
33. Gaudin (SB III) gives a vivid description of a performance of the Moresca staged for Count and Countess Marbeuf; Comte Savelli de Guido has recorded the words and music of a version performed in the Balagne until the First World War, 'La Moresca' (*EC*, nos. 13, 14, 1957). The choreography, a type of sword dance, was probably of great antiquity; Alford and Gallop, in *The Traditional Dance*, relate dances of this type to a widespread pre-Christian symbolic representation of the contest between summer and winter.
34. See Boswell, *Private Papers ...*, vol. vii; Pottle.
35. *The Cambridge Modern History* (1902–11), vol. vi, 13.
36. For Boswell's efforts to help the Corsicans see *Private Papers ...*, vols. vii, viii; Pottle; Boswell's unsigned items in the *London Chronicle*, January 1766–September 1769.
37. Villat (SB IV, 1, B) vol. i, is at pains to point out that the annuity represented arrears in subsidies promised by France to Genoa in 1755 and 1756, and that therefore no sale took place; but in fact this skilful transaction amounted to nothing else. For the text of the treaty see *ibid.*, vol. ii, appendix.
38. Nasica (SB IV, 3); see also Chuquet (SB IV, 3), vol. i. Napoleon recalled this speech at Saint Helena; see Emmanuel Comte de Las Cases, *Mémorial de Sainte-Hélène* (Paris, Lebègue, 1823), 16–21 August 1815.
39. See Bettinelli, *op. cit.*
40. Voltaire, *Précis du Siècle de Louis XV*, 2nd edn, 1769; see also Villat (SB IV, 1, B), vol. i.
41. Dumouriez (SB III). Livre i. He writes of the war: 'It is astonishing that this handful of islanders, without artillery, without fortresses, without stores, without money, should have held the French nation in check during two campaigns.... Liberty doubles the valour and strength of man.'

CHAPTER XVI: *The End of an Epoch*

1. Dumouriez (SB III).
2. In May 1768 Pembroke asked Boswell for a letter of introduction for his intended visit to Corsica (Boswell, *Private Papers ...*, vol. vii). He stayed in Corsica 12–21 April 1769 (Villat, SB IV, 1, B, vol. i). He accompanied Paoli to Pisa with the British Consul at Leghorn, Sir Alexander Dick (*London Chronicle*, 8–12 July 1769).

3. Bettinelli, 'Observations . . .'.

4. Boswell, *Life of Samuel Johnson*.

5. Franklin was present when Paoli called on Robert Wood, Under-Secretary of State, on his arrival in London, 20 September, and announced the news to Boswell when they met at the Honest Whigs Club the following day (see Boswell, *Private Papers* . . ., vol. viii; Carl van Doren, *Benjamin Franklin*, New York, Viking Press, 1938). The quotation given is from a letter to the *Public Advertiser*, 17 January 1769, reprinted in the *Pennsylvania Chronicle*, 3 April 1769; see *Benjamin Franklin's Letters to the Press, 1758–1775*, collected and edited by Werner W. Crane (University of North Carolina Press, 1950). Paoli's health was drunk at the first anniversary of the Sons of Liberty in Boston, 14 August 1766; but his great popularity in America, 1768–70, must be attributed to the success of Boswell's book, which ran into a third edition in 1769. The toasts quoted were to celebrate Paoli's birthday, 10 April 1769, at a meeting of the Sons of St Patrick at Philadelphia. The Paoli Tavern, twenty miles north-west of Philadelphia, was founded August 1769; Paoli is now a residential town of 2500 inhabitants. See George Pomeroy Anderson, 'Pascal Paoli, an inspiration to the Sons of Liberty' (Boston, *Publications of the Colonial Society of Massachusetts*, 1927), Transactions 1924–6.

6. See Rossi (SB II), vol. xiii.

7. See Chuquet (SB IV, 3), vol. ii; S.-B. Casanova (SB IV, 2), vol. ii.

8. The figure of 10,000 is estimated by the historian Médecin-Général P. Santini. For Napoleon's orders for conscription see 'Lettres de Napoléon relatives à la Corse' (*BSSHNC*, 1911); for his Corsican generals, P.-L. Albertini and G. Rivollet, *La Corse Militaire* (Paris, Peyronnet, 1958).

9. The uprising, 1798, known as the 'Révolte de la Crocetta', was a popular reaction against the reinforcement of anti-clerical legislation following the left-wing *coup d'état* of Fructidor; see Gai (SB IV, 1, A), the best guide to Corsican 19 c. history.

10. Corsican Royalist *émigrés* had joined forces with exiled Paolists and supporters of Britain to form an active counter-revolutionary group in Tuscany. General Suvarov, commanding Russian forces in western Europe, may have assisted them, but it is uncertain whether the Emperor Paul I, was consulted. The rebels landed on the east coast at the end of 1799; the revolt spread rapidly through the Sartenais and to the north (see Gai).

11. Miot de Melito's brief mission in Corsica, in 1801–2, is however better remembered for the introduction of tax concessions by the Arrêtés Miot (see chap. I, n. 4). Morand, appointed Military Governor in 1801, remained in office till 1811. See 'Lettres de Napoléon . . .'.

12. Emigration gathered volume from *c.* 1850, being first most noteworthy in Cap Corse and Balagne, prosperous areas which had become overpopulated in relation to their resources. The movement increased through the century, affecting every part of the island, was resumed after the First World War and again after the Second World War, causing a drop in the population from its peak, *c.* 280,000 in 1891 to *c.* 150,000 in 1954. Between 1946 and 1952 departures numbered *c.* 4300 a year; today they are estimated at *c.* 2000–2500. The loss is however more than compensated by the non-Corsicans – refugees from North Africa, foreign workmen and others – who have settled in the island, in large numbers since 1962. The population is now estimated at *c.* 200,000. See Lefebvre (SB IV, 5) and Renucci, (SB IV, 5).

13. See Marien Martini, *Les Corses dans l'Expansion Française*.

14. See S.-B. Casanova, vol. iv.

15. See Moracchini-Mazel, *Les Eglises romanes* . . ., vol. i (SB IV, 8, D); della Grossa (SB II); the victory was supposedly won by Ugo della Colonna (see chap. v, n. 4).

16. Glatigny was arrested, when walking to Ajaccio on the road from Corte, on New Year's Day 1869, the gendarmes having mistaken him for a notorious bandit. In spite of this experience he wrote of Corsica with sensitive appreciation in his prose work, *Le Jour de l'An d'un Vagabond* (Paris, Lemerre, 1870). See also Ricord, *Découverte Littéraire de la Corse*; G. Roger, *L'Ame de la Corse* (Baconnier, Alger, 1947).

17. *The Babylonian Epic of Creation* (Enuma elish), trans. S. Langdon (Oxford University Press, 1923).
18. The *zappone* is a double-headed mattock with a pick on one side and an adze-shaped blade on the other, formerly used for breaking the soil on the narrow terraces.
19. In 1849 (Versini, SB IV, 6, A).
20. Petit Bastiais, 'Le Rapport Clemenceau . . .' (SB IV, 5).
21. Diane de Cuttoli, 'Février, printemps blanc', in *La Houle des Jours* (1938).

SELECTED BIBLIOGRAPHY

THE following bibliography offers a selection of major works on Corsica and of the sources that have most contributed to the writing of this book. Other works consulted are cited in notes.

Abbreviations:

ADC   Archives Départementales de la Corse.
BSSHNC *Bulletin de la Société des Sciences Historiques et Naturelles de la Corse.*
EC   *Etudes Corses.*
REC   *Revue d'Etudes Corses.*
CH   *Corse Historique.*

I ORIGINAL SOURCES

ADC. The collection provides ample sources from the late 15 c. together with a few earlier documents. Of particular interest for this book were: FRANCIS MOLARD *Rapport sur les Archives provinciales de Pise* . . . (Ministère de l'Instruction Publique, Archives des Missions Scientifiques, 1873); documents in *Fonds Genois* (*Série C*), particularly *Civile Governatore*, of which a summary has been made by DE FREMINVILLE and A. TOURANJON, *Inventaire sommaire des Archives Départementales antérieures à 1790* (3 vols. Ajaccio, 1906–53); documents in *Fonds Paoli* and in *Série F.* Much use has also been made of *Le Plan Terrier*, a descriptive survey of the island carried out by the French government, 1770–94, with large-scale maps.

II CHRONICLERS

Histoire de la Corse comprenant la description de cette île d'après A. Giustiniani, les chroniques de Giovanni della Grossa et de Monteggiani, remaniées par Ceccaldi, la chronique de Ceccaldi et la chronique de Filippini, translated from Italian, with introductions, by ABBÉ LETTERON (*BSSHNC*, Bastia, 1888–90). Consists of a description of the island by the bishop A. GIUSTINIANI, written *c.* 1531, and the works of four successive Corsican chroniclers covering the history of Corsica from the earliest times to 1594: DELLA GROSSA, lived 1388–*c.* 1464; MONTEGGIANI, covers period 1465–1525; CECCALDI, lived *c.* 1521–60; FILIPPINI, lived 1529–*c.*1594. Filippini revised and added to the work of his predecessors and published the whole at Tournon in 1594 as *La Historia di Corsica* . . . Unrevised texts of DELLA GROSSA and MONTEGGIANI are published by LETTERON, in the original Italian, *Chroniche di Giovanni della Grossa e di Pier'Antonio Montegiani* (*BSSHNC*, 1910).

PIETRO CIRNEO, *De Rebus Corsicis*, history of Corsica from the earliest times to the author's death in 1506. Translated from Latin by Letteron (*BSSHNC*, 1884).

FRA PAOLO OLIVESI D'ISTRIA, *Serafici e cronacali ragguagli della provincia minore osservante di Corsica* (Luca, 1671).

CARLO ROSTINI, 'Memorie dell'Abate Rostini', account of the national rebellion, 1729–41, published with French translation (*BSSNHC*, 1881–3).

AMBROGIO ROSSI, *Osservazioni storiche sopra la Corsica* (*BSSHNC*, 1895–1906). Rossi (1754–1820) was the author of a history of Corsica to 1814 in 17 volumes, of which 13 are published in *BSSHNC*, covering the period 1705–1814.

III EARLIER WRITERS

FELICE PINELLO, 'Annotazioni particolari per il governo di Corsica' (*BSSHNC*, 1887).

SAN LEONARDO DA PORTO MAURIZIO, 'Missions du Père St Léonard de Port-Maurice en Corse . . .' (*BSSHNC*, 1889).

JEAN FRANÇOIS GOURY DE CHAMPGRAND, *Histoire de l'Isle de Corse* . . . (Nancy, Cusson, 1749).

JAMES BOSWELL, *An Account of Corsica, the Journal of a Tour to that Island and Memoirs of Pascal Paoli* (London, Dilly, 1768).

FRANÇOIS RENÉ JEAN DE POMMEREUL, *Histoire de l'Isle de Corse* (2 vols. Berne, Société Typographique, 1779).

'Mémoires historiques sur la Corse par un officier du régiment de Picardie, 1774–1777' (*BSSHNC*, 1889).

JACQUES MAURICE GAUDIN, *Voyage en Corse . . . par M. l'abbé Gaudin* (Paris, Lefévre, 1787).

CHARLES FRANÇOIS DU PERIER DUMOURIEZ, *La Vie et les Mémoires du Général Dumouriez* (Paris, 1795; edn used, 4 vols. Paris, Baudouin, 1822–3).

EMMA ELEANOR ELLIOT, *Life and Letters of Sir Gilbert Elliot* . . . (3 vols. London, Longmans, 1874), vol. ii.

'Correspondance de Sir Elliot Vice-Roi de la Corse avec le gouvernement anglais' (*BSSHNC*, 1892, 1895). The only published version of this correspondence, from originals communicated by Sir Gilbert's grandson, translated into French by S. de Caraffa.

ROBERT BENSON, *Sketches of Corsica* (London, Longmans, 1825).

VALÉRY (pseud.), ANTOINE CLAUDE PASQUIN, *Voyages en Corse, à l'Ile d'Elbe et en Sardaigne* (2 vols. Paris, Bourgeois-Maze, 1837), vol. i.

PROSPER MÉRIMÉE, *Colomba* (Paris, Magen et Comon, 1841).

GUSTAVE FLAUBERT, visited Corsica in 1840. His travel journal was published in *Par les Champs et par les Grèves* (Paris, ed. Conard, 1910).

ALEXANDRE DUMAS, *Les Frères Corses* (Paris, Souverain, 1845).

FERDINAND GREGOROVIUS, *Corsica in its Picturesque, Social and Historical Aspects* . . . (London, Longmans, 1855). First published in German (Stuttgart, Cotta, 1854).

ABBÉ JEAN-ANGE GALLETTI, *Histoire illustrée de la Corse* . . . (2 vols. Paris, Pillet, 1863).

THOMASINA CAMPBELL, *Southward Ho!* . . . (London, Hatchard, 1868).

ALPHONSE DAUDET, Sketches and stories in *Lettres de Mon Moulin* (Paris, Hetzel, 1869) and *Etudes et Paysages* (Paris, Dentu, 1874).

EDWARD LEAR, *Journal of a Landscape Painter in Corsica* (London, Bush, 1870).

GUY DE MAUPASSANT, Stories in *Contes du Jour et de la Nuit* (Paris, Marpon et Flammarion, 1885) and *Le Père Milon* (Paris, Ollendorff, 1899); reports for *Le Gaulois*, 1880, reprinted in *Au Soleil* (Paris, Victor-Havard, 1884).

GASTON VUILLIER, *Les Iles Oubliées* . . . (Paris, Hachette, 1891).

HENRY SETON MERRIMAN, *The Isle of Unrest* (London, Smith, Elder, 1899).

IV MODERN WORKS

I POLITICAL HISTORY

A *General works*

XAVIER POLI, *La Corse dans l'Antiquité et dans le haut Moyen Age* . . . (Paris, Fontemoing, 1907).

P.P.R. COLONNA DE CESARI ROCCA, *Histoire de la Corse écrite pour la première fois d'après les sources originales* (Paris, Bonvalot-Jouve, 1907).

A. AMBROSI, *Histoire des Corses et de leur Civilisation* (Tours, Deslis, 1912).

P.P.R. COLONNA DE CESARI ROCCA and LOUIS VILLAT, *Histoire de la Corse* (Paris, Boivin, 1916).

DOM J. B. GAI, *La Tragique Histoire des Corses* (Paris, SPERAR, 1951).

B *Special periods*

ANDRÉ LE GLAY, *Histoire de la Conquête de la Corse par les Français. La Corse pendant la Guerre de la Succession d'Autriche* (Paris, Picard, 1912).

LOUIS VILLAT, *La Corse de 1768 à 1789* (2 vols. Besançon, Millot, 1925).

MAURICE JOLLIVET, *Les Anglais dans la Méditerranée 1794–1797. Un Royaume Anglo-Corse* (Paris, Chailley, 1896).

PIERRE TOMI, 'Le Royaume Anglo-Corse' (*EC*, nos. 9–14, 1956–7).

Also consulted: EMILE VINCENS, *Histoire de la République de Gênes* (3 vols. Paris, Firmin Didot, 1842).

2 RELIGIOUS HISTORY

CHANOINE S.-B. CASANOVA, *Histoire de l'Eglise Corse* (4 vols. Ajaccio, Bastia, 1931–8).

3 BIOGRAPHY

P.P.R. COLONNA DE CESARI ROCCA, *Don Juan Corse* ... (Paris, Société Générale d'Editions, 1917).

ESTHER VAN LOO, *Le Vrai Don Juan, Don Miguel de Mañara* (Paris, Sfelt, 1950).

J. THEODORE BENT, 'King Theodore of Corsica' (*The English Historical Review*, vol. i, 1886).

ANDRÉ LE GLAY, *Théodore de Neuhoff, Roi de Corse* (Paris, Picard, 1907).

Paoli. Valuable biographical material is provided by ABBÉ LETTERON 'Pascal Paoli avant son élévation au Généralat ...' (*BSSHNC*, 1885), in Paoli's correspondence, published in *BSSHNC* between 1881 and 1931, and by N. TOMMASEO, *Lettere di Paoli* (Florence, Vieusseux, 1846). By far the best life of Paoli is by PETER ADAM THRASHER, *Pasquale Paoli* ... (London, Constable, 1970), although the author has not had access to the Corsican archives and his account of Paoli's constitution is therefore necessarily incomplete.

J. M. P. MCERLEAN, *The Formative Years of a Russian Diplomat: Charles-André Pozzo di Borgo in Corsica, 1789–1796* (University Microfilms, U.S.A., 1968).

T. NASICA, *Mémoires sur l'Enfance et la Jeunesse de Napoléon* ... (Paris, Ledoyen 1852).

FRÉDERIC MASSON and GUIDO BIAGI, *Napoléon inconnu* ... (2 vols. Paris, Ollendorff, 1895). Contains previously unpublished early writings of Napoleon, included an unfinished history of Corsica written 1789–90, 'Lettres sur la Corse...'

ARTHUR CHUQUET, *La Jeunesse de Napoléon* (3 vols. Paris, Colin, 1897–9).

J.-B. MARCAGGI, *La Genèse de Napoléon,* ... (Paris, Perrin, 1902).

LEON MAESTRATI, 'La généalogie des Bonapartes de Corse' (*CH*, nos. 5/6, 7, 1962).

ABBÉ LYONNET, *Le Cardinal Fesch* (2 vols. Lyon, Perisse, 1841).

4 LEGAL AND CONSTITUTIONAL HISTORY

GIOVANNI CARLO GREGORJ, *Statuti civili e criminali di Corsica* (Lyon, Dumoulin, Ronet et Sibuet, 1843).

PIERRE LAMOTTE, 'La déclaration d'indépendance de la Corse' (*EC*, no. 2, 1954). 'La formation du premier gouvernement corse autonome' (*CH*, no. 2, 1953).

MATHIEU FONTANA, *La Constitution du Généralat de Pascal Paoli en Corse (1755–1769)* (Paris, Bonvalot-Jouve, 1907).

To appear shortly: DOROTHY CARRINGTON, 'The Corsican Constitution of Pasquale Paoli (1755–1769)', study presented at the Thirteenth Congress of Historical Sciences, Moscow, 1970, to be published by the International Commission for the History of Representative and Parliamentary Institutions.

5 SOCIAL AND ECONOMIC HISTORY

ANTOINE CASANOVA, 'Essai d'étude sur la seigneurie banale en Corse' (*EC*, nos. 17, 18, 21–4, 1958–9). 'Caporaux et communautés rurales ...' (*CH*, nos. 9/10, 11, 1963; no. 16, 1964; no. 26, 1967).

PIERRE LAMOTTE, Studies on the collective organisation of the rural communes in *E.C.*, nos. 9, 10, 11, 1956.

PIERRE EMANUELLI, *Recherches sur la Terra di Comune* ... (Aix-en-Provence, Tacussel, 1958).

FRANCIS POMPONI, *Essai sur les Notables ruraux en Corse au XVIIe siècle* (Aix-en-Provence, La Pensée Universitaire, 1962).

FERNAND ETTORI, Studies on the Genoese encouragement of agriculture in *E.C.*, nos. 6, 9, 15/16, 1955-7.

ANTOINE ALBITRECCIA, *Le Plan Terrier de la Corse au XVIIIe siècle* (Paris, Presses Universitaires de France, 1942).

ALBERT GAUDIN, *Le Régime fiscal de la Corse, Les Arrêtés Miot* (Ajaccio, Massel, 1896).

M. F. ROBIQUET, *Recherches historiques et statistiques sur la Corse* (Paris, Le Frère de l'Auteur, 1835).

ANTOINE ALBITRECCIA, *La Corse. Son Evolution au XIXe siècle et au début du XXe siècle* (Paris, Presses Universitaires de France, 1942).

PETIT BASTIAIS, 'Le Rapport Clemenceau sur la situation actuelle de la Corse' (29 septembre; 1, 2 octobre 1908).

M. DELANNEY, 'Commission extraparlementaire et interministerielle chargée d'étudier la situation de la Corse . . .' (*Journal Officiel de la République Française*, 4 juillet, 12 septembre, 1 octobre, 10 novembre 1909).

PAUL LEFEBVRE, 'Situation démographique du Département de la Corse' (*EC*, nos. 2, 4, 1954).

YERAHMIEL KOLODNY, *La Géographie urbaine de la Corse* (Paris, SEDES, 1962).

Comité technique . . . *Plan de la mise en valeur de la Corse . . . 1949* (Paris, Alépée, 1950).

L. NEUWIRTH, *Rapport d'Information . . . sur le situation économique de la Corse . . .* (Imprimerie de l'Assemblée Nationale, 1961).

Etude d'Armature urbaine de la Corse. Compte économique, 1968 (SOGREP, 1970).

To appear shortly: JANINE RENUCCI, *Corse traditionelle et Corse nouvelle, Etude de Géographie d'une Ile.*

6 TRADITIONAL LIFE

A *Vendetta and bandits*

PAUL BOURDE, *En Corse* . . . (Paris, Calmann Levy, 1887).

J. BUSQUET, *Le Droit de la Vendetta et les Paci Corses* (Paris, Pedone, 1920).

J. B. MARCAGGI, *Bandits Corses d'Hier et d'Aujourd'hui* (Ajaccio, Rombaldi, 1932).

XAVIER VERSINI, *Un Siècle de Banditisme en Corse, 1814–1914* (Paris, Les Editions de Paris, 1964).

B *Marriage customs*

CAROLINE SPINOSI, *Le Droit de Gens mariés en Corse du XVIe siècle au XVIIIe siècle* (Aix-en-Provence, La Pensée Universitaire, 1956).

MADELEINE-ROSE MARIN–MURACCIOLE, *l'Honneur des Femmes en Corse du XIIIe siècle à nos jours* (Paris, Cujas, 1964).

C *Popular poetry and songs*

F. ORTOLI, *Les Voceri de l'Ile de Corse* (Paris, Leroux, 1887).

J. B. MARCAGGI, *Les Chants de la Mort et de la Vendetta de la Corse* (Paris, Perrin, 1898).

AUSTIN DE CROZE, *Le Chanson populaire de l'Ile de Corse* (Paris, Champion, 1911).

D *Legends and popular beliefs*

F. ORTOLI, *Les Contes populaires de l'Ile de Corse* (Paris, Maisonneuve, 1883).

DOROTHY CARRINGTON and PIERRE LAMOTTE, 'Les Mazzeri' (*EC*, no. 15/16, 1957).

7 GEOGRAPHY, GEOLOGY, BOTANY

MARIO C. ASCARI, 'La Corsica nella carte geografiche di Tolomeo' (Archivio Storico di Corsica, April–June, 1938).

A. BERTHELOT and F. CECCALDI, *Les Cartes de Corse de Ptolemée au XIXe siècle* (Paris, Leroux, 1939).

GEORGES DENIZOT, 'La Structure géologique de la Corse' (*EC*, no. 19/20, 1958).

MARCELLE CONRAD, *Promenades en Corse parmi ses Fleurs et ses Forêts* (Revue Corse Historique, Numéro special, 1962).

8 ARCHAEOLOGY AND ART

A General works

PROSPER MÉRIMÉE, *Notes d'un Voyage archéologique en Corse* (Paris, Fournier, 1840).

GENEVIÈVE MORACCHINI avec la collaboration de DOROTHY CARRINGTON, *Trésors oubliés des Eglises de Corse* (Hachette, 1959).

B Prehistoric archaeology

A. DE MORTILLET, *Rapport sur les Monuments mégalithiques de la Corse* (Paris, Leroux, 1893).

SIBYLLE VON CLES-REDEN, *The Realm of the Great Goddess* (London, Thames & Hudson, 1961). General study of megalithic monuments with an important chapter on Corsica.

ROGER GROSJEAN, *Filitosa, et les monuments protohistoriques de la vallée de Taravo* (Collection: Promenades Archéologiques, 1, Paris, 1960).

ROGER GROSJEAN, *Filitosa et son contexte archéologique* (Paris, Presses Universitaires de France, 1961).

ROGER GROSJEAN, *La Corse avant l'Histoire* (Paris, Klincksieck, 1966).

ROGER GROSJEAN, Studies in *EC*, nos. 6, 7/8, 1955; nos. 10, 11, 12, 1956; no. 13, 1957; nos. 17, 18, 1958; no. 22, 1959; *REC*, no. 1, 1961; *CH*, no. 8, 1962; nos. 9/10, 1963; nos. 13/14, 1964.

ROGER GROSJEAN, 'Les armes portées par les statues-menhirs de Corse' (*Revue Archeologique*, no. 11, 1962).

ROGER GROSJEAN, 'Classification descriptive du Mégalithique Corse' (*Bulletin de la Société Préhistorique Française*, t. LXIV, fasc. 3, 1967).

PIERRE LAMOTTE, 'Une nouvelle statue-menhir découverte sur le territoire de Tavera' (*REC*, no. 2, 1961).

MICHEL-CLAUDE WEISS, Studies in *CH*, nos. 13/14, 15, 1964.

ENRICO ATZENI, 'L'Abri sous roche D' du village préhistorique de Filitosa . . .' (*Congrès préhistorique de France . . . Ajaccio . . . 1966*, Paris, Société Préhistorique Française, 1966).

G. PERETTI, 'Une sépulture . . .' (*Congrès préhistorique de France . . .*, Paris, Société Préhistorique Française, 1966).

FRANÇOIS DE LANFRANCHI, 'La grotte sépulchrale de Curacchiaghui . . .' (*Bulletin de la Société Préhistorique Française*, t. LXIV, fasc. 2, 1967).

To appear shortly: FRANÇOIS DE LANFRANCHI, *Le Peuplement du Bassin de l'Ortolo et du Rizzanese du Néolithique à l'Age du Fer*.

C Graeco-Roman archaeology

A. AMBROSI, *Carte archéologique de la Gaule romaine . . . Carte et texte du département de la Corse . . .* (Paris, Leroux, 1933).

JÉRÔME CARCOPINO, *Les Leçons d' Aléria* (Bastia, Costa, 1963).

JEAN JEHASSE, *Aléria grecque et romaine* (Lyon, Audin, 1963, revised edition, 1964).

To appear shortly: JEAN and LAURENCE JEHASSE, *La nécropole pré-romaine d'Aléria.*

D *Middle Ages and later periods*

GENEVIÈVE MORACCHINI-MAZEL, *Les Monuments paléo-chrétiens de la Corse* (Paris, Klincksieck, 1967).

GENEVIÈVE MORACCHINI-MAZEL, *Les Eglises romanes de Corse* (2 vols. Paris, Klincksieck, 1967).

J. LEBLANC, *La Collection du Cardinal Fesch au Musée d'Ajaccio* (La Revue Française, Paris, 1965).

DOROTHY CARRINGTON, 'Cardinal Fesch, a grand collector' (*Apollo*, London, November 1967).

INDEX